KITCHEN BASICS & SOLUTIONS

BY

DR. MYLES H. BADER

MORE USABLE FOOD INFORMATION THAN ANY BOOK EVER PUBLISHED

THE ULTIMATE CHEFS GUIDE TO FOOD SECRETS

KITCHEN BASICS & SOLUTIONS
BY
DR. MYLES H. BADER

Published by:
Creative Product Concepts, Inc.
1435 Walnut Street
Philadelphia, PA 19102

Distributed by:
Creative Product Concepts, Inc.
1435 Walnut Street
Philadelphia, PA 19102

Illustrations by:
Debora Rose Peek

Printed in the United States of America
First Printing May 2002

ISBN: 1-929199-10-4

TABLE OF CONTENTS

CHAPTER 10

CHAPTER 11

CHAPTER 12

CHAPTER 13

WEBSITES

CHAPTER 1

SECRETS OF COOKING AND PREPARATION

VEGETABLE COOKING

BAKING

Leave the skins on to preserve most of their nutrients. Make sure that the vegetable has high enough water content or it will dry out in a very short period of time. The harder root vegetables are more suited to baking; these include potatoes, winter squash, jicama, and beets.

STEAMING

Cooking vegetables in a short period of time retains most of the nutrients. Start with the more solid vegetables such as carrots then add the softer to the steamer after. The following are approximate steaming times for the more common vegetables:

Artichokes	6-10 minutes
Green Beans	45 minutes
Beets	45 minutes
Broccoli with stalk	25 minutes
Brussels Sprouts	20 minutes
Cabbage	15 minutes
Carrots	25 minutes
Cauliflower	12 minutes
Celery	20 minutes
Corn on Cob	15 minutes
Green Peas	20-40 minutes
Green Peppers	5 minutes
Onions	20-30 minutes
Potatoes (all)	35 minutes
Tomatoes	15 minutes

PRESSURE COOKERS

Needs to be controlled more. Can be too difficult for vegetables and overcooking is a common occurrence.

WOK

This is a fast method providing the pan is well heated with a very small amount of vegetable oil first. The only problem that may occur is that if you cook the vegetables too long in oil some of the fat, soluble vitamins may be lost.

WATERLESS COOKWARE

Best for green leafy vegetables and uses only the water that adheres to the leaves after washing. Usually takes only 3-5 minutes.

BOILING VEGETABLES

WHEN BOILING VEGETABLES THERE ARE A FEW GOOD RULES TO FOLLOW:

- Vegetables should always be placed in the water after it has started to boil. The shorter the time in the water, the more nutrients that will be retained. Vitamin C is lost very quickly.
- The water should be allowed to boil for 2 minutes to release a percentage of the oxygen, which will also cause a reduction in nutrients.
- Leave the skins on and the vegetables in large pieces. The more surface you expose, the more nutrients will be lost.

CROCK-POT

Vegetables should never be placed in a crock-pot for prolonged cooking. Most of the nutrients will be lost to the heat and the liquid.

MICROWAVE

Usually results in short cooking times which retains the nutrients. The water content of the vegetables will determine just how well they will cook. Microwave ovens should have a movable turntable so that the food will not have "cold spots." This can result in the food being undercooked.

If you wish to brown foods in the microwave, be sure and use a special dish for that purpose. The dish should always be preheated first for the best results. If you don't have a browning dish, try brushing the meat with soy or teriyaki sauce.

- A steak will continue cooking after it is removed from the microwave and it is best to slightly undercook them.

MEASUREMENT FACTS

60 drops	= 5 ml.	= 1 tsp	3 tsp	= 1 tbl
2 tbl	= 30 ml.	= 1 fl. oz.	8 tbl	= $^1/_2$ cup
Juice of 1 orange	= 5-6 tsp.		5 large eggs	= 1 cup
2 tbl butter	= 1 oz		1 oz	= 30 g.

COOKING TEMPERATURES

	DEGREES FAHRENHEIT
Ground Beef, pork, lamb	160
Beef, lamb, veal	
Rare	140
Medium Rare	145
Medium	160
Medium-Well	165
Well-Done	170
Pork	
Medium	160
Well-Done	170
Precooked	140
Poultry	
Ground Meat	165
Whole Birds	185
Parts	175
Stuffing (alone or in bird)	170
Egg Dishes	165
Leftovers	170

THERMOMETERS

DEEP-FAT/CANDY
The bulb should be fully immersed in the candy or food and should never be allowed to touch the bottom of the cooking container. To check the accuracy of the thermometer, place it in boiling water for 3-4 minutes. The temperature should read 212°F or 100°C.

FREEZER/REFRIGERATOR
These thermometers read from −20° to 80°F. Frozen foods should always be stored at 0°F or below to slow nutrient loss and maintain the quality of the food.

MEAT
Insert the thermometer into the center or thickest part of the meat making sure that it is not resting on a bone.

OVEN
It is wise to check your oven temperature accuracy at least once a month. If the temperature is not accurate, it can affect the results of the food being prepared, especially baked goods. The thermometer should be placed in the middle of the center rack.

KEEP YOUR SUNNY SIDE UP

If you want to keep food wrapped in aluminum foil from over-browning, keep the shiny side of the foil out.

OIL CHANGE

If you need to place a thin layer of oil on food, try using a spray bottle with oil in it. Beats using a brush and reduces the amount of oil used.

CRISP IT

If you would like a crisp topping on your casserole, try leaving the lid off while it is cooking.

SAFETY FIRST

If a child accidentally turns on the microwave, damage may occur. To avoid a problem, just keep a cup of water in the microwave when it is not in use.

KEEP THE ENERGY FOCUSED

If the meat has a bone, microwave cooking will send more energy to the bone than the meat and the meat may not cook evenly. If possible remove the bone and give it to the dog or cat (only if it's a really big one).

KA BOOM

A microwave oven is just as safe as a regular oven. However, make sure you never place a sealed container in a microwave.

WHAT IS THE FORMULA FOR AN ALL-AROUND BREADING?

The following blend should make any food taste better and enhance the flavor. Mix all ingredients together well and store in the refrigerator until needed. Allow the blend to stand at room temperature for 20 minutes before using.

2   cups of whole, wheat pastry flour
½   tablespoon paprika
1   tablespoon of dry mustard
¾   teaspoon of finely ground celery seed
1   teaspoon ground black pepper
1   teaspoon dried basil
1   teaspoon dried marjoram
¾   teaspoon dried thyme

DON'T BE AN EGG POPPER

When cooking eggs in the microwave, remember that whole eggs may explode and when cooking an egg with a whole yolk intact, place a small hole in the yolk with a pin to allow for expansion.

HELP! I'M FALLING APART

The best oil for deep fat frying is canola. It has the highest smoke point and will not break down easily. Oils can only be cooked to 400ºF before serious deterioration starts to occur.

RAPESEED TO THE RESCUE

To use butter, margarine, or lard for frying or sautéing add a small amount of canola oil to them to raise the smoke point. This will allow you to cook with them without their breaking down for a longer period of time.

A LITTLE DAB WILL DO YA

If you need to place a thin layer of oil on food, try using a spray bottle with oil in it or PAM™. Beats using a brush.

NOT AN OLD WIVES TALE

If you are having problems keeping a pot from boiling over, try placing a toothpick between the lid and the pot. Other tricks include placing a wooden spoon across the top and rubbing butter around the inside lip of the pot. Also, if you add 1½ teaspoons of butter to a cooking pasta or soup, it will not boil over. This doesn't work with vegetable oil and of course, adds calories and cholesterol.

LE PEW

If odors are a problem with a particular dish, try placing a cloth that has been dampened with ½ water and ½ vinegar over the pot. Be sure and make sure that the edges are not near the flame or intense heat.

FAT REDUCTION

Cooking meat in oil will not lower the fat content to any great degree. However, all other methods of cooking will lower the fat content.

WOK IT, WIPE IT

Depending on the type of metal your wok is made of, it may rust. Always wipe off the inner surface with vegetable oil after each use.

HOW DRY I AM

To avoid foods splattering when fried, be sure and dry them thoroughly before placing them into the hot oil. Also, place all fried foods on a piece of paper towel for a few minutes before serving to allow the excess oil to drain off.

GIVE ME AIR

Always use a shallow pot for cooking roasts, this will allow air to circulate more efficiently. Placing fresh celery stalks under the roast also helps.

AN UPLIFTING EXPERIENCE

A frequent problem that occurs when frying is trying to fry too much food at once. The fat may overflow (bubble over) from the temperature difference of the cold food and the hot fat. Also, to avoid food from sticking together, the basket should be lifted out of the fat several times before allowing it to remain in the fat.

PUNCTUATION

When baking potatoes, try piercing the skin with a fork to allow the steam to escape. This will stop the skin from cracking. Also, rubbing a small amount of oil on the skin helps.

JUST POP YOUR TOP

To develop a crisp topping on your casserole, try leaving the lid off while it is cooking.

NO SKINHEAD HERE

If you want to eliminate the skin forming on your custard, just cover the dish with a piece of waxed paper while it is still very hot.

CHOP, CHOP

If you want to save money when purchasing canned tomatoes, just buy a can of whole tomatoes and when you need chopped tomatoes, place sharp scissors or a knife in the can and slice away.

HELP, I'M DROWNING

Most foods should be refrigerated as soon as possible to help retain the potency of the nutrients. An example of nutrient loss is boiled carrots, which if allowed to remain whole will retain 90% of their vitamin C and most of their minerals. However, if they are sliced before cooking, they will lose almost all of the vitamin C and niacin content.

NUTRIENT DAMAGE CONTROL

Baking soda should not be added to foods while it is cooking, since it may destroy certain B vitamins.

DOUBLE DUTY

It's very handy to keep a shaker of $^3/_4$ salt and $^1/_4$ pepper next to the range or food preparation area.

LOW HEAT IS BEST

To avoid curdling when cooking with dairy products, always cook at a lower temperature setting.

POSITION IS EVERYTHING

The thicker, tougher areas of the food should always be placed toward the outer edges of the cooking pan to obtain the best results in a microwave oven.

PREPARATION OF FOODS

WASHING/SOAKING

The water soluble vitamins are very delicate and can be lost if the vegetable or fruit is allowed to remain soaking in water for too long. Carrots or celery stored in a bowl of water in the refrigerator may cause the loss of all the natural sugars, most of the B vitamins, vitamin C, and vitamin D as well as all minerals except calcium.

PEELING/SLICING/SHREDDING

When you shred vegetables for salads you will lose 20% of the vitamin C content. Then if you allow the salad to stand for 1 hour before serving it you will lose another 20%.

SKIN 'EM

There should no concern about removing the skin from fruits and vegetables just before eating them. Less than 10% of the total nutrients are found in the skin. Removing the skin may be a good thing to do with many foods since pesticide and fertilizer residues are usually found in the skin.

COOKWARE, CURRENT 2002 FACTS

There are a number of materials that are used to manufacture pots and pans, many of which do not really do the job adequately. Remember, the thicker the gauge of the metal, the more uniformly it tends to distribute the heat. The finish on the metal will also affect the efficiency of the cookware.

COPPER

These will not react with any food and are safe to cook in. Copper is one of the best heat conductors and is preferred by many chefs. Copper pans, however, should only be purchased if they have a liner of tin or stainless steel to be safe, otherwise they may leach metals into the food. When you cook in glass, remember to reduce the oven temperature by 25°F.

One of the worst types of cookware is the thin stamped stainless steel pots with a thin copper-coated bottom. The copper coating is approximately 1/50th of an inch in thickness and too thin to distribute the heat efficiently and uniformly.

The "real" copper cookware provides excellent heat distribution on the bottom as well as the sides of the pan. The copper, however, needs to be kept clean and if black carbon deposits form to any degree it will affect the heat distribution significantly. These pots are usually lined with tin which must be replaced if it wears out otherwise excess copper may leach into the food causing a health risk. Foods that are high in acid will increase the release of copper. The metal ions in copper will also react with vitamin C and reduce the amount available.

ENAMELED COOKWARE

While the enamel does resist corrosion, it is still metal coated with a thin layer of enamel. The coating is produced by fusing powdered glass into the metal surface, which is in most instances cast iron. The cookware can chip easily if hit against another object and can even shatter if placed from a very hot range into cold water.

GLASS COOKWARE

Rapid temperature changes may cause the glass to crack or break in many brands. Glass has a very low "heat-flow" efficiency rating and when boiling water is poured into the glass cookware, the actual heat that is transferred from the boiling water to the bottom of the cookware will travel slowly back to the top of the pot. Because of this, the bottom of the pot will swell and the top of the pot does not expand creating a structural type of stress and a crack is very possible. Corningware® and Pyrex™ in that order would be the only choices for glass cookware, since both will resist most stresses.

ALUMINUM

The majority of cookware sold in the United States in 2001 was aluminum, which is an excellent heat conductor. Current studies report that there is no risk from using this type of cookware unless you are deep scraping the sides and bottoms of the pots continually, allowing aluminum to be released into the food. Rarely does anyone do this. Excessive intake of aluminum may lead to Alzheimer's disease.

Aluminum cookware stains very easily, especially if you are using hard water to cook with. Certain foods, such as potatoes, will also cause the pans to stain easily. If you cook a high-acid content food such as tomatoes, onions, wine or if lemon juice is used in aluminum, it will probably remove some of the stain. If a pan is already stained when the acidic foods are cooked, it may transfer the stain to the food possibly turning your foods a brownish color.

Aluminum pans also tend to warp if they are subjected to rapid temperature changes, especially if they are made of thin gauge aluminum. If they are made of a thick gauge, they will have excellent heat-flow efficiency and will not rust, thus making the thick pan, the best pan for use as cookware.

Water and cream of tartar will clean aluminum. Just fill the pan with water and add 1 tablespoon of cream of tartar then boil for 15 minutes before washing.

Lime-soaked pickles should never be made in an aluminum pot even though the instructions state that aluminum is recommended. A chemical reaction takes place which is not healthy.

CAST IRON/CARBON STEEL

May only supply a small amount of iron in elemental form to your diet, but not enough to be much use nutritionally. Certain acidic foods such as tomato sauce or citrus fruit may absorb some iron but not enough to supply you with adequate daily supplemental levels. Iron does, however, conducts heat fairly well.

These are both non-stainless steel, iron-based metals that have a somewhat porous, jagged, surface. These pots need to be "seasoned." To accomplish this, you need to rub the cooking surfaces with canola oil and heat it at 300°F for about 40-50 minutes in the oven, then allow it to cool to room temperature before using. The oil has the ability to cool and seal the pores and even provide a somewhat non-stick surface. Another factor is that when the oil is in the pores, water cannot enter and possibly cause the formation of rust.

These pots should be washed daily using a mild soap and dried immediately. Never use salt to clean the pot, since this may cause rusting. If a cleaner is needed, be sure it is a mild, one. Iron pots tend to release metal ions that react with vitamin C and reduce its potency.

Cast iron pots can be cleaned by just filling the pot with warm water and dropping in 3 denture cleaning tablets, then allow the pot to sit for 1 hour. This method will not affect the seasoning. To remove rust, just use sand and vegetable oil and rub lightly.

NON-STICK

These include Teflon™ and Silverstone™ and are made of a type of fluorocarbon resin that may be capable of reacting with acidic foods. If you do chip off a small piece and it gets into the food, don't be concerned it will just pass harmlessly through the body.

Never allow any brand of "non-stick" surface pan to heat to a high temperature dry. The pan may release toxic fumes if heated above 400°F for more than 20 minutes. This could be a serious problem for small pets and birds. Proper vegetable oil seasoning of most pots will produce a non-stick surface without risk and last for months.

These non-stick surfaces are the result of a chemically inert fluorocarbon plastic material being baked on the surface of the cookware or other type of cooking utensil. Silverstone™ is the highest quality of these non-stick items. The food is actually cooked on jagged peaks that protrude from the bottom, which will not allow food a chance to stick to a smooth surface. The surface is commercially "seasoned" producing the final slick surface.

The major contribution of a non-stick surface is that of allowing you to cook without the use of fats, thus reducing the calories of foods that would ordinarily be cooked with fats. The less expensive non-stick cookware usually has a very thin coating and will not last very long with everyday use. With heavy usage and continual cleaning, the coating will eventually wear thin.

STAINLESS STEEL

To be a good heat conductor, they need to have a copper or aluminum bottom. High acid foods cooked in stainless steel may leach out a number of metals into the food, which may include chlorine, iron, and nickel.

MULTI-PLY PANS

The bottoms of these pans usually have three layers. They are constructed with a layer of aluminum between two layers of stainless steel. Stainless steel does not have the hot spot problem and the heat will be more evenly diffused by the aluminum.

CLAY POTS

Remember to always immerse both the top and the bottom in lukewarm water for at least 15 minutes prior to using. Always start to cook in a cold oven and adjust the heat after the cookware is placed into the oven. If sudden changes occur, the cookware may be cracked. Never place a clay cooker on top of the range directly on the heat.

CONVECTION OVEN

This method utilizes a fan that continuously circulates the hot air and cooks the food more evenly and up to three times faster than conventional oven methods. It is great for baked goods and roasts. Make sure you follow the manufacturers recommendations as to temperature since you will be cooking at 20^0 to 75^0 less than you would normally. Baked goods, however, are easily over-browned and need to be watched closely.

BARBECUING FOOD FACTS

ONION TRICK

Try burying an onion wrapped in aluminum foil in the coals for 1 hour. Try it, you'll like it.

GREAT FLAVOR TRICK

A number of different herbs can be placed on the coals to flavor the food. The best are savory, rosemary, or dried basil seedpods. Lettuce leaves can be placed on the coals if they become too hot or flare up.

BUILDING A GREAT FIRE

- Always use high quality hardwood charcoal to make the hottest, long lasting fire.
- Line the bottom of the fire bowl with aluminum foil.
- Allow the starter fluid to remain on the coals for 1 minute before lighting.
- Let the coals burn for 35 minutes before placing food on the grill.
- Wood chips on the coals will add flavor.
- Nut shells, will also add flavor when placed on the coals.
- Allow 1 inch of space between the coals.

HELP! THERE'S NO OXYGEN IN HERE

Charcoal briquettes should always be stored in airtight plastic bags since they will absorb moisture very easily.

BYE, BYE, EYEBROWS

Coat your grill with a spray vegetable oil before starting the fire, then clean it shortly after you are through. Never spray the oil on the grill after the fire has started, as it may cause a flare-up.

A CLEAN GRILL IS A HEALTHY GRILL

Window cleaner sprayed on a warm grill will make it easier to clean.

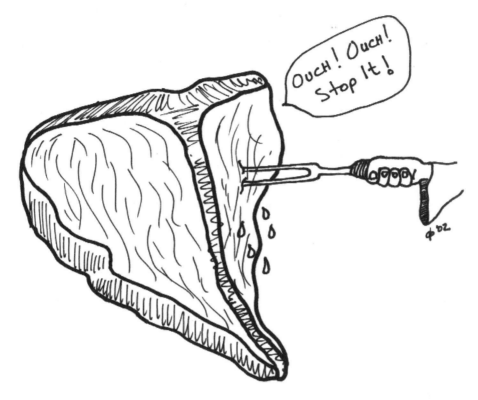

TONGS FOR STEAKS

Always turn steaks with tongs to avoid puncturing the steak and allowing the juices to run out.

HEALTH HINT:

If you are using real charcoal briquettes, be aware that if the fat from meat drips on a briquette, a chemical reaction will take place sending a carcinogen called a "pyrobenzine" onto the surface of the meat from the smoke. This dark-colored coating should be scraped off before you eat the meat, otherwise consuming a 12 oz. steak can provide you the same cancer risk as smoking 15 non-filtered cigarettes. There is no risk if you use artificial charcoal or a gas grill. Americans spend over $400 million dollars each year on charcoal briquettes.

CASSEROLES

HINTS & TIPS FOR GREAT CASSEROLES

- Keep pre-cut and peeled veggies in the freezer.
- Use dried herb instead of fresh herbs because of cooking times.
- Keep the casserole lid off if you want a browned topping.
- If you re-heat a casserole, defrost it in the refrigerator, cover and bake at 350°F.
- Make casseroles in advance allowing enough time for flavors to release and mingle.

SAUTÉING

- When sautéing, make sure that you only use a small amount of oil. If you wish to have the food turn out crisp you need to heat the oil to a high temperature before adding the food. To test the temperature of the oil, try dropping a small piece of food into the pan, if it sizzles it is ready for you to sauté.
- Remember to always have the food at room temperature if you wish the food to brown faster and more evenly. Cold foods tend to stick to the pan. During the sautéing process, the pan should be moved gently back and forth a number of times to assure that the browning will be even.
- Before sautéing carrots, potatoes or any dense food, try parboiling them first. This will assure that all the food will be done at the same time.
- Foods that are to be sautéed should be dry. Never salt any food that is to be sautéed, salt tends to retard the browning of foods.
- Before sautéing meats, try sprinkling a small amount of sugar on the surface of the meat. The sugar will react with the juices, caramelize, and cause a deeper browning as well as improving the flavor.
- Never overcrowd a pan that you are sautéing in. Overcrowding causes poor heat distribution resulting in food that is not evenly browned.
- If the fat builds up from the foods that are being sautéed, remove the excess with a bulb baster.
- Never cover a pan when sautéing. Steam tends to build up and the food may become mushy.

DIGITAL COOKING?

We are all aware that if you place your hand into a pot of boiling water at 212°F you will definitely get burned. However, when you place your hand into a 325°F oven all you feel is the intense heat and do not get burned. The reason for this is that air does not transfer nor retain heat as well as water.

THE CHEMISTRY OF COOKING

When you use heat to cook food, basically you are increasing the speed of the molecules of that food. The faster they move, the more they collide, the more heat is generated, and the hotter the food gets. This changes the texture, flavor, and even the color of the food. For every 20°F you raise the temperature over the normal cooking temperature you will actually increase the molecular activity by 100 percent, not 20 percent.

NUTRIENT LOSSES

When you boil vegetables, they will lose about 42% of their mineral content, however if you steam them, they will only lose 2% of their mineral content.

CAKE PANS MUST RISE TO THE OCCASION

Cake pans are a very important part of making a cake. Some factors will influence the outcome more than others, such as the thickness of the pan which is not very important. However, the finish of the pan and its relative volume to the size of the cake is very important. If a cake is heated faster, the gas cells will expand faster and the better the batter will set. The perfect pan for the job should be the actual size of the finished product. If the sides of the pan is too high; the unused area can shield the batter from needed radiant energy and slow the rate at which the batter is heated making the cake drier. This is also the cause of humps in the cake. Never use a baking pan with a bright surface since they will reflect radiant heat and transmit the heat too slowly and thereby slowing the baking process.

DANGEROUS BUTCHER BLOCKS

Any cutting surface has the potential of harboring dangerous bacteria. Cutting boards and especially butcher-block surfaces are often used to place hot pots down. When this occurs, some of the heat is transferred to the surface and into the wood where bacteria may be lurking. Bacteria, like heat, which may activate them for a longer period of time or provide an area for them to survive as you prepare food.

MOIST HEAT OR DRY HEAT?

Foods that contain a large percentage of connective tissue, such as meat, or have a tough fibrous structure, such as those found in certain vegetables, should be cooked using moist heat. These foods are not naturally tender, therefore, they must be tenderized by the moist heat. There are, of course, exceptions to the rule, one of which is if the meat is heavily marbled or frequently basted.

QUICK, SHUT THE DOOR

If anyone has ever driven you crazy because you opened the oven door when something was cooking, this is your chance to explain why you do that. When the door is opened or left ajar for a few minutes, it only takes 40-50 seconds for the temperature to return to the preset temperature. It is not really a big deal and will not affect the food.

WHO BARBECUES: MOM OR DAD?

When it comes to slaving over the hot barbecue in the backyard, its dad who gets the chore 60% of the time. However, its mom who chooses what is to be barbecued almost 100% of the time. The most common items to barbecue are burgers, chicken, hot dogs, and corn on the cob.

PUT A LID ON IT

When you are boiling water, place a lid on the pot and the water will come to a boil in a shorter period of time. However, this is only true after the water reaches 15⁰F. Before this point, it doesn't matter if the pot has the lid on it or not. The water will not produce enough steam until it hits the 150⁰F level and at that level, it is best to trap the steam in the pot. To raise 1 gallon of water from 60⁰F to 212⁰F (boiling) on a gas range top, takes 23 minutes with the lid on, without the lid it takes about 35 minutes.

COOKING IN A RECREATIONAL VEHICLE, IT MAY BE A HAZARD

Over 236 Americans were killed and thousands have become ill from carbon monoxide (CO) poisoning while cooking and using heaters in motor homes in 1999. The gas is odorless is produced from faulty heating and cooking units. Every motor home should be equipped with a CO detector which sounds an alarm like a smoke detector and costs $45-$80.

ARE THERE DIFFERENT TEMPERATURES OF BOILING?

When we see water bubbling either lightly or more rapidly, the temperature will always be the same 212⁰F(100⁰C). There is, however, the possibility of 1⁰F difference at times but for the most part it remains constant. The only difference in the rapidly boiling water is that the food may cook somewhat faster due to the increased activity of the heat-carrying molecules. The food will cook more evenly and the food will retain more nutrients if the water is not rapidly boiling. Hard water, due to its high mineral content will boil 1-2⁰F above soft water.

NEVER SALT FOODS TO BE FRIED

Salt tends to draw moisture from foods. If a food is salted before placing it in the fryer, it will draw moisture to the surface and cause spattering when the food is placed into the heated oil.

NEVER REUSE FRYING OIL

When oil is used for frying the temperature is raised to such a high level that a percentage of the oil is broken down (begins smoking) and decomposes into Trans-fatty acid oil as well as turning a percentage of the polyunsaturated oil into saturated oil. Trans-fatty acids even though edible, tends to cause an increase in free radicals (abnormal cells) in the body and may also raise the bad cholesterol levels (LDL) and lower the good cholesterol levels (HDL). Best to use fresh canola oil every time you fry.

SMOKE, FLASH, & FIRE POINTS OF OILS

The smoke point of oil is the point at which the oil starts deteriorating. All oils have different smoke points; canola oil having one of the highest makes it the best oil for frying. Flavor would be another determining factor in using oil with a lower smoke point. The smoke point is the point at which the oil is starting to convert a percentage of the oil into Trans-fatty acids. The flash point is the point that the oil starts to show a small amount of flame emanating from the surface of the oil; this usually occurs at about 600°F and should tell you that the oil has reached a dangerous level. The fire point is about 700°F, which is the point that you had better have a fire extinguisher ready and remember never to use water on a grease fire. The fire needs to be smothered to extinguish it.

SMOKE POINTS OF FATS

FAT	SMOKE POINT
Canola Oil	525° F.
Safflower Oil	510° F.
Soybean Oil	495° F.
Corn Oil	475° F.
Peanut Oil	440° F.
Sesame Oil	420° F.
Animal Lard	400° F.
Vegetable Shortening	375° F.
Unclarified Butter	50° F.

JUST HOW HOT, IS HOT!

Your gas range at home will burn at 3,000°F. It is an easily controllable heat and therefore the heat of choice for almost all chefs. Electric ranges will only heat up to 2000°F and is more difficult to control small temperature changes. Depending on the dish, this can become a problem, especially with boiling over.

NEVER CROWD WHEN DEEP FRYING

When food is added to hot oil, it tends to lower the temperature. Foods will absorb too much oil when this occurs unless the oil is returned to the normal frying temperature in a very short period of time. To reduce the effects of a lower frying temperature one of two methods are recommended. First, never add too much food to the oil at once. It not only lowers the temperature, it can cause overcrowding and will not allow all the food to be fried evenly. Second, start the temperature about 15°F above the recommended frying temperature so that when you do add the cold food it will still be approximately the desired temperature. Whenever possible food should be left out for a short period before placing it into the fryer, the closer to room temperature the higher the frying temperature after the food is added. If the food is too cold the oil may drop down to the greasy range of about 300°-325°F and the oil may never get to the proper temperature.

CANDY-MAKING SECRET

Sugar crystallization is one of the more frequent problems when making candy. This usually occurs when the slightest grain of sugar that may be trapped on the side of the pan falls down into the syrup mixture. This can easily be prevented by heating the sugar over low heat and do not stir, until the sugar is completely dissolved. If any sugar crystals are still clinging to the sides of the pan, tightly place the lid on the pan and continue cooking the syrup for 3-4 minutes. The steam that is generated will melt the clinging sugar grains.

HOT SPOT, COLD SPOT

Your cooking pans should be made of a material that will dissipate the heat evenly throughout the bottom of the pan so that the food will cook evenly. Unfortunately many pans do not have this ability and develop cold spots. To check your pan, place a thin layer of about 4-5 tablespoons of sugar that has been mixed with 2 tablespoons of water on the bottom of your pan and spread it out as evenly as you can. The sugar over the hot spots will caramelize and turn brown forming a pattern of the hot spots. Hopefully, you will not have a pattern and the sugar will caramelize all at about the same time. If you do have a problem, use a heat diffuser under the pan or try the same test using a lower heat setting.

BURNED ON GREASE REMOVER

Fill the pot with tap water and add 6 Alka-Seltxer® tables, then allow it to sit for 1 hour before scrubbing.

CRUCIFEROUS COOKING

When you cook a cruciferous vegetable such as cauliflower, never use an aluminum or iron pot. The sulfur compounds will react with the aluminum turning the cauliflower yellow. If cooked in an iron pot, it will turn the cauliflower brown or a bluish-green.

THE PRESSURE OF PRESSURE COOKING

Pressure cooking is more desirable for people that live at higher altitudes since water boils at 203°F at 5,000 feet elevations instead of the standard 212°F at or near sea level. Normally, a food would take longer to cook at the higher elevations. With a pressure cooker, it allows the water to reach a temperature of 250°F by increasing the atmospheric pressure in the pot and using the steam to cook the food faster. Steam conducts heat better than air and forces the heat into the food.

COOKING WITH ALCOHOL

The boiling point of alcohol is 175°F, much lower than the boiling point for water of 212°F. When alcohol is added to a recipe it will lower the boiling point until it evaporates. For example, if you decide to change your recipe by adding some wine to replace some of the water, you will need to increase your cooking time by about 10 percent.

SALTING YOUR COOKING WATER

If you add 1 teaspoon of salt to your cooking water, it will raise the temperature 1-2° F. Sugar and many other ingredients will also raise the temperature of the water. Unless the recipe calls for this raise, it is best not to add salt because salt has the tendency to cause many foods to become tough.

BOILING POINT VS. ALTITUDE

As the altitude increases, the atmospheric pressure decreases placing less pressure on water that is trying to boil. When this occurs, it makes it easier for the water to boil and the water molecules are released more easily. Water will boil at a lower temperature at the 5,000-foot elevation. For every 1,000 feet, water will boil at approximately 2°F. less than at sea level.

ALTITUDE (feet)	FAHRENHEIT	CELSIUS
0	212°	100°
1,000	210°	99°
2,000	208°	98°
3,000	207°	97°
4,000	205°	96°
5,000	203°	95°
10,000	194°	90°

HOW A CONVECTION OVEN WORKS

The standard oven and the convection oven, work very similar to each other. The notable difference in the convection oven is that it has a fan that increases the distribution of the heat molecules providing heat to all areas more evenly and faster. Because of the fan and the efficiency of the heat circulation, a lower temperature is usually required, thereby conserving energy. Roasts, especially do well in a convection oven because of the lower heat, the meat tends to be juicier.

MAKING THE BREADING STAY PUT

Preventing the breading from falling off foods can sometimes create a real headache unless you follow a few simple rules. First, make sure that the food that is to be breaded is very dry and use room temperature eggs, over-beating the eggs will also cause a problem. Second, after you apply the breading place the food into the refrigerator for 1 hour before allowing the food to remain out for 20 minutes before frying. Homemade breadcrumbs are the best because of their uneven texture they tend to hold better.

WHY PANS WARP

Metal pans have higher heat-flow efficiency rating than other materials as well as having a tougher internal structure. Metal pans warp due to structural stress that is caused by sudden changes in temperature. The thinner the metal pan, the more easily it will warp and the thicker the pan the less likely to warp.

NATURAL NO-STICK PANS

Your pans can be protected from foods sticking to them by just boiling white vinegar in the pan for a few seconds to season the pan. This should last for 4-5 months before you need to do it again.

HOW DOES HEAT COOK FOOD?

There are three main methods of transferring heat to food; radiation, convection, and conduction. Basically, you are transferring heat from a hot object to a cold one. Radiant heat is in the form of electromagnetic waves, such as those from a toaster to the toast. It does not require any assistance from air and water. The energy travels at 186,000 miles per second, the speed of light. Convection cooking employs circulating molecules, which are propelled by either gas or liquid. The heat is placed at the bottom of the food or liquid and as the heat rises, it allows the colder food or liquid to fall toward the heat. The air or water currents provide the convection cooking as a vehicle for the heat. Conduction cooking utilizes an oven where the hotter molecules pass along the heat from the surface to the interior of the food. When an aluminum spike is inserted in a potato, the heat is allowed to pass more easily to the inside and heat the food from both the inside and the outside at the same time.

NEVER USE PLASTIC WRAP IN A MICROWAVE

When foods become hot, chemicals from plastic wrap may be released and migrate into the food. The wrap may also stick to the food, especially fatty or sugary foods. Waxed paper, paper towels, or a plate work best.

SOLVING PROBLEMS THAT MAY OCCUR IN SAUCE BEARNAISE

Sauce bearnaise is one of the most popular sauces in the United States restaurants. It is an emulsion sauce that combines oil and water. It was developed in France in the 1830's and goes well with meats and fish dishes. When preparing the sauce the most frequent problem is that of overheating. One of two problems may occur; the first is that if the egg proteins are overheated they tend to coagulate forming small curds in a liquid that is supposed to be creamy. The second problem is that overheating may cause a breakdown of the emulsion causing it to separate. To prevent the protein from coagulating, try placing a small amount of vinegar in the sauce to lower the pH.

WHY CHEFS LEAVE THE BROILER DOOR AJAR

When the door is left ajar, it will actually improve the broiling aspects and reduce the roasting aspects. When the door is left ajar the pan and the air inside the broiler doesn't become as hot as it normally would and reduces the effects of conduction heat cooking. It still allows the same heat intensity to occur and improves the flavor and imparts a more crusty texture to meats.

WHY YOUR POT LID MAY STICK

When you are cooking a food the air space that is inside the pot increases in pressure and raises the lid very slightly allowing the heated air (gas) to escape. When the heat is turned off, however, the pressure and temperature is decreased and with the help of water molecules sealing around the rim of the lid pulls the lid tightly shut. The longer the lid is left on, the tighter the seal. If this occurs never place the pot in cold water, just place the pot on moderate heat for a minute or so to return the pressure to a more equal level with the outside.

IS GAS OR ELECTRIC COOKING BEST?

There is no contest here, it is definitely gas that wins on the range top, since you are able to change the temperature quickly, as well as have instant heat control, which is preferred by all chefs. Boiling over is more easily controlled with gas than electric in all instances. The oven, however, is a different story. Electric ovens will reach the desired temperature more rapidly and hold it more evenly with excellent accuracy.

MICROWAVE MAGIC?

A microwave oven actually works by emitting high-frequency electromagnetic waves from a tube called a "magnetron." This type of radiation is scattered throughout the inside of the oven by a "stirrer." The "stirrer" is a fanlike reflector, which causes the waves to penetrate the food, reversing the polarity of the water molecules billions of times per second, causing them to bombard each other and creating friction that heats the food.

DO I, OR DON'T I MICROWAVE IT?

Microwave cooking is less expensive than most other methods of cooking, however, it is only desirable for certain types of foods. If you are baking a dish, it will rise higher in a microwave oven, however, meats do not seem to have the desired texture and seem a bit mushy. When it comes to placing something frozen in the microwave, it will take longer to cook since it is difficult to agitate the water molecules when they are frozen.

CAN'T TOP A RESTAURANT WOK

The big difference is the more intense heat that is developed in a professional wok. Your home gas range is only capable of producing less than 10,000 BTU's. The BTU's produced in a professional wok is almost twice that high due to a larger gas feeder line and larger burner opening diameters. Also, the specially built wok has a series of burners, not just one. The higher heat tends to seal the juices and flavors in and the amount of juice that remains in the wok is less, allowing the juices that are there to stick to the vegetables more readily. Beware of special woks built with flat bottoms for electric ranges. The flat bottoms make it very difficult to stir and cook the vegetables properly.

SELF-CLEANING OVENS, IT'S HOTTER THAN HADES

Electric ovens are capable of much higher temperatures than gas ovens. Since the electric ovens go as high as 1000° F. during the self-cleaning phase, it literally disintegrates any food or grease particles and turns them into dust that only needs to be wiped away.

AS IGOR WOULD SAY, WOK THIS WAY

Cooking in a wok originated in China over 2,000 years ago during the Han Dynasty. It was prompted by the lack of cooking oil. It cooked the food fast and was an energy saver. There are a few things that every cook should be aware of when stir frying foods:

- Before cooking beef, pork, or chicken, partially freeze the meat for about 1 hour so that it will be easy to slice thin, even-sized pieces.
- Place the meat in a marinade for great flavor for a few minutes while you are preparing the vegetables. Adding a small amount of cornstarch to the marinade will protect the meat from the high heat and make the meat more tender and juicy.
- Vegetables should be cut into uniform bite-size pieces to insure that they will cook evenly. If vegetables are preferred in different sizes, then they will have to be added at different times, which makes the cooking more difficult.
- Oil should be used very sparingly; approximately one tablespoon is all that is needed for four servings, which is just enough to place a thin coating on the bottom of the wok..
- Never stir-fry more than $\frac{1}{2}$ pound at a time for the best results.

WOKS: A GOOD SOURCE OF IRON

Most woks are made from steel, which is 98% iron. A study performed at the Texas Tech University found that if you stir-fry in a steel wok; it will increase the iron content in foods by as much as 200-500%. The amount of iron in a $3\frac{1}{2}$-ounce portion of vegetables may rise from 0.4 mg. to 3.5 mg. when cooked in a wok. If the wok is made of stainless steel it will only release an insignificant amount of iron.

QUICK, QUICHE ME

Quiches should be served right from the oven to the table and never allowed to cool. Quiches are usually made with onions and mushrooms, both of which have a high water content. Because of this fact, the quiche will lose a large amount of moisture as it cools causing the crust to become soggy and weepy.

WHEN WAS THE MICROWAVE OVEN INVENTED?

In 1946 Dr. Percy Spencer, an engineer at Raytheon Laboratories, was working with a magnetron tube, which produces microwaves. He had a candy bar in his pocket, which he went to eat and found that it had melted and there was no heat source for that to occur. The only thing he could think of that would cause this to occur was the magnetron tube he was working with.

He then tried placing a small amount of popcorn near the tube and the popcorn popped in a few seconds. He then tried focusing the beam through a box at an egg, which exploded on one of his associates much to both of their surprise. The result was the first microwave oven called the Amana Radar Range™ introduced in 1977. The use of the word "radar" was used since the actual beam was invented in England and used as microwave radar to detect Hitler's planes in 1940.

WHO INVENTED THE TOASTER?

The first people to toast bread were the Egyptians in 2500BC using long-handled forks. The inventor of the toaster as we know it today was Charles Strite who received a patent for the toaster in 1919. However, the toaster didn't really work as well as he would have liked and it took him a few more years after a number of poor field tests to produce the first pop-up toaster in 1926 with the brand name of Toastmaster. The toaster had a darkness timer and sales went wild. Congress was so impressed they declared March 1927 as National Toaster Month.

CROCK POT AKA SLOW-COOKER

The Crock Pot was invented in 1971 by Rival. Many consumers still question whether the pot is safe or a breeding ground for bacteria since it advocates all day cooking at a low temperature. The fact is that most slow cookers have settings that range from 170^0 to 280^0F. Bacteria die at 140^0F, which is below the lowest possible temperature that can be used. However, if the lid is left off it may cause a problem with food not being fully cooked and harboring bacteria that is still alive. To minimize the risk of food poisoning, the following should be followed:

- All foods should be at refrigerator temperature. No frozen or partially thawed foods.
- Only cook cut up pieces of meat, not whole roasts or fowl to allow the heat to penetrate fully.
- Make sure that the cooker is at least $^1/_2$ to $^2/_3$ full or the food will not absorb enough heat to kill any bacteria.
- The food must be covered with liquid to generate sufficient steam.
- The original lid should always be used and should be tight fitting.
- When possible, allow the cooker to cook on the high setting for the first hour then it can be reduced.
- Never use the cooker to reheat leftovers. A number of bacteria are usually found on leftovers and it takes a high heat to kill them.
- Always follow the manufacturers directions for temperature settings.

THE CUTTING EDGE

One of the most important utensils in a kitchen is your knife. There are a number of different materials used in knife blades, many of which are relatively new and need to be evaluated as to which will suit you best. Make sure the handle is secured with at least three rivets. It should feel comfortable and always avoid plastic grips. When cutting foods the best surface would be a soft wooden cutting board. Hardwoods and plastic boards tend to dull the blade faster and also reduce the life of the knife.

Carbon Steel
This is, by far, the best for taking the sharpest edge and is the preferred knife for the serious chef. However, if the blade is not constantly kept dry it will rust. Acids in foods may also take their toll and turn the blade black, which can be imparted back to foods.

Super-Stainless Steel
This is not one of the better quality blades. Once it dulls and loses its original well-honed sharpness, it is almost impossible to restore to a decent level of sharpness. However, it does resist rust and staining.

Stainless Steel

Has the ability to resist rust and the acid effects from foods. Will take a sharper edge than the super stainless steel, but will dull and does not really take a very sharp edge.

High-Carbon Stainless Steel

This is the most expensive of the four types mentioned here and will not rust nor stain. It does not have to be washed and dried continually when in use. Can be sharpened to a sharper edge than either of the other stainless steel knives.

HOW DO YOU SHARPEN A KNIFE?

The one method that should never be used on a good kitchen knife is that of allowing a coarse grinding wheel to be used. The blade will only last a few years if you do and will become thinner and thinner. Rotating steel disks are not recommended either. The preferred method is the "butcher's steel." This is just a rough-surfaced, hard metal rod with a protective handle. If the butcher's steel is used frequently it will keep the edge on the knife.

If you have a problem keeping the edge it may mean that you are not using the sharpener as frequently as you should and you may have to use a "whetstone" to return the edge. The whetstone is made of silicon carbide (carborundum).

WHAT IS THE PROPER WAY TO STORE A KNIFE?

One of the best ways to store a quality knife is to keep it in a wooden countertop knife holder that was made for the knife. However, not all wooden, holders are quality ones and the holder should not have a hard surface for the blade to lie on. The higher quality holders will have a protective liner that allows the edge of the blade to rest free. When a knife is stored in a drawer with other utensils it will end up with small nicks on the blade and that will eventually ruin a high quality knife.

WHAT SHOULD I LOOK FOR WHEN BUYING A KNIFE?

Purchasing a knife is an investment that you need to make. It is a kitchen tool that is indispensable and unless you buy a quality knife, you will not have it very long and not be very satisfied with the results. Purchase either carbon-steel or high-carbon steel knives. The manufacturer should be a recognized name such as Trident, Wusthof, or Heckles and be sure that the blade and the handle are one piece and that the handle is not attached to the blade. If the knife has a plastic hilt, it is not recommended.

BOILED FOODS TAKE LONGER TO COOK ON BAD WEATHER DAYS

When the weather is bad and stormy, the atmospheric pressure goes down. The lower the pressure, the lower the boiling temperature of water becomes. The decreased temperature is usually about 1-2 degrees and it will take a little longer to cook boiled foods.

HOW TO CHECK YOUR OVEN TEMPERATURE WITHOUT A THERMOMETER

Place about 1 tablespoon of flour on the bottom of a cookie sheet and place it into a preheated oven for about 5 minutes. When the flour turns a light tan color, the temperature is between 250^0 to 325^0F. If the flour turns a golden brown, the oven is at 325^0 to 400^0F. When it turns a dark brown, the temperature is 400^0 to 450^0F and almost a black color the oven will be 450^0 to 525^0F.

CHAPTER 2

THE COLD FACTS AND FOOD STORAGE

SHOULD I FREEZE IT?

There is always an uncertainty in the public's mind regarding whether or not to freeze or refreeze a food and if it is frozen, how long it will retain its nutrient value, as well as its flavor and consistency. Many foods do not do well when frozen, some get tough, some develop ice crystals shortly after being place in the freezer, while others get mushy when defrosted.

FREEZING ALCOHOL

If you are going to try and freeze any dish that has alcohol in it, remember alcohol will not freeze like water and may need to be frozen at a lower temperature.

SAVE THOSE NUTRIENTS

The longer a food is frozen the higher the nutrient loss. Seal all freezer stored foods as well as possible to retain the nutrient level and avoid freezer burn as well as the formation of ice crystals. While ice crystals are not a serious problem they can affect the quality of the food as it is being thawed and makes the food mushy.

OUTSMARTING A POWER FAILURE

A good trick when you go away on vacation is to place a baggie with a few ice cubes in the freezer. If a power failure occurs while you are gone and the food thaws and re-freezes, it can affect the quality of the food as well as increase the bacterial growth. You need to be aware of this fact and discard the food.

COLD DAMAGE

There are a number of foods that should never be refrigerated since the cold causes either loss of flavor, sprouting, or the starch turning to sugar. These include garlic, onions, shallots, potatoes, and tomatoes.

FREEZING SANDWICHES

Frozen sandwiches will thaw by lunchtime. If the bread is buttered prior to freezing, the bread will not become soggy and absorb any filling.

FREEZER TEMPERATURE AND FOODS

FREEZER TEMPERATURE	QUALITY CHANGES AFTER
30° F.	5 DAYS
25° F.	10 DAYS
20° F.	3 WEEKS
15° F.	6 WEEKS
10° F.	4 MONTHS
5° F.	6 MONTHS
0° F.	1 YEAR

FOOD PRESERVATION

The preservation of food is possible only if some method is used to destroy or control the growth of microorganisms that cause spoilage. There are a number of methods, which include drying, dehydrating, salting, smoking, radiation, heating, freezing and the use of chemical agents (preservatives, etc.).

The microorganisms that cause food spoilage can be found everywhere. They are in the water, air, counter surfaces, brought home on foods, and even in the product itself. In many cases the food is contaminated as a natural occurrence, such as salmonella being present in the chicken ovaries. Microorganisms can exist in two forms, either visible to the naked eye such as in colonies or in small spores, which are for the most part invisible to the naked eye and carried by the air.

There are three divisions of microorganisms, molds, yeast, and bacteria.

MOLDS, YEAST, AND BACTERIA

Molds are usually airborne "spores" or "seeds" that may light on a food product and start to multiply. They may also send out "feelers" or "filaments" and grow in colonies, which may be seen in many colors depending on their food source. Mold spores will move from one food to another, especially fruits, so it would be wise to check your foods when you bring them home to be sure that none has any mold on them. Foods with a high acid content, such as tomatoes, pickles and fruits are especially susceptible to the growth of mold.

Yeast is a small one-celled fungus that produce enzymes, which convert sugars to alcohol and carbon dioxide in a process, called fermentation. It is also an excellent dietary source of folic acid. Yeast and molds can be destroyed by processing the foods at boiling temperature.

Bacteria need only a small amount of organic material and some moisture to grow and multiply. They grow by splitting their cells and may develop either acid or alkaline properties. Bacteria grow rapidly between 40° and 140° F. The longer the food is kept in this zone, the more the bacteria will multiply. High temperature cooking will destroy most bacteria.

When there is no moisture or the available moisture is used up, growth in all of these microorganisms cease and they dry up and become dormant until moisture is again introduced.

COOKING TO KILL BACTERIA

Egg in the shell . . . . .145° F. for 15 seconds
Fish, beef . . . . .145° F. for 15 seconds
Pork . . . . .155° F. for 15 seconds
Poultry, ground beef . . . . . . .165° F. for 15 seconds

WAS NAPOLEON RESPONSIBLE FOR FOOD PRESERVATION?

Napoleon's army was becoming sick and many of his men were dying from scurvy and other diseases related to lack of essential nutrients. Because of their long marches far from the food sources all they could bring with them was salted meats. Napoleon talked the rulers at the time to offer a reward equal to $250,000 in today's money if anyone could develop a method of preserving foods. Nicholas Appert, a Paris confectioner, after 14 years of trial and error finally invented a method of preservation. His method was to place food in a glass jar, allowing for expansion, and place a hand-hewn cork in the jar attached firmly with a piece of wire. Each jar was then wrapped in a burlap sack and lowered into a pot of boiling water. The length of time the jar was left in seemed to vary with the type of food. He was successful in preserving eggs, milk products, fruits, vegetables, and meats. He was awarded the prize money in 1810 by Napoleon and was labeled as "the man who discovered the art of making the seasons stand still."

WHO MADE THE FIRST TIN CAN?

Canning was invented in 1810 by Peter Durand, an Englishman, who called it a "tin canister." This would be an improvement over the glass jar, especially for transportation to outlying areas without breakage. The first "tin cans" had to be made by hand with workers cutting the can from sheets of tin-plate then soldering them together leaving a small hole in the top to place the food in. The hole was then covered with a small tin disc and soldered closed. A tin worker was able to produce about 60 cans a day. The United States started a canning operation in the 1820's and within 20 years the canning of foods was being done all over the country. In 1860 Isaac Solomon in Baltimore found that if he added calcium chloride to the water when it was boiling he could raise the temperature from 212° F. to 240° F. and thus reduce the processing time from about 6 hours to 45 minutes. A processing plant could now produce 20,000 cans a day instead of 2,500. The longest food to date that has been eaten safely was canned meat that was 114 years old.

FREEZING BAKED GOODS

Certain foods need care when freezing and also special preparation techniques after they have been removed from the freezer. The following foods are some of the more popular that most people freeze.

Biscuits
Prepare as per instructions, then freeze in a well-sealed bag. Should be heated unthawed at 350⁰F for about 20 minutes.

Coffee Cake
Bake until the cake is a light brown only, then cool as quickly as possible and freeze. Thaw at room temperature in freezer wrapping. If the cake has been frozen in aluminum foil, heat at 400⁰F.

Muffins
Prepare as per package directions, then freeze. Thaw at room temperature then heat at 300⁰F for about 15-20 minutes.

Doughnuts
Prepare as usual and freeze. Remember that raised doughnuts will freeze better than the cake type. Glazed doughnuts do not freeze well. Thaw at room temperature for about 10 minutes before placing in a 400⁰F oven to heat.

Bread (homemade)
Prepare as usual and allow the bread to cool before placing in freezer. Thaw at room temperature and if wrapped in aluminum foil, bake at 300⁰F for about 10 minutes.

Sandwiches (closed)
If you are going to freeze sandwiches use day old bread and spread butter, margarine or salad dressing to the edge of the bread before adding any filling. Do not use crisp vegetables, cooked egg white, preserves, mayonnaise or tomatoes. Package in aluminum foil and freeze. Thaw at room temperature in original wrapping for about 3-4 hours or in a lunch pail.

WHO CAME UP WITH THE NAME BIRDSEYE?

The Birdseye Food company was founded by Clarence Birdseye, an American businessman who invented the process of freezing food in small packages. He discovered the process by accident while hunting in Labrador in 1915. Some portions of caribou and fish were frozen by the dry Arctic air and when thawed were tender and still tasty. He developed a process that duplicated the Arctic conditions and started a company. Birdseye Seafood was founded in 1923 and by 1929 had expanded its product line to other foods. In 1929 Birdseye sold the company to General Foods.

NEGATIVE EFFECTS OF FREEZING FOODS

When food is frozen a percentage of the cells tend to burst releasing their liquids. This will occur in all foods regardless of the method of freezing or the type of wrap. Ice crystals are formed from the lost liquid and the food never has the same texture or exactly the same flavor as it originally had when it was freshly prepared. Biologically, the process that occurs is referred to as "osmosis." Osmosis is the process by which a liquid passes through a semi-permeable membrane (cell wall) in order to equalize the pressure. When the food is frozen the solids inside of the cell cause the water to become more concentrated allowing the liquid from outside the cell to enter, form crystals, and eventually cause a number of the cells to burst. Since some of the flavor of the food is contained in each cell a percentage of the flavor is also lost. Meats, fruits, and most seafood are more negatively affected than vegetables.

BE SMART WHEN FREEZING FOODS

There are a number of important facts that should be adhered to if you wish to freeze foods successfully:

- When preparing any vegetable for freezing, be sure and undercook it. Re-heating will complete the cooking.
- Freezing tends to intensify the flavor in spices such as garlic, pepper, oregano, and cloves so you should use less then add more before serving. Additional onions can be used since freezing tends to cause the flavor to be lost. Salt should be used in moderation or not at all. Salt tends to slow down the freezing process.
- Never use quick-cooking rice in a dish that will be frozen, as it tends to become mushy. Use regular or converted rice.
- Artificial flavorings and sweeteners do not do well when frozen.
- Toppings should always be added before serving. Cheeses and bread, crumbs on foods do not do well.
- Freezing causes old potatoes to fall apart, always use new potatoes in dishes that are to be frozen.
- Gravies and sauces need to be made somewhat thicker than normal since they will usually separate.
- Cool foods first in the refrigerator before freezing.

WHY IS A FULL FREEZER MORE ENERGY EFFICIENT?

A freezer that is full will use less energy than a half-full freezer because frozen foods retain cold air for a long period. The freezer will run fewer hours per day and save considerable money in electricity.

FREEZER BURN, JUST THE FACTS

Freezer burn makes the surface of the food a lighter color than normal, dries out the food, makes it tough and takes away its flavor. Freezer burn may be caused by a damaged package, food that has been packaged in product that is not moisture or vapor resistant or too much air was allowed into the package. Before sealing up foods to be frozen, be sure and remove all the air you possibly can.

BLANCHING BEFORE FREEZING, A MUST

When vegetables are frozen, enzymes may still remain active and cause changes in the color, texture, and taste in the vegetable even if they have been previously stored under refrigeration. Freezing will slow the changes down, however, it will not totally inactivate the enzymes. If vegetables are blanched by either boiling them in water that has boiled for 2 minutes first (to release oxygen) or steaming them for 3-4 minutes it will not cook them but will inactivate the enzymes and the vegetables will retain their color, texture, and taste. Of course, the enzymes are important to good nutrition and it would be more desirable to only purchase enough for a few days at a time.

CHEST FREEZER Vs UPRIGHT FREEZERS

This debate has been around for a long time, however, the answer has always been a fairly simple one. The chest freezer, even though the door may be larger, will retain its cold setting longer when the door is opened since cold air is heavier than hot air and tends to stay put. The upright freezer tends to release most of its cold air the minute the door is opened. Chest freezers will maintain and hold the preferred 0^0 F. freezer level to maximize food storage times before spoilage.

WHY IS THERE A GUMMY LIQUID IN MY FROZEN FRUIT?

There are a number of reasons why this may occur. The fruit may have been frozen too slowly; the freezer temperature was not maintained at 0^0 F. or the temperature fluctuated too much by having the door opened too often while the fruit was freezing.

SMOKE CURING FOODS

The use of smoke to cure foods is one of the oldest methods of food preservation and one that provides a number of risks to the body from the toxins that may be placed into the food from the smoke. Smoke may contain as many as 200 different chemical components, which include alcohol, acids, phenolic compounds, pyrobenzine, and other carcinogenic chemicals. Many of these toxic substances do, however, retard microbial growth. Salt curing methods and smoking are frequently combined to minimize the oxidation of the fats that cause rancidity.

NEW STORAGE BAGS, A MUST FOR EVERY KITCHEN

A new plastic storage bag for fruits and vegetables is now on the market. The bag contains hundreds of microscopic holes that allow air to circulate around the produce. The bag is also impregnated with "oya" which is a natural substance that will absorb ethylene gas, which is released by the produce as it ripens and helps the produce, ripen. Unfortunately, the more ethylene gas the produce expels and remains around the food, the faster the food ripens and spoils. The bags are tinted green to lessen the effects of light reducing the potency of the vitamins. The bag is marketed under the name "Evert-Fresh."

Produce stored in these bags will last 10 times longer than standard plastic storage bags and in tests over a 12 day period 50% more of the vitamin C was retained. If you are unable to locate them: call (800) 822-8141 to order your supply.

STORING MARGARINE

Margarine will absorb odors from foods that are stored nearby very readily. It should be sealed as tightly as possible and should store for 4-6 months in the refrigerator. Margarine freezes well and will keep for 1 year if the temperature is kept at 0^0 F.

FREEZER STORAGE TIMES AT ZERO DEGREES FAHRENHEIT

FOOD . . . . .MONTHS

MEATS

Beef, Lamb	6-12
Chops, Cutlets, Beef Hamburger	3-5
Ground Pork	1-3
Sausage	1-2
Bacon (unsliced)	3-5
Bacon (sliced)	1
Fish	3-6
Ham	3-4
Liver	3-4
Poultry	4-6
Giblets	3
Duck, Goose	5-6
Rabbit	9-12
Shrimp or Shellfish (cooked)	2-3
Turkey	6-8
Hot Dogs	2-3
Luncheon Meats (ready-to-eat)	0

DAIRY PRODUCTS

Milk	2 weeks
Ice Cream	4 weeks
Cream (40%)	3-4
Eggs (not in shell)	7-10
Margarine	2-4
Butter	2-4
Cheddar Cheese	5-6

FRUITS

Apples (sliced)	10-12
Apricots	10-12
Berries	11-12
Cherries (sour)	12

REFRIGERATED STORAGE TIMES FOR VEGETABLES

VEGETABLE . . . . .DAYS IN REFRIGERATOR

ARTICHOKE	6-7
ARUGULA	3
ASPARAGUS	4-6
BAMBOO SHOOTS	7
BEANS, LIMA	2-3
BEANS, GREEN	3-5
BEETS	7-10
BITTER MELON	5
BLACK-EYED PEAS	2-3

BOK CHOY .3-4
BROCCOLI 4-5
BRUSSELS SPROUTS 3-5
CABBAGE 8-14
CARROTS 7-14
CAULIFLOWER 4-7
CELERY .7-14
CELERY ROOT 2-3
CHICKPEAS 2-3
CHICORY .3-5
CHINESE CABBAGE 4-5
COOKED FRESH VEGETABLES 3-5
CORN 1
CUCUMBERS 4-5
EGGPLANT 3-4
ESCAROLE 3-5
FENNEL .7-14
GINGER .7-14
GREEN ONIONS 7-14
GREENS, DANDELION, MUSTARD . . .1-2
HORSERADISH 10-20
JICAMA .7-14
KALE 2-3
KOHLRABI 4-5
LEEKS 7-14
LETTUCE, ICEBERG 7-14
LETTUCE, ALL OTHERS 6-10
MUSHROOMS 4-5
OKRA 2-3
ONIONS .7-14
PEAS 7-10
PEPPERS, GREEN & CHILI 4-6
PEPPERS, SWEET RED & YELLOW . .2-3
RADISHES 2-3
RUTABAGAS 7-14
SALISIFY 7-14
SAUERKRAUT, FRESH 6-7
SOYBEANS 2-3
SPINACH 2-3
SPROUTS 2-3
SQUASH, SUMMER 4-5
SWISS CHARD 2-3
TOMATOES 3-5
TOFU 3-10
TURNIPS 5-7
WATER CHESTNUTS 6-7
WATERCRESS 2-3

- NOTE: Unless otherwise noted in this chapter, all vegetables should be in perforated plastic bags.

STORAGE TIMES FOR FRESH FRUIT

FRUIT	RIPEN AFTER HARVESTING	REFRIGERATOR STORAGE TIME
APPLES	YES	2-4 WEEKS
APRICOTS	YES	2-3 DAYS
AVOCADOS	YES	10-14 DAYS
BANANAS	YES	1 WEEK
BERRIES	NO	3-7 DAYS
MELONS	YES	7-10 DAYS
CHERRIES	NO	2-4 DAYS
CRANBERRIES	NO	1 MONTH
CURRENTS	NO	1-2 DAYS
DATES	NO	1-2 MONTHS
FIGS,FRESH	NO	1-2 DAYS
GRAPEFRUIT	NO	10-14 DAYS
GRAPES	NO	3-5 DAYS
GUAVA	YES	2 WEEKS
KIWIFRUIT	YES	1 WEEK
KUMQUATS	NO	3 WEEKS
LEMONS	NO	2-3 WEEKS
LIMES	NO	3-4 WEEKS
LITCHIS	NO	1 WEEK
MANGOES	YES	2-3 DAYS
NECTARINES	YES	3-5 DAYS
ORANGES	NO	10-14 DAYS
PAPAYAS	YES	2 WEEKS
PEACHES	YES	3-5 DAYS
PEARS	YES	3-5 DAYS
PERSIMMONS	YES	1-2 DAYS
PINEAPPLE	YES	3-5 DAYS
PLUMS	YES	3-5 DAYS
POMEGRANATES	NO	2-3 WEEKS
PRUNES	YES	3-5 DAYS
RHUBARB	NO	4-6 DAYS
STAR FRUIT	YES	5-7 DAYS
UGLIFRUIT	NO	10-14 DAYS
WATERMELONS	NO	1 WEEK

STORAGE TIMES FOR NUTS IN THE SHELL

NUTS	CUPBOARD	REFRIGERATOR	FREEZER
ALMONDS	1 YEAR	1 YEAR	1 YEAR
BRAZIL NUT		9 MONTHS	9 MONTHS
CANNED NUTS	1 YEAR	1 YEAR	1 YEAR
CASHEWS		6 MONTHS	9 MONTHS
CHESTNUTS		6 MONTHS	9 MONTHS
COCONUTS		1 MONTH	
FILBERTS	3 MONTHS	9 MONTHS	1 YEAR
MACADAMIA NUT		6 MONTHS	1 YEAR
MIXED NUTS		9 MONTHS	1 YEAR
PEANUTS, RAW	2 MONTHS	6 MONTHS	1 YEAR
PEANUTS, ROASTED	1 MONTH	3 MONTHS	9 MONTHS
PECANS	2-3 MONTHS	6 MONTHS	1 YEAR
PINENUTS		1 MONTH	6 MONTHS
PISTACHIOS		3 MONTHS	1 YEAR
PUMPKIN SEEDS	2-3 MONTHS	1 YEAR	1 YEAR
SUNFLOWER SEEDS	2-3 MONTHS	1 YEAR	1 YEAR
WALNUTS	2-3 MONTHS	1 YEAR	1 YEAR

STORAGE TIMES FOR REFRIGERATED DAIRY PRODUCTS

PRODUCT	DAYS UNDER UNDER REFRIGERATION	MONTHS IN FREEZER 0° F.
BUTTER	45-90	7-8
BUTTER, Clarified	60-90	7-8
BUTTERMILK	7-14	3
CREAM	3-5	3
CREAM, WHIPPED		
Commercial	30	DO NOT FREEZE
Homemade	1	2
EGGS (in shell)	20	DO NOT FREEZE
EGGS (hard boiled)	7	DO NOT FREEZE
EGGS (yolks)	2-4	12
EGGNOG	3-5	6
HALF & HALF	3-4	4
ICE CREAM, Commercial		2-3
FROZEN DESSERTS		1-2
MAYONNAISE	60	DO NOT FREEZE
MARGARINE		
Regular & Soft	120	12
Diet	90	
MILK	3-7	3
NON-DAIRY CREAMER	21	12
NON-DAIRY TOPPINGS		
Container	7	12
Aerosol can	90	DO NOT FREEZE
SOUR CREAM	14	
YOGURT	14	2

STORAGE TIMES FOR CHEESES

CHEESE	WEEKS UNDER REFRIGERATION
APPENZELLAR	4
BEL PAESE	4
BLEU CHEESE	2-4
BRICK	4-8
BRIE	3-5 DAYS
CAMEMBERT	3-5 DAYS
CHEDDAR	5-8
CHESHIRE	5-8
COLBY	4-8
COLD PACK CHEESE	2-3
COTTAGE CHEESE, all curds	1
CREAM CHEESE	1-2
DERBY	4-8
EDAM	4-8
FARMER'S	1-2
FIRM-TYPE CHEESES	4-8
FETA	8-12
FONTINA	4
GOAT	2-4
GORGONZOLA	2-4
GOUDA	4-8
GRUYERE	2-4
HAVARTI	3-4
HERKIMER	4-8
JARLSBERG	4
LIEDERKRANZ	3-5 DAYS
LIMBURGER	1-2
MASCARPONE	1
MONASTARY TYPE	2-4
MONTEREY JACK	2-4
MUENSTER	1-3
MOZZARELLA, fresh	2-3 DAYS
MOZZARELLA, dry	2-4
NEUFCHATEL	1-2
PARMESAN	10-12
PORT DU SALUT	2-4
POT CHEESE	1
PROCESSED CHEESE, opened	3-4
PROVOLONE	8-12
RICOTTA	1
ROQUERFORT	2-4
SEMISOFT TYPE	2-4
STILTON	2-4
SWISS	4-5
TILLAMOOK	4-8
TILSITER	2-4

- NOTE: The unprocessed natural cheeses will freeze for 4-6 months and retain most of their flavor.

STORAGE TIMES FOR MEATS

MEAT		DAYS UNDER REFRIGERATION	MONTHS IN FREEZER
BEEF	Roasts, Steaks	3-5	9
	Ground, Stew	1-2	2-4
	Organs	1-2	2-4
VEAL	Roasts, Chops, Ribs	3-5	6-9
	Ground, Cutlet, Stew	1-2	3-4
	Organs	1-2	1-2
PORK	Roasts, Chops, Ribs	2-4	3-6
	Ham (fully cooked)	5	1-2
	Ground, Sausage	1-2	1-2
	Organs	1-2	1-2
	Bacon	7	1
LAMB	Roasts, Chops, Ribs	2-4	6-9
	Ground, Stew	1-2	3-4
	Organs	1-2	1-2
POULTRY	Chicken, Fresh	1-2	12
	Ground Chicken	1-2	2
	Chicken Broth	1-2	1
	Fried Chicken	3-4	
	Chicken Salad	3-5	
	Chicken Hot Dog	7 after opening	6 unopened package
	Turkey (pieces)	1-2	9

STORAGE TIMES FOR BAKING STAPLES

PRODUCT	SHELF LIFE
ARROWROOT	1 YEAR
BAKING POWDER	3-6 MONTHS
BAKING SODA	18 MONTHS
CORNSTARCH	1 YEAR
CREAM OF TARTAR	1 YEAR
EXTRACTS	1 YEAR
GELATIN, BOXED	1 YEAR
SALT	FOREVER IF KEPT DRY
TAPIOCA	1 YEAR
VINEGAR	1 YEAR
YEAST	DATE ON PACKAGE

PROBLEMS WITH ALUMINUM FOIL

Foods wrapped in aluminum foil may be subjected to two problems. The first is that since aluminum foil is such a great insulator it tends to slow down the heat transfer and the food will not freeze as fast as you may want it to. Bacteria may grow and not be killed when the food is re-heated. Secondly is that when you crinkle the aluminum foil to place it around the food, micro-cracks develop which may allow air and moisture to penetrate the food. If you plan on storing food for more than 2-3 days in the refrigerator in aluminum foil you should probably wrap the food in plastic wrap first. Aluminum foil will also react with foods that acidic or salty and may impart a strange taste to the food.

WHICH IS BETTER, A THERMAL BOTTLE OR A VACUUM BOTTLE?

When a hot beverage is placed in a container for storage, the heat is lost to the colder air through conduction, and a cold beverage will lose the cold and gain heat from its surroundings. Both, a thermal or vacuum bottle will slow the transfer of heat and cold between the beverage and its surroundings by placing a barrier between the food or beverage and the environment. A vacuum bottle places the food in a space within a vacuum surrounding the food. The unit is hermetically sealed between the bottle's inner and outer glass lining. In the thermal bottle, the exterior is solid and a poor conductor of heat, but not as poor as a vacuum bottle. Thermal bottles will not break as easily since they do not have the glass interior.

THE DANGERS IN RAW FOODS

The bacteria salmonella comes from the intestines of humans and animals and is often found in raw meats and eggs. Salmonella can be present after foods are dried, processed, or frozen for long periods. The bacteria can also be transferred to food by insects or human hands, especially infants and people with poor cleanliness habits. Salmonella is easily killed with high heat, which is why raw meats need to be cooked thoroughly. Food preparation surfaces that are not cleaned adequately after preparing raw meats and egg dishes are usually the cause of most cases of salmonella related illnesses.

COLD FACTS

If ice cream thaws it should not be re-frozen. Jelly, salad dressing, and mayonnaise do not freeze well on bread products. The freezer in your refrigerator is not the same as a supermarket food freezer. It is best used for storing foods for short periods only. Foods should be frozen as quickly as possible and temperatures should be 0ºF or below. Potatoes become mushy when frozen in stews or casseroles. Their cells have high water content and break easily when frozen. However, mashed potatoes freeze well. Any bakery item with a cream filling should not be frozen. They will become soggy. Custard and meringue pies do not freeze well. The custard tends to separate and the meringue becomes tough. Waffles and pancakes may be frozen, thawed and placed in the toaster.

KEEPING FROZEN FOODS MORE PALATABLE

Meats & Fish
Rancidity is always a factor in meats and fish even though you freeze them. Meats with a higher level of saturated fat will freeze better than those with a higher level of unsaturated fat. Hamburger will have the shortest fresh-life of any meat due to the grinding and exposure of more muscle surface and fat to the air.

Vegetables
Since raw vegetables have enzymes, it is necessary to blanch the vegetables to kill the enzymes before freezing or they will turn the vegetables into mush.

Freezing Salsa
Uncooked salsa can be frozen without any problem if you drain as much water from the salsa as possible. If the salsa is not drained well, it will end up with a layer of ice on top.

Fruit
The cell wall of fruit contains pectin, which hold the fruits together. When you freeze fruit, the pectin tends to dissolve and the fruit loses its shape. To avoid this problem, just add some sugar or calcium to the fruit and it will retain its shape.

Eggs
You can freeze raw egg whites but not the yolk. The yolk will turn into gelatin, however, cooked yolks will freeze well. Egg whites that have been cooked tend to get rubbery when frozen.

Dairy Products
Milk products that have less than 40% butterfat cannot be easily frozen. Heavy whipping cream can easily be frozen because of its high butterfat content. Cakes with icings that contain egg should not be frozen.

Emulsified Sauces
Products that have been emulsified do not freeze well. The water in the products tend to produce ice crystals and also they tend to separate. Mayonnaise and salad dressings are good examples of products that should not be frozen.

Starchy Sauces
Any sauce or custard that has been thickened with flour or cornstarch should not be frozen. If the product has been thickened with arrowroot or tapioca you can freeze it without a problem.

Starchy Foods

High starch foods such as potatoes, pasta, rice and most grains after they have been cooked should not be frozen. Most will turn mushy and not be very palatable.

Baked Goods

Baked goods that are low in moisture will freeze well with little or no change in texture. Pies that have not been baked also do very well.

Soups & Casseroles

Because of their high water content, both of these foods do well when frozen. The texture does not change enough to matter when thawing. Do not freeze these products, however, if they contain any dairy products.

COLD AND FREEZING FACTS

THERE ARE ICICLES IN MY ICE CREAM

Icicles or ice crystals in ice cream are usually formed from opening the door to the freezer too often. It doesn't take very much of a temperature drop to force the water molecules out of some of the ice cream cells and form the ice crystals. If the ice cream is stored for a prolonged period of time at 0°F(-17.8°C), the crystals will change their form again. Just scrape the crystals away since they are harmless.

WHY ICE MUST FLOAT

When water freezes, the hydrogen molecules and oxygen combine in a loose fashion creating air pockets, which causes the frozen water to rise. When water remains in its liquid form the air pockets do not exist making water denser than ice.

SCRUB THOSE ICE CUBES

When ice cubes remain in the freezer tray or the icemaker for more than a few days they may pick up refrigerator odors or contaminants from the air when the door is opened. It would be best to wash the ice cubes before using them for the best results.

MASHER TO THE RESCUE

If you need to use frozen juice concentrate, just use a potato masher to soften it.

A COLD SOLUTION

When you place a bowl of ice cubes out for a party and don't want them to melt too fast, try placing a larger bowl with dry ice under the cubes. The ice cubes will last through the entire party.

HOW CLEAR I AM

To make clear ice cubes. Boil the water first before placing the water in the ice cube trays. This will eliminate the impurities that make the ice cubes cloudy. Never use cloudy ice cubes in a gin and tonic. This is probably against the law somewhere.

BOY, AM I SHAPELY

If you would like to make different shaped ice cubes, just freeze water in small cookie cutter, then place the frozen shapes into a pan of very hot water for a few seconds to loosen them up.

SPEEDY ICE CUBES

Believe it or not, if you use boiling water to make ice cubes, they will freeze faster. Even though cold water is closer to the freezing point, the hot water evaporates faster leaving less water to freeze. The evaporation also creates an air current over the ice cube tray, which tends to actually blow on the water, similar to the cooling effect when you blow on a hot spoonful of hot soup before tasting it.

YOU'RE FREEZING MY ENZYMES

When foods are frozen the enzymes go into hibernation, however, they are not destroyed. If enzymes were not inactivated by freezing, they would cause flavor and color changes in the foods. When blanching, the enzymes are destroyed. Blanching must be done if you want to produce top quality frozen vegetables. Enzymes in fruits are the cause of browning and can be neutralized with the use of ascorbic acid.

RANCIDITY CONTROL WHEN FREEZING

Products that are frozen with higher fat content can become rancid to a certain degree and ruin the flavor of the food. Air is the guilty party, which means that the food must be wrapped properly to avoid air coming into contact with the food. If you use a freezer bag, try and squeeze as much of the air out of the bag as possible.

HELP! MY TEXTURE IS CHANGING

When you freeze foods, you are actually freezing the water that is in the food cells. As the water freezes it expands and a number of the cell walls rupture releasing their liquid, which then freezes into ice crystals, thus resulting in the food becoming softer. These changes in texture are more noticeable in fruits and vegetables since they have higher water content than most other foods. Certain vegetables such as tomatoes, lettuce and celery are so high in water content they literally turn into mush when frozen.

When cooked products are frozen, their cell walls are already softened, therefore they do not burst as easily. This is especially true when high starch vegetables such as corn, lima beans and peas are included in dishes.

QUICK, FREEZE ME FASTER

The damage to foods when freezing them can be controlled to some degree by freezing them as fast as possible. When foods are frozen more rapidly, the ice crystals that are formed are smaller and cause less cell wall rupture. If you know you will be freezing a number of items or a food that you really want to keep in good shape, try setting the freezer at the coldest setting a few hours before you place the food in. Some freezer manuals also will advise you which shelves are in the coldest area.

IT FEELS LIKE A ROLLER COASTER IN HERE

The temperature of your freezer should never fluctuate more than a few degrees to keep foods at their best. The temperature should be kept at least 0° F. or below for the best results. Thawing and re-freezing is the worst thing you can do to foods. Every time the temperature drops in the freezer, some of those small ice crystals will convert to larger ice crystals and little by little, the dish will be ruined.

MICROBE ALERT, MICROBE ALERT

Most microorganisms are not destroyed by freezing and may even be present on fruits and vegetables. Blanching does help lower the microorganism count significantly but enough of them do survive and are ready and waiting to destroy the food as soon as it thaws. Inspect all frozen foods, which may have accidentally thawed by leaving the freezer door open or from an electrical failure. The botulism microorganism does not reproduce at 0° Fahrenheit.

QUICK GET THE ALOE, I'VE GOT FREEZER BURN

Poorly wrapped food or slow freezing allows moisture to evaporate and cause freezer burn. This produces a grainy, brown spot on the food and that area becomes dry and very tough. The area will lose its flavor, however, the food is still safe to eat (if you really want to).

YOU WON'T LIKE ME IF YOU FREEZE ME

There are number of foods that have a high liquid content. When these foods are frozen they are not very palatable.

FOOD	PROBLEM AFTER FREEZING
Apples	Becomes, soft and mushy and may turn dark
Celery	Becomes soft and only good for cooking
Cooked egg whites	Turns rubbery
Cooked macaroni and rice	Mushy; loss of taste
Cheese in blocks	Tends, to crumble too easily
Cheese, crumbled	Soggy
Cucumbers	Limp, water-logged, poor flavor
Custards	Gets watery
Cream cheese	Becomes grainy and crumbly
Cream pies	Gets watery
Custard fillings	Easily separates, watery
Egg whites (cooked)	Soft, tough, rubbery
Fried foods	Loss of crispness, soggy
Gelatin	Weeps
Grapes	Becomes soft and mushy
Gravy	Need to be re-heated if fat separates
Icings made with egg whites	Weepy
Jelly on bread	Tends, to soak into the bread
Lettuce	Loses shape and very limp
Mayonnaise	Separates

Meringue	Toughens
Milk sauces	Tends to curdle or separate
Onions, raw	Becomes; watery and very limp, but OK for cooking
Potatoes, Irish	Soggy when frozen in soups or stews
Potatoes, raw	Texture is lost and they may darken
Radishes	Texture is poor and they become pithy
Salad greens	Lose crispness
Sauces with milk or cream	May separate
Sour Cream	Separates, watery
Tomatoes, raw	Watery and tend to lose their shape
Whole milk	Separates
Yogurt	Separates

THAWING 101

- Thawing is best done in the refrigerator at about 41° F. (5° C.). This will not expose foods to the temperature danger zone.
- Many foods can be thawed under warm water at about 70° F. (21.1° C.) providing it takes less than 2 hours. This method is usually reserved for poultry.
- If you thaw in the microwave, the food should be cooked immediately to be on the safe side.
- Room temperature thawing should never be done since it allows the food to reach a temperature that may cause bacterial growth.

PROTECT ME, I'M VALUABLE

It is necessary to use the proper packaging materials if you want to keep your food in good condition when you freeze them. Foods will lose color, flavor, nutrients and moisture unless you are careful. The wrapping material or container will vary depending on the type of food or dish you are freezing. Never freeze fruits or vegetables in containers over ½ gallon, since they tend to freeze too slowly and usually do very poorly. If you wish to have the best results use packaging with the following characteristics:

- Should be resistant to oils, grease and water.
- Strong and leak-proof.
- Easy to seal up.
- Has a space to write date on.
- Needs to be moisture proof.
- Should not be too porous.
- Should not become brittle and crack at freezing temperatures.

FOILED AGAIN

Aluminum foil should never be used next to a warm or hot meat product and frozen. It keeps the food warm for too long a period and bacteria may grow and if the food is not re-cooked to a high enough temperature after it is thawed the bacteria may be re-activated. Also aluminum foil develops micro cracks and is only good next to a cold food in the refrigerator for no more than 1-2 days. Also, never place aluminum foil on top of a meatloaf with tomato sauce. It will deteriorate from the acid in the tomato sauce. The acid in citrus fruits will also eat away aluminum foil.

WERE BREAKING UP, ALL FOOD OVERBOARD

Standard glass jars are not recommended for the freezer and break very easily. If you do use glass jars, use only the ones that are made special for freezing. Plastic containers are very good for freezing. When using a plastic container, remember to place a piece of plastic wrap next to the food after it has cooled or is newly frozen. This will slow any moisture loss and may prevent the formation of larger ice crystals. Also, use freezer tape whenever possible to seal around the lids of all containers.

I'M EXPANDING, I HOPE I DON'T BURST

Other than most vegetables that normally will pack loose, most foods should have a small air space to allow for expansion.

THE POWERS GONE; WERE LOST

If you lose power, never open the freezer door unless you really have to. If the freezer is full, the foods will remain frozen for 2-4 days without thawing depending on the size of the freezer. Half-filled freezers will only remain frozen for about 24 hours. Cover the freezer with a blanket and tape it around as best you can. Tape all around the door after placing aluminum foil in the door cracks. Place a baggie with ice cubes in the freezer to see if has thawed and re-frozen the food.

YOU CAN GROW OLD IN HERE

When foods are kept past the recommended freezer storage time, the food is still OK to eat, however, the taste, texture and nutritional quality will be reduced significantly. Rotating frozen foods are a must.

WELL ZIP MY LOCK

Zip-type bags should not be used for freezer storage unless they specifically state that they are made for freezer use. Most are too porous and the seal is not airtight enough to really do the job.

I WANT MY SWEETS

Fruits can be frozen without sugar. Sugar is only used to maintain the sweet flavor, help retain the texture and stabilize the color and is not needed as a preservative.

I'M NOT ALL ARTIFICIAL

If you plan on using a sugar substitute with foods that are going to be frozen, it is not a problem, however, you should follow the directions for equivalents very closely. While the artificial sweeteners do provide sweetness, they do not provide the syrup and color stabilization that the real thing will.

ELIMINATING BROWN OUT #1

The best method of reducing or eliminating the browning of fruits can be achieved with the use of ascorbic acid or vitamin C. Pure ascorbic acid is available in most supermarkets or drug stores. While some people tend to use lemon juice, it is not as effective and may impart more of a lemon flavor, which may not be desirable for many foods.

ELIMINATING BROWN OUT #2

To stop potatoes, apples and pears from browning when they are cut and exposed to the air, just dip them into a bowl containing water and 2 tablespoons of white vinegar. This also works well with avocados.

BLANCHING IN A MICROWAVE

If you choose to blanch in a microwave, I suggest you read up on the procedure in your manual. It is not as efficient as boiling water blanching and cold spots are possible, which will not kill the enzymes that must be destroyed.

I DIDN'T BLANCH AT ALL

Vegetables that are frozen and not blanched are still good to eat, however, the quality, color, texture and flavor will be considerably lower than those that have been blanched before freezing.

FREEZING YOUR CORN

Corn must be handled just right or it will not be very edible. Corn should be blanched according to directions and chilled immediately in a bowl of ice water until the cobs are completely cooled down. Before you cook the ears, allow them to partially thaw at room temperature and place a small amount of sugar in the water.

COOKING FROZEN VEGGIES

Vegetables should be cooked right from the freezer for the best results. The only exception is corn-on-the-cob and leafy greens.

COOKING MEATS THAT HAVE BEEN FROZEN

Meat and fish may be cooked directly from the freezer.

FREEZE THAT COMMERCIAL

Commercial fruit juice concentrates can be frozen at 0° F. for 1 year and most vegetables for 8 months. Bread can be frozen for 3 months and ground beef for 4 months, roasts and steaks for 1 year. Whole chicken can be frozen for 1 year, while parts are only good for 6 months.

TO RE-FREEZE OR NOT TO RE-FREEZE, THAT IS A HEALTH QUESTION

Meat & poultry	May be re-frozen if freezer temperature was maintained at 40° F. (4.4° C.) or below and the meat has no odor and is not discolored.
Vegetables	May be re-frozen only if ice crystals are present or if the freezer temperature was 40° F. (4.4° C.) or below.
Fruits	May be re-frozen providing they do not show any signs of spoilage. If they have fully thawed it would be best to use them in cooking or preserves.
Cooked foods	May be re-frozen only if ice crystals are present or the freezer was 40° F. (4.4° C.) or below. If questionable the food should be discarded.
Ice cream	If even partially thawed, discard it. If temperature was above 40° F. (4.4° C.) the ice cream could be dangerous.

FREEZER AND REFRIGERATOR STORAGE TIMES

Product	Days Under Refrigerator (40° F.)	Months in Freezer (0° F.)
Butter	45-90	7-8
Butter, Clarified	60-90	7-8
Buttermilk	7-14	3
Cream	3-5	3
Cream (half & half)	3-4	4
Eggnog	3-5	6
Frozen Desserts		1-2
Ice Cream (commercial)		2-3
Margarine (all types)	90-120	12
Milk (all types)	3-7	3
Non-Dairy Creamer	21	12
Sour Cream	14	0
Yogurt	14	2
Whipped Cream (commercial)	30	DO NOT FREEZE

CHAPTER 3

CONDIMENTS,. SAUCES AND SUCH

HOW FOODS BECOME EMULSIFIED

Emulsification is the process of combining two liquids that do not normally wish to come together. A good example of this is oil and water. Oil and vinegar is another example and if they are used to make salad dressing you know that it takes a bit of shaking to bring them together before you can pour the dressing out of the bottle. When the oil and vinegar solution is shaken the oil is broken into small droplets for a short period of time. There are a number of emulsifying agents that help keep the liquids in suspension. One of the best emulsifiers for oil and vinegar is lecithin. Lecithin, a natural fat emulsifier, can be obtained at any health food store in ampoules and only one or two of the ampoules emptied into the mixture will place the ingredients into suspension. Lecithin is found naturally in egg white, which is why egg whites are used in many sauces to keep the ingredients in suspension.

GELATIN, THE GREAT THICKENER

Gelatin can be acquired from a number of different sources, however, the most common source in animal hoofs, muscle, bones, and connective tissue. Other sources include, seaweed from which agar-agar is produced and Irish moss from which carregeenan is made. Both of these are popular commercial thickeners, carregeenan is especially useful for thickening ice cream products.

Gelatin granules have the capability of trapping water molecules and then expanding to ten times their original size. The firmness of a product will depend on the gelatin/water ratio. If the product becomes too firm, a small amount of heat is all that is needed to change the firmness closer to a liquid, if you chill the product it will become firm again. Since gelatin is high in protein you can never use fresh figs, Kiwi, papaya, or pineapple in the product since these contain an enzyme that breaks down protein thus ruining the product. The enzyme in pineapple (bromelain) can be neutralized, by simmering the pineapple for a few minutes.

When using gelatin for a dish, be sure and moisten the gelatin first with a small amount of cold water, then use the hot water to completely dissolve the gelatin. When hot water is poured into the dry gelatin a number of the granules will lump and some will not totally dissolve which may cause your dish to be somewhat grainy. The hot water should never be over 180°F for the best results. If your recipe calls for an equal amount of sugar to gelatin, the cold water step is not required since the sugar will stop the clumping. However, you still never pour the hot water into the gelatin, place the gelatin in the water.

WHO REALLY INVENTED KETCHUP OR IS IT CATSUP?

The original name for what we call "ketchup" was "ketsiap." The sauce was invented in China in the seventeenth century and mainly used on fish dishes. It was made from fish entrails, vinegar, and hot spices. The Chinese imported the sauce to Malaya and it was renamed "kechap." The Malaya's sold the kechap to the English sailors during the eighteenth century, the sailors brought it back to England and mushrooms were substituted for the fish entrails. In 1792 a cookbook by Richard Briggs "The New Art Of Cookery" named the sauce "catsup" and included tomatoes as one of the main ingredients. Ketchup became popular in the United States in 1830 when Colonel Robert Gibbon Johnson ate a tomato on the courthouse steps in Salem, New Jersey and didn't die. Tomatoes at that time were thought to be poisonous. H.J. Heinz started producing ketchup in the early 1870's; the company today is a $6.6 billion dollar company.

HANDY CONTAINERS

Empty plastic ketchup and mustard containers are great for holding icings and oils. Allow a mixture of warm water and baking soda to sit overnight in the containers then rinse thoroughly with hot water.

HOW DID HEINZ BECOME THE NUMBER ONE KETCHUP?

In the 1940's Hunt's was the number one selling ketchup in the United States, mainly because it poured more easily and this was viewed as a real asset since you didn't have to fight with the bottle to get the ketchup out. Heinz was also selling ketchup but sales were lagging far behind the Hunt's product. In an effort to change the public awareness that just because the Hunt's ketchup poured more easily that doesn't necessarily mean that it is the best product. In the 1950's Heinz placed simple TV ads stating that "Heinz, Slowest ketchup in the West....East....North....South." The public then started viewing the quality of ketchup as a measure of the viscosity and Heinz with the thickest product took the market away from Hunt's and Hunt's has never regained it back even though all ketchup is now slow. Quality ketchup now flows at 4-6.5 centimeters in 30 seconds. Government, standards (USDA) for ketchup flow is 3-7 centimeters in 30 seconds. Ketchup is a $600 million dollar industry with sales of seven 14-ounce bottles sold per person in the United States annually.

THE JELLY THICKENER

Pectin, a carbohydrate, is the most common thickener for jellies. If your jelly doesn't set it will probably be the result of too little pectin or the wrong proportions of other ingredients. For certain types of fruit jellies only a small amount of pectin may be needed since most fruits are relatively high in pectin. Some of the higher pectin fruits include all citrus fruits, apples, and cranberries. The ones with less pectin include peaches, cherries, raspberries, apricots, and strawberries. To get the most out of the pectin that is found in the fruit, the fruit should be very fresh. The fresher the fruit, the more active pectin will be available for processing the jelly. Jelly requires a number of ingredients to set properly. Pectin is only one of the most important. The acid and sugar content will, both affect the properties of the product in regard to setting up. Cooking the jelly at too high a temperature will destroy the pectin.

NEW SALT SUBSTITUTE

A new salt substitute that actually tastes exactly like salt will be available to United States markets by 2002. The substitute was created at Michigan State University and will be called "HalsoSalt®." The new salt was a product of research into alternative uses for corn and produced lysine, which is a nutrient that has a salty flavor and is capable of masking the metallic flavor of potassium chloride.

HERBS TO BATTLE HARMFUL BACTERIA

New studies are showing that certain herbs can reduce the bacterial count in certain foods. Seasoning foods may reduce the risk even from E. coli in meats and other foods. Herbs such as cloves, cinnamon, garlic, oregano and sage were all good active herbs. The most effective herb, however, in the study was garlic. The addition of 7.5% garlic and clove herbal mixture killed 99% of the pathogen that was added to the food. More studies are underway and by 2002 we may be able to purchase an herbal blend that protect our foods from bacterial contamination.

NEW DRESSING TO CONTAIN FISH FLAKES

A new dressing that will be used on vegetables will be produced from a soy sauce base and will contain fruit, mushrooms and dried cured Bonita fish flakes. The dressing is presently being sold in Japan and should be in United States markets.

The recipe has hardly changed from the original 1835 one using anchovies layered in brine, tamarinds in molasses, garlic in vinegar, chilies, cloves, shallots, and as a sweetener sugar. The mixture must still age for 2 years before being sold, the solids are filtered out, and preservatives and citric acid are added.

HOT PEPPER SAUCES

One of the most common hot sauces is salsa. These sauces are very popular in Mexico and most of South America. They may be served either hot or cold.

CHEF'S SECRETS:

When handling hot peppers, always wear light rubber gloves and be careful not to touch your eyes. The chemical capsaicin in peppers can be very irritating to your skin and especially your eyes. The same chemical is used in police pepper sprays. One drop of pure capsaicin diluted in 100,000 drops of water is still strong enough to blister your tongue.

To reduce the hotness, remove the seeds and the ribs then wash the peppers in cold water.

TABASCO, THE WORLD'S FAVORITE

Only three ingredients go into producing the most popular hot sauce in the world: they are fiery, hot Tabasco peppers, vinegar and salt. Sales total over 76 million bottles annually. The Tabasco pepper seeds were originally planted in the United States on Avery Island, Louisiana around 1865 and the product produced today is still using peppers planted from the first strain. The salt used in Tabasco Sauce is from the same island. The peppers need to be fermented for 3 years before they can be used in the sauce. Tabasco was first marketed in 1868.

THIS DOG WILL TAKE A BITE OUT OF YOU

If you really want fire hot, try Mad Dog Liquid Fire Hot Sauce. Just use it a drop at a time or it will take your toupee off and send it flying. The product contains jalapeno peppers and African Bird's Eye chili pepper. There are a few other secret ingredients and I think it's best we don't know what they are.

HOT CAN BE ICE COLD

Salsa can be frozen, however, it must be uncooked and freshly prepared. Drain as much liquid off as you can from the tomatoes or a layer of ice will be formed on the top.

HOW HOT IS HOT

The following peppers have been graded as to their level of hotness. A grade of 10 will knock your socks off and curl your toes, 6-9 will only knock your socks off, and below 6 will still give you a pretty good kick, but are palatable for most people. If your mouth is on fire, try to drink a small amount of milk or beer, since both will neutralize the hot bite. Most dairy products will work well. Peppers are graded on a Scoville Scale for their level of hotness. The hottest pepper is the Habanero at a 200,000-300,000 Scoville unit rating.

Pepper	Grade	Scoville
Habanero	10+	(200,000-300,000)
Thai Piquin	10	(100,000)
Jalapeno	9	(85,000)
Cayenne	8+	(50,000)
De Arbol	8	(25,000)
Hungarian Wax	7	(20,000)
Serrano	6+	(12,000)
Cherry	6	(7,500)
Cascabel	5	(5,000)
Ancho	3+	(1,500)
Anaheim	3	(1,000)
Pimiento	2	(500)
Peperoncini	1	(100)

KETCHUP

Ketchup was originally called "ketsiap" and was invented by the Chinese in the 1600's. It was used as a sauce for fish and was composed of fish entrails, vinegar and hot spices. The sauce was exported to Malayan's who sold the sauce to English sailors during the 1700's. In 1792 the sauce was altered and tomatoes were added and it was renamed "catsup." The sauce became popular in the United States in 1830 and H.J. Heinz started producing the commercial product in 1870.

VINEGAR

The earliest record of vinegar use dates back almost 7,000 years ago to ancient Babylonia when dates were made into wine and vinegar. Vinegar was used as a medicinal as well as a flavoring for a number of dishes. Other fruits became popular around the same period and these included grapes and figs. Laborers in ancient times were given small amounts of wine vinegar and water with a dash of salt to pep them up and work more hours. The Roman army was given vinegar rations to give them more stamina. In World War I vinegar was used to treat wounds. Vinegar does have certain antibacterial and antiseptic properties.

ALL ABOUT VINEGAR

Vinegar is commonly produced from ethyl alcohol utilizing the bacteria, acetobacter, which feeds on the alcohol, converting it into acetic acid (vinegar). Vinegar, however, can be made from a number of other foods, which is the preferred variety to use such as, apples or grains. The distilled vinegars are best used for cleaning purposes and not as a food additive. Vinegar tends to stimulate the taste buds and make them more receptive to other flavors.

The varieties of vinegar are endless depending on the food that is used to produce it. It is a mild acid called "acetic acid." The actual amount of acid in vinegar varies from 4-7 percent with the average being 5 percent. Common types include apple cider vinegar, plain white distilled, red and white wine, barley, malt, rice, and balsamic. The acetic acid content of vinegar is referred to by "grains". A 5 percent acetic acid content is known as 50-grain vinegar. The 50-grain means that the product is 50% water and 50% vinegar. A 6-7 percent vinegar will keep foods fresher longer because of the higher acid content. Vinegar will have a shelf life and retain its effectiveness for about 18 months.

Studies have found that excessive use of vinegar, which contains a mild acid may cause digestive problems, liver disorders, ulcers and destroy red blood cells prematurely. In moderation there should be no problem, however, if you can substitute apple cider vinegar in a recipe it would be healthier. Apple cider vinegar contains malic acid, which is actually friendly to the human digestive process.

One cup of vinegar is composed of 98.8% water, hardly any protein, no fat, 14.2 grams of carbohydrate, 14 mg. of calcium, 22 mg. of phosphorus, 1.4 mg. of iron, 2 mg. of sodium and 34 calories.

SOME DIFFERENT TYPES OF COMMERCIAL VINEGAR

Apple Cider Vinegar
Produced from whole apples that have been ground into pulp, then cold-pressed and fermented in wooden barrels. It can be used in salad dressings, pickling and any dish that calls for white vinegar. Be sure and purchase a good brand since some apple cider vinegar is produced from apple cores and peelings and poorly processed. The best flavoring herb combination is dill, garlic and bay.

Balsamic Vinegar
Historically, balsamic vinegar can be traced back to 1046. A bottle of balsamic vinegar was given to Emperor Enrico III of Franconia. During the Middle Ages balsamic vinegar was used as a disinfectant.

Most is produced in Italy and aged 3-12 years before being sold. The aging produces mellow, brown vinegar that is relatively sweet. Balsamic vinegar is produced from the unfermented juice of the Trebbiano grape. Some balsamic vinegar may be 50 to 100 years old and still be usable. It is one of the best cooking vinegars and is great for a salad dressing, bringing out the flavor of many vegetables.

BALSAMIC GRAPE BREW

There are two varieties of balsamic vinegar: artesian-made and commercial. True balsamic vinegar is more of a liqueur than vinegar and is almost like syrup. True balsamic vinegar can only be produced in the provinces of Modena and Reggio in northern Italy. Artisan-made balsamic vinegar can be traced back over 1,000 years. It is made from boiled-down grape must and legally cannot contain any wine vinegar. The aging process is complex and the juice must be passed down through a series of progressively smaller wooden barrels for at least 6 years, which are kept in a cool, dry location.

These special wooden barrels have small holes in their tops, which encourage evaporation, thus allowing the flavors to concentrate. This process also allows special enzymes to assist in the production of complex flavors. The vinegar must be aged between 12 and 20 years and the cost for a $1/2$ ounce bottle is between $60.00 and $250.00 for certain aged "aceto" balsamic vinegar. The best brands to purchase are Malpighi, Cavalli, Mamma Balducci and Giusti.

COMMERCIAL BALSAMIC PAINT REMOVER

Commercial balsamic vinegar is not regulated and the amount of aging can vary. It may be a blend of artisan-made or even boiled grape-must combined with good quality wine vinegar. The real inexpensive commercial balsamic is produced from cheap wine vinegar, colored and flavored with caramel. The poor quality can be compared to a quality paint remover and might substitute for one.

Cane Vinegar
Produced from sugar cane extract and water that has been fermented. The acid level of cane vinegar is just barely within the legal limits of 4% acidity. Can only be purchased in some oriental groceries and is mainly used in the Philippines.

Champagne Vinegar
This is really not made from champagne, but from the grapes that are used to make champagne. These include Chardonnay and Pinot Noir. The methods used are the same methods that are used to produce wine vinegar. Acidity levels, in champagne vinegar is relatively high and runs around 6%. Most have excellent flavors and are usually used in delicate sauces. Flavoring herbs are lemon balm, lemongrass and lemon zest.

Coconut Vinegar
Tends to leave an aftertaste and has a very low acidity level of 4%. May only be found in Asian grocery stores. Frequently used in Thai cooking.

Distilled Vinegar
May be prepared from grain, wood pulp or oil by-products. Distilled vinegar has a somewhat harsh flavor and acidity level of 5%. Usually used in commercial processing of pickles and related foods. Best used for cleaning purposes around the house.

Fruit Vinegar
Prepared using good quality cider vinegar, which has fruits such as strawberries, peaches, or oranges added.

Herb Flavored Wine Vinegar
Produced from white wine or a quality cider vinegar with the addition of any herb that is compatible. The most popular are basil, rosemary, dill, chive and oregano. Tarragon wine vinegar is commonly used by chef's for shellfish dishes, and poultry. Rosemary wine vinegar is excellent with lamb dishes.

Malt Vinegar

Originally prepared using soured beer and was called "alegar" in Europe. Traditionally it is used on fish and chips in England. Presently it is produced from malted barley and grain, mash, which is fermented and then combined with wood shavings, then placed into large vats with a vinegar bacteria. Acidity levels in malt vinegar is normally 5%. The best flavorings are a combination of tarragon, whole cloves and garlic.

Raspberry Vinegar

Produced by soaking raspberries in white wine providing the vinegar with a pleasant fruity flavor. Commonly used with pork dishes, poultry, as a salad dressing, and on fruits. Vinegar can be produce from almost any fruit, however, the flavor of raspberry vinegar seems to be the most acceptable for a large majority of the public.

Rice Vinegar

The Chinese have produced rice vinegar for over 5,000 years. It has a mild, somewhat sweet taste and is produced from rice wine or sake. This is very robust vinegar that is somewhat bitter. The Japanese produce rice vinegar that is sweeter and much milder using cooked rice. The Japanese rice vinegar is capable of neutralizing lactic acid in the body, which may relate to increasing endurance levels for athletes.

Sherry Vinegar

This is very mellow vinegar with a somewhat nutty flavor. A more expensive vinegar it is produced similar to the methods of producing balsamic vinegar. Acidity levels in sherry vinegar is 6-7% and blends especially well with olive oil in salad dressings. Chefs use the vinegar to de-glaze pans. The best flavoring combination is thyme, rosemary, oregano and basil.

Wine Vinegar

Wine vinegar is produced from white, red or rose wine and is common vinegar for salad dressings. White wine vinegar is milder than the red and goes well with fish and lighter dishes. The best flavoring combination for red wine vinegar is rosemary, savory sage, bay leaf, garlic and basil. The best for white wine is dill, tarragon, basil and lemon balm.

I'LL HAVE A SHOT OF VINEGAR WITH MY PEARLS

Cleopatra dissolved pearls in a glass of vinegar and drank it to win a wager that she could consume the most expensive meal ever.

I WAS PUNGENT

Vinegar has the tendency to lose its pungency when heated. For this reason, when you add vinegar to a dish, it should only be added when you remove the dish from the heat. If the level of acidity in vinegar is not desired, just add the vinegar while the dish is cooking and the acidity will dissipate.

MOTHER CAN BE A PRODUCER

If you purchase a better quality wine cider or malt vinegar, they may be used for a starter if the vinegar has not been filtered or pasteurized. Bacteria or "mother" may form on the surface, then sink to the bottom. If this occurs, the "mother" can be used to prepare another batch of vinegar similar to a sourdough starter.

VINEGAR TASTING PARTY

One method of tasting vinegar is to place a square sugar cube into the vinegar for about 5 seconds then suck out the vinegar. It is best not to try and taste more than 4-5 different varieties before drinking a small amount of pure mineral water to clear your taste buds.

LIVENING IT UP

If the dish you are preparing lacks the flavor you would like it to have, just add 1-2 teaspoons of balsamic vinegar to it.

I'M TOO SWEET FOR YOU

If you over-sweeten a dish, try adding a small amount of vinegar until the flavor is more to your liking.

VINEGARCOPTER

If you want to eliminate cigarette smoke from a room, just very lightly dampen a dishtowel and swirl it around over your head, keeping your feet on the floor. This will clear the room of cigarette smoke as well as the smoker.

PHOOEY, I FORGOT TO ADD VINEGAR

When cooking cabbage, add a small amount of vinegar to the cooking water and it will eliminate about 70% of the cooking odor. If you get fish or onion smell on your hands, just rub a small amount of vinegar, toothpaste, salt or coffee grounds on to remove the odor (lemon juice works too).

OLD FASHIONED REVIVAL

When vegetables become slightly wilted, they can be revived by placing them into a vinegar and water bath. Make sure the water is ice cold.

FRESHER WATER WITH VINEGAR

Next time you go on a camping trip and want your water to remain fresher longer, just add a few drops of cider vinegar to the water to keep it fresher longer and it will also have a cleaner taste.

NICE LITTLE MOLD, HAVE A SUGAR CUBE

If you want to store cheese for a longer period of time to avoid the cheese becoming moldy, just place the cheese brick into a well sealed plastic container with a piece of paper towel on the bottom that has been lightly soaked with vinegar, then add 3-4 sugar cubes. If any mold spores are lurking around after you seal it, they will be killed by the vinegar or go to the sugar cube.

HOUSEHOLD CLEANING USES FOR VINEGAR

Remove Water Rings

Mix vinegar and olive oil in a one-to-one ratio and apply with a soft cloth using slight pressure in a circular motion.

Polish Leather Furniture

Boil 2 cups of linseed oil for 1-minute then allow it to cool before stirring in 1 cup of white vinegar. Apply with a soft cloth then allow it to stand for 1-2 minutes and then rub off gently.

Remove Carpet Stains

Only works well if the stain is fresh. Combine 1 part of white vinegar to 3 parts of water and allowed to remain on the stain for 3-4 minutes. Using a sponge, rub the area gently from the center out then dry with a clean soft cloth. Try an area that is out of the way to be sure that the carpet is colorfast.

Chewing Gum Remover

White vinegar is capable of dissolving and softening chewing gum from a number of fabrics and carpeting.

Decal Remover

Apply warm vinegar on a sponge and allow it to stand for a few minutes then wipe with a soft dry cloth.

Mildew Remover

For severe buildup of mildew, use white vinegar full strength. For all other mildew buildup, use a solution of vinegar and water.

Plastic Upholstery Cleaner

Combine vinegar and water one to one and wipe the furniture with a dampened soft cloth. Follow with a dry cloth to buff.

Metal Cleaner

Use a small amount of vinegar, baking soda or salt to prepare a paste and use the paste to clean bronze, copper or brass pots or utensils.

Clean Aluminum Pot Stains

Black stains on aluminum pots can be removed by boiling white vinegar in the pot up to the area of the stain. For large pots boil the vinegar in a small pot and pour it on the stain.

Wash Windows

Mix one tablespoon of white vinegar to one quart of water.

Grease Cutter

Place a capful of vinegar in the dishwasher to cut grease.

Crystal Clear Glassware

If you want your crystal to sparkle, just rinse them in a solution of: one part white vinegar to three parts warm water.

Remove Lime Residue

Coffee pots, tea kettles and irons are notorious for hard water residue buildup. When they get really bad, fill them with white vinegar and run them through a cycle.

Drain Cleaner I

Boil 2 cups of vinegar and pour it down the drain a small amount at a time. Allow the vinegar to remain in the drain for about 5-10 minutes before pouring a pot of very hot water down the drain. The alternative is to use $\frac{1}{2}$ cup of baking soda poured into the drain followed by $\frac{1}{2}$ cup of warm vinegar, cover the drain and allow to stand for 5-10 minutes before running cold water down the drain.

Drain Cleaner II

Drop 3-4 Alka-Seltzer® tablets down the drain, the pour a bottle of white vinegar down. After 3-5 minutes run hot water down.

Clean Shower Head

Remove the head and place it in a container that will allow you to cover the head with vinegar. Allow soaking overnight, rinse and replace.

Weed Killer

Pour white vinegar on weeds in sidewalk or driveway cracks and they will be killed.

Pet Flea Killer

Add 1 teaspoon of cider vinegar to every quart of water. Fleas will not go near your pet.

Cement Remover

When you are working with concrete or cement, try cleaning your hands with vinegar, works great.

Ant Remover

If you are having a problem with ants, just wipe your counters off with a solution prepared from equal parts of vinegar and water. Crawling insects hate vinegar.

Remove Scorch Marks

If you rub a scorched mark with a clean soft cloth that has been lightly dampened with vinegar it may remove a scorch mark if it not too badly imbedded.

Brighten Clothes

If you add $1\frac{1}{2}$ cups of white vinegar to your rinse water it will brighten up the colors. If you are dying a fabric, add 1 cup of vinegar to the final rinse to set the color.

Remove Crayon Stains

Moisten a toothbrush with white vinegar and rub the area lightly until the crayon is removed.

Eliminate Deodorant Stains

Perspiration stains can be removed by rubbing the area with vinegar before laundering.

Ink Stain Remover

Vinegar will remove most ink stains if they are fresh.

Rust Remover

To remove rust, just moisten the fabric with white vinegar then rub the area lightly with salt. Place the garment in the sun to dry, then launder.

MEDICINAL USES FOR VINEGAR

Dandruff
Massage white vinegar into the scalp 3-4 times per week, then shampoo.

Nail Polish Saver
To make nail polish last longer, just soak the fingernails in a solution of 2 teaspoons of white vinegar and $1/2$ cup of warm water for 1-2 minutes before applying the polish.

Sunburn Reliever
Place a piece of cloth that has been lightly dampened with apple cider vinegar on the burn. Replace every 20-30 minutes.

Athletes Foot
Rinse your feet 3-4 times per day in apple cider vinegar.

Morning Sickness
When morning sickness occurs, just combine 1 teaspoon of apple cider vinegar in a glass of water and drink it.

Indigestion
To relieve indigestion, just place 2 teaspoons of apple cider vinegar into a glass of water and drink during a meal.

A BUNION SANDWICH

In a small bowl, soak 2 slices of white bread, 2 slices of red onion in 1 cup of vinegar for 24 hours. Place the bread on the corn (bunion) and place a slice of onion on top. Wrap with a bandage and allow it to remain overnight.

AROUND THE KITCHEN WITH VINEGAR

Storing Pimientos
If you want to store pimiento peppers after opening a can or jar, just place then into a very small bowl, cover them with vinegar and refrigerate. They will last for 2-3 weeks.

Keeping Ginger Fresh
Prepare a clean jar filled with balsamic vinegar and add the grated ginger, seal tight and refrigerate.

Flavor Enhancer
When preparing soup or tomato sauce, add one or two tablespoons of vinegar to the soup or sauce during the last 5 minutes of cooking time. This will really enhance their flavor.

Over-Salted Foods
Add 1 teaspoon of vinegar and 1 teaspoon of sugar then reheat the dish or sauce.

Mold Eliminator
Always remember to wipe down the outside of canning jars with vinegar to eliminate the possibility of mold growing.

Vegetable and Fruit Wash
Mix 2 ½ tablespoons of vinegar in 1 gallon of water and use the mixture to wash the outsides of fruits and vegetables before peeling or slicing into them.

Stops Food Discoloring
If you add 1-2 teaspoons of vinegar to the water you are boiling potatoes in, they will not discolor for a longer period.

Great Mashed Potato Trick
Once you have mashed the potatoes and added the hot milk, try adding a teaspoon of vinegar and beat a little bit more. It will fluff them up and they will hold their shape.

Firm Gelatin
In warmer weather, gelatin tends to lose its shape. Just add 1 teaspoon of vinegar to the gelatin to keep it firm.

BETTER WEAR DARK SHADES

If you would like the crust on your fresh baked bread to have a great sheen, just brush the top of the bread with vinegar about 5 minutes before the bread has finished baking. Remove the bread before brushing on the vinegar as the oven can get very cramped.

ALL CRACKED UP OVER EGGS

To keep the whites where they belong when an egg cracks during boiling, just add some vinegar to the boiling water.

FISH MASSAGE

Before you try and scale a fish, give the fish a vinegar massage and the scales will come off easier as well as keeping your hands from becoming smelling fishy.

VINEGAR, RISING TO THE OCCASION

Next time you steam vegetables, try adding 2 teaspoons of vinegar to the boiling water. It will prevent unwanted odors and stabilize the color of the vegetables.

WELL PICKLE MY EGGS

Pickled eggs are found in every English pub and will be sitting in a big jar of malt vinegar and spices.

STEAK SAUCE

A-1 STEAK SAUCE, RATED ONE OF THE BEST TASTING

The ingredients are: tomato puree, high fructose corn syrup, distilled vinegar, corn syrup, salt, raisins, spices, orange base (combination of orange, lemon and grapefruit juices), orange peel, dried onion and garlic, xanthan gum and caramel color.

NEW KID ON THE BLOCK

Grande Gusto™ is a new flavor enhancer that has been approved by the FDA and contains all-natural flavor and has no yeast or MSG.

WORCESTERSHIRE SAUCE

WHO INVENTED THE SAUCE?

John Lea and William Perrins invented Worcestershire Sauce in England in 1835 by accident. They were managing a small drug store in Worcester, England when a customer, Lord Marcus Sandys asked them to reproduce his favorite Indian sauce that he had liked when he was in Bengal. They mixed up a batch of sauce prepared from vegetables and fish but didn't like the aroma it gave off and placed the mixture in their cellar for storage.

While cleaning the cellar two years later they accidentally found the mixture and were surprised at the taste. Lea & Perrins Worcestershire Sauce is now one of the most popular steak sauces in the world. The recipe has barely changed from the original one using anchovies layered in brine, tamarinds in molasses, garlic in vinegar, chilies, cloves, shallots and sugar to sweeten it up. The mixture must still age for two years before being sold. The solids are filtered out and preservatives and citric acid added.

SOY SAUCE

Soy sauce is one of the most popular condiments in the world. It is prepared from roasted soybeans and wheat (or barley), which have been fermented. The Chinese claim that ketchup was originally produced from a Chinese soy sauce recipe. There are four varieties of soy sauce:

- Light soy sauce that we normally see in the supermarkets.
- Dark soy sauce which is not as salty but has a very strong flavor.
- Chinese black soy sauce; which is very thick and the color of blackstrap molasses.

- Japanese tamari soy sauce; which is very dark, thick and has a lower salt content that the Chinese variety.

THE SOY SAUCE LEADER

Kikkoman International, Inc. is the largest producer of soy sauce in the world. Their latest product is a clear soy sauce that can be used in recipes without altering the color of the food. The company also produces soy sauce that is preservative-free and reduced-sodium, both available in either powered or liquid forms.

MUSTARD

The mustard we know today can be traced back to 1726, and was produced by Adam Bernhard Bergrath in Dusseldorf. He combined strong brown mustard seeds with a milder yellow seed and added vinegar, water and salt. One of the finest quality mustard's produced in the world is made by Appel & Frenzel under the name Lowensenf Mustard.

MARINADES

Marinades are usually prepared with one or more acidic foods, which are used to soften the food and allowing the flavors to be more easily absorbed. They are usually thin liquids, however, most utilize oil as a carrier of the flavorings into the food. Marinades may be used for as little as 30 minutes and as much as 2-3 days depending on the type of food and the recipe.

LOVE ME TENDER.........

Most marinades are used to both flavor the food as well as tenderize it. The more common tenderizing acids are: papaya (papain), pineapple (bromelain), kiwi, lemon or lime juice, apple cider vinegar and wine.

A TASTY MORSEL

The number of seasonings used in marinades is endless and really depends on a person's taste. The most common seasonings used are black or red pepper, garlic and onion.

HELP! THE MARINADE IS DRYING OUT MY ROAST

Marinades will provide a small amount of moisture to a piece of meat, however, one of the major components of a marinade is acid. Acid will reduce the ability of the meat to retain its natural moisture when the meat is cooked. In some meat, the addition of the marinade will balance off this process and you will not notice any dryness. Always remember to allow your roast to rest for 10 minutes after you remove it from the oven so that the liquids that are left can return to the surface of the roast.

CHEF'S SECRETS:

Many chefs use a plastic bag to apply the marinade to meats and fish. Just pour the marinade into the bag, add the food and seal it up well with a rubber band, plastic strap or metal tie. The bag can easily be turned occasionally to be sure that all areas of the food are well marinated.

Sometimes a chef will simmer the marinade after removing the food, thus reducing it and concentrating the flavors and use the marinade as a sauce. One note of caution; if the marinade was used for raw meats of any kind or raw fish, it would be best not to use the marinade for a sauce unless it is boiled.

MAYONNAISE

Mayonnaise may be made using any type of vegetable oil. The preferred oil would be one that is low in saturated fat and ideally one that is high in monounsaturated fat, which would be olive or canola oil. If you wish to have a somewhat nutty flavor, you can use walnut or almond oil. Always use the highest quality of the oil you choose.

WHO INVENTED MAYONNAISE?

Mayonnaise was invented by a German immigrant named Nina Hellman in New York City in 1910. Her husband Richard Hellman operated a deli in the city where he sold sandwiches and salads. He soon realized that the secret to his success was based on Nina's recipe for her dressing she put on the sandwiches and salads. He started selling the spread he called "Blue Ribbon" for ten cents a dollop and did so well that he started a distribution business, purchased a fleet of trucks, and in 1912 built a manufacturing plant. The rest is mayonnaise history with Hellman's Mayonnaise becoming one of the best selling spreads in history. At present, we consume 3 pounds of mayonnaise per person annually. To date Hellman's has sold 3.5 billion pounds of mayonnaise without changing the original recipe.

STEP BY STEP, DROP BY DROP AND SLOWLY I STIR

When preparing mayonnaise, always remember to add the oil drop by drop, which gives the emulsification enough time to fully form up. As soon as the mixture begins to become more solid and looks somewhat white, you can then add the oil in a slow, thin, steady stream. Adding the oil too quickly will result in separation.

CURING A SEPARATION

If the oil that is being added does cause a separation, the problem can be solved by either adding ½ teaspoon of prepared mustard or 1 teaspoon of vinegar to the mixture. If this doesn't work, try using an egg yolk that has been beaten well. Whisk the egg yolk into the mixture a small amount at a time just until the mixture is emulsified again. The balance of the oil then needs to be added in, a small amount at a time.

TASTY SENSATIONS

Once all the oil has been added to the mayonnaise, flavorings can be added if desired. If you would like a more tart sauce, just add 1 teaspoon of lemon juice. Additional mustard may be added or any other condiment that appeals to your taste. Always serve mayonnaise at room temperature for the best flavor.

I DON'T LIKE THE COLD

Emulsions, such as mayonnaise do not freeze well. The water in the products tends to freeze into ice crystals and separates from the oil. This causes the sauce to break up when thawed and cannot be put back into suspension easily.

MAKING MAYONNAISE? CHECK THE WEATHER REPORT FIRST

When the temperature or humidity is high, it will cause the mayonnaise to come out heavier and greasier than normal.

SHORT LIFESPAN

Fresh mayonnaise will only remain fresh for about 3 days under refrigeration and should not be frozen. After 3-4 days the mayonnaise will start to separate and there is no method to bring it back into a separation.

PLEASE DON'T FREEZE ME

Mayonnaise will stay fresh in the refrigerator after it is opened for about 2 months, but does not freeze well.

Standard Mayonnaise Recipe:

1   egg yolks (large)
1   teaspoon of lemon juice
1   cup extra virgin olive oil (cold pressed)
1   teaspoon quality mustard (your favorite)
1/8   teaspoon crushed sea salt (if desired)
1/8   teaspoon freshly ground black pepper (if desired)

Combine the egg yolks, lemon juice, mustard, salt and pepper in a bowl and whisk. After they are blended, add the oil a few drops at a time, allowing the mixture to thicken and obtain a yellowish-white color. Then continue to add the balance of the oil slowly in a thin stream. If the mixture becomes too thick, add small amount of lemon juice to thin it out.

Russian Dressing Recipe:

1   cup Standard Mayonnaise
1/3   cup quality mild chili sauce
1   tablespoons chives (chopped fine)
1/2   teaspoon finely minced pimentos

Combine all ingredients, mixing thoroughly and chill for 2-3 hours in the refrigerator. Best if served chilled.

Tartar Sauce Recipe:

1   cup Standard Mayonnaise
3   tablespoons chopped dill pickle
2   tablespoons chopped parsley
1   tablespoon tarragon
2   tablespoons finely chopped scallions or red onion
2   tablespoons very dry white wine (optional)
  Ground sea salt and ground fresh black pepper, as desired

Combine all ingredients in a medium bowl and place into refrigerator for 2-3 hours to allow the flavors to blend well. Best when served chilled.

Thousand Island Dressing Recipe:

1   cup Standard Mayonnaise
1   tablespoon finely chopped green bell pepper
1/4   tablespoon finely chopped red bell pepper
1   cup chopped canned whole tomato (no seeds)
3/4   teaspoon chopped pimentos
1   hard-boiled egg, finely chopped
1/2   teaspoon Worcestershire sauce
3   tablespoons mild chili sauce

Combine all ingredients in a medium bowl and chill in the refrigerator for 2-3 hours. Whisk well before serving chilled.

SALAD DRESSING

CHEF'S SECRETS:

The standard ratio followed by most chefs when preparing an oil and vinegar salad dressing is to use 1 part apple cider vinegar (or lemon/lime juice) to 3 parts of extra virgin olive oil (cold processed). A vinaigrette salad dressing can be made by just adding $1/2$ teaspoon of quality mustard and using red wine vinegar instead of the cider vinegar.

To prepare a creamy olive oil salad dressing, just pour the oil into a running blender with a variety of seasonings and herbs already in it. Pour the oil very slowly.

SAUCES

Sauces are only meant to complement the flavor or provide moisture for the dish. Sauces should never detract from the original flavor of the food. French cooking schools classify sauces in five categories: Espagnole, which is a brown, stock-based sauce; Velote, which is a light, stock-based sauce; Bechamel, which is a white sauce and usually milk-based; Hollandaise or mayonnaise, which are emulsified sauces and Vinaigrette, which is considered an oil and vinegar sauce. However, we place mayonnaise in the condiment class because it is usually always purchased as a commercial product and vinaigrette as a salad dressing.

THICKENING 101

To thicken any sauce, you will need to increase the solids and reduce the amount of liquid. This can be accomplished by boiling away some of the liquid, however, this will reduce the amount of useable sauce and may concentrate the flavors too much. If the sauce is high in water content, cooling it causes the water molecules to lose energy and they relax, thus thickening the sauce. There are, however, a number of good substances that will thicken sauces and depending on the type of sauce you are preparing one will surely be just right for the job. These include pureed vegetables, egg yolk, flours, gelatins, tapioca, pectin, okra, cornstarch, arrowroot, potato starch, kneaded butter, emulsified butter, cream, peanut butter, etc.

A FEW OF THE COMMON THICKENING AGENTS

Arrowroot:
Purchased as a fine powder that is derived from the root stalks of a tropical tuber. It is prepared by dissolving a small amount in water. These stems are mainly composed of complex carbohydrates, which have the tendency to thicken at a lower cooking temperature than most other starches. The advantage of arrowroot is that there is less likely the chance of burning the thickener due to its low protein content.

Tapioca:
Extracted from the tropical cassava root and best used as a thickener if it is diluted with water before being added to a dish just before serving. The roots are finely grated, left to ferment. Then pressed into cakes and baked. The baked cakes are then powdered into a pure starch. Tapioca is best when it is moistened, then heated and immediately used.

Vegetable puree:
Healthier method of thickening gravies and sauces. Purees may be made with any assortment of vegetables that compliment the dish it is to be used in. Vegetables need to be cooked first; some need to be sautéed fist then pureed in a blender or food processor. Once the vegetables are pureed, they should be put through a sieve or fine mesh before using.

Cornstarch:
Produced from the endosperm of a kernel of corn and should always be dissolved in cold water before using for the best results. May become cloudy when cooked and satiny when fully set. When used in place of flour the sauce will be clearer.

All-Purpose Flour
Made from the endosperm of wheat and tends to turn opaque when cooked and somewhat pasty when set: very effective in thickening gravies.

Rice Starch
This is sold in a fine white powder and is made from ground rice. It will turn white when cooked and creamy when it sets up. Usually found at Asian markets. Use only half as much as cornstarch for the same results.

Mung Bean Starch

Produced from dried ground mung beans. Becomes very clear when it is cooked and somewhat gelatinous when set. Commonly used throughout Asia to prepare jellied dishes.

PECTIN

When using pectin in preserves, be sure and only use the pectin specified in the recipe. Different brands are prepared with different ingredients that will make a difference in the final product. Some pectin needs acid and sugar to set, while others need acid and a small amount of sugar. Some pectin never needs acid or sugar to set.

REAL EASY AND THICK TOO

A relatively new thickener Thick & Easy® is now available. The thickener is made from modified food starch and maltodextrim with no additives or preservatives. The product can be used to thicken any type of cold or hot food, either solids or liquids. The product can be frozen and reheated by microwave oven. The thickening activity stops after one minute and it retains its consistency. It is fully digestible, does not bind fluids, releasing 98% for consumption, while most competitive products only release 50%. For additional information call (800) 866-7757.

COMMERCIAL THICKENERS

One of the better commercial thickeners is Textra™. Textra™ is a modified tapioca starch that has been designed to improve mouthfeel and texture of foods. It does not impart any taste to the product while providing thickening for drinks, sauces and syrups. It is one of the more stable thickeners and will assist particles, such as fruit pulp to remain in suspension.

INSTANT STARCH

There are two "jel" products that will do a great thickening job. These are ClearJel-310® and Rice Gel®. ClearJel-310® will thicken as soon as it is added to either water or milk and will provide a smooth, fully hydrated texture as well as being heat and acid resistant. Rice Gel is produced from pre-cooked rice flour with no noticeable taste of its own. It has a high water capacity and blends well with dry foods and is non-allergenic.

THICKENING A SAUCE OR MAKING GLUE FOR THE KIDS

The easiest method to thicken a sauce is to prepare a small amount of "paste." The paste should be prepared separate from the sauce. Never try and add the paste ingredients to the sauce to hasten the procedure. The paste needs to be smooth and the consistency will vary depending on the level of thickening needed. If the sauce is very thin, you will need a thick paste, etc. Add the paste gradually, allow the sauce to boil and stir until the desired texture is obtained. These pastes will work especially well with gravy and most other sauces.

Thin Paste . . . . .Use 1 tablespoon	flour + 1 cup of liquid
Medium Paste . . . . .Use 2 tablespoons	flour + 1 cup of liquid
Thick Paste . . . . . . .Use 3 tablespoons	flour + 1 cup of liquid

Use whatever liquid is compatible with the sauce you are preparing.

HEAR YE, HEAR YE, HOT SAUCES HATE EGG YOLKS

If your recipe calls for egg yolks, never add them to a sauce that is too hot. The instant change in temperature, resulting from placing the cool egg into the hot liquid is just enough of a change to curdle the egg yolk and may ruin the sauce. To eliminate the possible problem, remove a small amount of the sauce and allow it to cool for a few minutes before mixing the egg yolk in. The cooled sauce can then be added to the hot mixture.

WHISK ME A RIBBON

When sauce is finished cooking, it should fall from the whisk in a wide ribbon or sheet. This should take about 5 minutes of cooking.

WHY DOES STARCH THICKEN A SAUCE?

Starch granules are a solid, which just by being there will cause a certain degree of thickening. However, the small starch granules tend to trap water molecules, thus reducing the percentage of free-flowing water that is in the sauce or soup. When you heat the starch it has the ability to expand and is capable of absorbing even more water.

NERVOUS PUDDING

Kids call gelatin "nervous pudding" because it always shaking. Gelatin has been used as one of the primary thickeners for hundreds of years and is capable of increasing ten times its original size. Gelatin is the best water-trapping medium we have found. Care, however, must be taken when adding other ingredients to gelatin. Sugar reduces the absorption capacity of gelatin significantly and fruits such as pineapple and papaya, which contains the enzymes bromelain and papain and will eliminate gelatin's thickening ability.

AVOIDING A SEPARATION

If your egg-based sauce separates, remove the pan from the heat and beat in two tablespoons of crushed ice to reduce the heat and place the eggs back into suspension, thus saving the emulsion. You can also change pans and add one tablespoons of ice water to a small amount of the sauce while slowly whisking back the balance of the separated sauce. Additional ice water can be added slowly, but only as needed.

TWO TIMES THE POWER OF FLOUR

Cornstarch, arrowroot and potato starch should only be used just before you are finishing the sauce, since they have twice the thickening power of flour and can only be cooked for a few minutes before losing their thickening power.

NEED, KNEADED BUTTER?

This is an excellent thickener, especially at the last minute. If you wish to make a sauce from leftover liquids that have remained in the pan, just place an equal amount of butter (unsalted) and flour in another pan and then mix them together to make a thick paste. Use small amounts of the paste adding it gradually to the leftover liquid.

THE FATS IN THE FLOUR

Flour will not lump if you add the flour to any fat that is already hot. In fact, you can add flour to any hot liquid without the flour lumping.

REGULAR FLOUR VS. INSTANT FLOUR

Regular flour tends to turn into a form of gelatin when it comes into contact with hot water that tends to block the water from entering. Instant flour contains smaller irregular-shaped granules that allow space for the water to enter.

HOW ABOUT A QUICKIE

If you would like a hollandaise sauce that can be prepared in 10 minutes or less, try Knorr® Hollandaise Sauce Mix. The ingredients include modified food starch, wheat flour, non-fat dry milk, hydrolyzed vegetable protein, partially hydrogenated peanut oil, lactose, salt, fructose, onion and garlic powder, citric acid, vegetable gum, yeast extract, soup stock, spices and a natural flavor. It really is not too bad tasting, but nothing like the "made-from-scratch" original.

DON'T MOCK MY HOLLANDAISE

To prepare a "mock" hollandaise sauce, just use 1 cup of white sauce and add 2 slightly beaten egg yolks and cook until just 2 bubbles (not 3 or 4) appear on the surface. Remove the pot from the hot burner and beat in 2 tablespoons of unsalted butter and 2 tablespoons of pure lemon juice. Voila, fake hollandaise sauce that will fool everyone but a chef.

SAUCE TOO SALTY? SUGAR CUBES TO THE RESCUE

One easy method of reducing the salt level in sauces and soups is to dip a sugar cube into the dish and run it back and forth covering the surface only once and before the cube melts. Salt is attracted to sugar and a percentage of the salt will adhere to the cube, then discard the cube.

HOT IS NOT REALLY HOT, IT'S WARM!

Sauces are never served hot, always warm. High heat will melt the butter too fast and ruin the emulsification and cause separation. You want the butter to turn into a foamy mixture, not a liquid. Start with cold butter, which will keep the mixture cool and reduces the risk of the butter melting instead of foaming. Keep the pan moving on and off the heat if necessary while beating the butter with a whisk. You can also use a double boiler, which is easier for the person who is not used to making a white sauce.

I'M GOING BAD, MY STARCH IS FREEZING

Most sauces and custards that are thickened with flour or cornstarch do not freeze well. The starch, amylase, which is commonly found in grain starches such as wheat flour and cornstarch tend to freeze into a very firm, spongy-texture and allows the liquid to drain out. If the food is thickened with a root starch, such as arrowroot or tapioca they can be frozen and thawed without any problem.

I'LL NEVER COOK AGAIN

If you accidentally burn your dessert sauce, don't fret just add a small amount of pure vanilla or almond extract in the sauce to cover up the burnt taste.

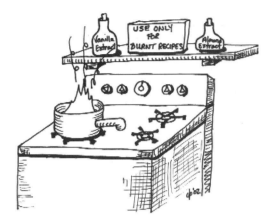

CHEF'S SECRET TO A SAFE HOLLANDAISE

Since eggs may be contaminated even if they are not cracked, it would be wise to microwave the eggs to be sure that there is no contamination before you make the sauce. The procedure will not harm the eggs and they will still be in good shape for the sauce. The procedure can only be done with 2 large yolks at a time and in a 600-watt microwave oven.

The first step is to separate the egg yolks from the white and remove the cord. Then place the yolks in a small glass bowl and beat them until they are well mixed. Next, add 2 teaspoons of real lemon juice and mix thoroughly. The bowl should then be covered and placed into microwave on high and the surface observed. When the surface starts to move allow the mixture to cook for no more than 10 seconds. Remove the bowl and whisk with a **clean** whisk. Return the bowl to the microwave and cook until the surface moves again and then another 10 seconds. Remove and whisk again with a clean whisk. Allow the bowl to sit for one minute before you use it for the sauce and it will be salmonella free.

ARE YOU GOING TO DO IT AGAIN?

There are a number of rules to remember when re-heating soups, sauces and stews. Foods that contain fats tend to oxidize more readily and this may impart a less than desirable flavor. When re-heating, never place the food in an aluminum or iron pot and never add salt until the food is almost completely warmed back up. Soups and gravies should only be simmered for about 2 minutes. Creamed soups should only be re-heated at a slow simmer after it has reached a slow boil for about 2 minutes.

AM I REALLY THAT BITTER, I TRY TO BE SWEET

Occasionally, sauces tend to taste a bit bitter and the reason escapes you. It may be from a tomato seed or two that ended up not being strained out. A crushed tomato seed will cause a sauce to become bitter.

WHY IS MY MELTED CHEESE SOLID?

When melting cheese, never cook it for too long a period or at too high a temperature. When this occurs, the protein separates from the fat and the cheese gets tough and rubbery. Once a cheese hardens, especially in a sauce, it would be wise to discard the sauce and start over. When you melt cheese, it would be wise to grate the cheese first. The cheese will then melt in a shorter period of cooking time.

MAKE YOUR CHEESE HAPPY, GIVE IT SOME WINE

The reason cheese tends to form lumps or strings, is that the calcium phosphate present in the cheese binds with the protein. This can be avoided if a small amount of wine, which contains tartaric acid, is added to the melting cheese. The tartaric acid prevents the calcium phosphate from linking the cheese proteins. If you prefer not to use wine, just use a small amount of lemon juice and the citric acid will accomplish the same thing.

WHITE SAUCE, THE RIGHT WAY

There are two types of white sauces: *Bechamels,* which is made from whole milk or cream and Veloute, which is made from chicken or fish stock to be sure it retains a white color. All white sauces are made with a *roux* – which is made by combining flour in clarified butter (or almost any fat) while cooking slowly until it combines. This is always done before adding any liquid, however, be sure the mixture doesn't brown and that it does foam up slightly and remains a light color.

As soon as this occurs, add the liquid at once and stir continually until it starts to boil, reduce the heat and allow the mixture to simmer for 5-8 minutes. The simmering is important since it will remove the taste of the flour.

Cajun roux is cooked until the mixture of flour and fat turns black but does not burn. This is a very slow process.

CHEF'S SECRETS TO THE PERFECT WHITE SAUCE:

1 When you stir the liquid into the roux and lumps are formed, strain the mixture through a fine sieve before continuing.
2 If the sauce is too thick, add a small amount of liquid while stirring slowly. If too thin, just simmer longer until it thickens.
3 If you are preparing the white sauce and need to allow it to sit for a period of time, rub the top of the sauce lightly with the end of a stick of butter. This will result in a thin layer of melted butter on the top preventing a skin from forming.
4 If a skin does form, skim it off carefully to remove it all.

FREEZING WHITE SAUCE

If you do not use cream or eggs, the sauce will freeze well for 2 weeks but will only last for one day in the refrigerator. If you do freeze the sauce with egg, the yolk will separate from the sauce when thawed. Cream in the sauce may be too thin when thawed and will require 1-2 teaspoons of arrowroot to be added.

WINE SAUCE TIP

When wine is added to any sauce, be sure and heat the sauce long enough for the alcohol to evaporate thus leaving the flavor only.

GIDDYUP BUTTER

Mounted butter sauces gain body from both the emulsification process and air that is beaten in.

SPEEDY, ALMOST INSTANT SAUCES

Beef Sauce: Whisk 1 cup of heavy cream with 2 tablespoons of a mildhorseradish sauce, 1^1/$_2$-tablespoons of lemon juice and a small amount of salt and pepper as desired.

Chicken Sauce: In a small saucepan on low heat, whisk 8 ounces of sour cream with one can of cream of mushroom soup, then add one cup of de-fatted chicken broth.

Fish Sauce: Whisk together, one cup of mayonnaise with 2 tablspoons of minced sweet pickles, 1 tablespoon of minced onions and 1 tablespoon of minced stuffed green olives.

Lamb Sauce: In a small saucepan over low heat, melt one cup of mint jelly with one cup of pure, pulp-free orange juice and one tablespoon of mild prepared mustard. Heat and serve warm.

Low-fat Sauce: Combine one can of quality light evaporated milk with one package of onion soup mix and one tablespoon of cornstarch in a small saucepan over low heat. Whisk in your favorite minced herbs or onion, remove from the heat and add one cup of non-fat sour cream.

Pork Sauce: In a small saucepan over low heat, melt one cup of current jelly with ^{1}/$_2$ cup of ketchup and 1 teaspoon of pineapple juice. Serve warm.

Vegetable Sauces: Melt 6 or more ounces of Velveeta with just enough milk to make a smooth mixture, serve while it is warm.

Slowly melt 6 or more ounces of regular or any flavored cream cheese with a small amount of milk on low heat in a small saucepan.

Whisk one pint of heavy cream and one cup of mayonnaise and blend well.

LOWER-FAT SAUCES

Barbecue Sauce
The American-style barbecue sauce is made with tomato sauce, mustard, onions, garlic, brown sugar or molasses and apple cider vinegar.

Bordelaise
Prepared with wine, brown stock, bone marrow, shallots and herbs.

Bourguignonne
French sauce prepared with red wine, onions, carrots, flour and bacon.

Coulis
Usually prepared as a vegetable puree.

Demi-Glace
Prepared as a reduced stock made with either sherry or Madiera wine.

Marinara
Prepared from tomato sauce, onion, garlic and oregano.

Sweet and Sour
Prepared with sugar, vinegar and seasonings.

Veloute
Stock-based white French sauce.

HIGHER-FAT SAUCES

Alfredo
An Italian sauce prepared from cream, butter and Parmesan cheese.

Bechamel
White sauce prepared from butter, milk and flour.

Bernaise
French white sauce prepared from white wine, tarragon, vinegar, shallots, butter and egg yolk.

Bolognese
Italian meat sauce prepared from meat, vegetables, wine, cream and herbs.

Hollandaise
Prepared with butter, egg yolk and lemon juice.

Mole
Mexican sauce prepared from onions, garlic, hot chilies and chocolate.

Pesto
Italian sauce prepared from fresh basil, pine nuts, garlic and Parmesan cheese.

Ragu
Prepared from tomato sauce, ground beef, onions, celery, white wine and herbs.

Vinaigrette
French oil sauce prepared from olive oil, vinegar and herbs.

TOMATO SAUCES

The French were the first to utilize tomato sauce in recipes after the tomato was discovered in Peru and brought to France by the Spanish Moors in the 1500's. If you are going to use fresh tomatoes in a recipe, be sure they are at room temperature for the best results. Tomatoes can be refrigerated for storage, however, they lose almost all of their aroma and flavor when cold. Allow the tomatoes to remain at room temperature for 30 minutes before using them. This will re-activate the aroma and flavor.

CHEF'S SECRETS:

Since most recipes call for removing the skin and seeds of tomatoes, there is an easy method of accomplishing this. Just place the tomatoes in a large pot of boiling water for 2-3 minutes. This will loosen the skin then remove them with a slotted spoon. To remove the seeds, cut the tomato in half and squeeze the halves into a fine strainer. This will catch the seeds and allow the juice to be saved.

Homemade tomato sauce can be stored in the refrigerator for 2 days and will freeze for 3-4 months.

Classic Old Fashioned Spaghetti Sauce Recipe:

4   tablespoons of extra virgin olive oil (cold processed)
1   teaspoon of Canola oil
³/₄ cup red onion, chopped
2   cloves of garlic, chopped
1   large carrot, chopped
1   large stalk of celery, chopped
1   pound of lean ground round
½   cup Chianti (optional)
4   large ripe tomatoes, skinned, seeded and chopped
1   tablespoon fresh thyme
2   cups of brown stock
Add salt and ground black pepper as desired

Place the olive and canola oil in a large pan over medium heat and sauté the onions for about 5 minutes but do not allow them to burn. Add the carrot, garlic and celery and sauté for another 5 minutes. Add the ground beef and cook until the meat is well browned, then stir in the tomato, wine (optional), thyme and brown stock. Lower the heat and simmer for 50 minutes. Add the salt and pepper as desired.

BARBECUE SAUCE

Barbecue sauces are prepared to provide a particular flavor to the food and is usually brushed on meat and chicken. They are not designed to tenderize the food and do not penetrate very deeply into the food. Almost all barbecue sauces contain oil, which keeps the surface of the food moist and helps avoid burning. The sauce is applied a number of times during the cooking process with a natural bristle brush or a special barbecue brush.

Grandma's Barbecue Sauce Recipe:

2   cups ketchup or seasoned tomato sauce
3   tablespoons of extra virgin olive oil (cold pressed)
1   teaspoon canola oil
1/2   cup finely diced red onion
4   cloves of garlic, finely minced
1/2   cup unsulfured molasses
1/4   cup apple cider vinegar
1   teaspoon powdered cayenne pepper
1   tablespoon lemon juice
1/4   cup quality mustard
1   teaspoon soy sauce

Using a medium-sized pan, heat the olive oil with the small amount of canola oil (to raise the smoke point) over medium heat. Stir in the garlic and onion and sauté for 6-8 minutes before adding the rest of the ingredients. Mix the balance of the ingredients into the sauce, then allow it to simmer for about 15-20 minutes. The sauce may be applied either warm or cold.

COMMERCIAL TERIYAKI SAUCE

Commercial teriyaki sauce should contain the following ingredients if the quality is superior: Soy sauce, dried garlic, concentrated pear or grape sweetener, dried onion, sesame seed, garlic powder, ginger powder, onion powder and natural vegetable gum. There should be no added salt.

MOLE SAUCE

This sauce is of Mexican origin and can probably be traced back to the Aztecs who used chocolate to sweeten dishes. However, originally a mole sauce was any sauce that contained hot chili peppers. The sauce is traditionally served with poultry dishes, but can be found on almost any dish in a Mexican restaurant.

Mexican Mole Sauce Recipe:

1   *tablespoons of extra virgin olive oil (cold pressed)*
½   *teaspoon of canola oil*
½   *cup red onions, sliced*
2   *large ripe tomatoes, peeled and seeded and diced*
1   *Poblano chilies, remove seeds, ribs, skin and cut up*
2   *cloves of fresh garlic, sliced*
¼   *cup regular or seasoned bread crumbs*
½   *cup roasted peanuts, finely chopped*
¼   *teaspoon powdered cinnamon*
½   *teaspoon ground black pepper*
2   *cups chicken stock*
2   *ounces of chopped quality unsweetened chocolate*
1   *tablespoon toasted sesame seeds*
Add salt as desired

Place the chilies, nuts, tomatoes, breadcrumbs and onion in a blender or food processor and chop them up on a fine setting. Be sure not to make mush, just chop them up fine. Place the mixture in a medium bowl and stir in the black pepper, cinnamon, salt and chocolate. Place a medium-sized pan over medium heat and heat the olive and canola oil for 2 minutes, then whisk in the bread crumb mixture and allow to simmer for about 5-7 minutes or until the chocolate has melted and the mixture has thickened.

Add the chicken stock and simmer for about 15-20 minutes or until the mixture is very hot and thick, but workable. Add the sesame seeds and the sauce is finished. This sauce should be served as soon as it is prepared for the best results.

SWEET SAUCES

CUSTARD

One of the most popular sweet sauces is a custard sauce, which can be made in a number of great flavors such as chocolate, vanilla, raspberry, mint, blueberry, apricot and lemon.

CHEF'S SECRETS:

When preparing custard, eggs are sometimes a problem if not handled properly. The eggs should be beat first with sugar and set aside. The milk or cream must then be scalded until small bubbles form around the edges of the pot. Pour a small amount of the hot liquid into the eggs mixing thoroughly, slightly cooking the eggs. Add the egg mixture into the hot milk and heat on low heat until it starts to thicken. The custard should then be strained into a bowl to remove any solidified egg or film that had formed.

Custard must be stirred continually to prevent the bottom burning. Chefs always use a wooden spoon when stirring custard since some of the eggs minerals may react with certain types of metal spoons. When stirring always stir in a figure eight pattern to cover the complete bottom.

CHOCOLATE SAUCE/SYRUP

When preparing chocolate sauces there are a number of tips that you should be aware of. The following will help you obtain the perfect sauce:

CHEF'S SECRETS:

If a liquid is used in the recipe, always melt the chocolate in the liquid, not separate for the best results. Use low heat and stir continuously.

The microwave is excellent for melting chocolate. Just place the chocolate in a large measuring glass and cook until melted while keeping an eye on it to be sure it doesn't cook too much.

Most chefs melt chocolate in a double boiler over simmering (not boiling) water.

Always use the type of chocolate called for in a particular recipe and always use the highest quality chocolate you can find.

FINGER LICK'N GOOD

Ganache is one of the finest blends of chocolate sauce you will ever taste when made properly. It consists of melted semi-sweet chocolate, heavy cream and unsalted butter. It is definitely not a healthy food since it is high in fat, cholesterol and calories.

Ganache Recipe:

In a small saucepan heat 1 cup of heavy cream and 2 tablespoons of butter to boiling. Place a 12 ounce bag of chocolate semi-sweet morsels into a medium bowl and pour the hot butter cream mixture over the chocolate and stir until smooth. When it is cool, it will remain somewhat soft and should not harden.

NOTE: Do not use vanilla purchased in Mexico for any of these recipes. The purity of this type of vanilla may be suspect and may affect the quality of the recipe.

Grandma's Hot Fudge Heaven Sauce Recipe:

4   ounces of bittersweet chocolate (4 squares)
12   ounce can of quality evaporated milk
3   tablespoons of salted butter
2½ cups confectioner's sugar
2   teaspoons of pure vanilla extract

Combine the chocolate, sugar and evaporated milk on the top of a double boiler with simmering water in the bottom. Stir occasionally until the chocolate has melted completely. Remove from the heat and whisk in the pure vanilla and butter until the mixture is smooth. Enjoy!

CONTROLLING YOUR TEMPER WHILE TEMPERING

Tempering chocolate is the process of melting it, cooling it, and then melting it again. This process produces a more lustrous, glossy and stable mixture and is called for in many chocolate recipes. This is an exact science to obtain the right consistency and takes some practice. However, there is a "quick-tempering" method that utilizes a small amount of oil that will speed the process up considerably. The end product will be a little thinner, but will not make a difference in most recipes and decorative uses.

WE LOVE CHOCOLATE

The United States is the largest purchaser of cocoa beans in the world. We average about 170,000 tons annually.

FINALLY LOW-FAT CHOCOLATE SYRUP

New low-fat chocolate syrup has hit the markets, which has all the flavor and taste of the real thing and 5 times less fat. The product is produced by New-Market Foods of Petaluma, California and consists of brown-rice syrup, honey, molasses and cocoa. The topping is syrupy and buttery and found in health food stores.

' THE QUICK-TEMPERING METHOD:

Use 1 tablespoon of vegetable oil, (preferable a neutral oil such as Canola or safflower) also clarified butter is often used by some candy chefs, even a solid shortening. Stir 1 tablespoon of the oil into every 3 ounces of melted chocolate you use over low heat. Quick-tempered chocolate will only hold up for 2-3 days, but the candy is usually long gone before that.

COOKING EXTRACTS

VANILLA EXTRACT

The FDA has established guidelines for vanilla extract and if you use vanilla extract in your cooking you should know the differences in the various ones that are sold. To be called a "pure vanilla extract" the list of ingredients must read "extractives of vanilla beans in water, alcohol (35%). This will probably be the more expensive brand. Other labels may read "water, alcohol (35%), vanilla bean extractives and corn solids." The better brands may still use a small amount of corn solids, however, they will always have the vanilla bean as the first ingredient on the list of ingredients.

To produce one gallon of pure vanilla extract it takes 13.6 ounces of vanilla beans, 35% alcohol and water. The alcohol evaporates when you bake or cook with the vanilla. Sugar should never be listed on the label and may affect the product. Time (aging) will improve the flavor of pure vanilla extract.

Vanilla sold in Mexico has been implicated in numerous studies as containing contaminants from the harvesting of the bean and the processing procedures. Since there is no way of telling which are good and which are bad, it is recommended not to purchase any Mexican vanilla.

The Unites States purchase more vanilla beans than any other country in the world, about 1,500 tons of vanilla beans annually.

WELL, EXCUSE MY INFUSION

Almost everyone is familiar with a simple "infusion" by just placing a tea bag in a cup of water and releasing the flavors and compounds. However, there are a number of other liquids that can be infused with essences, cinnamon sticks, vanilla beans, nuts, spices, dried fruits, and even flower petals. Hot liquids tend to cause the herb or essence to release its flavors and occasionally their colors more readily than a cold liquid. The following is a simple method of infusion:

- Place the liquid you wish to infuse and the flavoring in a saucepan over moderate heat. The liquid may be milk, soup stock, sugar syrup, cream, etc. When the liquid is just about ready to boil, remove the saucepan from the heat, cover the pan and allow the mixture to steep until the flavor you desire is achieved. This process usually takes about 30-60 minutes. The mixture should then be strained and pressed hard through the strainer to extract all the liquid. The liquid is now ready to be used in your recipe.

CHAPTER 4

GOOD FATS, BAD FATS & OILS

FATS (LIPIDS)

Fats are substances such as oils, waxes, lard, butter and other compounds that are insoluble (unable to mix with) in water. Some fats are readily visible, such as fat on meats, butter, cream cheese, bacon, and salad dressing. Other fats are less visible, such as fat in egg yoke, nuts, avocado and milk.

Fats are a combination of "fatty acids" which are their "building blocks" or basic "sub-units." The type of fat depends on the specific mixture of these fatty acids. The body uses fat as its energy storage reserves, padding to protect organs, as a constituent in hormones, an important building block of a healthy cell wall, and insulation.

FATS FALL INTO THREE MAIN CATEGORIES

1. Simple Fats — These are basic fats called a triglyceride and are composed of a glycerol base with three fatty acids.

2. Compound Fats — These are a combination of fats and other components. One of the more important being the lipoproteins: which are fats that combine with proteins. Lipoproteins are the main transport system for fats. They may contain cholesterol, triglycerides, neutral fats, and fatty acids. Since fat is insoluble it needs a vehicle to carry it around the body.

3. Derived Fats — Produced from fatty substances through digestive breakdown.

THE FATS YOU EAT ARE COMPOSED OF THREE CHEMICAL ELEMENTS:

Carbon C
Hydrogen .... H
Oxygen .... O

The carbon atoms are like a skeleton and can be compared to the framework on a house. In a saturated fat, all the carbons are completely surrounded by hydrogen and oxygen atoms. Since the carbons are totally saturated this type of fat is solid at room temperature.

In polyunsaturated fat some of the carbons have a free space where an atom of hydrogen could be attached. It is because of these openings that polyunsaturated fat is liquid at room temperature. If all the carbons have hydrogen atoms attached, the fat is saturated and solid at room temperature. There is also a middle of the road fat called a monounsaturated fat, which the body likes better than any other type of fat.

THE THREE MAJOR TYPES OF FATS

POLYUNSATURATED FATS (PUFA) **GOOD FATS**

Always remains a liquid at room temperature. Examples are safflower, corn, and peanut. Studies have shown that some PUFA and MUFA fats may have a tendency to lower blood cholesterol levels.

MONOUNSATURATED FATS (MUFA) **GOOD FATS**

These tend to thicken when refrigerated but are still liquid at room temperature. Examples are olive and canola oil. Recent studies show that MUFA oils may be more effective in lowering blood cholesterol levels than PUFA oils.

SATURATED FATS (SFA) **BAD FATS**

Normally, these are either solid or semi-solid at room temperature. Examples are butter, lard, shortening, and hard margarine. The exceptions to the rule are coconut oil and palm oil, which are liquid at room temperature and may be listed on the list of ingredients as "tropical oils." SFA's have the tendency to raise cholesterol levels even though they may not actually contain cholesterol.

MEDIUM CHAIN TRIGLYCERIDES (MCT)

This oil is derived from vegetable oils and cannot easily be stored by the body. MCT oil does not raise cholesterol levels and contains 8 calories per gram instead of the normal 9 calories per gram in other fats. The oil has shown to have anti-bacterial properties and can reduce the size of breast tumors in laboratory animals. The oil is extracted from coconuts, which contain about 15% MCT oil. MCT's, when ingested, tend to circulate until needed as a source of energy instead of being stored. The major supplier of the oil is Mead Johnson and sells for $40 per quart. Wholesale suppliers, however, such as Stephen and Huls America sell the oil for about $10 per quart wholesale.

Studies are underway to relate the MCT oil to thermogenesis, which is the process by which the body creates heat by mobilizing fat stores. Presently margarine is available in England that utilizes MCT oil as the main ingredient. By 2001 some ice cream manufactures may be substituting MCT oil for milk fat. MCT oil has too low a smoke point at 375^0 F. to be used for frying.

GOOD FAT?

Medium-chain triglycerdides (MCT) are sold in health food stores for people who have trouble absorbing fats. They are for the most part produced from coconut oil, have a very low smoke point, and can be used for cooking without producing trans-fatty acids. Body builders tend to use this fat to increase caloric intake, but studies to date are not conclusive.

ESSENTIAL FATTY ACIDS (EFA)

The essential fatty acids are a part of the polyunsaturated fats and are considered a "good fat." They play a role in keeping the body tuned up and in good shape. If you are deficient in these good EFA fats you may have symptoms that include: loss of hair, elevated cholesterol and triglyceride levels, high blood pressure, nerve abnormalities and reduced immune system efficiency. Our bodies cannot produce these acids and they must arrive by way of the foods we eat. Some of the more important EFA's include Linoleic Acid, Linolenic Acid, vitamin F and the Omega group of fatty acids.

Foods that are high in EFA's include seeds, grains, nuts and cold-water fish. There are also a number of foods and disease processes that interfere with the breakdown and utilization of these fats, such as alcohol consumption, diabetes, a poor diet and aging. Supplements that are available include oil of evening primrose, flaxseed oil, black current oil and fish oils.

The more popular sources of Linoleic Acid (Omega-6) are soybeans, corn, sesame seeds, wheat germ and safflower. The best source of Linolenic Acid (Omega-3) is best found in soybeans, walnuts, canola oil, pumpkin, and flaxseed oil.

HYDROGENATION

Many vegetable and baked good product labels state that they are hydrogenated. This simply means that the manufacturer has added hydrogen atoms from water to harden the fat in the product and make it more "saturated," thus adding a different texture to the food to make it more palatable and possibly last longer. A liquid fat can be turned into a solid in this manner, however, what you are doing is changing a good fat into a bad fat. The more hydrogenated a product the higher the saturated fat level.

Rearrangement can also be achieved during this process combining two different oils to produce a product with different melting points.

THE BAD PARTS OF A GOOD FAT

We have now covered a number of important points regarding fats and their relationship to the foods we eat, however, we now need to discuss the fact that those "good guys", the polyunsaturated fats and the monounsaturated fats may have a bad side to them.

An example of this is eating at a fast food restaurant and ordering a potato patty for breakfast. Since it is early morning and the frying vat has just been filled with a good fresh vegetable oil (we hope); the majority of the fat will probably be a good polyunsaturated fat.

However, when you go back to that same restaurant for lunch, they have now fried in that oil for four hours and the majority of the oil has converted to bad oil called a trans-fatty acid. Studies have implicated this oil in the acceleration of the aging process, raising the bad cholesterol, and lowering the good cholesterol.

When you purchase oil from the supermarket for the most part you're buying good oil or the "cis" form. The "trans " form should be avoided as much as possible.

Cis-Form Fatty Acids

A horseshoe shaped molecule of polyunsaturated fat that occurs naturally in nature and is normally incorporated into a healthy cell wall. The health of the cell wall depends on a supply of "cis" form fatty acids. When these acids are not available the cell wall is constructed with abnormal openings (ports of entry) that may allow foreign substances to enter and cause a disease process to start.

Trans-Form Fatty Acid

Instead of the normal horseshoe form, trans-fatty acids are found in a straight-line shape. This form of the fat is difficult for the cell to utilize in the construction of a healthy wall. The blueprint calls for a horseshoe shape, not a straight line. Margarine may contain up to 54% trans-fatty acids and shortenings as much as 58%. Heating and storage of these fats increases these percentages.

COMMON COOKING OILS

The following are some of the more common oils that are used for cooking and baking. Oils will vary as to the type of fats they are composed of, color, aroma, nutrients, and smoke points. Oils may be categorized in many different ways, such as how refined the oil is, the plant or animal it was extracted from, the method of extraction (cold or hot), smoke point, consistency and color. All fat content figures are for one tablespoon of fat or oil. Saturated fatty acids (SFA), polyunsaturted fatty acids (PUFA), monounsaturated, fatty acids (MUFA).

Almond Oil

Unrefined almond oil is commonly used in many dishes and is commonly substituted for butter. It adds an amber color to foods and has a mild sweet flavor. Refined almond oil is produced by crushing almonds and heating them until a thick, golden-colored paste is produced. The paste is then squeezed to produce the oil. This extensive processing makes almond oil one of the more expensive oils. Some people who are allergic to aspirin may be allergic to almonds and almond oil. The French almond oil is the highest quality.

SFA . . . . .3.2 g   PUFA . . . . . .3.3 g.   MUFA . . . . . .5.7 g.

Avocado Oil

A light, nutty tasting fruit oil that is usually only used on salads. The oil does contain a small amount of saturated fat, but is mostly monounsaturated. The smoke point is too low to be considered for cooking and frying. Avocado is the highest fat fruit and should be used in moderation.

SFA . . . .1.6 g.   PUFA . . . . . .1.9 g.   MUFA . . . . . . .9 g.

Canola Oil

Produced from the rapeseed plant, which is a relative of the mustard family. It is normally found in the refined state, has a very high smoke point making it one of the best all-around oils. This is the best oil for frying since it does not breakdown as easily as most other oils. The oil is high in monounsatuated fat and low in saturated fat. It is also one of the lowest priced oils. Canola oil is one of the few oils that contain omega-3 fatty acids. The name canola was derived from the word Canada and oil. The source of canola oil, rapeseed, is mostly grown in Canada.

SHOOT THAT RAPESEED PLANT

Human genes are being shot into rapeseed plants to attempt to produce a plant (canola oil plant) that will be able to reduce the level of soil contamination. The plant is being forced into mating with the human genes.

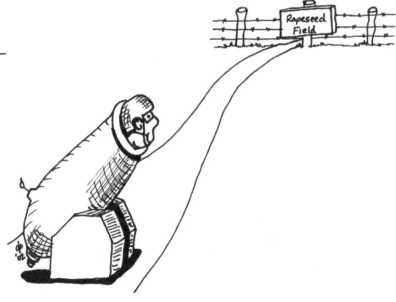

SFA . . . .1.0 g.   PUFA . . . . . .4.1 g.   MUFA . . . . . .8.3 g.
Smoke Point – 525° F. (273.9° C.)

Coconut Oil

This oil is very high in saturated fat and may be capable of raising cholesterol levels. Normally, not sold for home cooking uses, it is present in numerous products, especially baked goods, candy and margarine. The oil has the ability to extend the shelf life of foods and it would be best to read labels to see if the product contains coconut oil or as it is sometimes called "tropical oil."

SFA ....11.8 g.   PUFA ......0.2 g.   MUFA ......0.8 g.

Corn Oil

One of the most common oils that is manufactured in large quantities and extracted from the corn germ, a by-product that is obtained from cereal and corn syrup producers. The oil is a light yellow color and has a mild flavor, which does not overpower recipes. This makes corn oil excellent for baking, pastries, and most recipes that call for vegetable oil. A darker corn oil is sold that is extracted from the whole corn kernel and has a stronger aroma, similar to that of popcorn.

Other types of corn oil include unrefined, expeller-pressed oil that has a strong aroma and not recommended for delicate dishes since it will overpower the flavors. This type of oil, however, is good for baking, in sauces and dressings. This type of oil cannot be used for frying since it tends to foam and boil over easily.

A highly refined corn oil can be used for frying and has a relatively high smoke point. Corn oil is about 87% polyunsaturated fat and contains about 60% of the essential fatty acid, linoleic acid. Corn oil also contains more vitamin E than most other oils after processing, which normally reduces the vitamin E content significantly.

SFA ......7 g.   PUFA ......7.9 g.   MUFA ....3 g.
Smoke Point – 475° F. (246.1° C.)

Cottonseed Oil

This oil is normally not sold to the general public since it may be easily contaminated. The oil is heavily used in many products such as shortening, baked goods, margarine and dressings. It was one of the most popular oils in the United States until the 1940's when more efficient processing methods were invented.

SFA ....3.5 g.   PUFA ......7.0 g.   MUFA ......2.4 g.

Flaxseed Oil

One of the best sources of the essential fatty acid omega-3. Has a strong golden color. And the flavor is not overpowering. The oil mixes well with most foods and imparts a pleasant flavor. Health food restaurants tend to use the oil in salad dressings, Cole slaw, dips, marinades and sauces for vegetarian dishes. Best not to cook the oil as it tends to lose its flavor and aroma. The essential fatty acids are more active in this oil if it is not heated.

Grape-seed Oil

A light colored oil that is produced from grape seeds. The majority of the oil sold in the United States is imported from Europe, however, the United States is starting to produce larger amounts of the oil. Grape-seed oil has a very high smoke point and can be used for frying and in dishes that need to be cooked at high temperatures. Excellent for stir-fried foods.

SFA . . . . .3 g.   PUFA . . . . . .9.5 g.   MUFA . . . . . .2.2 g.

Hazelnut or Filbert Oil

It is strong, full-flavored oil with a roasted nutty aroma. This oil has been used in France for hundreds of years and is one of the more popular oils. The unrefined hazelnut oil is difficult to refine, hard to find in the United States and very expensive. It is used by European chefs when preparing special hot sauces and for breading. The refined oil; is produced by crushing the nuts, then heating them before squeezing out the oil.

SFA . . . . .1.0 g.   PUFA . . . . . .1.4 g.   MUFA . . . . . .10.6 g.

Hemp Oil

An excellent source of essential fatty acids since it contains a balance of omega-3 and omega-6 fatty acids. The color of hemp oil tends to turn most people off since it is a green color, but has a mild flavor and good texture. Like flaxseed oil, hemp oil is best when it is not heated and can be used in the same dishes and dressings as flaxseed oil.

Olive Oil

Olive oil is high in monounsaturated fat (77%) and is gluten-free. One tablespoon contains 8% of your daily requirement of vitamin E. Greece is one of the largest producers of olive oil with an annual output of 300,000 tons. The oil produced is of the highest quality, which is the low acid, extra virgin variety.

Most of the Mediterranean countries produce olive oil of such poor quality that it must be refined to produce an acceptable flavored product. Look for oil from Greece or California that states "cold-pressed, extra virgin, pure organic."

Smoke Point – 375° F. (190.6° C.)

Palm Oil

This is one of the highest saturated fat oils and may raise cholesterol levels. May also be listed on the list of ingredients as a "tropical oil" and is frequently found in baked goods with coconut oil. This oil is one of the most popular oils used for making soap. The oil is extracted from the pulp of the oil palm plant. Palm oil is normally a solid at room temperature due to its high degree of saturated fat.

SFA..........6.7 g.   PUFA............1.3 g.   MUFA.........5.0 g.

Peanut Oil

Peanut oil is one of the more popular oils and one of the easiest to extract oil from since peanuts are about 50% fat. They tend to maintain their nutty flavor in recipes and especially stir-fried foods. Many chefs tend to mix the oil with unrefined sesame oil, which will compliment each, others flavors and aromas. Peanut oil has a high smoke point and is a common oil for most cooking purposes, especially frying. However, 90% of peanut oil is saturated fat, which is higher than almost every other vegetable or nut oil. Also, peanut oil is low in vitamin E, trace minerals and essential fatty acids. Peanuts are actually from the legume or bean family and not from the nut family.

Peanut oil is produced from pressed, steam-cooked peanuts and will not absorb or transfer flavors to other foods. Peanuts are also one of the ingredients in the manufacturing of dynamite.

SFA...........2.3 g. PUFA..........4.3 g. MUFA.........6.2 g.
Smoke Point – 440° F. (226.7° C.)

Safflower Oil

Popular all-purpose oil that is relatively inexpensive and has a mild flavor. The thistle-like plant was used to produce a dye for garments in ancient times. Since the oil lacks flavor it can be used in almost any dish that requires liquid oil without the risk of flavoring the dish. Unrefined safflower oil is best, used cold in dressings, salads and sauces. The oil is high (80%) in essential fatty acids, especially linoleic acid. The oil is difficult to extract because of a very hard husk and hydraulic presses are required to extract the oil.

The lower-priced safflower oil is usually extracted with the use of chemical solvents, however, the method of extraction is not required to be placed on the label, which means that you don't know whether you are purchasing a high quality product or not. Safflower oil is second only to canola in its vitamin E content. The refined oil has a high smoke point and is good for frying. Cold-pressed is the best oil to use in salads or dishes that are not heated.

SFA .....1.2 g. PUFA ......10.1 g. MUFA ......1.7 g.
Smoke Point – 510° F. (265.6° C.)

Sesame Oil

Sesame oil can be purchased in two distinct varieties; the type that is produced from roasting the bean, which is the dark oil and the lighter oil that is recommended for use in salads and dishes that are not cooked. The more popular of the two is the dark variety, which is commonly used in many Chinese dishes producing a nutty flavor. The lighter oil is produced from pressed, raw sesame seeds and is considerably milder and used when you desire just a hint of the sesame flavor. It only takes a few drops of sesame oil to add flavor to vegetables, soups, or salad dressings.

One of the major advantages is that sesame oil is very stable and does not turn rancid easily even in hot, humid climates. It is considered one of the more healthful oils and is high in polyunsaturated fats and especially essential fatty acids.

SFA . . . . .1.9 g.   PUFA . . . . . .5.7 g.   MUFA . . . . . . .4 g.
Smoke Point – 420° F. (215.6° C.)

Soybean Oil

Unrefined soy oil is one of the more difficult oils to extract, which makes the oil somewhat expensive. The oil is used in baking and contains an excellent amount of lecithin, which is an emulsifier. The oil is also high in essential fatty acids and polyunsaturated fats. Unrefined soy oil tends to become rancid rather easily and should be used shortly after purchase and should be stored in the refrigerator.

The highly refined soy oil is lower in price and used extensively in the baking industry. Almost 80% of all oil that is used for baking is soy oil. If you see "vegetable oil" on the label it is probably soy oil. Good source of omega-3 fatty acids.

SFA . . . . .2.0 g.   PUFA . . . . . .7.9 g.   MUFA . . . . . .3.2 g.
Smoke Point – 495° F. (257.2° C.)

Sunflower Oil

Most sunflower oil is produced by a cold-pressed method, which only mulches the sunflower seeds then presses the mulch to obtain the oil. Heat and chemicals are not used thereby producing healthy, high nutrient oil. New Zealand is one of the major producers of sunflower oil. Russia produces as much as 80% of their usable oil from the sunflower. It has a low smoke point and not recommended for high temperature cooking or frying.

SFA . . . . .1.4 g.   PUFA . . . . . .8.9 g.   MUFA . . . . . .2.7 g.

Walnut Oil

This is another expensive oil when purchased in the unrefined state. The finest grades of this oil are produced in the Perigord and Burgundy provinces of France. To produce unrefined walnut oil the nuts are dried and cold-pressed. The oil is high in polyunsaturated fat and has a pleasant nutty flavor. Walnut oil tends to become somewhat bitter when heated and is best, used cold in salads. Refined walnut oil is produced by crushing the nutmeats and heating them to produce a paste. The paste is then squeezed to extract the oil.

SFA . . . . .1.2 g.   PUFA . . . . . .8.6 g.   MUFA . . . . . .3.1 g.

GOING UP IN SMOKE – QUICK REFERENCE

Knowing the smoke point of the oil you are going to cook or fry with is very important. Since certain foods need to be fried or cooked at certain temperatures, the last thing you want is for the oil to break down and ruin the dish. The following are the smoke points of the more common oils used for frying:

Canola Oil	.525° F. (273.9° C.)
Safflower Oil	.510° F. (265.6° C.)
Soybean Oil	.495° F. (257.2° C.)
Corn Oil	.475° F. (246.1° C.)
Peanut Oil	.440° F. (226.7° C.)
Sesame Oil	.420° F. (215.6° C.)
Olive Oil (blend)	.375° F. (190.6° C.)
Vegetable Shortening	.375° F. (190.6° C.)
Clarified Butter	.350° F. (176.7° C.)
Butter	.250₀ F. (121.1° C.)

METHODS OF REFINING AND EXTRACTING OILS

The extraction method is very important and will determine the color, level of nutrients remaining, flavor, and stability of the oil. Manufacturers do not have to state on their label, which method is being used leaving the consumer in the dark as to whether the oil is really of a higher quality or not. The higher quality oils do state the method such as "cold-pressed" and charge a premium for their product.

When oils are heat-extracted, all oils will lose a percentage of their nutrients. When processed at over 300°F all proteins and vitamin E is destroyed. When processed at 120°F to 160°F almost all the protein and nutrients are retained in usable form. However, there is less usable oil produced making these products more expensive. When vitamin E is retained in the oil, the oil will not become rancid as easily and will have a better shelf life. To overcome this problem many companies add antioxidants to the oil.

REFINED OILS

These are the best oils for frying and cooking dishes at higher temperatures since they do not break down easily. Oils that are highly refined have very little flavor and usually have a light color. These oils are neutralized, bleached, deodorized and are low in nutrients. The **neutralization process** removes any "free fatty acids", which have separated from the triglyceride molecule. If the acids were allowed to remain in the oil they would react with oxygen and produce rancidity. A washing and drying process to remove any moisture, which produces deterioration of the refined oil, further neutralizes the oil.

The **bleaching process** involves removing impurities using an absorbent earth as a filter leaving the oil clear. Another process called fractionation can also be done to refined oils. This process can take liquid oil and cool it down under special controlled conditions separating high melting point triglycerides from the low melting point triglycerides providing solid, liquid fat at room temperature. The product can then be sold as margarine or liquid oil.

The **deodorization process** involves removing any smell or taste that is not desired and is achieved by blowing steam through heated oil. A vacuum then removes the steam, which has trapped the smells and any off-taste.

UNREFINED OILS

These oils are not heavily processed and cannot be used for high temperature cooking and frying. The only exception to this rule is safflower oil. Unrefined oils are by either cold-processed or expeller-pressed methods. Because of these methods of processing the oils will retain their flavors and aromas. Many unrefined oils are used to flavor dishes that require the stronger oil flavors. Most of the unrefined oils retain a high level of essential fatty acids and nutrients.

EXPELLER-PRESSED EXTRACTION

The seeds or grains are squeezed under pressure of about 15 tons per square inch, which generates considerable heat. Temperatures commonly exceed 300ºF, which destroys all the protein and vitamins. Most of the oils sold in the United Stated are expeller-pressed extraction oils.

COLD-PRESSED EXTRACTION

This oil is still expeller-pressed, however, the process is not allowed to reach the high temperatures that are produced from the full extraction processing. Only three oils: olive oil, peanut oil and sesame oil, can be processed by this method and obtain enough oil to sell commercially. The low heat processing reduces the quantity of oil obtained significantly. Cold-pressed oils are the highest quality oils and contain the highest levels of nutrients.

CHEMICAL SOLVENT EXTRACTION

The less expensive brands of oils, especially the supermarket brands may use solvent extraction methods. This is an inexpensive method of oil extraction using the chemical "hexane" or another petroleum product to separate the oil from a food source. After the extraction takes place, the toxic solvent is boiled off. The oil is then refined, deodorized and bleached to an acceptable color at temperatures of over 400ºF leaving literally no nutrients in the oil. Preservatives and antioxidants must be added to give the oil a good shelf life and retard rancidity.

PACKAGING OILS

If you would like to obtain the highest level of nutrition from oil, packaging is one of the most important factors to consider. Oils should be packaged in containers that do not allow any air or light to reach the oil.

Airtight Black Glass Containers

If you wish to obtain the highest level of essential fatty acids from the oil, then the oil must be packaged in a very dark or black container that are well-sealed. The oils should also be stored in the refrigerated section of the market. Quality oils processed at low temperatures will lose their nutrients very quickly.

Metal Cans

Metal containers have been used for many years to protect oils from the air and light. Most of these containers are of a very high quality and should not impart any metallic taste to the oil. Olive oil is the most common oil sold in metal containers. These containers are more common in Europe. Only metal container that the oil is sold in is safe for oils. These metal containers are specially lined with plastic polymers to prevent the oil reacting with the metal. Metal containers will cause rancidity very quickly if not coated.

Plastic Bottles

Almost all plastic bottles that are used to sell the lower quality oils are usually clear or translucent allowing the light to penetrate the bottle. The oil will not retain its freshness for any length of time. Frying oil may be purchased in these bottles; however, these oils are rarely recommended for cold dishes or salads.

STORING OILS

Generally, all oils should be resealed as tightly as possible and stored in a cool, dry location. The best location, however, is the refrigerator. Cloudiness is common when an oil is refrigerated and the oil will return to normal if allowed to remain at room temperature for about 15-20 minutes. If a container of oil is left out of the refrigerator for even a short period of time on a hot, humid day, the oil will start to become rancid very quickly.

Oil that has been opened is only fresh for about 4 months and should be discarded after that. It would be wise to date the oil container when it is purchased. Rancidity will usually begin about 4 months after the oil is purchased regardless of the method of storage. Exposure to light for long periods will cause almost any oil to turn brown. Oil that is in a sealed, unopened bottle will stay fresh for 1 year.

When oil is poured out of the bottle into any other container for any reason, it should never be returned to the original container and mixed with the clean oil. Contamination is possible and may ruin the balance of the oil left in the container.

Unrefined oils high in essential fatty acids only have a high quality shelf life of 3-6 weeks and must be refrigerated. If you wish to freeze the quality oil, it will be good for about 12 months.

FLAVORED OILS

Flavored oils are sold in all food specialty stores and natural food markets, however, it is easy to prepare your own. The best base oils to use are olive, sesame or peanut oil. Any herb or combination of herbs can be added to the oil. All herbs should be thoroughly washed and dried before adding them to the oil since cleanliness is an important factor to reduce the possibility of contaminating the oil.

The most common herbs used in flavored oils are garlic, cayenne peppers, fennel, bay leaf, rosemary, oregano, cloves or citrus wedges. The herb needs to remain in the oil until the desired level of flavoring is reached.

When preparing flavored oils, it is necessary to be aware of the potential health problems that are associated with these oils. The botulism bacteria is commonly found in the soil and brought into the home on vegetables and herbs. Certain precautions need to be taken when preparing flavored oils. Since the botulism bacteria, thrives in a low acid, anerobic atmosphere (low level of oxygen) environment, it is necessary to heat the oil with the herb to 240°F(116°C) to destroy any potential bacteria that may be present.

If you are serious about making flavored oils, then you should purchase a book on the subject and adhere to the recipes and preparation and storage methods.

CHILE OIL RECIPE

The following ingredients will be needed:
2   Cups of olive oil
1   Cup of red New Mexico chile (crushed)

Place the oil and chile in a heavy pan and place on medium heat until the olive oil starts to lightly bubble. Reduce heat to low and continue cooking until the chiles darken, but do not allow them to burn or heavily blacken, then remove from the heat and allow to cool, then strain through cheesecloth. Place into a sterilized well-sealed jar in the refrigerator for 1 month before using.

DIGESTION OF FATS

The following is an example of how fats are digested:

Mouth
No digestion takes place here. Fats are just broken down into smaller particles by chewing action.

Stomach/Pancreas/Duodenum
Fat is separated from other foodstuffs by the action of hydrochloric acid, which make it easier for it to be broken down by pancreatic lipase.

Small Intestines
The presence of fat in the duodenum (first section of the small intestines) stimulates the gall bladder to release bile salts. The fat globules are then further broken down by bile salts, which allows the enzymes to go to work and release diglycerides and monoglycerides and a few fatty acids. The bile salts then combine with pancreatic lipase, which helps to accomplish the breakdown process of the fats. Fats are then absorbed into the intestinal wall and are carried throughout the body by lipoproteins.

Liver
This is the main site of fat metabolism.

ESSENTIAL FATTY ACIDS

Essential fatty acids (EFAs) are building blocks of all "good fats" and are necessary for optimum health. The body is unable to produce these "essential fats" and a quality source of the fat is required. The EFAs help the body to maintain a healthy cell wall around our cells and are critical to healthy functioning of the central nervous system and our blood vessels. The majority of EFA oils are derived from fish oils and plant oils. While a low fat diet is recommended we should not lose sight of the body's need for an adequate supply of EFAs. EFAs may also be sold and called vitamin F in some literature. Basically, the two most common EFA oils are linoleic and linolenic acids.

OMEGA 3 FATTY ACIDS

This group of EFAs are derived mainly from fish oils and studies have shown that this type of oil has the ability to lessen the risk of a heart attack by reducing the chances of a clot forming in an artery that has built up plaque on the walls. The omega-3 fatty acid also has the ability to reduce the level of bad cholesterol (LDL) circulating in the bloodstream. Some arthritis sufferers have found that by increasing their intake of omega-3 fatty acids it tends to have an anti-inflammatory effect and relieves some of the discomfort. However, people who are taking any anticoagulant medications need to consult their physicians before taking this supplement

OMEGA-6 FATTY ACIDS

This group of EFAs tends to compliment the omega-3 fatty acids and assist them in working more efficiently. These fats have been studied in relation to the same medical concerns with the addition of relieving pre-menstrual tensions and improving skin tone. The omega-6, group of oils is usually always derived from plant sources, the best of which are; black currents, evening primrose and starflower.

FLAXSEED OIL

This plant has been around for over 5,000 years and the benefits are too numerous to mention in relationship to a healthy body. The oil is one of the best sources of EFAs and contains 60% omega-6 and 20% omega-3 oils. Studies have shown that the oil can reduce blood triglyceride (fat) levels.

SALAD DRESSING MAY BE GOOD FOR YOUR HEART

The latest information from a Harvard University study relates the use of salad oil to lowering the risk of heart disease by providing a good source of essential fatty acids. The salad dressing consisted of oil from a quality plant source and vinegar. Fat-free dressings on a consistent basis may not be in a person's best health interests. Alternating between a quality plant-oil based dressing and a fat-free dressing may be the best way to go.

TRANS-FATTY ACIDS

Trans-fatty acids have been getting a lot of press in recent years, especially since a high percentage was found in margarine. An explanation of what trans-fatty acids are was explained in the first chapter, however, additional information is necessary to cover the topic. Basically, trans-fatty acid, are a product of processing foods that contain fat. When fat is heated, a percentage of fat converts to bad fat called a trans-fatty acid, which is really an artificial chemical. Chemical, that is found in our foods in such abundance to make it the number one artificial chemical in our food supply.

PROCESSED FOODS, A MAJOR PROBLEM

Burgers, fried chicken, french fries, baked goods, pastries, etc. may contain up to 25% of their fat in the form of trans-fatty acids. It doesn't matter whether the fat in the product is listed as polyunsaturated or saturated fat, it is possible that that the 25% will include some of the good fats that have been converted.

EUROPEANS MAY BE SMARTER THAN AMERICANS

European countries and the World Health Organization after investigating trans-fatty acids have determined that they are a significant health problem and reducing them in our foods would substantially lower the incidence of heart and related diseases. The FDA and the United States food industry don't feel that the proof is insufficient and nothing need be done at this time.

MEDICAL TEST TO BE USED ON FOODS

Magnetic Resonance Scanning (MRI) equipment using a lower level of magnetic resonance will soon be used to investigate how water molecules react in foods. There are a number of foods that could be used to produce other products if we knew at what point water molecules change and affect the product quality. This information could influence spoilage and change fat-containing foods significantly.

HYDROGENATION TO BE A PROCESS OF THE PAST

New oil processing techniques are being studied that will change oil and create an oil that is a high-saturate oil. This will eliminate the need to hydrogenate oil and eliminate the trans-fatty acid. This new fat science will create fat that will have the same desired properties of the hydrogenated oil.

STABILE OIL A REALITY BY 2001

Oil has the tendency to breakdown when used for prolonged periods or if heated to very high temperatures. This problem will be to a great degree solved with the increase of the oleic fatty acid content. The process of producing high-oleic oil has been too costly, however, by 2001 scientists feel that the problem can be solved. This will provide oil for frying that will be a healthier oil and not breakdown to trans-fatty acids as easily.

CANOLA OIL TO BE MODIFIED FIRST

The first oil to be genetically modified will be canola oil. The modified oil will have a higher level of "high-laureate" fat. This will increase the level of "good" usable polyunsaturated fat and reduce the level of saturated fat.

NEW STARCH WILL BE REPLACING FAT

When food is processed, a product that is produced is "modified starch." This unusual starch can act as a food thickener and especially a fat substitute. The modified starch can provide the "mouthfeel" that people react favorably to when they eat a high-fat food. In the near future, however, chemically modified starch will not be needed. Plants are being developed that will make a new "modified starch," which will actually be harvested, then used as a natural fat replacer.

PRICEY OLIVE OIL

Because of a drought in olive growing areas of the Mediterranean, olive oil prices have risen about 30-35%. The increasing demand for the high quality oil in North America is fueling the price hike.

FAT-FREE PRODUCTS NOT FAIRING WELL

Manufacturers jumped on the bandwagon in 1997 and started to produce hundreds of fat-free foods. However, the trend has turned out to be more of a fad than anything else is. The weight conscious public found out that they needed to give up too much taste, texture and flavor and has opted to shift toward the low-fat and reduced-fat foods instead.

FAT-FREE COOKING TO BE A REALITY

You will not have to purchase expensive non-stick coated pot and pans ever again. A new substance that will be sold in sheets will be available in early 2002. The new product consists of a specially treated anti-sticking sheet that is placed into the pan or baking tin or any other type of pot. You will be able to cook any dish or food on the sheet without the food sticking and it will allow uniform cooking. This will also eliminate the messy spray oils, which are being used to reduce fat intake. The sheet will not stick to the pan and can easily be cleaned and re-used over and over. The product is produced by Mapelli Srl and will be sold under the brand name, Maplon.

NEW BUTTER WILL SPREAD LIKE MARGARINE

A new spreadable butter may be available in the United States by 2002. Studies in Australia are having excellent success with altering a cow's diet to include more polyunsaturated and mono-unsaturated fats; they have developed butter with almost the same consistency but more spreadable and lower in saturated fat. The butter still possesses the same "mouth feel" and flavor as the standard high saturated fat, hard-to-spread butter that has been produced for 7,000 years.

FRYING OIL TO BE MADE INTO DIESEL FUEL

Researchers at the U.S. Department of Energy in Idaho have discovered a method of re-cycling frying oil into a bio-diesel fuel. This environmentally friendly fuel can be produced through a less expensive process than is used to produce the standard diesel fuel and will be 100% biodegradable. The new diesel oil burns cleaner and will not polluting the air as well as having a nice aroma. In fact the aroma is almost too pleasant, since it smells just like fried chicken. The new bio-diesel fuel is presently being tested by the National Park Service in some busses and seems to be working as well as the standard polluting diesel oil they had been using. Their only fear was that the park bears would chase the busses since they smelled like fried chicken, luckily this did not happen.

SEAWEED TO BE MORE POPULAR IN 2002

Monsanto is making progress in the development of new oil that will be used for baking. The "seaweed oil" will mainly be used in cakes and cookies and the company is hoping that the new products will contain some of the healthy nutrients found in fish.

MARGARINE AND TRANS-FATTY ACIDS

Margarine may contain the bad fat produced from the heat processing, trans-fatty acids, and butter has cholesterol. My preferred choice would be whipped, unsalted butter in moderation. The harder the margarine, the higher the percentage of saturated fat it contains. Even though margarine does not contain any cholesterol, saturated fats may assist in the production of cholesterol. The softer the margarine, the lower the level of trans-fatty acids since air and water tend to replace a percentage of the fat.

MARGARINE SUBSTITUTE IN SUPERMARKETS

The FDA has approved a new product called "Benecol" to replace margarine and even lower cholesterol. The product is made from a plant, "stanol ester" and was invented in Finland. It has been sold in Finland since 1995 where studies have shown that the product actually blocks the absorption of the bad cholesterol, LDL. Johnson & Johnson's McNeil Healthcare has purchased the international rights to market the product. "Take Control™" is another new product that is also a margarine replacement that is already on the shelves.

HEALTH RISK

Diets high in total fat and especially trans-fatty acids (from heated fats) have been related to cancer of the colon, the prostate and breast. Studies are also showing that the efficiency of the immune system may be depressed by high fat diets. Recommended dietary fat levels are 20-25% of your total daily calories, however, a person can actually survive on only 5% dietary fat if the fat is of the essential fatty acid type.

WHO INVENTED MARGARINE?

Margarine was invented by a French chemist in 1870 upon the request of Napoleon III who wanted a low-cost fat. Originally, it was produced from animal fat; however, today it is made from vegetables oil (mainly soy), milk solids, salt, air, and water. The name margarine came from the original chemical used in the production of margarine, which was "margaric acid."

Margarine was brought to the United States in 1873 and the production of "artificial butter" was started by the U.S. Dairy Company in New York City. By 1886 there were 30 manufacturers producing margarine. The United States government placed special taxes on margarine to protect the dairy industry, which almost eliminated the product.

Many of the color restrictions and taxes regarding margarine: were eliminated by the 1950's and by the early 1960's supermarkets began selling tub margarine and vegetable oil spreads. In 1967 Wisconsin was the last state to repeal bans on margarine sales. It wasn't until 1996 that all restrictions of the sales of margarine were repealed.

THE LURKING KILLER

An article written in Michigan Today states that trans-fatty acid is involved "in 30,000 premature deaths from heart disease per year." The major source of trans-fatty acids in the American diet is from French fries, burgers, margarine and commercial baked goods.

HOW MUCH IS TOO MUCH

As a general rule most products that state: "hydrogenated oil" on the list of ingredients have 30-40% of that oil as trans-fatty acid oil. The following is the approximate percentages of trans-fatty acids found in some of the more common foods:

```
French fries  . . . . . . . . . . . . . .40%
Cookies . . . . . . . . . . . . . . . . .35%
Crackers . . . . . . . . . . . . . . . .39%
Doughnuts  . . . . . . . . . . . . . .38%
Hamburgers . . . . . . . . . . . . .45%
Potato Chips . . . . . . . . . . . . .38%
```

GOOD FATS IN JEOPARDY

Trans-fatty acids have been found to interfere with the conversion of some of the good essential fatty acids the body requires to remain in optimum health. The trans-fatty acids tend to block the conversion of omega-3 and omega-6 fatty acids into a form that is required by the body.

AVOIDING TRANS-FATTY ACIDS

The following are a few tips how to avoid trans-fatty acids:

- Don't buy foods that contain "vegetable shortening" or "hydrogenated oils."
- Avoid fried foods as much as possible.
- Purchase low-fat or liquid margarine.
- Limit your intake of commercial cookies, pastries, cake and crackers.
- Purchase foods that are low in saturated fats or state "low or cholesterol-free."

A FEW OF THE HARMFUL EFFECTS

Trans-fatty acids have been implicated in the following:

- Lowers the blood levels of good cholesterol, HDL.
- Raises the blood level of the bad cholesterol, LDL.
- Raises the level of the type of fats that may increase risk of heart disease.
- Has the ability to raise cholesterol levels.
- Tends to lower the amount of available milk in lactating females.
- Tends to lower the quality of mother's milk.
- May affect the birth weight leading a lower weight.
- Increase the risk of diabetes.

TRANS-FATTY ACID-FREE MARGARINE

A number of companies are now producing a margarine that does not contain any trans-fatty acids. Processing of the oil to protect it from high heat for a prolonged period make this possible. The following are some of the more popular brands:

- Brummel and Brown Soft
- I Can't Believe It's Not Butter – Fat-Free
- Shed's Country Crock Light & Squeezable
- Spectrum Naturals with canola and olive oils
- Smart Balance (light and regular)
- Smart Beat Fat-Free
- Promise Fat-Free
- Fleischman's Fat-Free
- Parkay Squeeze

CHOOSING THE RIGHT MARGARINE

The lower fat margarine is produced by adding additional water, thickening agents, such as gelatin, rice starch or guar gum to the mixture. Additional air may be pumped in to create addition volume. By changing the texture and consistency of margarine it may not be suitable for all cooking needs. The following will provide a guideline to using margarine in a variety of cooking needs:

Baking and general cooking:
Use the standard margarine, which is about 80% oil. The lower fat margarine has approximately 55% fat and does not work as well.

Spreading on bread:
The light or low-fat margarine, which contain about 50% oil are fine.

Sautéing and frying:
Never use the fat-free margarine, which has only about $\frac{1}{2}$ gram of fat per table-spoon. Stick margarine may work in some cases, but butter is preferred for sautéing. High smoke point oils such as canola or peanut oil is best for frying.

CHEF'S FRYING SECRETS

TEMPERATURE CONTROL

If frying temperatures are not controlled properly, the food will absorb more fat, the batches will not be consistent and the flavor will vary. The oil will also break down faster. The following are a few facts that should be followed when frying foods:

- A thermometer should be used to check the temperature of the oil and the oil should never exceed 380°F.
- If a time period is going to elapse between batches, it would be best to reduce the oil temperature to 250°F to slow down the deterioration of the oil.
- When using shortening to fry with, always heat the shortening slowly. If you heat shortening too quickly, it will scorch. Always start shortening at 225° F and keep it there until it the shortening has completely melted, then you can turn the heat up.
- Too low a temperature will result in a poor coloring and usually a greasy product.
- When frying batches, remember to allow the temperature to go back up or return to the normal frying temperature before adding more food to be fried.

WHY FRYING OIL DARKENS PREMATURELY

The following are the more common reasons for frying oil darkening:

- Your frying pan or fryer is not as clean as it should be.
- When you did clean it, you failed to rinse it well and there was some soap film left in the fryer.
- You are overcooking the food.
- The fat has been broken down and is mostly trans-fatty acids.
- The temperature has been consistently too high.

WHY FAT WILL SMOKE

The following are the most common reasons:

- Foreign material has gotten into the fryer and burning while you are frying.
- Too much breading has fallen off and is building up.
- The fat has broken down and is no longer good.
- The temperature is too high.

THE CASE OF THE FOAMING FRYER

There are a number of reasons why foam will form on the top of foods being fried. The following are a few of the more common ones:

- The fryer is not as clean as it should be and was not rinsed properly leaving soap scum.
- Too much salt or food particles accumulating in the fryer.
- Using brass or copper utensils in the fryer, which react with the oil creating foam.
- Poor quality fat or old worn out fat.

LESS GREASY FOODS

To make fried foods less greasy, just add 1 tablespoon of white vinegar to the pan or deep-fat fryer before adding the oil.

FAT FACTS

AIR-POPPED POPCORN MAY BE A GOOD SNACK

It would be wise to read the label on air-popped popcorn packages before you buy the product if you're trying to cut down on fats. Some products are now sprayed with oil.

GOOD SNACK FOOD

A great new snack food is now available on the market shelves. It is called "Seaweed Crunch. A serving has only 3 grams of fat and 130 calories. The texture and flavor is excellent. The snack food is being sold through health food stores and produced by Soken Natural Foods.

SNACK FOOD: HISTORY TIMELINE

1853	Chips invented by accident by George Crum in Saratoga Springs, New York
1861	Pretzels were brought to the United States from Germany where they were called "bretzels."
1885	A gasoline-powered popcorn popper was invented for commercial use making popcorn a popular and accessible snack food.
1892	In Cleveland potato chips were delivered house to house by horse-drawn wagons making them easily accessible.
1906	Planter's started selling Planter's Peanuts and invented the commercial process to produce them at a reasonable cost.
1926	The first potato chip bag was invented by Laura Scudder. The bags were filled with waxed paper, filled then ironed shut.
1950	Korn Kurls were invented by the Adams Corporation. Pork rinds also hit the snack scene.
1960	Frito-Lay started producing corn chips and Cheetos cheese snacks. Lay's Potato Chip were sold in 1965.
1964	Doritos corm curls were introduced and were a big hit.
1983	The thicker, ridged chips made for dipping were produced by Frito-Lay.
1995	The low-fat snack foods appeared in all categories.

1998   Fat substitutes become popular and attract new snack converts only to find out that the artificial fats may be harmful.

FAT AND CHOLESTEROL IN YOUR FAVORITE SNACKS

FOOD	TOTAL FAT(g)	CALORIES FROM FAT(%)	CHOLESTEROL(mg)
Apple Pie(2 crusts ¹/₈)	13.8	42	0
Cheesecake (¹/₆)	18.0	63	44
Chocolate Bar (1 oz.)	8.7	54	6
Chocolate Cake(frosted ¹/₈)	10.5	40	9
Chocolate Pudding (¹/₂ cup)	5.7	27	5
Fudge (1 oz.)	2.4	20	10
Frozen Yogurt (¹/₂ cup)	3.2	25	10
Ice Cream (vanilla ¹/₂ cup)	7.3	50	29
Ice Milk (¹/₂ cup)	2.3	19	9
Lemon Meringue Pie (¹/₆)	9.8	9	51
Popcorn (with oil 1 oz.)	8.0	51	0
Potato Chips (1 oz.)	9.8	58	0
Pumpkin Pie (¹/₆)	10.4	41	22
Orange Sherbet (¹/₂ cup)	1.9	13	5

PUREES TO THE RESCUE

One of the easiest methods of reducing fats in baked goods is to use fruit or vegetable purees to replace a percentage of the fat. The recipe will determine what type of puree you choose to use and it should relate to the other ingredients and compliment them. For example if you are making banana bread, you could use banana puree and only use about 2 tablespoons of oil per loaf.

THE FLIP-N-FRY™ DOES THE BREADING

If you bread your food, you may want to try a handy gadget for breading almost any kind of food. The plastic bowl has an inner core and a well-sealed lid that makes it easy to completely bread your food without a mess.

THE EGG BINDER

Many recipes call for eggs to be used as binders to hold everything together, however, egg yolks are high in fat. Egg yolks can be eliminated in almost all recipes and it is not necessary to add additional whites to replace them. If additional whites are used it will make many dishes dry and tough. If the egg yolks are needed for flavor, just eliminate some of them to reduce the fat.

NEW MICROPROCESSOR TO CHECK FOR BAD OIL

Many people get ill after eating fried foods and feel that it is their system that does not handle these foods properly. However, new research has proven that in many cases it was the fault of the oil, not the person's digestive system. A newly invented microprocessor will soon be placed in all frying systems, even for home use that will alert the user when the oil is not fit for human consumption. As oil decomposes free-fatty acids are released, some of which may be harmful when consumed in large quantities.

WHOOOOSH

A good test to tell whether hot oil is still usable and not high in trans-fatty acids is to drop a piece of white bread into the pan. If the bread develops dark specs, the oil has reached an unsafe level of deterioration. Never allow oil to heat to the smoke point, as it may ignite. It will also make the food taste bitter and may even irritate your eyes. The oils with the highest smoke points are canola, safflower and corn.

SLOWS DOWN AGING

Cooking wine will stay fresher longer if you add a tablespoon of very fresh vegetable oil to the bottle.

SUCKING UP TO FAT

A few pieces of dried bread placed in the bottom of the broiler pan should absorb fat drippings. This will eliminate smoking fat and should reduce any fire hazard.

BUYER BEWARE

The best quality oil is "cold-pressed" extra virgin olive oil. It is made from the plumpest, "Grade A" olives, has the best flavor, and is processed by pressing the oil from the olives with as little heat and friction as possible. The next best is virgin olive oil then pure olive oil, which is a blend of both. Many companies are using "cold-processed" instead of "cold-pressed." Cold-processed may mean the olive oil is produced by using a chemical solvent to extract the oil. Chemical residues are not uncommon. Read the labels and watch for this intentional use of a similar phrase, which does not denote a quality processing.

LIGHTEN-UP

When you deep fat fry, try adding $\frac{1}{2}$ teaspoon of baking powder per $\frac{1}{2}$ cup of flour in your batter to produce a lighter coating and fewer calories.

MAYONNAISE: OR SALAD DRESSING?

Mayonnaise must contain at least 65% oil by weight, any less and it must be called salad dressing. Most fat-free mayonnaise contains more sodium than "real" mayonnaise. A tablespoon of mayonnaise contains only 5-10 mg. of cholesterol since very little egg yolk is really used.

INCREASING THE FAT

Fast food restaurants may deep fat or par-fry French fries before they arrive at the restaurant to save time. This may cause a higher level of trans-fatty acids in the fries. As much as 10 grams of fat may come from the par frying.

GOOD TO THE LAST DROP

If you really want to get all the shortening out of a can, try pouring 2 cups of boiling water into the container and swish it around until all the fat melts. Place the container into the refrigerator until it sets up and the fat is on the top: then just skim off the fat.

LOG JAM AHEAD

Used oil should never be poured down the drain. It may solidify and clog the drain. Save the oil in a metal can and dispose of it in the garbage.

KEEPING BUTTER, BETTER

If you would like to have your butter ready and easy to spread at all times, go to a kitchen store and purchase a "British" butter dish. It is a butter dish made from terra cotta, the top of which needs to be soaked in cold water every day.

ADDITIVE HELPS

Cooking wine will stay fresher longer if you add a tablespoon of very fresh vegetable oil to the bottle.

CHEF'S SECRET

If your recipe requires that you cream shortening with a sugary substance, try adding a few drops of water to the mixture. This will make it easier to stir. When creaming butter in the blender, cut the butter in small pieces.

BUTTER FACT

The highest quality butter is U.S. Grade AA, which is produced from fresh sweet cream. U.S. Grade A is almost as good but has a lower flavor rating. U.S. Grade B is usually produced from sour cream. The milk-fat content of butter must be at least 80%.

REDUCED FAT VS. STANDARD FOOD

The reduced fat and fat-free craze is more advertising than a real nutritional benefit to most people. What you are basically doing is giving up fat and in most cases
replacing the fat with sugar. The calories almost end up the same and in some cases
the calories are even higher or the taste suffers to such a degree that the public
refuses to buy the product.

REDUCED FAT FOODS	CAL.	REGULAR FOODS	CAL.
Non-fat frozen yogurt (1 cup)	380	Regular ice cream (1 cup)	360
Low-fat peanut butter (2 tbsp)	190	Regular peanut butter (2 tbsp)	190
Fat-free fig cookie (2 cookies)	140	Regular fig cookie (2 cookies)	200
Low-fat granola cereal (1/4 cup)	110	Regular granola cereal (1/4 cup)	130
Baked tortilla chips (2 ounces)	220	Regular tortilla chips (2 ounces)	260

SLOWS DOWN AGING

Cooking wine will stay fresher longer if you add a tablespoon of very fresh vegetable oil to the bottle.

BUYER BEWARE

The best quality oil is "cold-pressed" extra virgin olive oil. It is made from the
plumpest, "Grade A" olives, has the best flavor, and is processed by pressing the
oil from the olives with as little heat and friction as possible. The next best is virgin olive oil then pure olive oil, which is a blend of both. Many companies are
using "cold-processed" instead of "cold-pressed." Cold-processed may mean the
olive oil is produced by using a chemical solvent to extract the oil. Chemical
residues are not uncommon. Read the labels and watch for this intentional use of
a similar phrase, which does not denote a quality processing.

DON'T LET OLIVE OIL HAVE A BREAKDOWN

Olive oil is one of the healthiest oils to use in salads or for low temperature cooking. It has a low smoke point, which means that it will break down easily and start
smoking. You can extend the usable life of olive oil and slow its breakdown by
adding a small amount of canola oil to the olive oil. Canola has a very high smoke
point. This will also work well with butter when you are sautéing.

OLIVE OIL VS. CHOLESTEROL

Some nutritionists claim that olive oil has the ability to lower cholesterol levels, however, the only solid information reports that extra virgin olive oil tends to help the body
preserve the good cholesterol, HDL and in some cases may lower the bad cholesterol.
This is, of course is a good thing, but don't expect a cholesterol lowering effect from
any vegetable oil. Oat bran has been shown to lower the bad cholesterol by 26%.

GRANDMOTHER'S FRYING OIL TRICK, NOT A GOOD ONE

When my grandmother fried foods she always cleaned the oil out with a few slices of raw potato, then threw them away and stored the oil in the icebox to reuse it. When oil is reused the level of trans-fatty acid rises until it is 100%, which doesn't take too long. Oil should never be reused.

FATS IN THE FIRE

If the frying fat is not hot enough, food will absorb more fat. However, if you get it too hot it will smoke, burn, and produce trans-fatty acids. Use a thermometer; the temperature should be 360^0 to 375^{0}F.

NEW PRODUCT KEEPS OIL FROM BECOMING BAD

In Europe, cooking oil breakdown has prompted laws regulating the amount of polar substances (dirty oil with trans-fatty acids), which are created by the breakdown of good oil. If the oil has more than 25% polar substances, the oil must be discarded. A new product is being used in Europe called Frypowder® and has recently been approved by the FDA as being safe in the United States has the ability to reduce the breakdown elements and allow the oil to have a longer, healthier lifetime usage.

RECIPES HAVE FAT POINTS

Many recipes that utilize fats for texture and to lend moisture, however, there are a number of foods that can replace fat without the food losing its flavor or taste sensations. If you experiment with other products to replace the fat, you may be surprised at the results. The "fat point" is a point at which fat is not needed and a replacement food can take its place for the balance of the suggested fat. Some of the best substitutes are fruit and vegetable purees. Yolks can easily be omitted in many recipes as well and only the whites used as a binder. When omitting a yolk, don't replace it with additional whites or the dish may turn out on the tough side.

PIG ABS

Lard is derived from the abdomen of pigs and is used in chewing gum bases, shaving creams, soaps, and cosmetics. Future studies may implicate lard in shortened life span as well as a factor in osteoporosis. Leaf lard is derived from the kidney area of the pig and is a higher quality than all other types of lard (best for piecrust).

FATTY PATE

Pates are bordered with pork fat from the flank of the pig.

PUTTING ON THE RITZ

Some of the highest fat content crackers are Ritz, Town House, and Goldfish, which contain about 6 grams of fat per ounce.

LARD HAS LARGER FAT CRYSTALS

Lard can be stored at room temperature for 6-8 months. If you substitute lard for butter or shortening, reduce the amount you use by 25%.

LARD OIL REPLACES WHALE OIL

During the 1800's California lighthouses used "sperm oil" from whales to light their lights. By the late 1860's the sperm oil became too expensive as the Sperm whales became an endangered species and the lighthouses switched to lard oil.

GREAT EGG-SUBSTITUTE MAYONNAISE

If you want to enjoy mayonnaise without the cholesterol and fat in the eggs, the following ingredients will be needed:

2	*Tablespoons of a quality egg substitute*
1/2	*Teaspoon of standard prepared mustard*
Dash	*Table salt*
Dash	*Black pepper (powder)*
1	*Teaspoon of pure lemon juice*
1/2	*Cup of corn oil*
1	*Ampoule of lecithin (from market or health food store)*

Place the egg substitute, mustard, salt, pepper and lemon juice into a medium bowl and beat gently with a small wire whisk, then add the corn oil a small amount at a time while continuing to whisk. Continue adding a small amount of oil and whisking until the mayonnaise becomes somewhat stiff, then you can add the balance of the oil and possibly a little more seasoning after you taste it. To complete the mayonnaise, just break open an ampoule of lecithin and empty the small amount of emulsifier to the mayonnaise and beat. This will keep the oil in suspension. Another method if you do not have the lecithin is to add one tablespoon of boiling water, which will do the same thing, but won't last very long. This needs to be consumed when prepared.

CRISPY CRITTER

When you are greasing a pan, make sure you don't use too much grease or you may cause the food to over brown.

PIGS IN A BLANKET

The age-old favorite of small pancakes wrapped around sausages was 60% fat and almost all saturated fat.

A REAL WHOPPER

Every ounce of fat contains 250% more calories than an ounce of carbohydrate or protein.

NOT THE BOTTOM OF THE CHURN

Buttermilk can be substituted for 2% or whole milk in most recipes. Buttermilk is less than 1% fat, almost equal to skim milk, however, it has a thicker consistency.

AND AWAY IT GOES

A high fat intake has been related to calcium losses through the urine.

BEAT ME, BEAT ME

Butter will go farther and have fewer calories per serving if you beat it well, increasing the volume with air.

YOLKS AWAY

When preparing any recipe or omelet, try replacing the egg yolks with an equal amount of egg substitute or just reduce the number of yolks.

LONGEVITY

The most popular oil is olive oil with soy oil coming in second. Olive oil will stay fresh longer than most oils while soy oil tends to lose its flavor the longer it is stored due to the linolenic acid it contains.

YUMMY, YUMMY

Eight ounces of potato chips are the equivalent of eating 16-20 teaspoons of fat.

NEEDS SHADES

Only purchase oils in containers if you cannot see the oil. Oil is very sensitive to light and will become rancid. All oils with the exception of cold-pressed olive oil starts oxidizing as soon as it is heat processed, then continues to breaks down until it becomes rancid.

WHY CAROB?

When carob is made into candy products, fat is usually added to improve the texture. This usually brings the fat content close to real chocolate. In fact, cocoa butter used in real chocolate is 60% saturated fat while the fat used in a carob candy is 85% saturated fat.

MARGARINE FACT

Most margarine contains over 90% fat. Diet margarine usually contains 80% fat, 16% water, 2% salt, and 2% non-fat milk solids. Margarine is naturally white; colorings and additives are added to all margarine. Liquid diet margarine, however, may contain only 40% fat.

BUTTER BUDS

Butter Buds, are an all-natural, fat and cholesterol free granule that has a butter flavor. They are normally used in place of butter on baked potatoes or any other dish that you would normally sprinkle or add a pat or two of butter to. A serving (one teaspoon) only contains 5 calories compared with 65 calories for the same amount of butter. They are made of a carbohydrate derived from corn with the flavor coming from powdered butter oils, which only contribute the flavor and nothing else.

A FATTY SEPARATION

If you are going to make your own mayonnaise, be sure that the weather report is clear. If the temperature or humidity is too high it will cause the mayonnaise to come out heavier and greasier than normal.

NEW FRYING SHORTENING LOWERS CHOLESTEROL

This new fat is called Appetize 2 and is a shortening that has had the animal fat removed and then re-formulated to actually lower cholesterol levels. In the very near future, expect to see fast food chains advertising that their fried foods have been fried in Appetize 2. This should also eliminate the trans-fatty acid problems.

THE DEBATE

The margarine, butter controversy is still going on with neither side really winning. Margarine has the bad fat, trans-fatty acids due the method of heat processing they must go through and butter contains cholesterol. My preferred choice would be whipped, unsalted butter in moderation.

WHERE, OH WHERE, HAVE MY VITAMINS GONE

Refined corn oil is a chemical extraction, a triglyceride, with no relationship to the nutrients in a "real" ear of corn. The vitamins that would normally assist with the digestion of corn oil are absent, even the vitamin E is lost.

APPLESAUCE REPLACES FAT

In most recipes applesauce can be used to replace fat almost on a one to one substitution basis. If the recipe calls for 1 cup of oil, you can use 1 cup of applesauce, especially in baked goods.

DIETARY FIASCO

A burrito topped with sour cream and guacamole may contain up to 1,000 calories and 59% fat. Add cheese sauce for another 300 calories.

THE BIG "C"

Diets high in total fat and especially trans-fatty acids (from heated fats) have been related to cancers of the colon, prostate, and breast. Studies are also showing that the efficiency of the immune system may be depressed by a high fat diet. Recommended dietary fat levels are 20-25% of your total daily calories, however, a person can actually survive on only 5% dietary fat if the fat is of the essential fatty acid type. Dietary fats are being implicated as a key factor in over 300,000 cases of skin cancer reported annually.

GOOD FAT, BAD FAT?

Recent studies have shown that stearic acid, one of the saturated fats has little effect on raising cholesterol levels. As our laboratory tests become more sophisticated more information about which fats will actually raise your cholesterol will be forthcoming. Then we can then avoid only those foods that may be harmful.

SALAD AND COOKING OIL USE

1909 - 1.5 pounds per person
1972 - 18 pounds per person
1990 - 29 pounds per person
1995 - 33 pounds per person
1997 - 34 pounds per person
1999 – 36 pounds per person
2001 – 39 pounds per person

MARGARINE USE

1950 - 6 pounds per person
1972 - 11 pounds per person
1990 - 16 pounds per person
1995 - 18 pounds per person
1997 - 19 pounds per person
1999 – 22 pounds per person
2001 – 25 pounds per person

ASK FOR IT

Most non-dairy creamers are made from coconut oil, which is high in saturated fat. Mocha Mix is your best bet.

FATS ARE MORE SATISFYING

Studies now show that dieters miss fats more than sweets.

EDUCATION A MUST

Americans consumed 53 pounds of hard fats (meats, etc.), shortenings (baked goods, etc.) and cooking fats (oils, etc.) per person in 1972. In 2001 the consumption has risen to 74 pounds, not a good direction. Poor nutrition education and the increased eating at fast food restaurants is to blame. There are 312 fats that are available for use in frying alone.

TOP FRYING OIL

Rapeseed (canola oil) for years has been grown as a forage crop for animals in the United States and Canada. Originally, it was banned in the U.S. when imports from Canada showed high levels of "erucic acid." However, new varieties have shown to contain lower levels of euric acid and the oil is now being produced and sold in large quantities. It is high in monounsaturated fat and has a high smoke point, making it the preferred oil for frying.

THE COLOR OF FAT

Current studies show that if your body is higher in "brown fat" rather than "white fat" you have a higher percentage of the more active type, which may relate to why some people are able to control their weight easier than others. Studies are being conducted at Harvard University regarding these fats and their effect on human metabolism.

INSOMNIA

Most fat should be consumed either at breakfast or lunch, few, if any for dinner. High fat meals late in the day may cause the digestive system to overwork while you are sleeping, causing restless sleep patterns.

SUGAR IN, FAT OUT, CALORIES THE SAME

The new reduced-fat peanut butter has the same number of calories per serving as the regular peanut butter, about 190 per serving, sweeteners were added in place of the fat.

CREAM-IT

To make a creamy salad dressing, try pouring cold-pressed olive oil very slowly into a running blender containing the other ingredients and spices.

WORK LIKE A PRO

Purchase empty plastic ketchup bottles to use for your oils. The narrow spout makes it easy to pour oils when cooking. Label them with a permanent felt-tip marker.

FAT SCIENCE

When oils are refrigerated and become cloudy, it is due to the buildup of harmless crystals. Manufacturers will sometimes pre-chill the oils and remove the crystals in a process known as "winterization." These oils will remain clear when refrigerated. Lard has larger fat crystals than butter, which has a lot to do with the texture of these fats and is controlled during processing. The large fat crystals in lard will make it the choice for a number of baked goods where a flakier crust is preferred, especially pies. Moderation in eating these lard products, however, is the key word.

MORE FAT SCIENCE

Oxygen has been found to be eight times more soluble in fat that in water, which is why fats tend to oxidize so easily and turn rancid. Every time you open a bottle of oil, more oil leaves and is replaced by oxygen.

TYPICAL AMERICAN DIET

The average American diet is about 44% fat. Dietary guidelines suggest no more than 30% of total calories. My recommendation is no more than 20% or less with the type of fats leaning toward the PUFA and MUFA types. The 30% figure is workable if the fat calories are all of the best type of fat, which may be difficult for most people.

GOOD FAT?

Medium-chain triglycerdides (MCT) are sold in health food stores for people who have trouble absorbing fats. They are for the most part produced from coconut oil, have a very low smoke point, and can be used for cooking without producing trans-fatty acids. Body builders tend to use this fat to increase caloric intake, but studies to date are not conclusive.

OVERWORKING YOUR DIGESTIVE SYSTEM

One 8-ounce bag of potato chips contains 6 tablespoons of oil amounting to 80 grams of fat.

FAT-REPLACERS

In 2000, the new "fat substitutes" have been appearing in our foods. These synthetically produced products should be viewed with caution and used in MODERATION only. There are three categories of fat-replacers, protein-based, carbohydrate-based and fat-based.

PROTEIN-BASED FAT-REPLACERS

Simplesse®
This fat-replacer only contains 1-2 calories per gram and is made from whey protein or egg protein. The product is digested as a protein and is used in ice cream, salad dressings and many other dairy products. Dairy-Lo® is produced from a modified whey concentrate and used in dairy products, baked goods and salad dressings.

K-Blazer®, Lita®
Produced from milk and egg protein or corn protein and mainly used in frozen desserts and baked goods.

CARBOHYDRATE-BASED FAT-REPLACERS

Avicel®, Methocel™
Produced from a purified form of cellulose and has mouth feel and other properties similar to "real" fat. Used in dairy products, sauces and salad dressings.

Slendid™ (1991)
Produced from gums, such as guar gum, locust bean gum and carrageenan. Contains no calories and used in fat-free dressings, desserts and processed meat products.

Fruitafit®
Contains only 1 calorie per gram and used as a fat and sugar replacer. The main ingredient is inulin, which is extracted from chicory root and used in yogurt, cheese, baked goods, whipped cream and dairy products.

Oatrim, Beta-Trim™
This fat substitute is made from hydrolyzed oat flour and may even be good for you. It is oat flour that has been treated with water to break down the starches into individual sugars. This causes a change in the texture and provides the fat texture that people like in their foods. The flour is high in "beta-glucan" which may have a cholesterol-absorbing ability. The product; was developed by the USDA and contains only 1 calorie per gram instead of the usual 9 calories per gram in fat.

Studies have shown a definite cholesterol lowering correlation in the 24 volunteers that took part in the study. Over 40 new products are being developed and it will be necessary to read the label to find it. It may also be called "hydrated oat flour" or use the brand name "Oatrim." Currently, it may be found in cookies, cheeses, low-fat hot dogs, and low-fat lunch, meats. It is a safer alternative than the Olean products.

Z-trim™

Contains no calories and is produced from insoluble fiber extracted from soybeans, peas, oat or rice hulls. It is very heat stabile and used in baked goods, hot dogs and dairy products.

Nu-Trim™

Produced from oats or barley and contains beta-glucans, a soluble fiber. Beta-glucans have been known to lower the bad cholesterol LDL and the total cholesterol. Meets all specifications of the FDA for a food product.

FAT-BASED REPLACERS

Olestra (Olean®) (1996)

Olestra is a large synthetic fat molecule, so large that it passes through the intestinal tract undigested. This increase of undigested material may cause diarrhea. Olestra as it goes through the system, however, tends to attract the fat-soluble vitamins A, D, E, and K and may bind with them. Proctor and Gamble the inventor of the product is familiar with the problem and may have to fortify the products with vitamins, however, this may not solve the problem.

A more significant problem may be that the carotenoid family are also fat-soluble and the over 500 carotenoids may also be in trouble. A percentage of carotenoids may be washed out of the body. These include beta-carotene, alpha-carotene, lutein, lycopene, and the rest of the family. Since these are not considered to be essential nutrients P & G does not feel that they have to include them through fortification. The carotenoids are a nutrient that is under investigation as a possible cancer preventive nutrient.

The official name that will appear on products with olestra is Olean. Olean has only been approved for snack foods. It is being added to snack-chips, crackers, tortilla chips, cheese puffs, and potato chips initially. The FDA is requiring that a warning label be added which reads:

"This product contains Olestra. Olestra may cause abdominal cramping and loose stools. Olestra inhibits the absorption of some vitamins and other nutrients. Vitamins A, D, E, and K have been added."

The "**fake-fat chip**" will have a caloric reduction of about 34%. The downside to all of this is that people may consume more junk foods and still end up with the same number of total calories. P & G presently is marketing the product under the brand name "WOW."

A number of intestinal problems (diarrhea and abdominal cramping) related to products that contain Olestra are now being reported in medical journals and my recommendation is to consume the Olestra-containg products in moderation until further studies are concluded. Additional information that has been released in 1999 states that people who have bleeding disorders or persons taking blood thinning medication should avoid products that contain Olestra since vitamin K may be adversely affected.

Salatrim, Benefat™

This new fat substitute will be marketed under the brand name Benefat™. Salatraim is a complex mixture of specific triglycerides that only contain 5 calories per gram instead of the normal 9 calories per gram in fat. The product does not contain any trans-fatty acids and has excellent "mouth-feel." When used in baked goods the new fat substitute can be used 1:1 in relation to normal fat. Rearranging the fat molecules reduced the calories and produces better fat.

Caprenin™ (1992)

Produced from canola, coconut oil and palm-kernel oil. Contains no long-chain fatty acids unless they are natural. Presently used in Milky Way II candy bars.

FAT BY THE TEASPOON

Sometimes it is hard to visualize the amount of fat we really consume. The following chart will actually provide the amount of fats in some common foods in teaspoons. The fat content of foods is much easier to comprehend in teaspoons rather than grams. If you wish to calculate the fat content in the foods you eat in teaspoons, the rule is that 5 grams of fat equals about 1 teaspoon of fat.

FOOD	SERVING SIZE	TEASPOONS
Bacon	1 strip/thin	$1^1/_4$
Big Mac	1	7–9
Bologna	1 slice	2
Canadian Bacon	1 strip	1
Chicken Breast/No Skin	4 ounces	1
Chicken Breast/Skin	4 ounces	$2^1/_2$
Chicken TV Dinner	1 medium	7
Duck/Roasted	$3^1/_2$ ounces	7
Fried Oysters	1 average serving	$2^1/_2$
Frog Legs	2 large	$2^1/_2$
Goose	$3^1/_2$ ounces	$5^1/_2$
Hamburger	$^1/_4$ pound	$3^1/_2$
Ham/Lean	2 slices/thin	$1^1/_4$
Ham TV Dinner	1 medium	3
Hot Dog/All Beef	1 medium	$2^1/_2$
Lean Beef	3 ounces	2
Lobster Newburg	$3^1/_2$ ounces	$2^1/_2$
Medium-Fat Beef	3 ounces	$4^1/_2$
Pork Chop	$3^1/_2$ ounces	$6^1/_2$
Rabbit	$3^1/_2$ ounces	$1^1/_2$
Salmon/Canned	$3^1/_2$ ounces	$3^1/_2$
Sirloin TV Dinner	1 medium	7
Squab	$3^1/_2$ ounces	$5^1/_2$
Trout/Raw	$3^1/_2$ ounces	3
Turkey	$3^1/_2$ ounces	2
Turkey Pot Pie	12 ounces	6
Veal Cutlet	$3^1/_2$ ounces	4

FAT CALORIES IN COMMON FOODS

The following is information regarding fat in relation to total calories in a person's diet:

PERCENT OF FATS	FOODS
90-100	Bacon, butter, margarine, lard, mayonnaise, solid shortenings, cooking oils, olives, baking chocolate, cream cheese.
80-90	Macadamias, salad dressings, pecans, walnuts, avocados, sausages, corned beef, coconut.
65-80	Hot dogs, peanuts, most chips, bleu cheese, cashews, lunch meats, peanut butter, prime rib, tuna in oil, Swiss cheese, sunflower seeds.
50-65	Hamburger, rib steak, chicken with skin, canned ham, salmon, trout, bass, veal cutlet, eggs, ice cream.
35-50	Most baked goods, lean hamburger, ground turkey, Canadian bacon, ham, steak, whole milk, round steak.
20-35	Low-fat yogurt, 2% milk, veal chop, loin and rump cuts of beef, sweet breads.
10-20	Crab, baked chicken without skin, most shellfish, tuna in water, low-fat cottage cheese, low-fat broiled fish.
Very small amount	Buttermilk, skim milk, beans, rice, cereals, potatoes. pasta, fruits, vegetables, egg whites,

SOURCE: Nutritive Values of Foods, USDA 1994.

PERCENT SATURATION OF COMMONLY USED FATS

VEGETABLE OILS & SHORTENINGS	PUFA	MUFA	SFA
Safflower Oil	75%	12%	9%
Sunflower Oil	66%	20%	10%
Corn Oil	59%	24%	13%
Soybean Oil	58%	23%	14%
Cottonseed Oil	52%	18%	26%
Canola Oil	33%	55%	7%
Olive Oil	8%	74%	13%
Peanut Oil	32%	46%	17%
Soft Tub Margarine	31%	47%	18%
Stick Margarine	18%	59%	19%
Vegetable Shortening	14%	51%	31%
Palm Oil	9%	37%	49%
Coconut Oil	2%	6%	86%
Palm Kernel Oil	2%	11%	81%
ANIMAL FATS			
Tuna Fat	37%	26%	27%
Chicken Fat	21%	45%	30%
Lard	11%	45%	40%
Mutton Fat	8%	41%	47%
Beef Fat	4%	42%	50%
Butter Fat	4%	29%	62%

PUFA   - POLYUNSATURATED FATTY ACIDS
MUFA   - MONOUNSATURATED FATTY ACIDS
SFA - SATURATED FATTY ACIDS

SOURCE: National Heart, Lung, and Blood Institute

HIGH FAT VS LOW FAT LUNCHEON FOODS

HIGH FAT FOOD	CALORIES	FAT(g.)
Cheddar Cheese (1oz.)	110	9
Swiss Cheese (1oz.)	110	8
American Cheese (1oz.)	110	9
Provolone (1oz.)	100	7
Bologna (4oz.)	360	32
Sausage (2oz.)	140	11
Hot Dog (1 med.)	160	12
Cream Cheese (1oz.)	100	10
Potato Chips (1oz.)	150	10
Cream of Mushroom Soup (1 cup)	100	7
Cola Drink (12oz.)	145	0
Double Burger w/Cheese	695	45
Vanilla Shake (12oz.)	290	11
Onion Rings (reg. order)	270	16
Butter/Margarine (1 Tbl.)	85	9
Mayonnaise (1 Tbl.)	100	11
Tartar Sauce (1 Tbl.)	70	8
Avocado (1/2 Haas)	150	14
Croissant Roll (1 small)	170	9

LOW FAT FOOD		
Danish Ham (4oz.)	100	4
Turkey (3oz.)	110	3
Turkey Pastrami (3oz.)	100	4
Mustard (1 Tbl.)	12	0
Mayo Lite (1 Tbl.)	45	5
Ketchup (1 Tbl.)	16	0
Pickle Relish (1 Tbl.)	30	0
Pretzels (1oz.)	110	1
Diet Soda (12oz.)	1	0
Vegetable Soup (1 cup)	60	2
Lettuce (1 cup)	12	.2
Tomato (1 small)	15	.1
Mozzarella Cheese (1oz. skim)	80	5
Lite-Line American Cheese (1oz.)	50	2
Lit-Line Swiss Cheese (1oz.)	50	2
Hamburger (reg.)	275	12
Chicken Hot Dog (1 reg.)	125	8
Pita Bread (1 pocket)	75	.7

SHORTENING VS. OIL

Shortening is just a solid form of fat and is always a solid at room temperature. It can be made from either an animal or vegetable source or a combination of the two. Shortenings that are made from vegetable sources are hydrogenated, which is the addition of water to a liquid fat until it becomes the consistency that is desired by the manufacturer. The term "pure shortening" means that the product can contain either vegetable or animal sources or a combination of both. If the product is labeled "pure vegetable shortening" it has to be made from only vegetable sources. If the product does not have the word "pure" on the label then a number of additives were added to increase the shelf life, however, when this is done it does lower the smoke point and is not as good a product. One of the best shortenings is Crisco, which has a balanced saturated fat to unsaturated fat of one to one.

THE LONGEST SHELF LIFE OF ANY OIL

The shelf life of Crisco is 2-3 years, longer than any other shortening. Cold pressed olive oil; however, if stored in a cool dark location and in a glass colored bottle may last up to 10 years and still be useable.

WHY FRYING OIL LANDS ON THE INSIDE OF LENSES

If you wear eyeglasses and fry foods, you may have noticed that the oil droplets collect on the inner surface of the lens rather than the outer surface. The reason for this is because when you are frying the minute droplets become airborne and then fall back toward the floor. When you are bending over working at your cooking task the oil droplets fall on the inside of the lens.

WHY OIL CAN'T BE USED FOR BAKING

Because of its liquid nature, oils tend to collect instead of evenly distributing through the dough. This may cause the baked goods to become grainy. When solid fat is used, baked items tend to be more fluffy and retain their moisture better. Especially bad are the "all-purpose" oils, which even though they say that they can be used for baking and frying are not up to the standards that most cooks desire. To produce these oils a number of additives are used which may affect the flavor and taste of the food.

FRYING TEMPERATURES ARE CRITICAL

It is never wise to fry at too low a temperature, especially if the food is breaded. The oil will not be hot enough to seal the breading or outer surface of the food and too much of the oil is allowed to enter the food before the sealing takes place. When the oil is too hot then the food may end up being burned on the outside and not allow the insides to be cooked through. Most breaded foods that are fried are normally fried at 375°F, it is best to check the recipe for the particular food you are frying for the correct frying temperature. Chicken should be fried at 365°F for 10-20 minutes for the best results and meats at 360°F.

WHO INVENTED MARGARINE?

Margarine, was invented by the French chemist, Hippolyte Mege-Mouries in 1869 upon request by Napoleon III who wanted a low-cost fat. Originally, it was produced from animal fat, however, today it is made from vegetables oil (mainly soy), milk solids, salt, air, and water.

SOME CANOLA OIL IS NOW BEING RUINED BY BIOTECHNOLOGY?

Canola oil is now being altered through genetic engineering so that it contains high levels of the saturated fat "laurate." Laurate is not normally found in canola oil but by producing a high saturated fat product it may now be used in the baking industry to replace palm and coconut (tropical oils) which are more expensive to import. Since the public has recently become aware that canola oil is high in monounsaturated oil, which is good for the body in moderation, the public may view the product containing canola oil to be a product that contains "good oil." The new Canola oil will be used initially in non-dairy products such as coffee creamers and whipped toppings.

THE DIFFERENCE BETWEEN FATS AND OILS

The difference between fats and oils is basically that fat is usually solid at room temperature and oil is liquid. If the fat is from an animal source, it is usually solid and from a vegetable source, it is usually liquid. However, all fats are similar in their chemical structure and vary more due to their type of fat saturation.

Shortening is solid fat at room temperature and can be either an animal or vegetable fat. The best shortenings will have the word "pure" on the label, if the word pure is not on the label, the product may contain a number of additives that are capable of lowering the smoke point.

Fats and oils should be as pure as possible to obtain the best results when baking or preparing any dish.

VEGETABLE OILS

The best vegetable oils to use for cooking are those that are lowest in saturated fat. However, some dishes require that certain oils or fats be used to produce the desired flavor of the dish. In those instances, the recommended oil should be used. In all other instances, olive oil is highly recommended since it is high in monounsaturated fat, which is fat the body prefers over other types of fats. Throughout the book, when recipes call for cooking with olive oil you should note that a small amount of canola oil is usually recommended along with it. The canola oil raises the smoke point of olive oil just enough so that it slows down the breakdown of the olive oil.

SPRAY OILS - MONEY SAVER

For many years the only spray oil that was sold was Pam. The markets now are selling many different brands as well as different oils available in spray containers. The latest to hit the shelves has been olive oil. If you find these products too pricey, all you have to do is stop by a kitchen supply store and purchase an oil spray bottle. These are small pump action spray bottles that you can easily fill. Use any oil and an equal amount of lecithin to keep the oil in suspension. Lecithin may be found in the vitamin section of your market or any health food store.

Most of the market brands contain lecithin, which helps keep the propellant and the oil from separating, however, it is best to purchase the pump-type sprays to protect the ozone layer. Never spray the oils on too hot a surface or an open flame since they are flammable. Also, be careful of inhaling the oil spray as it is capable of coating the lungs and could be fatal.

OLIVE OIL STATISTICS

The United States presently imports about 140,000 tons of olive oil annually. The United States has only .02% of all olive trees worldwide, while the Mediterranean basin has 95%. Italy produces almost 600,000 tons of olive oil and uses over 800,000 tons. The surplus comes from Greece, Spain and Tunisia.

GARLIC/OLIVE OIL ALERT

The government has issued an alert regarding placing raw garlic in olive oil for more than 24 hours. Garlic may harbor bacteria: that tends to multiply in an atmosphere that lacks oxygen. Even though the risks are minimal it would be wise not to store garlic in this manner. For additional information regarding this problem call (800) 232-6548.

NUTTY OILS

THE HAWAIIAN NUT

Macadamia nut oil is now becoming more available. The oil is high in monounsaturated fat and is great in salad dressings and to sauté many dishes in for a great flavor. The smoke point is somewhat higher than olive oil so you may not have to add canola oil to it to raise the smoke point.

TOP OF THE NUT HEAP

If you wish to use nut oil, one of the best would be walnut oil. Walnuts are lower in saturated fat than the other nuts and high in polyunsaturated fatty acids. Peanut oil has twice the saturated fat than walnut oil.

ARE MY TASTE BUDS WORKING?

Peanut oil has very little flavor when used for cooking purposes. It has a relatively high smoke point, which makes it a good choice for frying. The mild nut flavor is popular with Asian cooks however, it is not flavorful enough for most American dishes. The oil will remain fresh for about a year under refrigeration and if it becomes cloudy will clear up if allowed to remain at room temperature in a short period of time.

GRAVY

Gravy is always best if you use the pan drippings, which contain the flavor of the meat or poultry. Many people avoid using the drippings because of the high fat content, however, the fat content can easily be reduced by separating the fat from the flavorful liquid using a separating cup to pour off the fat. Other methods include placing ice cubes in a piece of cheesecloth and swirling that around to trap the fat, or if time allows the drippings can be placed into the freezer for a few minutes until the fat rises and can easily be removed.

A LEGAL SEPARATION

A common problem with gravy is that it almost always separates, especially as it cools down. To keep the gravy in suspension, all you have to do is add a pinch or two of baking soda to the gravy and stir.

GETTING RID OF YOUR LUMPS

You will never have lumpy gravy if you just add a pinch of salt to the flour and mix it in before adding any liquid.

QUICK, PUT ME IN A SUNTAN BOOTH

If your gravy is not brown enough and you need a quick fix, just add 1 teaspoon of hot instant coffee. There will not be any flavor of coffee in the gravy.

THIS SALT IS KILLING ME

To improve the taste of over-salted gravy, just add $1/4$ teaspoon of brown sugar to the gravy.

REPAIRING BURNT GRAVY

If you accidentally burn the gravy, all you have to do is add a teaspoon of peanut butter to the gravy. You won't notice the taste of the peanut butter at all.

GRAVY PERKER UPPER

If you would like your gravy to have a rich, dark brown color, just spread the flour on a cookie sheet and cook over a low heat, stirring occasionally until the flour browns. Just before serving the gravy, add a teaspoon of coffee to the gravy to firm up the color permanently. Another method of browning the gravy is to add onion skins to the gravy while it is cooking.

Grandmother's Gravy Recipe:

The rule of thumb to remember is to use the same number of tablespoons of fat (need to use a little) drippings to flour. The pan drippings should be taken from the pan before you remove the fat. The following recipe is for about 2½ cups of gravy and should be adjusted depending on the number of people to be served. This amount usually serves 8 people comfortably. Unsalted butter may be used in place of the fat drippings and be sure to start with the butter at room temperature, do not microwave.

In a medium saucepan over low heat, place 4 tablespoons of pan drippings and 4 tablespoons of all-purpose flour. Cook the mixture until brown stirring occasionally. Add 2 cups of de-fatted drippings and continue to cook over low heat until the desired thickness is achieved.

FAT FACTS

GREECE-ING UP FOR HEALTH

In Greece, people consume 40% of their calories as fat, however, their risk of heart disease is low. They consume most of their fat as olive oil.

HOW MUCH FAT CAN YOUR STOMACH CLEAR?

Approximately 10 grams of fat is cleared from the stomach per hour. Two scrambled eggs, bread and butter, coffee, and milk = 50 grams of fat. Assimilation time is 5-6 hours. An example of high fat foods; are bacon and cheddar cheese. The percent of fat to calories in each is 75% fat. Americans spend $3 billion per year on bacon.

THE QUALITY OF BUTTER

Butter is sold in three grades depending on the flavor rating and milk-fat content. The best grade is U.S. Grade AA, next is U.S. Grade A, which has a lower flavor rating and U.S. Grade B, which is made from sour cream. The milk-fat rating of butter must be at least 80%.

SQEEEEZING THE LAST DROP FROM A CAN

If you want to get the last drop of shortening from a can, just pour boiling water in the can and place it in the refrigerator for an hour or until the fat rises to the top, then just skim off the fat.

GOING UP IN SMOKE

Oil will deteriorate very quickly depending on the smoke point of that particular oil. When any oil deteriorates it starts smoking and develops into bad fat called a trans-fatty acid. To test the oil while it is hot to check on the level of deterioration, just drop a piece of white bread in the oil. If the bread develops dark spots, the oil has gone bad.

NEVER RE-USE FRYING OIL

A common practice is to clean out frying oil and store it in the freezer for future use. While the oil can be cleaned using a raw potato, the oil is not healthy oil once it has been used at a high temperature. A percentage of the oil breaks down into bad oil (trans-fatty acid) and the more you use that oil, the more acids it contains.

TURN OUT THE LIGHTS

When purchasing liquid oil, only purchase oil that is packaged in opaque containers. Oil deteriorates very quickly and the light will hasten the process.

THE HOTTER THE OIL, THE FEWER THE CALORIES

Tests have been conducted that prove that the hotter the oil, the less oil will be absorbed by the food. The frying time is also lessened, which also contributes to the fewer fat calories retained.

THE HIGHER THE FRYER, THE LOWER THE TEMPERATURE

When you fry above sea level it is necessary to lower the frying temperature 3°F for every 1,000 feet increase in elevation. If you live in Denver, Colorado, you will need to lower your frying temperature by 15 degrees.

LEAF LARD, BEST FOR PIES

Leaf lard has large fat crystals, which will produce a flakier piecrust. The lard is derived from the kidney area of pigs instead of the abdomen, which is where lard is usually derived from. When substituting lard for butter or shortening in a recipe, reduce the amount of lard used by 25%.

FAT IN MARGARINE

The average margarine sold contains about 90% fat; diet margarine contains 80% fat, 16% water, 2% salt and 2% non-fat milk solids. Liquid margarine may contain only 40% fat and more air and water than other diet margarine.

FAT SUBSTITUTES

The 1990's were the decade when a number of fat substitutes were invented. The requirements for these substitutes were that they have the "mouth feel" of real fat and be able to enhance other flavors. Most of these are still in use today but only found in certain products that they are compatible with.

Simplease™ (1990) Whey (or egg whites) protein concentrates that are subjected to microparticulation. Used in Simple Pleasures brand frozen desserts and may be used in other frozen foods. Contains 1-2 kcal/g and is digestible.

Stellar™ (1991) Modified cornstarch + water and sheared into a smooth cream. Used in salad dressings, Danish pastries, hot dogs and sausage. Contains 1 kcal/g and is digestible.

Slendid™ (1991) Pectin + calcium chloride + water and sheared to form a gel. Used in cookies and cheese products. Contains 0 kcal/g and is digestible.

Oatrim™ (1991) Oat starch + fiber + water that is sheared. Used mainly for Healthy Choice brand beef products. Contains 1 kcal/g and is digestible.

Caprenin™ (1992) Derived from canola, coconut, and palm oils and contains fatty acids that are longer than those found naturally. Used in Milky Way II brand candy bars. Contains 5 kcal/g and is partially digestible.

Olestra™ (1996) Sucrose polyester: with fatty acids attached. Used in chips and cookies. May appear in other product. Contains 0 kcal/g and is indigestible. Government warning is placed on label.

NutriLipids™ Composed of: high-oleic sunflower oil, medium-chain triglycerides, and soy protein. It is used in beverage mixes to improve the flavor and texture. The product is trans-acid and lactose-free. It provides a good source of protein, calcium and iron. Look for it on the label: this is an excellent product.

NEW FAT-REPLACER

A new fat replacer; PAC-TILLA™, is being used to produce non-fat baked goods. The product is produced from specially processed rice flour and used primarily in wheat flour tortillas. The product provides a smooth texture and provides a similar mouth-feel to that of "real" fat. The new fat substitute will also provide a longer shelf life for the products.

APPETIZE® IS 100% NATURAL

This is a new natural shortening made from a patented blend of cholesterol-removed meat fat and vegetable oils. Appetize® provides a believable taste of "real" meat fat shortenings combined with an excellent nutritional profile. For more information call: (800) 828-0800.

THE LEGAL FAT: SUET

Suet is fat that is derived from the kidneys of sheep and cattle. It may be substituted for lard in many recipes and has large fat crystals similar to lard, which is why suet is very popular in certain baked goods such as piecrust.

MASHED POTATOES WITH SCMALTZ AND GRIBENES (UFO'S)

Schmaltz is a traditional Jewish food that is prepared from rendering down chicken fat and skin. The fat has an excellent flavor and after it has finished rendering the small UFO's (unidentified fried objects) are called gribenes. The gribenes are actually the remains of the skin that has been turned into small, crunchy, fat balls. In moderation these fats are very tasty when added into mashed potatoes. Don't knock it till you try it.

BROWN-OUT

When greasing a pan with oil or butter, try not to overdo the amount you are using. A common problem of over-browning baked goods and other foods is caused by placing too much of an oil in a pan.

HOW TO STOP UP YOUR DRAIN

Fat should never be poured down the drain unless you pour at least one quart of boiling water after the fat. Cold pipes will solidify animal fat very quickly.

SALAD AND COOKING OIL USE

In 1909 Americans used 1.5 pounds of salad and cooking oil per person annually. Corn oil and lard were the most popular oils. In 1998 Americans: used 35 pounds per person. Margarine use has increased from 6 pounds per person in 1950 when Oleo was invented, to 24 pounds per person in 2001.

WHY FAT IS USED IN BAKED GOODS

Fat is used to produce tender baked good products by coating the gluten strands. The more the strands are coated, the more tender the product. Fat is also needed to add texture to baked goods and other products. Chilled solid fat is recommended when preparing flaky pasty dough since it does not combine with the flour. This creates a flaky texture effect of alternating layers of fat and flour, which is why lard is the preferred fat for piecrusts.

FRIED FOOD PROTECTOR

Fried foods will not pick up and retain as much fat if you add a tablespoon of vinegar to the fryer or skillet before adding the oil. Coat the pan as best you can and leave the balance of the vinegar on the pan.

TRAPPING AIR

Room-temperature fat, when creamed with sugar has the capability of trapping air in a cake batter, creating very light-textured cakes.

FRYING FOODS? HIDE THE SALT SHAKER

Never salt a food before placing the food into a fryer. The salt tends to draw moisture out of the food and will cause splattering. The moisture will also cause the oil to decompose more readily.

TOGETHERNESS

When you shake oil and vinegar together, the oil breaks into smaller particles, which allows the two to mix together temporarily. As soon as you stop shaking, the mixture, the fat droplets start to combine again and come out of suspension rising back to the surface. However, if you use an emulsifying agent, it will hold the oil and vinegar in permanent suspension. The best substance to keep these two together is lecithin. Just break open two lecithin ampoules and mix the liquid into the oil and vinegar.

The shaking will break down the fat globules again into very small particles and the lecithin will grab them, encircle them and keep them from combining again. Lecithin is the emulsifying agent in egg yolks, which keeps Hollandaise sauce in suspension.

THERE GO THE EYEBROWS AGAIN

The danger level of oil is called the flash point, which is about 600°F(315.6°C). At this point the oil will start to show signs of catching fire, however, the actual fire point is around 700°F (371.1°C). When the oil hits 700 degrees it will flame up and a fire extinguisher will be needed. However, the easiest method is just to cover the pan and eliminate the oxygen. Another method is to pour baking soda on the fire suffocating it.

NOT JUST HOT, REALLY HOT

Frying at too low a temperature will cause the breading to fall off many foods. Also, too much of the oil will enter the food since the hot frying oil is supposed to seal the food. If the oil is too hot, the food may burn or not be fully cooked. Breaded foods need to be fried at 375°F(190.6°C). Chicken needs to be fried at 365°F(185°C) for 10-20 minutes depending on the thickness of the piece. Meats should be fried at 360°F(182.2°C).

FORCING YOUR BREADING TO STAY PUT

Chefs never have a problem making breading stay on a food. There are a few secrets that will really make the difference.

- When using eggs, make sure they are at room temperature.
- Always place the breaded food in the refrigerator for 45 minutes then allow it to return to room temperature before placing the food in the fryer.
- Never over beat the eggs, the more air you put in, the lower the binding ability of the egg.
- Always use the smallest breadcrumbs you can purchase, large breadcrumbs do not adhere well.
- Homemade breadcrumbs are coarser and always adhere better.

FAT FROM DOWN UNDER

Copha is a coconut shortening that is commonly found in Australia. If your recipe calls for copha, just use a solid shortening.

STOP CROWDING ME, WAIT YOUR TURN

One of the first rules a chef learns is not to place too much food in a deep-fat fryer. Smaller batches will not cause the frying temperature to drop too low. When you do fry, remember to always make sure the oil is about 15°F(-9.4°C) above the temperature that you want to fry in. Foods that are placed into the fryer at room temperature will cause a drop of about 15°F(-9.4°C). Never place food directly from the refrigerator into the fryer since this will cause splattering and may cause a 30°F(-1.1°C) drop in temperature

CANOLA OIL BEING KILLED BY BIOTECHNOLOGY

Canola oil which is a good oil and high in monounsaturated fat, which the body prefers is now being altered into a more saturated fat through the addition of "laurate." When you see canola oil on the baked goods package, be aware that it is probably not the good canola oil, but an altered one. Initially, the new oil is being used in non-dairy creamers and whipped cream.

PURE OR VIRGIN, WHAT'S THE DIFFERENCE

Law has set the standards for olive oil and the saturated fat levels it contains. Extra virgin olive oil must not contain more than 1% unsaturated fatty acid and virgin olive oil must not contain more than 3.3%. Pure olive oil is a combination of both oils.

CLARIFIED BUTTER

Clarified butter is far superior to regular butter because you are able to fry with it at higher temperatures and it will store longer, even at room temperature. One of the drawbacks, however, is that you do have to give up some of the butter flavor, which comes from the protein (casein) in the part of the butter that is lost during the clarification process. The smoke point of butter will be raised from 250°F to 350°F (121.1°C to 176.7°C) since it is the protein that tends to cause the butter to scorch and smoke. The protein also reduces the storage time of butter.

When you clarify butter you separate the fat from the non-fat ingredients. When butter is heated it tends to breakdown into three different ingredients: A layer of foam, the thick middle layer of fat (the clarified butter) and a light-colored bottom layer of water, carbohydrates and protein (casein). The bottom layer contains no fat at all. The top layer contains similar ingredients as the bottom layer and trapped air keeps it from falling to the bottom.

HOW TO MAKE CLARIFIED BUTTER:

- Cut up ¼ pound of *unsalted* butter into very small chunks.
- Place the butter into a clear ovenproof bowl
- Cover the bowl and place it in the oven on the lowest temperature setting possible.
- After the butter has completely melted, place the bowl in the refrigerator for one hour and do not disturb.
- The middle fat layer (clarified fat) should be solidified.
- Remove the middle fat layer, remove the top foam and the bottom slimy layer, then rinse the middle fat layer under cold water.
- Dry the fat layer gently with paper towel and will store in the refrigerator for up to 3-4 weeks.

GHEE, ITS BUTTER

Ghee is similar to clarified butter and is made using real butter. Ghee has a big advantage over butter in that you can cook and especially sauté with it without it breaking down and burning too easily. Therefore you are able to treat ghee similar to oil. The smoke point of ghee is around 375°F(190.6°C), which is still lower than most oils but it is still much better than plain butter. Ghee tends to impart a great flavor to many sautéed foods, which is not possible with standard butter.

To prepare ghee, just place some butter in a saucepan on high heat and heat until all the water evaporates. Butter is approximately 19% water. Continue cooking at the lowest heat point until the milk solids start to coagulate and caramelize (turn a light brown). The excellent flavor is released into the ghee when the milk solids turn brown. The milk solids are easily skimmed off and removed and you are left with the ghee. Strain the final mixture through a few pieces of cheesecloth to remove any remaining milk solids.

POPCORN WITH GHEE

If you want to give popcorn a new taste treat, just use ghee instead of the oil you are presently using. There will be no heavy oil taste and the popcorn will have a new light buttery flavor.

DRAWN BUTTER

When you see drawn butter used on a menu it means that it is clarified butter with the sediment drawn off. It is a very clear butter that has a refrigerator life of about 2 weeks.

COMPOUND BUTTER

A compound butter is just a butter that has added ingredients and flavorings. It is usually prepared from unsalted butter, however, unless you prefer a sweet slightly sour taste, you might prefer using salted butter for most recipe variations. Basically, the butter is softened and beaten and beaten to add air and create a degree of fluffiness before adding any ingredients. When preparing a compound butter, it would be best to start with the highest quality butter available. Many pasta dishes are served using a flavored compound butter instead of a sauce.

BROWN BUTTER

Basically, this is an unsalted butter that has been heated until it is light brown and has a somewhat nutty aroma. It is prepared just before serving the dish and usually used on vegetables and fish dishes. The butter is easily burned and should not sit after it is prepared since it may deteriorate very quickly.

BLACK BUTTER

Black butter is prepared the same as brown butter, except it is heated a little bit more and has a few drops of apple cider vinegar added and possibly a few capers. Care is necessary so that the vinegar will not cause splattering.

STORING MARGARINE

Margarine readily absorbs odors from the refrigerator and should always be stored in a tightly sealed container. Margarine will store under refrigeration for 4-6 months if not contaminated by someone placing a spoon in it that had been in his or her mouth. Margarine will freeze for up to 1 year if the temperature is kept at $0^{\circ}F(-17.8^{\circ}C)$.

BUTTERY SECRETS

CHEF'S SECRETS:

When softening the butter, always allow the butter to soften at room temperature. The butter should be soft enough to be stirred with a wooden spoon. Never soften butter in a microwave or in a pan on top of the stove, since these methods will affect the flavor of the butter.

When adding the other ingredients, never use a blender, mixers or food processor. This will affect the overall texture of the final product.

WOULD SOMEONE CAUL FAT

A "caul fat" is a strip of fat that is used to wrap meats. It is sold in French, Asian or Italian markets. A good substitute would be bacon strips.

SAUTÉING SECRETS

- Chefs will never use salted butter when they are sautéing. The salt in butter may separate from the butter and impart a somewhat bitter taste to the food being sautéed. Always use unsalted butter.
- Always use a small amount of oil and heat the oil to a high temperature before adding the food. Try placing a small sample of the food (at room temperature) into the pan, if it sizzles the fat is hot enough.
- If the food is cold it will stick to the pan.
- Move the pan gently back and forth while sautéing.
- Parboil any dense foods such as carrots or potatoes first. This will assure that all the food will be done at the same time
- Never salt food that is to be sautéed, that will retard the browning.
- Before sautéing meat, sprinkle a small amount of sugar on the meat. The sugar will help the browning and caramelize and will also improve the taste.
- Never overcrowd the pan.
- Remove any excess fat with a bulb baster.
- Never cover the pan or the food will become mushy.

ONE POUND OF FAT

One pound of solid shortening is equal to 2 cups.

CHAPTER 5

SPICES, SEASONINGS & HERBS

PROTECTING YOUR HERBS

The best location to store spices is in a cool, dry spot where they will not be around heat. Storing spices near a microwave exhaust fan or over the range are two of the worst locations. If you decide to store them in the refrigerator, make sure you remove them at least 30 minutes before you plan to use them. This will allow the herb to warm up enough to release its flavor and aroma. Herbs that contain oil readily oxidize and should always be stored in the refrigerator. The flavor of fresh herbs are milder than those from the supermarket that have been dried.

FRESH HERB PRESERVATION

Remove the fresh, undamaged leaves from the stems and lightly spray them with cold water. Place the leaves into small paper cups and fill the cup with fresh (filtered if possible) cool water, then freeze. To defrost the herbs, place the cup under cool running water until fully defrosted.

WHAT IS CAJUN STYLE?

The definition of "Cajun Style" cooking refers to cooking a dish that contains; onion powder/dehydrated onion, garlic powder/dehydrated garlic, white pepper, red pepper, and freshly ground black pepper.

TO SEASON OR NOT TO SEASON, THAT IS THE QUESTION

When you need to increase the amount of food in a recipe and are not sure if you should increase the seasonings in the same proportion as the original recipe called for, the answer is never increase the seasonings to the full degree. If you double the recipe, increase the seasonings only by $1\frac{1}{2}$, if you increase by three times, only increase two times the original. If the recipe is a complicated one, it would be best to make two batches. Never increase sugar in tomato sauce dishes. Never increase salt more than a pinch or two at the most.

REFRESHING, WHOLE PACKAGED SPICES

Place the spices in a 350°F oven spread out on a cookie sheet for 3-5 minutes or until they release their aroma. Remove from the oven and use as is or grind them up.

THAT'S A BLAST

If you crush dried herbs before using them it will intensify their flavor. You can also intensify their flavor by soaking them for a few seconds in hot water, especially before adding them to a salad. When doubling a recipe, never double the seasoning until you taste the dish. This also works well if they have lost their flavor.

THE WORLD OF SPICES

ALLSPICE

The flavor is similar to that of cinnamon, cloves, and nutmeg. The majority is imported from Jamaica, Central America, and South America and it is sold in both whole and ground forms. The spice is used in pickling, meats, fish, baked goods, relish, puddings and fruit preserves. Allspice is a common herb and can be found in number of ready-to-serve foods such as, hot dogs, soups, and baked beans.

ANISE

Gives licorice it's unique flavor and is mainly imported from Mexico and Spain. Usually sold as anise seeds and can be found in licorice candy, cookies, pickling, and in soft drinks. Also, used to make Anisette and can replace ginger in some recipes. Rabbits love the taste of licorice.

BASIL

There are more than 60 varieties of basil found worldwide. It is a common seasoning for fish, meat, tomato dishes, soups, stews, pizza sauce, dressings, and used on salads. Basil is a relative of the mint family and is usually imported from India. Basil is also grown in the United States and known as "sweet basil." Best to store fresh basil in the refrigerator in a slightly moistened plastic bag. It should retain its flavor and aroma for about 4 days.

Basil tends to lose much of its flavor after about 15 minutes of cooking and should be added about 10 minutes before the food is done for the best results. There are a number of varieties of basil, which include lemon and cinnamon basil, which have green leaves and opal basil, which has purple leaves.

PRESERVING FRESH BASIL IN OIL

Only fresh leaves should be used and removed carefully from the stems. Place the leaves into a jar and cover them with extra virgin olive oil. Seal the jar well and refrigerate until ready to use.

BAY LEAF

Usually sold as whole leaves and commonly used in vegetables, stews, sauces, soups, French dressing, dill pickles, meat dishes, veal, and poultry. Also, used in numerous ready-to-serve foods.

Remember to remove bay leaves from foods before you serve them. If someone eats a piece it will be like eating a mouthful of straw. Never crumble up a bay leaf when using it in a recipe and stir gently so as not to break the bay leaf up. The Turkish variety of bay leaf has a milder flavor than the California variety and is wider and shorter.

CAPERS

These are an unopened green flower bud of a wild cultivated bush grown in Italy, France and Algeria. Recently they are also being grown in California. After they are harvested, they are dried and pickled in special vinegar brine. They are normally sold either whole or pickled in brine. Commonly used on smoked fish, chicken dishes, eggs, or veal.

Capers provide piquancy, which is why they are used in special sauces and as a condiment.

CARAWAY SEEDS

Somewhat similar flavor to licorice (anise) and are harvested at night before the dew evaporates. The majority sold in the United States is imported from the Netherlands and commonly used in rye bread, cookies, organ meats, dips, cabbage, sauerkraut, soft cheese spreads, sweet pickles, Sauerbraten, and French dressing.

CARDAMOM SEED

A member of the ginger family, with a slight lemon flavor. Best used in pickling, pastries, grape jellies, hot dogs, pumpkin dishes, sweet potatoes, and Asian dishes. Usually imported from India and sold whole or ground. The seeds have a tendency to cover up bad breath very effectively.

CAYENNE PEPPER

A common spice also called capsaicin or red pepper. Sold in crushed, ground, or whole forms. Commonly used in curries, relishes, salsas, chili products, most Mexican dishes, Italian, Indian foods, sausages, and dressings.

CELERY SEED

Sold in the seed form and as celery salt and used in soups, stews, salad dressings, fish dishes, salads, pickling, and many vegetable dishes. Celery flakes are made from dehydrated leaves and the stalks and used in the same dishes.

CHERVIL

Imported from France and used in salad dressings and anything that you would use parsley for.

CHILI PEPPERS

The best method of preparing chili peppers for use in recipes is to first roast them. Just use a long handled fork on top of the stove and singe them until the skin blisters. Place the hot peppers on a cloth and cover them allowing them to steam making the skin relax and easily pull away allowing the seeds and veins to be removed. The pulp will be very spicy but the seeds and veins will be even hotter. Try not to use too many of the seeds unless you desire a hot fiery dish.

CHILI POWDER

BETTER GLUE YOUR HAT DOWN

Prepared from a combination of cumin seed, hot chili peppers, oregano, salt, cayenne pepper, garlic, and allspice. This will give you a jolt if you are not used to it. Have a glass of milk ready.

CHIVES

Chives have a light onion flavor and are commonly used in to flavor dips, sauces, soups, baked potatoes, or to replace onion flavor in a recipe. Chives are a good source of potassium, iron and calcium. Chives should be cut up only just before you are ready to use them to preserve their vitamins and minerals. Heating chives will also cause a big loss of nutrients. Frozen chives retain a larger percentage of their flavor than dried chives.

CILANTRO

Sold as fresh coriander as a fresh herb and looks a lot like parsley. Commonly used in Mexican dishes and in salad dressings and salsa. To keep cilantro fresh, just remove the fresh leaves from the stem and place then on a piece of barely moist paper towel in a single layer. Roll the paper towel up and wrap it in plastic wrap or a bag, making sure as much air as possible is removed. Store in the refrigerator and the cilantro should stay fresh for at least 3-5 days.

CINNAMON

Imported from China and Indonesia and is harvested from the bark of the Laurel tree. The variety commonly sold in the United States is usually imported from Vietnam and called the "cassia" variety and is used in its whole form for preserving, spiced beverages, chicken, meat, flavoring puddings, pickling, cider, and hot wine drinks. The ground form is used for baked goods, ketchup, vegetables, apple butter, mustards, and spiced peaches. However, the "real" cinnamon is from the Laurel tree. The color is the giveaway; true cinnamon is actually a light tan color, while "cassia" is a dark reddish-brown.

CLOVE

Imported from Indonesia and usually sold as whole cloves. A strong spice used in moderation in baked beans, pickling, ham roasts, sweet potatoes, baked goods, puddings, mustards, soups, hot dogs, sausages, and barbecue sauces.

CORIANDER SEED

A relative of the carrot family, it has a sweet musk flavor. The seed or ground form is used in gingerbread, cookies, cakes, biscuits, poultry stuffing, pork, spiced dishes, pea soup, and cheese dishes.

CUMIN SEED

Used mainly in its ground form in curry, chili powder, soups, stuffed eggs, fruit pies, stews, soft cheeses, and chili con carne.

CURRY POWDER

Curry powder is a blend of at least 20 spices, herbs, and seeds. Ingredients may include: chili peppers, cloves, coriander, fennel seed, nutmeg, mace, cayenne, black pepper, sesame seed, saffron, and turmeric. The yellow color comes from the turmic. Usually used in Indian cooking, poultry, stews, soups, sauces, and meat dishes.

DILL

Sold in whole or ground seed form or as a fresh herb. Usually used in cottage cheese, chowders, pickling, soups, sauerkraut, salads, fish, meat sauces, potato salad, green apple pie, and spiced vinegar. Great for livening up egg salad.

FENNEL

The flavor is similar to anise but is somewhat sweeter. Usually used in pork dishes, squash, Italian sausage, sweet pickles, fish dishes, candies, cabbage, pastries, oxtail soup, and pizza sauce. When you choose fresh fennel, make sure you choose clean, crisp bulbs that are not browning. The stalks and greenery should be removed before using. Fennel bulbs and the base may be used raw in salads.

FENUGREEK

The aroma is similar to curry powder and is mainly used to make imitation maple syrup, and a digestive aide as a tea.

GARLIC

Grown worldwide and sold in fresh clove form or as garlic salt or powder. It is commonly used in hundreds of dishes especially Italian cooking, sauces, chicken dishes, etc. Has been used as a medication for a number of illnesses throughout history. Americans consume 250 million pounds of garlic annually with a large percentage grown in Gilroy, California.

Garlic can be peeled easily by placing it in very hot water for 2-3 minutes. When actually peeling garlic, try rinsing the garlic under hot water first to loosen the skin. For a special flavor rub a clove of crushed garlic on the sides of your salad bowl before mixing your salad.

There are hundreds of varieties of garlic grown worldwide. Elephant garlic is not really a member of the garlic family, but is a form of leek with a milder flavor than most garlic.

If you wish to store garlic for an extended period do not peel it, just leave the cloves in tact, and it will store for 3 months in a cool, dark, dry location. When garlic sprouts, some of the garlic flavor will go into the sprouts, however, the sprouts can then be used for salads. Garlic should not be frozen. If garlic is damaged or nicked with a knife it must be used or it will develop mold very quickly.

Garlic vinegar can be made by placing 2-3 fresh cloves in each pint of white vinegar, then allow to stand for at least 2 weeks before using.

WARM ME UP!

Garlic will have better flavor if it is at room temperature.

HEAVY-HANDED WITH THE GARLIC

If you have used too much garlic in your soup or stew, just simmer a sprig or small quantity of parsley in it for about 10 minutes. To remove the garlic odor from your hands, try rubbing your hands with salt on a slice of lemon.

Read the label before you buy a garlic product. Garlic products should contain an antibacterial or acidifying agent such as phosphoric acid or citric acid. If this is not on the label the product must be sold and stored under refrigeration at all times. Garlic butter does not have a long shelf life and should be stored in the refrigerator for no more than 14 days. Most butter is not made with a preservative. Garlic, once processed, is more perishable than most other herbs.

GARLIC FLOAT?

When cooking with whole garlic cloves and you don't want them in the dish when you serve it, just place a toothpick firmly into the garlic and it will be easy to retrieve. Another trick is to use a tea infuser for a number of herbs that fall apart easily.

ALWAYS ADD GARLIC LAST

When a recipe calls for adding garlic, always add the garlic last. Garlic burns very easily and may taste bitter.

ZAP THAT GARLIC

If you place garlic cloves in the microwave for 15 seconds, the skins will come right off.

HELPING GARLIC KEEP IT'S COLOR

If you would like garlic to retain its color when cooking the garlic with onions, just sauté the onions first, and then add the garlic.

GARLIC, MORE THAN A REMEDY FOR VAMPIRES

Garlic has been under investigation for a number of years in relation to heart disease with studies published in The American Journal of Clinical Nutrition. Most studies were done using garlic oil in which the active ingredients were retained. Studies showed that garlic inhibited the coagulation of blood, reduced the level of LDL (bad cholesterol), and raised the level of HDL (good cholesterol). The subjects consumed the equivalent of 10 cloves of garlic daily, blood levels of cholesterol dropped 14% and the HDL levels were raised by 41%. Most garlic products in health food stores, it was stated, had most of their active ingredients removed by processing.

GARLIC MYTHS

- Wards off vampires
- Will cure the common cold
- Will cure warts
- Relieves fainting spells
- Helps improve blood circulation
- Will ward off the evil eye
- Grows hair
- An aphrodisiac
- Cures high blood pressure

GARLIC, THE PUNGENT COUSIN OF THE ONION

Storing garlic is relatively simple, all you have to do is place the garlic in a cool, dry location as close to 50ºF as possible or even at room temperature and it will easily last for about 1-2 months. Garlic will retain its flavor better if it not stored in the refrigerator, however, there is no harm in storing it there. Storing garlic in a small jar of olive oil is the chef's way of keeping the flavor in the garlic for 2-3 months. Garlic should never be frozen it will lose its flavor.

DOES COOKING CHANGE GARLIC?

When garlic is heated the chemical that gives garlic its unique flavor is partially destroyed. The chemical is "diallyl disulfide" which is a sulfur compound. If garlic is allowed to sprout most of the chemical will enter the new sprouts and the garlic will become milder.

THE GARLIC MAGNET

If your soup or stew has been overpowered by garlic, just place some parsley in a tea ball and swirl it around for a minute or so. Garlic is attracted to parsley and you can then discard the garlic laden parsley.

LIQUID GARLIC

Garlic vinegar is an excellent substitute for garlic clove. You can substitute 1 teaspoon of garlic vinegar for each small clove of garlic.

GINGER

Has a pungent spicy flavor and is grown in India and West Africa. Sold in whole or ground form and is used in pickling, conserves, dried fruits, gingerbread, and pumpkin pie.

MACE

Mace is the dried out husk of the nutmeg shell. It is sold in ground form and used in pound cake and chocolate dishes. In its whole form it is used in jellies, beverages, pickling, ketchup, baked beans, soups, deviled chicken, ham spreads, and French dressing.

MARJORAM

Related to the oregano family with a sweet nutty flavor. It can be purchased in leaves and is imported from France, Chile, and Peru. Usually, combined with other herbs and used in soups, Greek salad, potato dishes, stews, poultry seasoning, sauces, and fish dishes.

MINT FLAKES

These dehydrated flakes of the peppermint and spearmint plants have a strong sweet flavor. Grown in the United States and Europe and used to flavor lamb dishes, fish, stews, soups, peas, sauces, desserts, and jellies. For an instant breath freshener, try chewing a few mint leaves.

MUSTARD

Yellow or white seeds will produce mild mustard, while the brown seeds produce the more spicy variety. Powdered mustard has almost no aroma until mixed with a liquid. Mustard has hundreds of uses and is one of the popular spices worldwide. Most mustard will last about 2 years if kept under refrigeration.

If a recipe calls for a particular type of mustard, it would be best to use that one. Using the wrong mustard will make a difference in the taste desired. Mustard oil, which is pressed from brown mustard seeds, is extremely hot and sometimes used in Chinese or other oriental dishes.

TYPES:

American Mustard
The typical hot dog mustard is produced from a mild yellow mustard seed, sweetener, vinegar, and usually colored with the herb turmeric. It has a fairly smooth texture.

Chinese Mustard
Found in small ceramic dishes in all Chinese restaurants. It is produced from powdered mustard, water, and strong vinegar. The sweetener is left out and the mustard will only retain its bite for 1-2 hours.

Dijon Mustard
Originated in Dijon, France. Produced from brown mustard seeds, white wine, unfermented grape juice and a variety of seasonings. It has a smooth texture and is usually a grayish-yellow color.

English Mustard
This mustard is produced from white and black mustard seeds, a small amount of flour, and turmeric for coloring. This is one of the hottest mustards sold.

German Mustard
Produced from a variety of mustard seeds. The color varies and the flavor is somewhat mild due to a small amount of sugar used in the production.

NETTLE

Most commonly prepared as a tea and has been used historically as a blood purifier and diuretic. Some herbalists recommend the tea for arthritis and urinary problems. The tea is a good source of certain vitamins and minerals but is never recommended for people who have a weak heart or kidneys. Studies are presently being conducted related to prostate problems, especially in the relief of slow-stream.

NUTMEG

A relatively sweet spice, that is available in ground form and imported from the East and West Indies. Commonly used in sauces, puddings, as a topping for custards, creamed foods, eggnogs, whipped cream, sausages, frankfurters, and ravioli. The most pungent is the freshly ground nutmeg. Special nutmeg graters are sold in kitchen specialty shops.

OREGANO

A relative of the mint family, and may be found by the names origanum and Mexican sage. Commonly sold in leaf or ground forms. A common herb: on Italian specialties such as pizza and spaghetti sauces. Try oregano on a grilled cheese sandwich and you will never eat another one without it.

PAPRIKA

The best paprika is imported from Hungary in the form of ground pods. The milder variety, red sweet, is grown in the United States. It is commonly used in a wide variety of dishes such as cream sauces, vegetables, mustards, salad dressings, ketchup, sausages, and fish dishes. Makes an excellent powdered garnish.

PARSLEY

The best variety with an excellent flavor is the Italian flat-leaf. This variety is also grown in the United States and Southern Europe and used in cheese sauces, marinades, salads, soups, vegetable dishes, chicken potpies, herb dressings, and even peppermint soup. It is high in nutrients, especially vitamins E and K and will alleviate bad breathe. Store it in a plastic bag in the freezer. Parsley can be dried in the microwave then crumbled. Parsley also contains essential oil, the most important being "apiole," which has been used as a diuretic. Not recommended for pregnant women since it stimulates the kidneys.

Parsley should not be cooked since it tends to destroy a high percentage of its vitamins and minerals. Parsley should only be sliced or chopped just before you use it to preserve the flavor. To store parsley, sprinkle it with cold water and wrap it in a piece of paper towel, place it in a plastic bag and store in the refrigerator.

PEPPER

This one of the most popular spices in the world and is commonly sold in both black and white varieties. It is imported from India, Indonesia, and Borneo, is sold in whole or ground forms and used in almost any dish.

After pepper has been ground, it tends to lose its flavor rather quickly. Best to use a pepper grinder so that your pepper will be fresh and flavorful. Grind white pepper and you won't change the color of your dish.

Szechuan pepper berries are harvested from the prickly ash tree and have a very tiny seed and a somewhat hot taste. Cayenne pepper is produced from chili peppers. Pink peppercorns are harvested from the Baies rose plant and have a very pungent odor and a somewhat sweet flavor.

PEPPERCORNS

GREEN, BLACK, AND WHITE PEPPERCORNS

Basically, these are all the same with the only differences being that they are harvested at different times of maturity and the method processing. The green peppercorns are picked before they are fully ripe and are preserved and used mainly in the pickling industry and in dishes that do not require a strong pepper flavor. Black peppercorns are picked when they are only just slightly immature and are the wrinkled peppercorns we use in our household pepper, shakers or in the fresh pepper grinders. The white peppercorns are harvested when the peppercorn is fully ripe and have a smooth surface. These are used in dishes where the color of the black peppercorns would detract from the color of the dish, such as a white cream sauce.

PEPPERMINT

PEPPERMINT, AN HERB AND MORE

Peppermint is related to the spearmint family and contains the active oil, menthol. Menthol is used in cigarettes, candies, liquors, toothpaste, mouthwash, etc. Menthol in low concentrations can also be used to raise the threshold temperature of our skin making a warm area feel cool. It has also been used as an anesthetic or as an irritant. Menthol is the active ingredient that will also chase the rodent population from your house or property. A small amount of oil of peppermint on a cotton ball placed anywhere you have a problem will solve it instantly. Works great on underground rodents too.

POPPY SEED

Has a rich, nut-like flavor and used in salads, cookies, pastry fillings, Indian dishes, and baked goods.

POULTRY SEASONING

Commonly used in poultry dressings, and soups. The major ingredients are sage, thyme, marjoram, and Savoy.

ROSEMARY

A sweet, fragrant, spicy herb, with a very pungent aroma. Imported from Spain and Portugal and used in stews, meat dishes, dressings, and Italian foods.

SAFFRON

This is one of the more difficult herbs to acquire as well as one of the most expensive. It is extracted from the stigma of a flowering crocus and is only imported from Spain. It is used in moderation in poultry, baked goods and rice dishes. Saffron's color strength will determine the level of flavor and aroma. The best quality saffron is sold in saffron threads and not the powder. When working with saffron, it is best never to use a whisk, since the threads will become entwined in the whisk. Also, wooden utensils will absorb saffron and should be avoided.

Saffron quality is measured in "coloring strength" with the best strength being between 246-256. It is possible to purchase saffron with strength of only 110 but this will be an inferior product. Saffron should never be purchased with a level below 190 degrees. To use saffron properly the threads should be soaked to infuse the saffron before adding it to a recipe. Saffron threads should never be added to boiling water or directly into a dish.

SAGE

A very strong herb; that is a member of the mint family and available in leaf or ground form. Commonly used in veal dishes, pork products, stuffing, salads, fish dishes, and pizza sauces. Sage contains a number of essential oils, such as thujone, camphor and eucalyptol. Finely crushed sage has commonly been used as an additive to toothpaste, since it has antiseptic qualities, helps cure bleeding gums, is a disinfectant and also helps remove plaque.

SALT (SODIUM CHLORIDE)

While salt contains important minerals that are beneficial to the body, in excess it may be detrimental. Body fluids and their distribution in the body depend on the location and concentrations of sodium and potassium ions.

Our kidneys regulate the blood sodium levels and provide the bloodstream with the exact amount as needed. When blood levels rise due to excess sodium ingestion, the body's thirst receptors are stimulated and fluid intake increases to balance the sodium to water ratio. The excess sodium and water is then excreted by the kidneys. When this balance cannot be maintained the result may be higher blood pressure and an increased deposition of atherosclerotic plaque material.

When salt is processed the native minerals are stripped away and it is then enriched with iodine and dextrose to stabilize it, sodium bicarbonate to keep it white, and anti-caking agents to keep it "free-flowing." Morton's Special Salt is one of the only salts that has no additives. Salt is used in almost every food that is processed and is one of the best preservatives.

It is estimated by the National Institute of Health that over 10 million people over the age of 65 have some degree of high blood pressure problems. Since sodium is found in thousands of food items, it is recommended that "added salt" be avoided to help control your total sodium intake.

When preparing food and seasoning with salt the recommended amounts for certain dishes is:

1 teaspoon	for Soups and Sauces
1 teaspoon	for raw meat dishes
1 teaspoon	for every 4 cups of flour (dough)
1 teaspoon	for every 2 cups of liquid used in cooked cereals

40% of regular table salt is sodium: Lite salt has only 20% sodium content.

SALT INTAKE HIGH, BEWARE

If you eat a piece of bacon and it doesn't taste salty you are consuming too much salt. Excess sodium intake builds up in the bloodstream, kidneys are unable to clear the excess water it retains, an increase in blood volume occurs and the heart has to work harder causing higher blood pressure.

SALT, THE MICROBE INHIBITOR

For thousands of years salt has been used to preserve foods by inhibiting microbial growth. Salt has the ability to draw liquids from tissues and freeing water that is bound by breaking down proteins. The mechanism involves salts ability to create a concentration of "ions" (electrically charged particles) outside of the bacteria and mold cells encompassing the microbe drawing out its water and either drying it up and killing it or slowing down its replication. It is the drying out feature of salt that makes it such a good preservative. To preserve meats in England the meat was covered with very large grains of salt that resembled "corn" hence the name "corned beef" was coined.

Fast food restaurants may use high levels of salt to hide the offensive flavors of low quality foods.

Kelp can be ground up and used in a shaker to replace salt. It only contains 4% sodium and the taste is very close.

SALT OF THE EARTH

The average person consumes about 4,500 mg. of salt daily, which amounts to about 2 teaspoons. The body only requires 200 mg. daily unless we are perspiring heavily. Mother's milk, contains 16 mg. of sodium per 3½ oz. Canned baby food may contain 300 mg. per 3½ oz. Canned peas have 100 times the sodium of raw peas.

It is necessary to read labels and be aware that many foods contain ingredients that contain sodium, such as MSG. Many spices also contain sodium as a normal part of their makeup. The following are some spices and flavorings that are sodium-free:

ALLSPICE	ALMOND EXTRACT	BAY LEAVES
CARAWAY SEEDS	CINNAMON	CURRY POWDER
GARLIC	GINGER	LEMON EXTRACT
MACE	MAPLE EXTRACT	MARJORAM
MUSTARD POWDER	NUTMEG	PAPRIKA
PARSLEY	PEPPER	PIMIENTO
ROSEMARY	PEPPERMINT EXTRACT	SAGE
SESAME SEED	THYME	TURMERIC
VANILLA EXTRACT	WALNUT EXTRACT	VINEGAR

SODIUM DIETARY RESTRICTIONS

The following foods should be avoided, due to their high sodium content:

AVOID

Meats and Luncheon Meats
All pickled products
All smoked products
Ham/pork
Dried beef (jerky)
Pastrami
Sausages
Frankfurters
Luncheon meats
Canned meat/fish

Soups
Regular broth
Bouillion/cubes
Canned soups
Dehydrated soups

Seasonings/Condiments
Soy sauce
All salts including "Lite"
Tomato juice
Prepared mustard
Steak sauce
Worcestershire sauce
Chili sauce

Snack foods
Salted crackers
Salted nuts
Salted popcorn
Pretzels
Potato chips
Corn chips
Tortilla chips
Salt sticks
Candy bars/nuts

Vegetables in Brine
Sauerkraut
Pickles
lives
Pickle relish

Miscellaneous
Instant hot cereals
Fast food sandwiches
Ready-to-eat meals
French fries
Processed foods
Commercial sauces
Commercial gravies

Meat tenderizer	Softened water
MSG/Accent	Mineral water
Commercial salad dressing	Seasoned salts
Dried packaged seasonings	Packaged pasta mixes

SODIUM CONTENT OF COMMON FOODS

HIGH SODIUM FOODS

FOOD ITEM	SERVING SIZE	SODIUM MG.
Dill Pickle	1 large	1935
Turkey Dinner (frozen)	1 large	1830
Macaroni & Cheese (frozen)	1 cup	1090
Pretzels	1 oz.	890
Tuna (oil packed)	3$\frac{1}{2}$ oz.	800
Peanuts (roated in oil)	1 cup	662
Creamed Corn	1 cup	671
Beef Frankfurters	1 reg.	495
Tomato Soup	5 oz.	475
Bologna	2 slices	450

MEDIUM SODIUM FOODS

Food Item	Serving Size	Sodium MG.
American Cheese (processed)	1 oz.	447
Pancakes (mix)	3-4" cakes	435
Mashed Potatoes (instant)	$\frac{1}{2}$ cup	75
Cheese Pizza (frozen)	1 med. slice	370
Carrots (canned)	1 cup	366
Tomato Juice	$\frac{1}{2}$ cup	320
Cottage Cheese (creamed)	$\frac{1}{2}$ cup	320
Corn Flakes	$\frac{3}{4}$ cup	305
Buttermilk	1 cup	225
Doughnut (packaged)	1 med.	210
Oatmeal (cooked)	3 oz.	175
Green Olive	1 large	155
Angel Food Cake (mix)	$\frac{1}{12}$ cake	130
Whole Milk	1 cup	20

LOW SODIUM FOODS

Food Item	Serving Size	Sodium MG.
Graham Cracker	1 large	95
Mayonnaise	1 Tbl.	80
Egg	1 med.	70
Turkey (roasted)	3 oz.	70
Margarine (salted)	1 Tbl.	50
Cottage Cheese (unsalted)	$\frac{1}{2}$ cup	30
Fruit Cocktail	$\frac{1}{2}$ cup	7
Orange Juice (canned, fresh)	$\frac{1}{2}$ cup	2
Fruit (canned, most)	$\frac{1}{2}$ cup	1
Macaroni (cooked)	1 cup	1

GENERAL SALT INFORMATION

The majority of the salt used in the United States is mined from salt deposits that were laid down thousands of years ago and are readily accessible.

TYPES OF SALT:

Canning Salt
This is really pure salt and only salt. It is only found in canning sections of the supermarket.

Ice Cream Salt
Produced from large chunks of salt and is used for home ice cream making. It is also used to ice down large kegs of beer. This is normally not food grade salt.

Kosher Salt
Has an excellent flavor and texture as well as being additive-free. Kosher salt has larger salt crystals and a more jagged shape, which means that they will cling to food better. Because of its characteristics, kosher salt has the ability to draw more blood from meats, since kosher meats must be as free from blood as possible to meet the strict Jewish dietary laws.

Pickling Salt
A fine-grained salt: that is additive-free and used in the preparation of pickles and sauerkraut.

Rock Salt
A poorly refined salt that has a grayish appearance with large crystals. Combines with ice to make ice cream.

Sea Salt
Has a fresh flavor and is available in fine or coarse-grained varieties. It is usually imported and preferred by chefs. Sea salt; as its name implies is acquired by allowing salt water to accumulate in pools and having the sun evaporate off the water leaving a more, stronger flavored salt with a few more trace minerals than table salt. Actually, there is not that big of a difference to pay the extra price for sea salt.

Iodized and Non-Iodized Salt
This is the standard table salt with iodine added or excluded. Most table salts have a non-caking, agent added. Very fine-grained, making it free flowing.

REPAIRING OVER-SALTED FOODS

When you add too much salt to a dish, try repairing it by adding 1 teaspoon of apple cider vinegar and 1 teaspoon of sugar.

SAVOY

Has a slight peppery flavor and is a member of the mint family. Commonly sold in leaf and ground forms and is primarily used to flavor eggs, meats, poultry, and fish.

SESAME

Has a rich, nut-like flavor and high oil content. Commonly used as a topping for baked goods and in halavah.

TARRAGON

Has a strong flavor similar to licorice. It is native to Siberia with the majority imported from Spain and France. Commonly used in sauce bearnaise, meat dish, salads, herb dressings, and tomato casseroles.

THYME

Has a strong, very spicy flavor and is available in leaf and ground forms. Commonly used in tomato-based soups, stews, sauces, chipped beef (an old army favorite), mushrooms, sausages, clam chowder, herb dressings, and mock turtle soup.

TURMERIC

Imported from India and Peru and used in chicken, pickles, meat dishes, dressings, curry powder, Spanish rice, relishes, and mustards.

VANILLA

VANILLA BEAN RUSTLERS?

The vanilla pod is the only food produced by a plant member of the orchid family. The reason "real" vanilla is so expensive is that is hand pollinated when grown commercially. In the wild it is pollinated by only one species of hummingbird. Since they are so expensive to grow and over 75% of the bean is grown in Madagascar where the pods are actually branded with the growers brand because of "vanilla bean rustlers" stealing the crop. Pure vanilla extract can only be made by percolating the bean similar to making coffee. Imitation vanilla is produced from the chemical vanillin, which is a by-product of the wood pulp industry.

VANILLA BEANS

They are grown on trees and look like long, thin dark brown beans. They are expensive and not as easy to use as the extract. In order to use the bean you need to split it, then scrape out the powder-fine seeds. Seeds from a single vanilla bean is equal to about 2-3 teaspoons of extract. The beans need to be stored in a sealed plastic baggie; then refrigerated.

PURE EXTRACT

If it says "pure" then it must come from the vanilla bean, however, the taste will be less intense. It still has an excellent flavor similar to the real bean.

IMITATION EXTRACT

Imitation means just that: Imitation. It is produced from artificial flavorings and has a stronger, harsher, taste than pure vanilla. It should only be used in recipes when the vanilla flavor will not overpower the dish.

MEXICAN EXTRACT

This may be a dangerous product and not recommended for use. The product has been found to contain the blood thinner, coumarin, which is a banned drug in the United States. Other possible toxins have been found in the product as well.

SUBSTITUTING HERBS

HERB	SUBSTITUTE
ALLSPICE	Cinnamon+dash cloves
ANISE SEED	Fennel seed
BASIL	Oregano
CARAWAY SEED	Anise seed
CHIVES	Green onion
CINNAMON	Nutmeg
CLOVES	Allspice
CUMIN	Chili powder
FENNEL SEED	Anise seed
GINGER	Cardamom
MACE	Allspice
MINT	Rosemary
PARSLEY	Cilantro

HOW SHOULD HERBS BE ADDED TO A DISH?

Herbs are noted for their aroma more than for their taste in most instances. Chef's know how to appeal to your sense of smell when preparing a dish and will add either some or all of the herbs just before the dish is served, since many herbs lose some of their flavor during the cooking process.

CAN THE OIL OF THE SAME HERB BE SUBSTITUTED FOR THAT HERB?

This is never a good idea; however, it is tried all the time. Oils are so concentrated that it is almost impossible to calculate the amount that you will need to replace the herb to acquire the same taste. A good example is cinnamon of which the oil is 50 times stronger than the ground cinnamon. If you did want to substitute the oil to replace the cinnamon extract, you would only need to use 1-2 drops of the oil to replace ½ teaspoon of the extract in candy or frostings.

THE COLOR OF PESTO

Pesto sauce tends to turns brown in a very short period of time instead of remaining the pleasant medium green we are used to seeing. The browning, which is almost black at times is caused by enzymes in one of the herbal ingredients, basil. Both the stems and the leaves of basil will cause the pasta to quickly be discolored with brown spots as well as turning the sauce brown. When nuts are added such as walnuts, sunflower seeds, or pine nuts the sauce will turn almost black. There is little to be done unless the pesto and pasta are prepared and served as soon as possible. One method of keeping the pasta yellow is to add $1/4$ cup of lemon juice or 1 $1/3$ tablespoons of cream of tartar to each quart of cooking water. You may have to stir your noodles more frequently and keep the water boiling rapidly to keep the noodles from sticking together since the acid tends to cause excess attraction between the noodles.

LICORICE, SWEETER THAN SUGAR

The word licorice actually means "sweet root." The plant is a member of the legume family and was used by the Egyptians over 4,000 years ago as a medicinal. The most common form found today is in candy and tobacco. Licorice extract: is produced by boiling the yellow roots of the plant in water and then extracting the solid through evaporation. The black solid mass has two components, the oil "anethole" which contributes the flavor and "glycerrhetic acid" which is the sweet component. Glycerrhetic acid is derived from glycerrhizin found in the raw root, which is 50 times sweeter than table sugar (sucrose). The Egyptians used to chew the raw root for its sugary flavor.

GARLIC OR HERBS STORED IN OIL MAY BE HARMFUL

Many chefs and cooks have been known for years to store garlic or other herbs in oil for longer shelf life and to flavor their olive oil. The latest studies are showing some possible health hazards that may become serious from this practice. The mixture may contain the rare and deadly Clostridium botulinum bacteria, which is present in the environment and may be present on herbs. The bacteria, does not like an oxygen environment but loves a closed environment such as in the oil.

When the herb is placed in oil it gives the bacteria a perfect oxygen-free place to multiply. A microbiologist at the FDA has warned that a number of people have become ill from placing store-bought chopped garlic in an oil medium. This type of mixture should be refrigerated and used within ten days to be on the safe side. When purchasing an herb and olive oil mixture from the market they will be labeled to be refrigerated and will contain a preservative, probably phosphoric acid or citric acid.

THE TOP TEN SELLING HERBS/BOTANICALS

1. CHAMOMIL
2. ECHINACEA
3. EPHEDRA
4. FEVERFEW
5. GARLIC

6. GINGER
7. GINGKO
8. GINSENG
9. PEPPERMINT
10. VALERIAN

WHAT IS CHINESE FIVE-SPICE POWDER?

A common fragrant spice mixture, used in a number of Chinese dishes. It is a combination of cinnamon, aniseed, fennel, black pepper, and cloves. The formula is 3 tablespoons of ground cinnamon; 2 teaspoons of aniseed; $1\frac{1}{2}$ teaspoon of fennel seed; $1\frac{1}{2}$ teaspoons of black pepper; and $\frac{3}{4}$ teaspoons of ground cloves. Combine all the ingredients in a blender until they are powdered.

THE ROYAL BREATH CLEANSER

In the year 300BC the Chinese Emperor had a breath problem and was given cloves to sweeten his breath. Cloves contain the chemical "eugenol" which is the same chemical that is used in a number of mouthwashes. Eugenol (oil of cloves) is also used to stop the pain of a toothache.

SOME HERBS NEED TO BE ROASTED BEFORE BEING USED

Allspice berries and peppercorns should be roasted before being used to intensify their flavor. Roast them in a 325°F oven on a small cookie sheet for 10-15 minutes before using them and you will be surprised at the difference in their flavor and aroma. They can also be pan-roasted if you prefer over a medium-high heat for about 5 minutes with the same result.

UNSAFE HERBS

The following herbs are classified as unsafe for human consumption and should not be used in any food or beverage. This is only a partial listing of the hundreds of unsafe herbs.

BITTERSWEET, WOODY NIGHTSHADE, CLIMBING NIGHTSHADE

Scientific Name: Solanum dulcamara, Solanum nigrum
Danger: Contains the toxin glycoalkaloid solanine as well as solanidine and dulcamarin.

BLOODROOT, RED PUCCOON

Scientific Name: Saguinaris canadensis
Danger: Contains the poisonous alkaloid, sanguinarine as well as other alkaloids.

BUCKEYES, HORSE CHESTNUT

Scientific Name: Aesculus hippocasteranum
Danger: Contains the toxin coumarin glycoside, aesculin (esculin).

BURNING BUSH, WAHOO

Scientific Name: Euonymus atropurpureus
Danger: The actual poisonous chemical compound has not been identified as yet.

DEADLY NIGHTSHADE

Scientific Name: Atropa belladona
Danger: Contains the toxic solanaceous: alkaloids hyoscyamine, atropine and hyoscine.

EUROPEAN MANDRAKE

Scientific Name: Mandragora officinarium
Danger: Poisonous plant that contains a narcotic substance similar to belladonna, Contains the alkaloids hyoscyamine, scopolomine, and mandragorine.

HELIOTROPE

Scientific Name: Heliotropium europaeum
Danger: Contains alkaloids that may cause liver damage.

HEMLOCK, SPOTTED HEMLOCK, CALIFORNIA OR NEBRASKA FERN

Scientific Name: Conium maculatum
Danger: Contains a poisonous alkaloid (coniine). Slows the heartbeat and eventually coma and death.

HENBANE, HOG'S BEAN, DEVIL'S EYE

Scientific Name: Hyoscyamus niger
Danger: Contains the alkaloid hyoscyamine, and atropine.

INDIAN TOBACCO, ASTHMA WEED, EMETIC WEED

Scientific Name: Lobelia inflata
Danger: Contains the alkaloid lobeline.

JALAP ROOT, HIGH JOHN ROOT, ST. JOHN THE CONQUEROR ROOT

Scientific Name: Ipomoea jalapa
Danger: Usually found in Mexico, its resin contains a powerful poison.

JIMSON WEED, THORNAPPLE, TOLGUACHA

Scientific Name: Datura stramonium
Danger: Contains the alkaloid atropine.

LILY OF THE VALLEY, MAY LILY

Scientific Name: Convalleria majalis
Danger: Contains the toxic cardic glycoside convallatoxin.

AMERICAN MANDRAKE, MAY APPLE, WILD LEMON

Scientific Name: Podophyllum pelatum
Danger: A poisonous plant containing a polycyclic substance.

MISTLETOE

Scientific Name: Phoradendron flavescens, Viscum album
Danger: Contains the toxic pressor amines B-phenylethylamine and tyramine.

MORNING GLORY

Scientific Name: Ipomoea purpurea
Danger: Contains a purgative resin. Seeds contain lysergeic acid.

PERIWINKLE

Scientific Name: Vinca major, Vinca minor
Danger: Contains toxic alkaloids. Can injure the liver and kidneys.

POKEWEED, SKOKE, PIGEONBERRY

Scientific Name: Phytolacca americana
Danger: Contains unidentified poisons.

SCOTCH BROOM, BROOM

Scientific Name: Cytisus scoparius
Danger: Contains the toxin sparteine and other alkaloids.

SPINDLE-TREE

Scientific Name: Euonymus europaeus
Danger: Produces violent purges.

SWEET FLAG, SWEET ROOT, SWEET CANE, SWEET CINNAMON

Scientific Name: Acorus calamus
Danger: Jamma variety is a carcinogen. Prohibited by the FDA.

TONKA BEAN

Scientific Name: Dipteryx odorata
Danger: Seeds contain coumarin. Can cause serious liver damage.

WATER HEMLOCK, COWBANE, POISON PARSNIP, WILD CARROT

Scientific Name: Cicuta maculata
Danger: Contains an unsaturated higher alcohol called cicutoxin.

WHITE SNAKEROOT, SNAKEROOT, RICHWEED

Scientific Name: Eupatorium rugosum
Danger: Contains a toxic alcohol substance.

WOLF'S BANE, LEOPARD'S BANE, MOUNTAIN TOBACCO

Scientific Name: Arnica montana
Danger: Unidentified substances. Produces violent toxic effects.

WORMWOOD, MADDERWORT, MUGWORT

Scientific Name: Artemisia absinthium
Danger: Contains oil of wormwood, an active narcotic poison. Never purchase the liquor Absinthe unless it is produced in the United States.

YOHIMBE, YOHIMBI

Scientific Name: Corynanthe yohimbi
Danger: Contains toxic alkaloids.

CHAPTER 6

HIDDEN DANGERS IN ADDITIVES

GENERAL INFORMATION

The following additives and chemicals are some of the more common ones that may be recognized by the general public or ones that will easily be found on labels. The information contained in this chapter pertains only to the more pertinent facts regarding these substances and will not be overly technical. In 2001 over 854 million pounds of additives were used in the manufacture of foods. The USDA and FDA has classified food additives into 32 different categories.

Keep in mind that you are rarely aware of the quantity of additives you consume. Almost all these additives require vitamins and minerals to assist with their breakdown so that they can be properly disposed of, usually by the liver. These additional nutrients must be obtained from somewhere in the body that could use them more effectively.

Anti-caking and free-flowing agents
These are usually added to foods that are finely powdered or in a crystalline form to prevent them from caking or becoming lumpy.

Antimicrobial Agents
Substances used in food preservation to prevent the growth of bacteria, which might cause spoilage.

Antioxidants
Used to preserve foods by limiting their deterioration, rancidity, or discoloration caused by oxidation. Oxygen is one of foods worst enemies.

Coloring Agents
Used to enhance the color of foods and are classified as color stabilizers, color fixatives, or color retention agents.

Curing and Pickling Agents
Used to provide flavor and retard bacterial growth as well as increasing shelf life.

Dough Strengtheners
Used to modify starch and gluten to produce stable dough.

Drying agents
Substances that have a moisture-absorbing ability; which keep the humidity in the product at standard moisture levels.

Emulsifiers
Keeps oil and water in suspension so that they do not separate after being mixed.

Enzymes
Assist in food processing by helping the chemical reactions take place in an orderly fashion.

Firming Agents
Assist in the precipitation of residual pectin, strengthening the tissue that supports the food. This prevents the food from collapsing during processing and storage.

Flavor Enhancers
Added to either enhance or change the original taste or aroma of the food. The substance must not change the normal taste or aroma, just improve it.

Flavoring Agents
Add a specific flavor to food.

Flour-Treating Agents
Added to flour that has been milled to improve its color or baking qualities.

Formulation Aids
Used to bring about a desired physical characteristic or special texture in the food. These include carriers, binders, fillers, plasticizers, film-formers, and tableting aids.

Fumigants
Volatile substances that are used for pest and insect control.

Humectants
Substances added to foods to assist the food in retaining moisture.

Leavening Agents
Used to either produce or stimulate the production of carbon dioxide gas in baked goods. This helps give the food a light texture. A number of yeast or salts are used.

Lubricants and Release Agents
Added to surfaces that come into contact with foods to stop the foods from sticking to them.

Non-Nutritive Sweeteners
Sweetener, that contains less than 2% of the caloric value of sucrose (table sugar) per equivalent of sweetening capacity.

Nutrient Supplementation
Substances that are necessary for a person's metabolic and nutritional needs.

Nutritive Sweeteners
These must contain more than 2% of the caloric value of sucrose per equivalent unit of sweetening capacity.

Oxidizing and Reducing Agents
Chemically oxidize or reduce specific food ingredients to produce a more stable food.

pH Control Agents
Added to assist in the maintenance of acid/base balance in the food. These include buffers, acids, alkalis, and neutralizing agents.

Processing Aids
Used to enhance the appeal or the utility of a food or ingredient of a food and includes clarifying agents, clouding agents, catalysts, flocculents, filter aids, and crystalline inhibitors.

Propellants, Aerating Agents, and Gases
Used to add force in expelling a product or used to limit the amount of oxygen that will come into contact with the food during packaging.

Sequestrants
Substances that combine with certain metal ions which changes them into a metal complex that will blend into water or other liquid to improve the stability of that product.

Solvents
Used to extract or dissolve substances placing them into solution.

Stabilizers and Thickeners
Used to produce a blended solution or disperse substances to give foods more body, to improve the consistency, stabilize an emulsion, and assist in the setting of jellies.

Surface-Active Agents
Used to change the surface of liquid foods, other than emulsifiers. These include stabilizing agents, dispersants, detergents, wetting agents, rehydration enhancers, whipping agents, foaming agents, and defoaming agents.

Surface-Finishing Agents
Used to increase the palatability of foods, preserve their natural glean, inhibit discoloration, and also included are glazes, polishes, waxes, and protective coatings.

Synergists
Substances that will react with other food ingredients causing them to be more effective when incorporated into a food product.

Texturizers
Affect the appearance or "mouth feel" of the food.

YOUR OVERWORKED LIVER

The foods we consume today contain over $500 million dollars worth of additives. Americans eat approximately 6-9 pounds of these chemicals annually, which amounts to over 1 billion pounds of additives consumed every year. Your liver is in charge of detoxifying this garbage. It is the major organ that must breakdown and dispose of these chemicals. In many cases it requires a number of nutrients to assist in their breakdown, nutrients that would prefer to be useful in other roles.

HIDE AND SEEK

Many preservatives may be hidden in the wrappers of foods. White bread may have as many as 16 chemical preservatives and additives just to keep it fresh.

IT'S THE OTHER 2% THAT MAY GET YOU

Almost 98% (by actual weight) of food additives that are used in food are corn syrup, pepper, mustard, baking soda, baking powder, citric acid, salt, or a vegetable coloring agent.

COMMON FOOD ADDITIVES

ACETIC ACID

Known as the acid, which makes vinegar acidic. Vinegar is about 4-6% acetic acid. It is used as a solvent for resins, gums, and volatile oils, can stop bleeding and has been used to stimulate the scalp circulation. Commercially, it has been used in freckle-bleaching products, hand lotions, and hair dyes. In nature, it occurs in apples, cheeses, cocoa, coffee, oranges, pineapples, skim milk, and a number of other fruits and plants. A solution of about 14% is used in the pickling industry and as a flavor enhancer for cheese.

ACID-MODIFIED STARCHES

These starches: are produced by mixing an acid, usually hydrochloric or sulfuric with water and starch at temperatures that are too low for the starch to gelatinize. After the starch has been reduced to the desired consistency, the acid is neutralized; the starch is filtered, and then dried. The modification produces a starch that can be cooked and used at higher concentrations than the standard unmodified starches. The acid-modified starch is mainly used to thicken salad dressings and puddings.

ALUM

Alum may go under a number of different names such as potash alum, aluminum ammonium, aluminum sulfate, or potassium sulfate. Aluminum sulfate (cake alum) is used in the food industry to produce sweet and dill pickles and as a modifier for starch. The other chemicals are used in astringent lotions such as after-shave lotions to remove phosphates from waste, water, harden gelatin, and water-proof fabrics.

AMMONIUM BICARBONATE

Alkali, leavening agent: used in the production of baked goods, candies, and chocolate products. Prepared by forcing carbon dioxide gas through concentrated ammonia water. Also, used commercially in products that will break up intestinal gas.

AMMONIUM CHLORIDE

Has a mild salt taste and does not blend well with alkalis. It is mainly used in yeast foods, rolls, buns, and as a dough conditioner. Commercially, it is used in permanent wave solution, eye lotions, batteries, safety explosives, and medically as a diuretic.

AMYLASE

An enzyme that breaks down starch into sugar: commercially derived from the pancreas of hogs. It is used in flour and as a texturizer in cosmetics. Sometimes used medically to fight inflammations and is completely non-toxic.

BETA-CAROTENE

A natural substance found in plants and animals. Has the ability to produce vitamin A. Found in many fruits and vegetables and has a yellowish-orange color. Used as a food coloring agent in numerous food products and cosmetics. Recent studies have shown beta-carotene to be a potent antioxidant. Since there is no toxicity involved with it, it is usually recommended over vitamin A.

BHA AND BHT, FRIEND OR FOE

Both of these chemical substances are frequently found in foods and are potent antioxidants. They are used in beverages, ice creams, chewing gum, potato flakes, baked goods, dry breakfast cereals, gelatin desserts, and soup bases. It is used as a preservative, antioxidant to retard rancidity, and as a stabilizer. Some animal studies have shown that abnormal behavior patterns and brain abnormalities appeared in offsprings after ingestion of these substances by the adults. The percentages of BHA that are allowed in foods are 1,000ppm in dry yeast, 200ppm in shortenings, 50ppm in potato flakes, and 50ppm when BHA is combined with BHT. The percentages of BHT allowed are 200ppm in shortenings, 50ppm in breakfast cereals and potato flakes.

BROMELAIN

Is an extract of pineapple and used in meat tenderizers. It will breakdown proteins and liquefy them if allowed to work long enough.

CAFFEINE

This is the number one psychoactive drug in the United States. It is used as a flavor in some root beer and found naturally in coffee, tea, and chocolate. It affects the central nervous system, heart, and is a respiratory stimulant. It is capable of altering the blood sugar release system in the body and easily crosses the placental barrier. Other side affects are extreme nervousness, insomnia, irregular heart rhythm, ringing in the ears, and even convulsions in high doses.

CALCIUM CARBONATE

The main chemical compound constituent in common chalk, limestone, marble, and coral. Commonly used as an alkali to reduce acidity in foods. Also, used as a neutralizer in ice cream and cream syrups. Commercially, used as a carrier for a variety of bleaches. It's used as a white dye in foods and was withdrawn by the FDA in 1988. Medically, is used to reduce stomach acid and as an antidiarrheal medicine. Animal studies show that over-consumption may affect mineral absorption, especially iron.

CALCIUM HYPOCHLORITE

Used as a germicide and sterilizing agent, used in washing the curd on cottage cheese, kills algae, is a potent bactericide, and fungicide. When used in a 50% solution is valuable in sterilizing fruits and vegetables. Dilute hypochlorite is commonly found in household laundry bleach. Can cause serious damage to all mucosal membranes if ingested. Should never be mixed with other household chemicals as it may produce deadly chlorine gas.

CALCIUM LACTATE

A white odorless powder, which is commonly used as a bread dough conditioner and oxidizing agent. Nutritionally, it is used as a source of calcium for calcium deficient patients, however, it may cause intestinal and heart disturbances.

CALCIUM PROPIONATE

Preservative: that is used to reduce the prevalence of certain bacteria and molds. May also be used as sodium propionate depending on the food.

CALCIUM SULFATE

Also known as "Plaster of Paris." A powder: that is used as a firming agent and a yeast dough conditioner. Commonly used in the brewing industry as well as other alcoholic products that need fermentation. Commercially, it is used in jellies, cereal flours, breads, rolls, bleu cheese, and canned potatoes and tomatoes. Reduces acidity in cottage cheese and toothpastes. Industrially, it is used in cement, wall plaster, and insecticides. Because it tends to absorb moisture and harden quickly some known problems have been related to intestinal obstruction. When it is mixed with flour it is an excellent rodent killer.

CARRAGEENAN

Also known as Irish Moss. A common stabilizer used in oils, cosmetics, and foods. Used as an emulsifier in chocolate products, chocolate milk, cheese spreads, ice cream, sherbets, French dressing, and gassed cream products. It is completely soluble in hot water and is not coagulated by acids. It is under further study by the FDA since it has caused cancerous tumors in laboratory animals, however, in the present levels used in food it should be harmless.

CHLORINE GAS

A common, flour-bleaching and oxidizing agent. May be found naturally in the earth's crust and is a greenish-yellow gas that is a powerful lung irritant. It can be dangerous to inhale with only 30ppm causing coughing. The chlorine in drinking water may contain carcinogenic carbon tetrachloride, which is formed during the production process. Chlorine placed into drinking water may not be the safest chemical to use in water.

CHLOROPHYLL

Green color found in plants, that plays the essential role in photosynthesis. It is used in deodorants, antiperspirants, dentifrice, and mouthwashes. Also, used to give a green color to soybean and olive oil.

CITRATE SALTS

Mainly used in pasteurized process cheeses and spreads. May tend to mask the results of laboratory tests for pancreatic and liver function and blood acid-base balances. If you are going for extensive blood work, try not to consume these cheeses for at least one week prior to the test.

COLORINGS

Most of the colorings presently in use are derived from coal tars (carcinogens). As the years go by, more and more of these colorings are phased out and banned for use in food.

DIACETYL

A naturally occurring substance found in cheese, cocoa, pears, berries, cooked chicken, and coffee beans. It appears as a yellowish-green liquid and tends to assist in retaining the aroma of butter, vinegar, and coffee. Also used in chocolate, ginger ale, baked goods, and flavoring in ice creams, candy, and chewing gum. Certain diacetyl compounds have been found to cause cancer in laboratory studies.

DISODIUM PHOSPHATE

Used to trap mineral ions in foods that would cause the food to spoil and affect the color of foods. Mainly used in the processing of evaporated milk, pork products, in sauces, and commonly used as an emulsifying agent in cheeses spreads.

ETHYL ACETATE

This is a colorless liquid that has a pleasant fruity odor and occurs naturally in a number of fruits and berries. It is extracted and made into a synthetic flavoring agent and used in berry products, butter, a number of fruit products, rum, mint products, ice creams, baked goods, chewing gum, puddings, and certain liquors. Also used in nail enamels and nail polish remover. The vapors are an irritant to the central nervous system with prolonged inhalation leading to possible liver damage.

ETHYL VANILLIN

Has a stronger flavor than natural vanilla and is used as a synthetic flavoring agent in berries, butter, caramel, coconut, macaroon, cola, rum, sodas, chocolate, honey, butterscotch, imitation vanilla extract, and baked goods. Has caused mild skin irritations in humans and injuries to a number of organs in animals.

EUCALYPTUS OIL

Has a camphor-like odor and used in mint, root beer, ginger ale flavoring, ice creams, candy, baked goods, chewing gum, and some liquors. Medically, it has been used as a local antiseptic, expectorant, and vermifuge. Deaths have occurred from people consuming as little as one teaspoon and reports of coma from consuming one milliliter.

GLUTEN

Combination of the two proteins: gliadin and glutelin. They are obtained from wheat flour, are extremely sticky, and produced by washing out the starch in the flour. Responsible for the porous and spongy structure of breads.

GUAR GUM

Derived from the seeds of a plant found in India. It has 5-8 times the thickening power of starch and used as a stabilizer in fruit-drinks, icings and glazes. Frequently used as a binder in cream cheese, ice creams, baked goods, French dressing, etc. Has been very useful in keeping vitamin tablets from disintegrating. Also, used as an appetite suppressant and to treat peptic ulcers.

GUM ARABIC

This also called acacia and is the odorless, colorless, and tasteless sap from the stem of the acacia tree, which grows in Africa and areas of the Southern United States. It is considered a natural gum and has the ability to dissolve very quickly in water. It is mainly used to stop sugar crystallization, as a thickening agent in the candy-making industry, and to make chewing gum. Gum acacia is used in the soft drink and beer industry to retard foam.

HYDROGENATED OIL

Oil that has been partially converted from liquid polyunsaturated oil into a more solid saturated fat. This process is done by adding hydrogen molecules from water to increase the solidity of the fat. Basically, it turns relatively good fat into bad fat, which has more "mouth feel."

INVERT SUGAR

Composed of a mixture of 50% glucose and 50% fructose. It is much sweeter than sucrose (ordinary table sugar). Honey is mostly invert sugar. Invert sugar is mainly used in candies and the brewing industry. It tends to hold moisture well and prevents products from drying out. Medically, it is used in some intravenous solutions.

LECITHIN

It is a natural antioxidant and emollient composed of choline, phosphoric acid, fatty acids, and glycerin. It is normally produced from soybeans and egg yolk. Used in breakfast cereals, candies, chocolate, baked goods, and margarine.

MALIC ACID

Has a strong acid taste and occurs naturally in many fruits, including apples and cherries. Used to age wines, and in frozen dairy products, candies, preserves, and baked goods. Commercially, used in cosmetics and hair lacquers and is a skin irritant.

MANNITOL

Usually produced from seaweed and is sweet tasting. Used as a texturizer in chewing gum and candies. Commonly used as a sweetener in "sugar-free" products, however, it still contains calories and carbohydrates. Studies are underway and may show that mannitol is a significant factor leading to cancer in rats. It may also worsen kidney disorders and cause gastrointestinal upsets.

METHYLENE CHLORIDE

A gas used in the decaffeination of coffee. Residues may remain and coffee companies do not have to disclose their methods on the label. Best to drink decaf if the label states that it was decaffeinated with water.

MODIFIED STARCH

Modified starch is ordinary starch that has been altered chemically and used in jellies as a thickening agent. Since babies have difficulty digesting regular starch, modified starch is easier to digest since it is partially broken down. Chemicals that are used to modify the starch include propylese oxide, succinic anhydride, aluminum sulfate, and sodium hydroxide.

MONOSODIUM GLUTAMATE (MSG)

MSG is actually the salt of glutamic acid, which is an amino acid. It occurs naturally in seaweed, soybeans, and sugar beets. It has no taste of its own; however, its main purpose in foods is to intensify existing flavors especially in soups, condiments, candies, meats, and baked goods. MSG mainly affects the salt and bitter flavors and makes them taste stronger. MSG is synthetically produced from starch or molasses.

A number of symptoms have been reported after ingesting MSG, which include headaches, facial tingling, depression, mood changes, light flashes, and rapid pulse rate. A study released by the Federation of American Societies for Experimental Biology in 1995 stated that MSG was declared safe for most people. However, other reports indicate that people with asthma may be affected by as little as 0.5 grams, which is the minimum amount that would be absorbed through most foods. Should be consumed in moderation if at all. .

NITRATE

Potassium and sodium nitrate is also known as "saltpeter." It is mainly used as a color fixative for processed meat products. They tend to combine with saliva and food substances (amines) to form nitrosamine a known carcinogen (cancer-causing agent). Animal studies have proven that mice developed cancer after being given nitrosamines.

NITRITE

Potassium and sodium nitrite is used as a color preservative in meats as well as providing a chemical that will assist the meat product in resisting certain bacteria. Sodium nitrite will actually react with the myoglobin in meat and protect the red color for a long period of time. It is used in all processed meat products, which include: Vienna sausage, smoke-cured fish products, hot dogs, bacon, lunchmeats, and canned meats. Vitamin E as well as vitamin C will block the formation of nitrites after ingestion.

When nitrites are fed to lab animals, studies have shown that malignant tumors developed in over 90% within 6-months, and death approximately soon afterwards. A number of incidents have been reported that linked high levels of nitrites in food to "cardiovascular collapse" in humans and even death from consuming hot dogs and blood sausage that were produced by local processors in different areas of the country.

An Israeli study discovered problems related to brain damage in lab animals when they were fed an equivalent amount of nitrites that would be consumed by a person eating a large amount of processed meats products.

When nitrites in food are ingested by humans; there are two possible pathways they can take. Both of which can be harmful: (1) the nitrites may react with a person's hemoglobin to produce a pigment called meth-hemoglobin, which may seriously lower the oxygen-carrying capacity of the red blood cell. (2) There is a possible cancer connection when the nitrites are biochemically altered into a "nitrosamine," which usually occurs in the stomach if certain proteins are present when the nitrites arrive.

If you drink some orange juice or chew a 500mg. vitamin C tablet just before consuming foods that contain nitrites the adverse reaction by the nitrites may be reversed. Vitamin C can neutralize the reaction that takes place in the stomach by interfering with the protein combining with the nitrite. Due to recent studies relating to this neutralizing effect, some manufacturers of hot dogs are now adding ascorbic acid to their product.

PAPAIN

An enzyme that will break down meats. It is prepared from papaya and is an ingredient in a number of meat tenderizers or marinades. It is also used for clearing beverages and added to farina to reduce the cooking time. Medically, it is used to prevent adhesions. It is, however, deactivated by cooking temperatures.

PECTIN

An integral part of many plants, it is found in their roots, stems, and fruits. The best sources are derived from lemon or orange rind, which contains 30% of the complex carbohydrate. It is used as a stabilizer, thickener, and adds body to beverages, syrups, ice creams, candies, French dressing, fruit jellies, and frozen puddings. Mainly used in foods as a "cementing or binding agent."

PEROXIDE

Three forms of peroxide are used commercially: Benzoyl, Calcium, and Hydrogen. Benzoyl peroxide is mainly used as a bleaching agent for flours, oils, and cheeses as well as medically made into a paste and used on poison ivy and burns. It should not be heated as it may explode. Calcium peroxide is used as a dough conditioner and oxidizing agent for baked goods. Has also been used as an antiseptic. Hydrogen peroxide is used as a bleaching agent, a modifier for food starch, a preservative, and to reduce the bacterial count in milk products. It is a strong oxidant that is capable of injuring skin and eyes. Commercially, it is used in hair bleaches and rubber gloves should always be worn at all times when using this product.

POTASSIUM CHLORIDE

A crystalline odorless powder that has a somewhat salty taste. It is used in the brewing industry to improve fermentation and to assist in the jelling process with jellies and jams. It is also used with sodium chloride as a salt substitute. Should be used in moderation as testing is being done relating to gastrointestinal irritation and ulcers.

SODIUM BENZOATE

Used in acidic foods to reduce the microorganism count. Has been used to retard bacterial growth and act as a preservative in carbonated beverages, jams and jellies, margarine, and salad dressings. Sodium benzoate may be found naturally in cranberries and prunes.

SODIUM BISULFATE

Used as an anti-browning agent and a preservative in beverages, corn syrup, dehydrated potatoes, dried fruits, sauces, soups, and some wines. Tends to destroy vitamin B1 (thiamin) when added to foods.

SODIUM CARBONATE

An odorless crystal or powder that is found in certain ores, in lake brine, and seaweed. Has the tendency to absorb water from the air and is used as a neutralizer for butter, milk products, and in the processing of olives. Commercially, it is used in antacids, soaps, mouthwashes, shampoos, and foot preparations. If ingested may cause gastrointestinal problems, nausea, and diarrhea.

SODIUM CASEINATE

A protein used as a thickener and to alter the color of foods. Usually found in coffee creamers, frozen custards, and ice cream products.

SODIUM CHLORIDE

This is the chemical name for common table salt. It is used in numerous food products both as a preservative and taste enhancer. Readily absorbs water. Many breakfast cereals are high in salt, such as Wheaties with 370 mg. of sodium per ounce. Most potato chips have 190 mg. per ounce. Your daily intake should not exceed 1200 mg. or about $3/4$ of a teaspoon.

HOW TO TELL THE DIFFERENCE BETWEEN SALT AND SUGAR

If you have placed salt and sugar into canisters and didn't know which was which, there is an easy way if you don't want to taste them. The following ingredients will be needed:

1 Tablespoon of table salt
1 Tablespoon of granulated sugar

- Place the salt and sugar in separate small saucepans and place them on low heat. The sugar will melt and caramelize (brown). The carbon in sugar turns the sugar brown. The salt will just sit in the pan waiting for you to turn the heat off.

- Another method is to place some of each in separate glasses of water and add different colors of food coloring to each, then pour one in one end of a divided ice cube tray and the other in the other end. The sugar will freeze into cubes and the salt will remain a liquid.

SODIUM CITRATE

Used an emulsifier in ice cream, processed cheeses, and evaporated milk. Also, used as a buffer to control acidity and to retain carbonation in soft drinks. Has the ability to attach itself to trace minerals that are present in water and prevent them from entering live cells.

TANNIC ACID

May be found in the bark of oak and sumac trees and the fruit of plants as well as in coffee, cherries, and tea. It is used as a flavoring agent and to clarify beer and wine. It has been used medically as a mild astringent. Commercially, it is also used in antiperspirants, eye lotions, and sunscreens.

SORBITOL

A sweetener that is extracted from berries and some fruits. Basically, it is an alcohol that produces a sweet taste and is used in dietetic products as a replacement for sugar. It is also used as a food binder, thickener, texturing agent, humectant, and food stabilizer.

SULFITES

There are three types of sulfites that may be used as anti-browning agents; sodium, potassium, and ammonium. They may all be used on most foods except meats or a high vitamin B content food. Physiologic reactions to sulfites are numerous with the more common being an acute asthmatic attack.

Sulfites have been used for years to retard browning of fruits and vegetables, providing a level of preservation. The most common use was on salad bars. The outside leaves of lettuce should be discarded since they have been found to contain sulfites in some instances. The United States has limited the use of sulfites however, imported produce may still be hazardous.

SULFUR DIOXIDE

Produced from the chemical reaction of heating sulfur. Used as food bleach, preservative, antioxidant, and anti-browning agent. Found on a number of dried fruits such as yellow raisins and apricots. It has a tendency to destroy vitamin A and should not be used on meats or high vitamin A content fruits or vegetables.

CHAPTER 7

LIQUID FACTS

WATER

Water seems to be getting more complicated with each passing year. It used to be simply water! However, commercially, that was just too simple and water now has to be flavored, colored, oxygenated, caffeinated, softened, filtered, carbonated, fluoridated, ginsenged, and vitamin and mineral enriched. New studies now say that we should drink water with minerals for a healthy heart, while other studies say that we should filter as much as we can from the water. I don't know how our grandparents lived to a ripe old age without all these new-fangled preparations and filter systems

Almost every day, it seems as if we hear about another incident involving contaminated water supplies. Our concern about our drinking water is definitely warranted, especially with over 50,000 chemical dumpsites identified in the continental United States. These dumpsites are capable of leaching over 45,000 different contaminants into the water supplies, of which only about 100 are regulated. These thousands of contaminants may include heavy metals, salts, inorganic compounds and suspended solid particular matter.

Disease outbreaks in the United States are in the news almost daily and most can easily be traced to chemical or bacterial contamination of local water supplies. Remember almost all of our drinking water originates in streams, rivers, and lakes. Even if the water source is a mountain stream, it may have contact with impurities that are in suspension and released as the water flows down the mountain.

Surface water frequently contains fertilizers and insecticide residues as well as pollutants from manufacturing plants and motor vehicles. Then there is the problem of chemicals added to our water supplies such as: chlorine, fluorine, phosphates, and sodium aluminate for purification.

We should be able to rely on a safe water supply and not worry every time we take a drink of tap water whether it is safe or not. Water may contain a number of inorganic minerals, which cannot be utilized by the body and thus are deposited in our bones, joints and organs. Conditions, such as arthritis, hardening of the arteries and a variety of bone diseases may be related to unsafe drinking water.

Water assists the body in the elimination of wastes and is a constituent of every living cell. The average adult consumes approximately 191.3 gallons of liquids annually, unfortunately only about 38% is a liquid that the body prefers and can utilize efficiently. The human body is between 60%-70% water, which is found in all cells, organs, tissues, urine, perspiration, and blood.

Water is an excellent lubricant and keeps nutrients moving throughout the body. We do acquire water from some of the foods we eat, such as juices, milk, and soups; however, the best source for the body is pure water. A number of other liquids such as coffee, tea, and most carbonated beverages may act as a diuretic and cause our water supplies to be depleted.

However, it is possible to damage the body or even kill yourself if you drink too much water. Drinking 1½-2 gallons of water within a one-hour period will short circuit the body, possibly cause serious illness and could kill a very young child

The following is the breakdown of the average adult annual liquid consumption. You may not be drinking the amount mentioned in each category, however, someone else is making up for it.

```
SOFT DRINKS . . . . . . . . . . . . .46.7 GALLONS
WATER  . . . . . . . . . . . . . . . . .43.1 GALLONS
COFFEE . . . . . . . . . . . . . . . . .28.6 GALLONS
BEER . . . . . . . . . . . . . . . . . . .27.8 GALLONS
MILK . . . . . . . . . . . . . . . . . . .19.8 GALLONS
TEA, JUICE, LIQUOR, WINE  . .25.3 GALLONS
```

BOTTLED WATER

Sales of bottled water have never been higher due to the number of incidences of contaminated water supply scares in the United States. Many wells in all parts of the country have been found to be contaminated from industry dumpsites, abandoned mines, animal or human sewage and even by natural mineral contamination. Most U.S. water treatment systems were developed before 1915. Estimates are over 125 billion dollars to update our present water purification systems, as well as taking over 18 years to complete the project. It is a sad commentary that many bottled water companies just sell us back our own local tap water after they clean it up for us.

Bottled water is still the fastest growing beverage sold in the United States. In 2001 we consumed about 2.8 billion gallons of it. The quality of bottled water is regulated by the FDA (Food and Drug Administration) and is considered a food product. Most water bottlers are members of the IBWA (International Bottled Water Association). The bottled water industry is a $3.9 billion-dollar industry.

States also regulate water bottlers and are analyzing and inspecting facilities on a regular basis. States must also inspect the laboratories that perform the water testing. Approximately 75% of all bottled water originates from springs or wells, while the other 25% are usually from tap water sources. If the water is from a municipal water company source it must be labeled that it is.

If the water states that it is purified, then it must be distilled, deionized, demineralized, or run through a reverse osmosis system. If this is done then the water does not have to be labeled "tap water" even if it comes from that source. Most bottling companies have in-house testing capabilities and stringent controls. IBWA members which include almost all United States bottlers (1200) must also have unannounced inspections by the NSF (National Sanitation Foundation International) inspectors.

Source inspections are also performed on a regular weekly basis, especially for microbacterial contamination. Additional information can be found on the IBWA Web site at or by calling 1 (800) WATER-11.

FLOURIDE

This tooth decay-fighting mineral will not be found in high levels in bottled water. If you would prefer a higher level then check the label since there are a few bottled water companies that do add additional fluoride. Fluoride has been proven effective, especially in children in reducing the risk of cavities and promotes increased mineralization even into adult life. Fluoride supplements, however, are available at most health food stores.

CRYPTOSPORIDIUM

While there are many bacteria and other contaminants that may affect our water, cryptosporidium, a disease-carrying parasite, is one of the more common contaminants. This parasite resides in animals such as goats, cattle, rabbits, squirrels, wolves, and raccoons and is passed into the water through their wastes. The eggs of the parasites have been the cause of gastrointestinal problems in a number of areas of the United States. Symptoms may materialize that are similar to flu symptoms but the infestation may be fatal to persons with poor or underdeveloped immune systems such as the young and the elderly and especially persons suffering from HIV.

When you are in a forest hiking, or camping it is always wise to bring your water with you or at least use a water purification tablet or boil the water. Mountain steams, lakes, rivers, and ponds are easily contaminated.

Well water or deep spring water for the most part is free of this contaminant. Surface water is usually the culprit. Filtration systems in bottled water companies remove organisms such as cryptosporidium very effectively.

One of the most serious outbreaks of cryptosporidium water contamination was in 1993, when 110 people died and over 400,000 people became ill in Milwaukee, Wisconsin. Animal waste contamination or a sewage leak probably caused this problem.

ADDITIVES

Bottled water must not contain any form of chemical additive or preservative, not even a sweetener. They can, however, contain a natural extract derived from fruit or spices. Bottled water must not contain any calories, be sodium-free, and even natural flavors, when added must be less than 1% of the weight of the finished bottled water product.

STORAGE

There is no dated shelf life on bottled water. It can last forever if stored in a cool, dry location away from any solvents or other household chemicals that may produce fumes.

TYPES OF BOTTLED WATER

SPRING WATER:

This water is usually found in underground springs, which flow close to the surface. Usually this water is labeled with the name of the spring. Whether the spring water comes to the surface or is drilled for, the water must have the same physical properties and be tested before bottling. One of the purest spring waters is found in Iceland and comes from the Hesjuvalla Spring. This has been a pure water source for over 1,000 years.

ARTESIAN WATER:

This is water that is bottled from a specific underground water source called an "aquifer." The source may be a well or body of water found in a layer of rock. Artesian water is one of the purest natural waters.

MINERAL WATER:

This water that must have at least 250 parts per million of dissolved solids. It must contain a specific level of minerals and trace elements when it is harvested from its source. Bottled water companies must not add minerals to this water product. Latest studies show that drinking lightly mineralized water may be beneficial for your heart.

SPARKLING WATER:

Sparkling water is naturally carbonated by nature with carbon dioxide. Bottled water companies may re-carbonate the water if it has lost a percentage of carbon dioxide, but only to the waters original level. Seltzer (two cents plain) is not considered bottled water, is not regulated by the IBWA and can contain sugar and calories. Seltzer, soda water, tonic water, etc. are considered soft drinks and are regulated as such.

PURIFIED WATER:

Purified water is produced through distillation. This process removes all contaminants and minerals and is the purest water. If this were your water of choice it would be wise to take a mineral supplement. This water may be labeled as distilled water.

TAP WATER

It will probably be a long time and take billions of dollars to clean up all the tap water in the United States. The studies that have been done all report similar findings, which conclude that millions of Americans are taking either a small risk or a major risk from drinking tap water. This will not come as a surprise to anyone since the TV shows and articles are numerous on the subject.

Many of the risk factors are right in our own backyards and are not the fault of the water company's purification methods. In older homes the water pipes may be deteriorating allowing the metals contained in the pipes to leach out into our drinking water. If the water has a slight acid/base upset it can easily leach out these metals. If you live in an older home, you may have lead pipes and you tap water should be tested at least once each year. The tap water flowing into over 80 million homes in the United States may contain carcinogens (cancer-forming agents).

Even if your home has copper pipes, they may have lead-soldered joints, which could also leach lead into your water supply. The levels of possible carcinogens cancer causing agents found in tap water by the EPA was a real eye opener. The list of cities included most of the major cities in the United States. The worst being Tampa, Florida, Houston, Texas, Oklahoma City, Oklahoma, and Charleston, South Carolina.

SOFT WATER

Soft water contains very few minerals and in most areas of the country tap water is so high in mineral content and needs to be softened. When water is softened it creates high sodium water, which is not healthy to drink, especially for persons with high blood pressure or kidney problems. Using soft water may also leach lead out of pipes in older homes.

Water softeners utilize a method of ion exchange to remove hard minerals, such as calcium and magnesium while replacing them with sodium. Sodium then creates a softening effect on the water creating more soapsuds. This makes the water more efficient for doing laundry, bathing, and doing dishes.

HEALTH CAUTION:

The medical community has issued a health alert regarding the use of potassium-based water softening units or the use of a high potassium salt. Drinking water that is high in potassium can be a health risk to persons who suffer from high blood pressure, diabetes, and kidney disease. High levels may lead to muscle weakness, heartbeat irregularities, and even heart failure. Most products that are sold come with a warning label regarding the risks of the potassium-based units and products.

HARD WATER

Hard water contains different minerals. The mineral content of your water will usually depend on the area of the country you live in. The high mineral content allows residues of calcium magnesium to form in plumbing fixtures.

HEALTH CAUTION:

Two minerals, magnesium and calcium that are related to the level of hardness in drinking water may be beneficial to protect woman against heart disease.

OXYGENATED WATER

A number of companies are now producing oxygenated water. Some of the drinks are being marketed as a breath freshener due to the increased level of oxygen improving the oral ecology and having a cleansing effect. These beverages have oxygen dissolved into the drink under pressure, similar to the carbonation process of placing carbon dioxide into a beverage to make a carbonated soda.

The drinks are sold in both glass and plastic containers. The glass container may be more efficient in retaining the level of oxygen since the plastic containers may tend to lose the oxygen at a faster rate. The higher the concentration level of available oxygen in the drink the more effective the drink may be. The breath freshening effect is derived from the oxygen increasing the level of good bacteria, the ones that are called aerobic bacteria and need oxygen to survive and multiply. The anaerobic bacteria are the ones that are usually responsible for causing bad breathe and do not require oxygen to survive.

These oxygenated beverages may be a natural solution to eliminating bad breath in some individuals and are a better alternative than using an alcohol content mouthwash that is effective for a short period of time. Other mouthwashes utilize chemicals that may only mask the offensive odor for a short period of time. When you inhale oxygen you obtain about a small level of oxygen, which mixes with saliva to keep your mouth moist. However, a thin film may easily form on your tongue allowing the anaerobic bacteria to multiply and cause odors. Oxygenated water consumed on a daily basis will increase the oxygen level to about 70 parts per million of pure oxygen compared to only 7ppm pure oxygen in the air you breathe.

Quality mouthwashes should contain chlorine dioxide, which is an effective anaerobic bacteria killer. If an oxygenated beverage is consumed and you are using a chlorine dioxide mouthwash, the beverage should increase the effectiveness of the mouthwash.

The majority of oxygenated beverages do not contain any sweeteners, preservatives, calories, or artificial flavorings. There is no limit to the number of drinks you can consume per day since it is a natural beverage. If you prefer drinking the beverage over ice cubes or just cold, it will not reduce the effectiveness.

LIFE O2 SUPER OXYGENATED WATER

This drink contains 10 times the oxygen level (72mg) as standard bottled water. The company claims its water will increase the amount of oxygen in your blood. The beverage is supposed to provide increased energy levels with no aftertaste. It contains no artificial ingredients and may be worth a try during an exercise period or sports activity. It is one the best oxygenated waters on the market.

GINSENG SPRING WATER

This new water has only recently been introduced into the United States and most drinks contain about 100mg.of the herb ginseng. Ginseng has been a popular energy related herb for hundreds of years. Most drinks are very tasty and refreshing.

CAFFEINATED WATER

A number of beverage manufacturers are now producing caffeinated water, which will provide an alternative to drinking coffee to acquire caffeine. Most of the drinks have a very poor taste; however, do provide you with an adequate level of caffeine that may assist you in staying awake longer. Unless they figure out how to improve the taste I do not foresee this drink being around too long.

ACIDULATED WATER

This is a mixture of water and an acid usually a citrus acid derived from lime, orange or lemon. It is commonly used on fruits or fruit salads to prevent them from browning when their surfaces are exposed to the air. Oxidation takes place very rapidly in many fruits and vegetables. When oxidation takes place the vitamin C is lost in the brown areas. To prepare acidulated water, just use 1 part of the citrus fruit to 5 parts of pure water.

WATER PURIFICATION METHODS

There are numerous methods of home water purification systems. If you decide to purchase a system, be sure to investigate the different types and the availability of service for that particular system. A number of units only produce a minimal quantity of pure water, which would not be sufficient for many families while other units do not provide the level of desired filtration.

Activated Charcoal Filtration Units

A number of the more popular units filter the water through activated charcoal filters. This method is very efficient in filtering out insecticides, pesticides, chlorine, and organic matter. However, this type of filter is not very effective in filtering out bacteria and undissolved metals, such as lead, copper, iron and manganese. Filters need to be checked regularly and changed or the system will be useless. If you do choose this type of unit, be sure it does not contain silver to neutralize bacteria. Silver is not that effective and a percentage may end up in your drinking water.

Chlorination

Systems that utilize chlorine to kill bacteria usually produce water with a somewhat off-taste and odor to the water. The system must be functioning properly at all times or there is the possibility of the chlorine forming a dangerous element.

Multi-Stage Filtration

These units are one of the most effective and usually recommended above most other units. They utilize a number of filtration methods such as a pre-filter, which will remove iron, rust, dirt particles, and sediments as small as 5 microns. They also have a lead-activated carbon filter, which removes lead and chlorine as well as a carbon block filter to remove chlorine, improve taste, remove odors, and most organic impurities.

Microstrainers
A good method of filtration, however, it is not able to remove most nitrates and nitrites. It will remove almost all chemicals and bacteria.

Reverse Osmosis
This is one of the most popular units sold in the United States and utilizes a duel sediment filter system. The system is effective in removing up to 90% of the minerals and inorganic matter. The system works by forcing water through a thin membrane, which removes the inorganic metals. Most units only store 5 gallons of water or less. This system only produces 20% drinking water and discards 80% as waste. Commercial systems are used to remove salt from seawater producing drinking water.

Distillation
Distillation is one of the most effective methods of filtration. Water is boiled producing steam, which is then cooled to produce water vapor, which is then trapped. However, certain gasses are not removed through this method. The more efficient distillers utilize activated charcoal filters as an additional organic material remover. Be sure and de-scale your distiller regularly or the efficiency will be greatly reduced.

Aeration
Radon gas is a continuing water contamination problem, especially in the midwest United States. An aeration filter is the most effective type of filter to resolve this problem. A survey conducted by the Environmental Protection Agency estimated that over 8 million people are at risk from radon contamination.

Ultraviolet Radiation Purifiers
These types of filters are very effective in filtering out bacteria and are normally installed on wells in conjunction with other types of filtration units. This system does require a constant electrical line voltage. It does not remove cyst contamination.

Ozonators
These filters are being used more extensively than ever before and are frequently found on swimming pools built after 1992. They utilize activated oxygen that is capable of purifying and removing bacteria without chlorination. Recommended more for swimming pools rather than drinking water since the system may produce bromate, which may be related to tumors of the kidney.

Carbon Filters
These filters utilize carbon to attract the contaminants, which then adhere to the carbon. They are useful in removing odors, improving the taste of water, and eliminating organic chemical compounds. Their drawback is that they do not remove heavy metals.

Magnetic Water Conditioners
Since all home appliances or equipment that use water builds up scale over a period of time, these conditioners are a must for the homeowner who wishes to protect their investment with a minimum of repairs from water scale damage. These systems do not affect water purity; however, they condition the water

magnetically altering the physical characteristics of water-borne minerals. The mineral will no longer be able to cling to the insides of the water pipes and no scale can be formed.

CHECKING YOUR OWN TAP WATER

Hints that will help you evaluate you own tap water for possible contamination or problems:

- If your sink has a dark reddish-colored stain it may be the result of rust in your pipes.
- If your sink has greenish stains it is probably from copper leaching from the pipes.
- If you notice a rotten egg smell, it's probably hydrogen sulfide produced from bacteria.
- If the water is cloudy it can be from dirt particles, iron, or bacterial contamination.

Cloudy water can also result from small air bubbles forming when the water is under pressure as it leaves the tap and soon dissipates. This is harmless and no need for concern.

COMMON CONTAMINANTS IN TAP WATER

Copper	Usually more of a problem in older homes stemming from the metal leaching out of the pipes.
Fluoride	Water companies add fluoride to reduce the incidence of tooth decay. While fluoride does reduce the incidence of cavities, it is also a very toxic chemical and must be carefully controlled.
Chlorine	Sometimes added as a disinfectant. People who frequently swim in pools that are chlorinated have reported arthritis and immune system disorders.
Lead	Leached out into tap water from older pipes.
Chlorocarbons	If chlorine is present it may react with organic compounds producing a harmful contaminant.
Organic Molecules	Includes hydrocarbons, gasoline, and cleaning solvents.
PVC's	Plastic materials from water pipes.
Radon	A naturally occurring contaminant.

Mineral	Sodium content of some water may be too high.
Pesticides/Fertilizers	Filter through the ground and end up in our water supplies.
Microorganisms	Include fungi, bacteria, and parasites.
Nitrates	Residues from fertilizers.
Drugs	Residues from prescription pharmaceuticals

HEALTH FACTS

DEHYDRATION

A survey of 3,000 Americans showed that a significant number are suffering from dehydration brought on by drinking too little water and too many cups of coffee and soft drinks. Remember that you can't fool Mother Nature! The following are a few good tips to staying well hydrated and healthier.

- When you exercise, remember to drink 16 ounces of water for every pound you lose through perspiration. Keep a water bottle handy and drink regularly.
- For good health drink 8 cups of water each day, especially when ill. The body dehydrates more easily when you have a cold or fever.
- Never wait until you are thirsty before you drink water.
- Remember coffee, soft drinks, tea, and alcoholic drinks have a diuretic effect. Caffeine especially is an excellent diuretic. Your body must find 8 ounces of water to breakdown 1 ounce of alcohol.
- If the weather is hot, cool water is the best fluid, and will be more easily absorbed and utilized by the body.

WATER AND AGING, A SERIOUS PROBLEM

As we age dehydration becomes a serious health problem due to the fact that our body's thirst mechanism is not working as well and does not tell us when our body requires more fluid. We don't know why our bodies tend to lose this ability but it is common among seniors and leads to dehydration. Remember our body is about 70% water and all the cells, the joints, and the tissues that protect our organs all rely on a good water supply.

Many seniors worry about fluid retention, however, if your body is functioning normally, your body will not retain excess fluids. Adequate water helps the kidneys function more efficiently, which helps alleviate fluid retention and improves waste disposal. Lack of adequate water may also cause the heart to work harder and if it already weak can lead to heart failure.

WATER AND ATHLETES

There are numerous studies that discuss the need for adequate water relating to the efficiency of an athlete. If the body is dehydrated by 5%, physical performance may be reduced by as much as 25%. When working out or performing a sport at an average pace the body can lose up to one quart of water every hour.

For the average 150-pound adult you should drink about 100 ounces of water daily if you take part in an active sport or exercise on a regular basis. If you plan on a strenuous exercise regimen, you should drink about 2 cups of water 2 hours before starting the exercise or strenuous sports activity. To replace water losses through perspiration if you are exercising vigorously you need to drink about 1 cup of water every 15 minutes.

If you allow your water level to get too low it can cause headaches, lightheaded-ness, dizziness, and nausea. Since water is used to cool the body a number of increased body temperature problems can occur, especially heat stroke. Depending on the duration and intensity of the activity, a sports drink may be best.

WHERE IS YOUR WATER FROM?

If the source of your water is from a surface water source, such as a lake or a river, the water can be exposed to acid rain, storm water runoff, fertilizer, and pesticide runoff, or industrial waste residues. Exposure to sunlight will cleanse the water to some degree, but I would have it checked regularly. If your water supply is from a well or a company it takes longer to become contaminated but should still be checked at least every 6 months.

RISK OF DYING FROM PESTICIDES IN WATER SUPPLIES

The risk of getting cancer from drinking pesticide contaminated water is about 1 in 1 million if you drink 8-10 glasses per day. The chances of getting cancer from smoking cigarettes (1 pack per day) are about 80,000 in 1 million.

YOUR TAP WATER MAY BE DRUGGED

Reports are surfacing that show drug residues in tap water, surface water and groundwater. These residues are from antibiotics, chemotherapy agents, numerous pharmaceuticals, tranquilizers, hormones, etc. They are excreted by humans and domestic animals and may be spread by flushing toilets, manure fertilizers and most types of sewage. German scientists have identified 30-60 drugs in typical water samples.

WET FACTS

THE NATIONAL CANCER INSTITUTE REPORTS

In 9 recent studies water quality was related to the risk of cancer in Pittsburgh, New Orleans, cities in Ohio, New York, and New Jersey. Almost 66% of all households in the United States are presently using water that is violation of EPA standards.

RADIATION, A PROBLEM

Radiation contamination of water supplies is presently a problem for 1.8 million Americans. The problem is caused by radioactive elements such as radon and uranium leaching into the groundwater. If you would like to find out if there is a problem in your area, just call (708) 505-0160.

IT'S A FACT

The human body loses the same amount of water when sleeping as when awake.

WATER WEIGHT

Sometimes a recipe mentions the weight of water. The weight of 1 tablespoon = $\frac{1}{2}$ ounce and the weight of 2 cups = 1 pound of water.

ARE YOU STILL THIRSTY?

When you drink 12 ounces of pure water, you will only absorb about 8 ounces during a 15-minute period. If you drink a regular soft drink that contains about 10% sugar, your body will only absorb about 1 ounce of water.

OH, THE WEATHER OUTSIDE IS GLOOMY

A person requires the same amount of water in cold weather as they do in cold weather.

COOL, CLEAR, WATER

Symptoms that are associated with dehydration or low water intake include: skin irritations, itching, dry skin problems, lack of alertness upon arising, or the midday blues (energy loss). More serious symptoms may include blood pressure problems, the digestive upsets, and even poor kidney function.

ARE YOU AMONG THE FEW, THE HEALTHY

Statistics show that only one in every eight Americans drinks the required 8 cups of water daily.

UP, UP, AND AWAY

On the average day, the human body can lose 32 ounces of water. This will increase significantly if you exercise, are active, or the weather is very hot.

TOP OF THE HEAP

The top water bottlers are Evian, Perrier, Black Mountain Spring Water, Calistoga, Clearly Canadian, NAYA, Water Joe, Earth 20, Aqua Penn Spring Water, and Saratoga.

RISKY WATER AREAS

Approximately 15 million Americans may be drinking water that is below EPA standards. Higher risk cities include New York, Portland, West Palm Beach, New Orleans, Cleveland, San Diego, Denver, Houston, San Francisco, and Chicago.

NOT SOMETHING TO BRAG ABOUT

In 2001 Americans spent almost 4.3 times the dollars on soda pop than they did on milk and seven times more on alcoholic beverages.

IT'S A WONDER WE DON'T SLOSH WHEN WE WALK

A 180-pound adult contains over 100 pounds of water. The brain has 76% water and the lungs have 86%.

GOING UP, BUBBLE LEVEL

When water boils the bubbles that come to the surface are just pockets of water vapor that originate on the bottom of the pot. As soon as the bubble absorbs enough energy to overcome the weight of the liquid and the atmospheric pressure they rise to the surface.

STOP BOIL OVER COLD

When you add pasta or other food to boiling water the foods will contain a percentage of organic matter, especially proteins, which are released into the cooking water. These elements that are released accumulate on the surface and disrupt the surface tension that has been created by the boiling water. When this occurs, foam is formed and mixes with the water causing the bubbles to be somewhat stronger and not burst as easily, thus flowing over the top of the pot. To avoid this problem, just add a small amount of oil to the water, which does not mix well with the water causing tiny oil droplets to form on the surface. The oil acts as "bubble-breakers," does not allow the bubbles to become large and the pot will not boil-over.

HIDDEN DANGER

Never drink tap water first thing in the morning or if the water has not been run for 2-3 hours. The risk of contaminants is very high from the water that is allowed to rest in the pipes. Always run the tap for at least one minute before drinking or using the water for cooking. The hot water tap is even guiltier than the cold water tap.

WATER AND SEA LEVEL

The normal boiling point of water at sea level is 212°F (100°C). For every 500 feet in elevation over sea level the boiling point of water decreases by 1°F.

DON'T HARM THAT ICEBERG

Most of the fresh water on earth is in the glaciers. However, if we melt them, we better all grow gills and fins. Only 3-4% of the fresh water is available for human consumption and to grow crops. Best if we learn more efficient methods of desalinization. About 97.3% of all the water on the planet is in the oceans; that leaves 2.1% in the glaciers and 0.6% in fresh water.

WHY DON'T WE DRINK MORE WATER?

- 75% of Americans are chronically dehydrated
- Mild dehydration will slow a persons metabolism by 3%
- One glass of water will eliminate hunger pangs in 100% of dieters
- Lack of water is the #1 cause of daytime fatigue
- 8-10 glasses of water per day will ease back and joint pain for 80% of sufferers
- A 2% drop in body water can cause fuzzy short-term memory
- 5 glasses of water daily decreases colon cancer risk by 45% and breast cancer by 79%

ADDING SALT TO WATER - DO MICROSECONDS REALLY COUNT?

When sugar, salt, or almost any other solid are added to water, the boiling point is raised and the freezing point lowered. If you add one ounce of salt to a quart of water it will raise the boiling point 1°F. An example of this: If you lived at an elevation of 1 mile you would have to add 8 ounces of salt to water to reach 212°F (100°C). The molecules of either salt or sugar interfere with the natural breakdown of the water molecule.

Adding salt to water to cook pasta faster is a waste of time, since the amount needed would be too much to fit into the pot. If you added 1 tablespoon of salt to 5 quarts of boiling water to cook 1 pound of pasta, it would only raise the boiling point by 7/100th of one degree Fahrenheit. Cookbooks that advise you to add salt to the cooking water of pasta should advise you that it is only done for flavoring. However, other studies tell us that adding salt sometimes makes certain pasta get tough.

BRING A BIG CANTEEN

If you're planning to climb Mt. Everest, bring a good supply of water since the higher the altitude the more water the body requires. Water will evaporate much faster the higher you climb. The increased rate of breathing also has a lot to do with it.

DID CAESAR DRINK PERRIER?

The source of Perrier Sparkling Mineral Water can be traced back about 130 million years with the first known record dating back to Roman times. The first bottling of the water took place in 1863 and it has been imported into the United States since around 1900. The water is the result of rainwater flowing down hillsides in Southern France and being filtered through limestone, sand and gravel deposits. During the natural filtration process the water acquires certain minerals, which give it a unique flavor. Geothermal activity deep underground provides the natural carbonation. The water rises to the surface at a constant pressure and at 60°F (15.6°C).

Since the demand for the water worldwide was too much for the springs to supply, the French collected the water and the gas separately and brought them to a bottling plant and combined the ingredients there to increase production.

RAINDROPS KEEP FALLING.....

Rainwater may contain a number of contaminants and minerals. Acid rain is a good example of how we can even contaminate the clouds.

HOT, COLD, OR TEPID

The temperature of drinking water does make a difference to our bodies. When we are thirsty cold water will quench our thirst faster. Hot water tends to open the cells in the intestines and may allow allergens to enter. Tepid or room temperature water is best tolerated by the body and utilized more easily.

A WORD TO THE WISE

When in any foreign country try not to drink tap water, brush your teeth with tap water, use ice cubes, drink any beverage with ice cubes, drink any non-carbonated locally bottled water, or mixed alcoholic drinks.

WATER VS. IRON AND OIL

Just a bit of interesting trivia! Water is capable of absorbing a large quantity of energy to raise its temperature. For example: it takes 10 times the energy to raise one ounce of water 1⁰F than to heat one ounce of iron 1⁰F. A pot of water will take twice as long to heat up than the same pot of oil to the same temperature.

WATER CONTENT OF BUTTER

Butter is made up of 59% water, 40% fat (mostly saturated), and only 1% protein.

COOLING OFF

Blowing on your soup when it is too hot will cool the soup about 50% faster than if the soup is left alone. Blowing on the hot liquid encourages evaporation at a faster rate.

STOP SCALDING YOUR HANDS

When pouring off boiling water from a pasta pot or vegetables into the sink, try running the cold water in the sink while you are pouring to prevent the steam from burning your hand.

RELEASE ME

Water must be filtered if you want clear ice cubes. However, if you boil the water before placing it into the trays this will allow a number of minerals that cause the cloudiness to dissipate into the air.

SO WHAT'S NEW

A new bacterium water contaminant, Helicobacter Pylori, is now being studied as a possible link to stomach cancers. Studies are ongoing in attempts to control it.

GETTING HIGH ON WATER

If water is overly oxygenated (adding more oxygen) drinking it may give you a slight feeling of euphoria. The latest entry into the beverage field may be "Life 02" which will contain seven times more oxygen than regular water.

GLUB, GLUB

The average person consumes over 15,000 gallons of water if they live to age 68.

FLUID BALANCE

The human body is dependent on an adequate and especially healthy water supply. Air and water are two essentials that without which, we cease to live. Every bodily function and organ system relies on water. Water assists our bodies in dissolving foods, transports nutrients to the organ systems then cools the body through perspiration, while assisting in regulating overall body temperature. Water washes out contaminants through the kidneys in the form of urine.

Because of all the uses for water in the body and the fact that we eliminate a good percentage of our supply every day we require an intake of about 6-7 pints of water to replace these losses. If you are thirsty, remember the body prefers a cool supply of water, which it can absorb easily. Hot water in the form of tea or coffee is not absorbed as well and may act as a diuretic and actually cause the body to excrete more water.

About 70% of the human body is water. If you weigh 150 pounds, your body contains about 90 pounds of water. The following shows the percentage of water making up the tissues, organs, fluids, and bone:

Brain	76%	Kidneys	83%
Heart	74%	Bone	22%
Muscle	75%	Blood	82%
Lungs	86%	Saliva	94%
Liver	86%	Perspiration	95%

GIVE IT TO THE PLANTS

Tap water should always be allowed to run for 2-3 minutes first thing in the morning in case contaminants have seeped in during the night.

THIRSTY, GET OUT THE BLOWTORCH

The oceans contain 97% of the earth's water as salt water. Desalinization is becoming more important as new methods are being discovered. We are presently living on only about 3% fresh water of which 75% of that is frozen up in glaciers.

DON'T CHILL OUT

If you suffer from any form of cardiovascular disease it would be best not to drink ice cold water. The cold may cause a sudden drop in tissue temperature and may cause an unnecessary shock to the system. Also, the digestive system will function more efficiently if you drink tepid water. However, it is best if we do not drink any water with our meals since water will dilute stomach acids and digestive enzymes.

RELEASES ME......

There is a higher level of contaminants in hot tap water than cold tap water. The heat tends to hold the contaminants better. Boiling hot tap water, however, tends to release contaminants.

WHY DO WE NEED TO DRINK MORE WATER AT HIGHER ELEVATIONS?

Where we live will actually have an effect on the amount of water we need to drink to hydrate the body adequately. At higher elevations water tends to evaporate faster through your skin due to the lower atmospheric pressure making the air drier. Since the air is thinner we also tend to increase our rate of breathing and lose additional moisture through exhalation. You will need to consume approximately 3-4 extra glasses of water per day if you live in the mile-high city of Denver than if you lived in New York.

WHAT TYPE OF WATER SHOULD THIRST BE QUENCHED WITH?

There has been a debate going on for years whether it is best to drink ice water or room temperature water when you are thirsty. The answer is to drink ice water, which will quench your thirst faster because it will cause the stomach to constrict, thereby forcing the water into the small intestine where it will be absorbed into the bloodstream faster.

DOESN'T SAY MUCH FOR THE GOVERNMENT

The bottled water industry is a $4.2 billion dollar industry. Over $2.9 billion dollars were spent in 2001 on home filtration systems. Home filter systems are only capable of removing larger particulate matter still leaving a good percentage of the small ones, such as some bacteria and viruses. One out of twelve households in the United States use bottled water as their main source of drinking water.

RAINDROPS.....

Rainwater is still considered to be mineral water and may have a number of impurities. We have all heard of "acid rain." The purest water is distilled water.

ADD A GOOD ORGANIC CLEANER

Rinsing vegetables in a sink filled with water (instead of under running water) will save about 200 gallons of water per month for the average family. You will waste another 200 gallons waiting for the tap water to warm up. Best to save the cold water for the plants.

DOES DEHYDRATION AFFECT US MORE IN THE SUMMER OR WINTER?

It is a known fact that the human body will lose more water during the summer months but you are more likely to become dehydrated in the winter. In the winter you lose the conscious need to drink more fluids and water is still lost through sweat. Sweat will not linger and is absorbed more quickly by the dryness of the atmosphere in a heated room and the rate of absorption of heavier clothing.

WASTE NOT......

If you leave the water running, you will waste about 1 gallon of water every time you brush your teeth. The average family normally uses over 300,000 gallons of water annually for all personal hygiene, lawn watering, laundry, and cooking.

DRINK A VEGGIE

Some fruits and vegetables have high water content. Carrots are 90% water and iceberg lettuce is 96% water.

WHY ICE FLOATS

When water freezes its molecules of hydrogen and oxygen combine in a loose fashion, thus creating air pockets in the structure of the ice cube. When water is in its liquid form these pockets do not exist making water denser than ice.

THINK AGAIN!

Well water should be tested every 6 months, without fail! Many farmers never have their water tested and assume that well water is always clean and healthy.

YOU NEED TO GET THE LEAD OUT

Over 5 million private wells in the United States may be exposing millions of people to high levels of lead. A warning has been issued by the Environmental Protection Agency that certain types of submersible pumps may leach lead into the water. The problem pumps have fitting made from brass that contains copper and zinc and 2-7% lead. It is possible to drink water with 51 times the allowable limits of lead in water prescribed by the EPA. Pumps should be made from stainless steel or plastic to eliminate the risk. For more information call the EPA's Safe Drinking Water Hotline at (800) 426-4791.

SCRUB THOSE ICE CUBES

When ice cubes are allowed to remain in the freezer tray more than a few days they tend to pick up freezer odor from other foods, or even a degree of contamination from the air when the freezer is frequently opened. It would be wise to wash the ice cubes before using them to avoid any contamination or alteration of the flavor of the beverage.

BREAK TIME

When water is called for in a recipe, it should be between 60-80 degrees for the results. Allow water you are going to use stand at room temperature for about 30 minutes before using.

NATURE'S CARBONATED WATER

A number of "natural" beverages advertise that their drink contains naturally carbonated water. This water is created underground by the action of a somewhat acidic water comes into contact with limestone resulting in the production of the gas carbon dioxide. The gas is trapped by the water under high pressure underground. Artificially, carbonation is helped along with either phosphoric acid or citric acid in most soft drinks.

HEAVY WATER, NOT REALLY

Occasionally a recipe will require a weight of water be used. 1 tablespoon = $1/2$ ounce and 2 cups = 1 pound of water.

HAVE A SHOT OF WATER

When your drinking an alcoholic beverage it would be wise to drink a cup of water for every alcoholic drink you consume. For every ounce of alcohol it takes 8 ounces of water to metabolize it. If you have ever had a hangover a few of the common symptoms are the result of dehydration such as dry mouth, headaches, and of course an upset stomach.

WHERE OH WHERE HAS THE WATER GONE

To produce food for one person . . . . 1¹/₂ million gallons
To grow one large potato . . . . .18 gallons
To produce 1 pat of margarine . . . . .85 gallons
To produce 1 loaf of bread . . . . .56 gallons
To manufacture 1 pint of whiskey . . . . .110 gallons
To produce 1 pound of flour . . . . .350 gallons
To produce 1 pound of beef . . . . .4,850 gallons
To grow 1 ear of corn . . . . .61 gallons
To produce a lettuce dinner salad . . . . .6 gallons
To grow one tomato . . . . .3 gallons
To produce 1 cola soft drink . . . . .10 gallons
Taking a bath . . . . .30 gallons
Watering the lawn .200 gallons
Brushing your teeth . . . . .1 gallon
Washing a car . . . . .100 gallons

COOKING WITH WATER

WHAT TEMPERATURE IS SIMMERING?

Simmer at sea level at a normal barometric pressure is around 195°F (90.6°C). A high simmer is 210°F (99°C) and a low simmer is about 180°F (82.2°C). The simmer temperature can be important when the recipe asks for a specific type of simmer. Keeping a thermometer handy in the kitchen will improve the quality of your cooking.

WHEW, TURN DOWN THE STEAM

When water turns to steam, it must expand to 1,600 times its original volume. Steam is an important leavening agent for baked goods. This is especially important for piecrust and puff pastry. The more rapidly the steam develops, the better the product will turn out, therefore the higher the starting baking temperature, the better.

SPECIAL WATER FOR RECIPES

When a recipe calls for water, the water should be between 60°-80°F (15.6°C - 26.7°C) for the best results be sure that the temperature is correct and allow the water to stand at room temperature for about 30 minutes before using it.

I'M BOILING, THERE GOES MY OXYGEN

When boiling vegetables or meats, allow the water to boil for about 2 minutes before adding the food. This will allow a percentage of the oxygen in the water to be released. Oxygen has the ability to reduce the percentage of available nutrients found in the food. Also the shorter the cooking time for vegetables, the more nutrients that will be retained. Leaving the skins on also helps.

ADDING SALT TO YOUR COOKING WATER

If you add 1 teaspoon of salt to your cooking water, it will raise the temperature 1°F-2°F (17.2°C-6.7°C). Sugar and many other ingredients will also raise the temperature of the water. Unless the recipe calls for this rise in temperature, it is best not to add salt, since salt also causes some foods to become tough.

TO SALT OR NOT TO SALT

It is OK to salt the water for foods that have a short boiling time such as vegetables. Never salt the water when cooking corn or it will toughen the corn, instead add 1 teaspoon of sugar to the water to sweeten it. When cooking foods for a prolonged period of time, never salt the water, especially for stews, stocks and beans. Beans especially tend to get tough. The safest way to use salt on many dishes and foods is to salt the foods just before they are finished cooking.

BOILING POINTS AND ALTITUDE

As the altitude increases, the atmospheric pressure decreases, placing less pressure on the water you are trying to boil. When the pressure decreases, the water molecules are released more easily and it takes less time and a lower temperature to boil water. For every 1,000 feet increase in elevation, the temperature of boiling goes down about 2° F. (16.7° C.).

Altitude (feet)	Fahrenheit	Centigrade
0	212°	100°
1,000	210°	99°
2,000	208°	98°
3,000	207°	97°
4,000	205°	96°
5,000	203°	95°

BLANCHING FOODS

There are different methods of blanching or parboiling foods. The following are two of the more popular methods:

- Place the food in a bowl, then pour boiling water over the food and allow it to stand for 30-60 seconds. Drain off the water and immediately place the food into ice cold water to stop the cooking action.

- Place the food in a large pot of boiling water, add $1/4$ teaspoon of salt to the water and boil rapidly for 1 minute. Immediately drain and plunge the food into ice water.

Soft vegetables, such as tomatoes do not need to be boiled for one minute to be blanched. Tomatoes only require 15 seconds in the boiling water. Cabbage and spinach only requires 30 seconds. Use your judgement depending on the hardness of the food when blanching or parboiling.

POACHING

Both poaching and simmering are methods of cooking which require a large amount of water or stock. The liquid should be very hot, but not to the point of boiling. If the food is accidentally allowed to boil it may fall apart. The cooking pot may be covered or uncovered and are mainly used for softer foods such as fruits, eggs, fish and shellfish. Tougher cuts of meats and stewing chickens can also be tenderized using this method. Poaching is commonly used to cook and tenderize corned beef in delicatessens. When chefs wish to poach fish they will frequently place the fish in the cold water and bring the water up to a gentle simmer, remove the pot from the heat and allow the fish to cook off the heat.

When poaching fruits, the best method is to use sugary syrup with a spiced wine to poach in. If you are going to poach a whole fish the recommended technique is to wrap the fish in a small towel and lightly tied so that it will not fall apart. This will also make it easier to handle when removing the fish from the pot.

I'M TOO HARD FOR BAKED GOODS

When preparing dough for baked goods, hard water may cause a problem since too high a mineral content may result in the gluten not being able to develop properly. If the gluten does not develop properly, the crust will be tough.

MY FOOD IS IN A BAIN-MARIE

This is a French term used in cooking to denote that a dish of food has been placed in a shallow pan of water and cooking it in the oven. The food is continually cooked using a moist heat. Delicate dishes are usually cooked using this method, the most common being mousses and custards, which allows them to set without breaking or curdling.

WATER SUB

When making bread and the recipe calls for water, you can substitute milk and it will make the texture softer and the crust darker. The milk should be scalded first to improve the volume.

STORING WATER FOR EMERGENCIES

The following information is important to your entire family in case of an emergency. You cannot live without water, but you can live without food for a longer period of time.

Type of water to store:
There are two basic types of water, commercial and tap. Bottled waters are safer to store for drinking purposes and emergency storage. However, the bulk of your water supply will probably be tap water due to the difference in cost.

Quantity of water to store:
We require a minimum of 2 gallons of water per person per day to survive reasonably comfortable: one gallon of water for drinking and one gallon for cooking and washing. Two people will require 56 gallons of water to survive for two weeks. Forget the daily showers.

Choosing the proper container:
Be careful not to choose a container that will leach chemicals into the water. Glass is excellent and plastic is fine as long as both are thoroughly cleaned before being filled. Camping jugs are OK and so are empty soda bottles. A 2-liter soft drink bottle contains about 2 quarts of water.

Emergency purification:
If you are unsure of the water or need to use suspect water in an emergency, place 10 drops of liquid chlorine bleach (Clorox) into a gallon of water. Adjust the number of drops for smaller containers. Boiling the water is always preferred if you have heat available.

Emergency water sources:
Water can be used from a waterbed, pond, pool or hot tub, but should be purified before drinking. These sources may be best used for flushing toilets. The water in the hot water heater or the commode tank (not the toilet) may be used for drinking after purification. If you suspect a water shortage, clean the bathtub spotless and fill it with cold water.

Rotate your water:
Stored water should be rotated at least every 6 months. The containers should be emptied and cleaned thoroughly before you re-fill them.

SHORT HISTORY OF CARBONATED BEVERAGES

THE FIRST SODA POP IN THE UNITED STATES

In 1866 James Vernor invented Vernor's Ginger Ale, which was one of the most popular soft drinks of the 1800's. The extract to produce the ginger ale was aged for 4 years in an oak cask before it could be used. This aging process was continued until the 1980's. Ginger ale was the most popular soda until the 1920's. During prohibition dry ginger ale was introduced as a mixer and became very popular and ginger ale was associated with alcoholic beverages as a mixer, which reduced the sales, and popularity of the golden ginger ale produced by Vernor's. Vernor's is presently owned by 7 UP and the real Vernor's is very difficult to find and only sold through select distributors.

DO YOU HAVE THE MOXIE TO ORDER MOXIE?

The second oldest carbonated soft, drink, is called "Moxie." Moxie was introduced in the United States in 1884 by Dr. Augustus Thompson in Union, Maine. This drink was originally sold as a nerve tonic and is still available today on the East Coast. The soda is formulated using the root of the yellow gentian plant, which was thought to calm frazzled nerves. Moxie is still sold in orange cans with labels that resemble the original bottle. A Miss Moxie Pageant is held annually in Lisbon Falls, Maine. Presently, the Moxie headquarters is in Atlanta, Georgia within the Monarch Bottling Company. To order your Moxie call: (207) 353-8173.

THE THIRD SOFT DRINK

Dr. Pepper was manufactured in the United States in 1885 in Waco, Texas. A pharmacist Charles Alderton at Morrison's Old Corner Drug Store invented this new soda drink. The drink was kicked off at the 1904 World's Fair in St. Louis and was a big hit. Dr Pepper's dropped the dot after the "r" and its first slogan was "King of Beverages" in 1910. Diet Dr Pepper is presently the number one selling diet non-cola in the United States.

COKE CAME IN FOURTH

Dr. John Styth Pemberton in Atlanta, Georgia invented Coca-Cola in 1886. In 1891 Asa G. Candler purchased the control of the company for $2300. In 1915 the company patented the contour bottle. In 1919 the company was sold to Ernest Woodruff's investment group for $25 million. In 2001 more than 731 million servings of Coca-Cola products were consumed per day worldwide.

INGREDIENTS, 7 OUNCES, MUST BE 7 UP

The original name for 7 UP was "Bib-Label Lithiated Lemon-Lime Soda." The soda was invented in 1929 and may have contained seven ingredients and sold in 7 ounce bottles. The name was changed to 7 UP in 1936 since the word "Lithiated" was confusing the public. The inventor of 7 UP may have named the soda after a cattle brand or a popular card game of that era called "Sevens Up." The original formulation contained a small amount of lithium, a mineral now used to treat mental patients. The drink was popularized during the 1920's when it was sold to speakeasies as a drink mixer to compete with dry ginger ale.

During World War II the beverage became very popular since it could continue production at a high level due to the low level of sugar need to produce the drink. Other soda companies needed more sugar, which was being rationed reducing their production. In recent years due to the competition 7 UP has found a new method of extracting their flavorings providing their product with a new crisp taste to compete with other similar products.

KVASS

During the early 1900's many immigrants brought recipes with them for a number of unusual carbonated beverages. One of these beverages was "kvass" and originated in Russia. It is only slightly carbonated and does have very small alcohol level. The ingredients to produce kvass included black bread, sprigs of peppermint, boiling water, sugar, ale yeast, and sultanas (a member of the raisin family). Occasionally, rye bread is substituted for the black breads and used the kvass as stock for soups.

BROOKLYN ORIGINAL

One of the tastiest chocolate-flavored sodas ever produced was called the Egg Cream. Louis Auster who owned a candy store in Brooklyn, New York invented the Egg Cream in 1890. The beverage was extremely popular and the demand for the drink was so great he opened 5 stores to handle the business. In 1928 a large independent ice cream company made Mr. Auster an offer for his recipe that was too low and was refused. The company official then used a racial slur and Mr. Auster stated that he would take the recipe to his grave. All the members of his family were sworn to secrecy and no one has ever revealed the secret formula to this day.

There are a number of companies today that sell bottled egg cream soda and most are very good. If you are going to make an egg cream, use a 12 ounce water glass and fill it $3/4$ full of seltzer water, then add $1^1/2$ ounces of chocolate syrup (Fox's U-Bet), and 2 ounces of whole milk (not a low-fat milk).

THE HISTORY OF THE SODA FOUNTAIN

MINERAL WATER

Mineral water is produced by water percolating to the surface through layers of magnesium and calcium and other minerals. The water also passes through layers of carbon dioxide gas, which attaches to the minerals and is held in suspension.

The origination of the soda fountain really had its start in Europe, probably in the 1500's. Diseases were commonplace and the more affluent escaped to the countryside for cleaner air and a change of pace. They frequently went to spas where they drank water that was coming from natural underground sources and had a high mineral content and naturally carbonated in many instances.

The water made people feel better and seemed to improve their health and was eventually bottled and sold in the cities as mineral water. The carbonation seemed to neutralize acidic conditions and that really made the drink popular. The cost unfortunately was high, having to haul water great distances and a method was needed to carbonate local water.

THE ARTIFICIAL CARBONATION OF WATER

Dr. Joseph Priestley in Leeds, England produced the first glass of carbonated water that was drinkable, in 1767. In 1770, Swedish chemist Torbern Bergman improved on Dr. Priestley's work and invented an apparatus that produced carbonated water using chalk and sulfuric acid. He also dissolved a number of minerals, commonly found in popular mineral waters to make his product more closely related to the spa water. Since the spa water sources dried up at different times of the year, this was a significant development. Another plus was that the taste was always uniform.

As the years passed the method of producing the carbonated water improved and larger volumes of the water could be produced. In 1807 a patent was issued to Henry Thompson of Tottenham, England for impregnating water with carbon dioxide gas and minerals. The first United States patent for soda water was issued in 1810 to Simons and Rundell, of Charleston, South Carolina. Mass production of carbonated mineral water now was in full swing.

In 1832, however, the first carbonic acid gas and carbonating machine was built by John Mathew's known as the "Father of American Soda Water" and was granted a number of patents. He invented the method of liberating carbonic gas from marble dust and was able to produce 25 million gallons of soda water from the marble scraps left over from the construction of St. Patrick's Cathedral in New York City and from tombstone makers. Originally carbon dioxide was released from bicarbonate of soda, which is where the name "soda" is derived. The word "pop" was originated from the sound made when the corks were removed from soda bottles. A common word also used when referring to soda was "seltzer" which originated from the German spring, Brighton Seltzers. The bottles used to sell the spring water were called "seltzer bottles."

THE FIRST CARBONATED WATERING HOLE

In 1808 Professor Silliman, opened a business that sold carbonated mineral water in New Haven, Connecticut. In 1809 a pharmacy in Philadelphia started selling the water and in 1810 a similar business was opened in New York City. The word "fountain" and its relationship to carbonated mineral water originated when fountains of soda water were to be exhibited at city hall in New York City. Most establishments in the 1800's that served the soda water were men's clubs and pharmacies. Pharmacies were more like meeting places and the drink was served to the upper crust of society for the most part.

It wasn't until 1825 when a French immigrant named Elie' Magliore Durand opened a high-class pharmacy in Philadelphia that artificial mineral water was sold as a soda beverage. Since the beverage was regarded as a health-related drink other pharmacies soon copied Durand and started selling the mineral soda water. The water was sold as a cure for overweight people who were told to drink a glass 20-30 minutes after every meal to lose fat.

The area of the pharmacy where the water was sold was called a soda fountain after the New York soda "fountain" displayed at city hall in 1810. It was not a true soda fountain and the true soda fountain was not invented and used until 1863.

FLAVORFUL CHANGE IN SODA WATER

A perfume dealer in Philadelphia in 1838 named, Eugene Roussel who sold soda water in his shop decided to add lemon juice and sugar to the soda water. Lemonade was a very popular drink at the time and he thought that he could improve his sales with a new drink. He found that adding lemon juice and sugar did not work well because of the stirring needed to place the sugar in suspension he lost most of the carbonation.

He then prepared syrup made of lemon juice and water, then added the sugar to the syrup. The syrup dissolved more easily and he had invented the first flavored carbonated beverage. The popularity of the beverage was phenomenal and bottling plants sprung up in Philadelphia almost overnight. By 1843 a number of bottling plants opened in New York City. The only flavor that was available until 1850 was lemon soda. After 1850 the flavors came fast and furious with vanilla leading the way and strawberry, raspberry, and pineapple following close behind.

The only other close relative to soda water during this period, which had been around for a few hundred years, was sarsaparilla. Sarsaparilla was produced from beer that did not ferment well and sugar was added turning it into probably the closest relation to soda pop as far back as the 1500's. Both root beer and sarsaparilla are related to beer as their originator.

THE REAL SODA FOUNTAIN ARRIVES

The first soda water dispenser was invented in 1819 and looked like a beer keg with a curved spout. Next came an urn-shaped device that sat on a counter. In 1858 another urn-shaped device was invented that dispensed the soda water with the addition of syrup. The "real" soda fountain dispenser; was invented by G.D. Dows in 1858 which was part of a marble box with one arm to dispense the soda and eight syrup dispensers as well as a shaved ice unit to provide cold soda pop. He patented the "soda fountain" in 1863 and it became the industry standard for 50 years.

The person to really commercialize the soda fountain industry was James W. Tufts of Somerville, Massachusetts. He invented an easily produced a soda fountain unit that he patented in 1863 and established a factory in Boston. He patented a number of significant improvements to the fountain and dominated the industry producing and selling over 25,000 "Tufts Fountains" by 1893. In 1876 Tufts paid $50,000 for an exclusive to sell soda water at the Philadelphia Centennial Exposition with the most elaborate 30-foot high soda machine ever built.

One of the most popular drinks other than soda pop sold at the soda fountain was the ice cream soda, which was invented in 1874 by Robert M. Green. Mr. Green was selling sodas that required cream and when he ran out of cream he substituted ice cream and a number of customers could not wait for the ice cream to be melted and took their drink with the ice cream in a somewhat solid state. The customers were excited about the taste of the drink and Mr. Green increased his income from $6.00 per day to $600.00 per day selling ice cream sodas.

THE SODA FOUNTAIN MOVES FORWARD

Until 1902 soda fountains were all designed to be functional only against the back wall and supported by a refrigeration unit and workspaces. In 1903 a literal revolution occurred with the design of a new soda fountain sold by the American Soda Fountain Company. New syrup pumps were incorporated into the new unit that delivered measured amounts of syrups. The units were placed in a counter, which a person could stand in front of and dispense the products more easily. This forced owners of all the older units to upgrade as fast as the units could be produced and increased their business since they were now able to handle a larger volume of traffic.

Another great innovation occurred in 1908 when L. A. Becker invented an "iceless" soda fountain. This new type of refrigeration unit did not require ice to cool the soda water. Another giant move forward was in 1888 when Jacob Baur invented a method liquefying carbonic acid gas. This eliminated the production of gas on-site using sulfuric acid. All that was needed was to purchase a tank of carbon dioxide from the Liquid Carbonic Company.

Eventually, food was served at the soda fountains and many were then called luncheonettes. By the 1930's it was a common occurrence to go to a pharmacy or diner for a meal not just a soda.

THE SODA FOUNTAIN CALL, AN AMERICAN ORIGINAL

Taking an order for food was one thing, but having to write it down was considered a waste of time since the soda dispenser was too busy. The dispensers developed a code system that was easy to remember and funny, which made it even easier to remember the orders. These "calls," were a unique part of Americana history and unique to the United States.

The first recorded instance of a soda fountain call was in 1880 when Preacher Henry Ward Beecher ordered food from a soda fountain drink dispenser. The first order ever recorded was when Preacher Beecher ordered two medium eggs on a piece of toast. The dispenser promptly called out to the cook to make one *"Adam and Eve on a raft."* Finding this interesting he then changed his order to scrambled eggs and the dispenser called out to change the order and said, *"and wreck 'em."* Also, some customers would order a laxative and did not want the other patrons to hear what they were ordering so the dispenser would call out for a *"Mary Garden."*

The following is a list of the more common calls that were used at soda fountains from the 1880's through the 1930's:

THE CALLS	THE MEANING
"Bucket of mud"	Large scoop of chocolate ice cream
"Jerk a bridge"	Four Chocolate sodas
"Through Georgia"	Jerk was the term for an ice cream soda, Bridge was four, and through Georgia, told the dispenser to add chocolate syrup.
"Ninety-five"	Customer leaving and not paying their bill
"Fix the pumps"	Checkout the girl with the large breasts
"Dog and maggot"	Cracker and cheese
"Black and white"	Coffee and cream
"Filet one and mode, mode"	Fudge cake with 2 scoops of vanilla ice cream
"Filet one all the way"	Fudge cake with chocolate ice cream
"Lacy Cup"	Hot Chocolate
"Eighty one"	Glass of water
"Eighty two"	Two glasses of water
"Shoot One"	A small glass of Coca Cola
"Shoot a left"	Glass of coke with lemon
"Burn a crowd of van"	Three vanilla milk shakes A malted milk was referred to as a burn, which would be chocolate, a crowd is three, and van refers to vanilla. If the call was just "Burn a crowd" it would mean three chocolate milk shakes.
"Shoot one through Georgia"	Coca Cola with chocolate syrup
"Shoot one and stretch it"	Large glass of Coca Cola
"Mug of murk"	Black coffee
"Hail a crowd in the air"	3 large glasses of ice
"Bucket of hail in the air"	Large glass of ice
"Draw some mud"	Coffee with cream
"Sinkers and suds"	Doughnuts and coffee
"Eye opener"	Castor oil in sarsaparilla
"Two cents plain"	Carbonated water
"Black cow"	Chocolate milk
"Oh gee"	Orangeade
"Squeeze one"	Orange juice
"Patch"	Strawberry ice cream
"Burn it and let it swim"	Chocolate ice cream float
"Fish eggs"	Order of tapioca pudding
"Nervous pudding"	Jell-O
"One all the way"	Chocolate soda with chocolate ice cream
"Tune in one"	Tuna sandwich
"Chewed fine with a breath"	Hamburger with onion
"Ground hog"	Hot dog on a bun

"Bellywash" . . . . .Soup
"Cackle berries" . . . . .Eggs
"Hen fruit" . . . . .Eggs
"Whistle berries" . . . . .Beans
"Hounds on an island" . . . . .Hot dogs and beans
"Fly cake" . . . . .Raisin cake
"Red paint" . . . . .Ketchup
"Rabbit food" . . . . .Lettuce
"Skid grease" . . . . .Butter
"Sand" . . . . .Sugar
"Dog biscuit" . . . . .Cracker
"Dough well done, cow to cover" . .Toast with butter
"Creame de goo" . . . . .Milk toast
"Graveyard stew" . . . . .Milk toast
"Cackle berries on slice of squeel" . .Ham and eggs
"Sea dust" . . . . .Salt
"Wart" . . . . .Olive
"Looseners" . . . . .Prunes
"Shake one in the hay" . . . . .Strawberry milk shake
"Black stick" . . . . .Chocolate ice cream cone
"Houseboat" . . . . .Banana split
"Bovine extract" . . . . .Malted milk
"Bird seed" . . . . .Grape Nuts cereal
"Bossy in a bowl" . . . . .Beef stew
"Twelve alive in a shell" . . . .One dozen oysters
"Choker holes" . . . . .Doughnuts
   "Twins" . . . . .Salt and pepper shakers
   "14" . . . . .Special order
   "Gravel train" . . . . .Sugar bowl
   "Lumber" . . . . .Toothpick
   "Salt water man" . . . . .The ice cream mixer
   "Souvenir" . . . . .Stale egg
   "86" . . . . .Don't have the item
"Echo" . . . . .Repeat the order
"Pittsburgh" . . . . .Toast is burning
"Saturday night special" . . . .Easily dated girl
"Pest" . . . . .Assistant manager
"George Eddy" . . . . .A non-tipper
"13" . . . . .One of the big bosses around
"Let it walk" . . . . .Take out order
"Spike it" . . . . .Add lemon flavor
"Break it and shake it" . . . . .Add eggs to a drink
"Slab of" . . . . .A piece of the item
"Load of" . . . . .A plate of the item

BY THE NUMBERS	THE CALL
One	Just one
Two	A pair
Three	A crowd
Four	A bridge (bridge players)
Five	A handful
Six	A handful plus one
Seven	A handful plus a pair
Eight	A handful plus a crowd
Nine	A handful plus a bridge
Ten	A real handful

THE DEMISE OF THE SODA FOUNTAIN

Soda fountains managed to hold on until the late 1950's, however, there were too many factors that hastened their demise into the history of Americana. The soda fountain and luncheonette provided the public with somewhere they could go for lunch and get a relatively fast meal before heading back to work. With the coming of fast food restaurants, Coca-Cola manufactured a soda machine that could be placed in any restaurant or theatre. Home refrigeration units and the loss of teen patronage created another problem. The teens were now going home to watch TV or hang out at the mall, making it inevitable that the soda fountain would suffer and thus the end of an era came swiftly.

Also, cars were becoming more readily available and the public was not providing foot traffic, which the drug stores depended upon and to top it all off, the super-markets started carrying soda and ice cream.

CARBONATED BEVERAGES IN 2002

Carbonated beverages in 2001 accounted for more than 35% of all beverages con-sumed in the United States. Sales are expected to increase to about 39% in 2003. The majority of these drinks were soft drinks with sales over $59 billion and 16.4 billion gallons. Coca-Cola is one of the largest sugar purchasers in the world. Almost 21% of all 2-year-old children drink soft drinks on a regular basis. Baby bottles are now being sold with soft drink labels and some in the shape of the actu-al bottles.

Both adults and adolescents are encouraged to drink more soft drinks by offering the larger size drinks at an excellent discount. Carbonated beverages are the num-ber one source of sugar in the American diet providing about 7-8 teaspoons per day. Soft drinks are presently providing about 6% of the total adult caloric intake. In teens soft drinks provide about 9% of their calories every day. Dr. Pepper has increased their sales by almost 60% over the last 5 years.

Presently, the natural soda market is coming on strong. Some of the major brands are New York Seltzer and Clearly Canadian.

THE TOP TEN SODAS IN THE UNITED STATES

1. Coca Cola
2. Pepsi Cola
3. Snapple
4. 7 up
5. Dr. Pepper
6. Jolt Cola
7. Surge
8. Shasta
9. Jones Soda
10. A & W Root Beer

ADVERTISING BUDGETS OF SOFT DRINK COMPANIES

1. Coca Cola ....$ 84.7 million
2. Pepsi Cola ......$ 110.5 million
3. Diet Coke ....$ 21.8 million
4. Dr. Pepper ....$ 37.7 million
5. Mountain Dew ....$ 29.8 million
6. Sprite ....$ 51.7 million
7. 7 UP ....$ 15.2 million

CAFFEINE CONTENT OF SOFT DRINKS (12 OUNCE SERVINGS)

1. Jolt ....71.5 milligrams
2. Sugar-Free Mr. Pibb ......58.8 milligrams
3. Pepsi One ....55.5 milligrams
4. Mountain Dew (reg. & diet) .55.0 milligrams
5. Kick Citrus ....54.0 milligrams
6. Mellow Yellow ....52.8 milligrams
7. Surge ....51.0 milligrams
8. Tab ....46.8 milligrams
9. Coca Cola (reg. & diet) .....45.6 milligrams
10. Shasta Cola (reg. & diet) ...44.4 milligrams
11. Mr. Pibb ....40.8 milligrams
12. Sunkist Orange ....40.0 milligrams
13. Dr. Pepper ....39.6 milligrams
14. Storm ....38.0 milligrams
15. Pepsi Cola ....37.2 milligrams
16. Aspen ....36.0 milligrams
17. RC Cola ....36.0 milligrams
18. Barq's Root Beer ....23.0 milligrams
19. Diet Rite Cola ....0.0 milligrams
20. 7 UP ....0.0 milligrams

As a comparison, the average cup of coffee contains 120 milligrams and the average cup of tea 50 milligrams of caffeine.

CALIFORNIANS, HEAVY DRINKERS

More than 12 billion soft drinks are consumed by Californians every year. The good news is that 9 billion containers made of aluminum, plastic, and glass is recycled in California annually.

ATHLETES AND CARBONATED BEVERAGES

Studies are underway to determine if carbonated soft drinks will impair an athlete's physical ability. The premise is that the CO_2 may overload the body and interfere with CO2 utilization. To date there is insufficient evidence to support this claim but who knows what the future will show.

HOW TO PRODUCE THE WORLD'S BIGGEST BELCH

A new soda pop has been released that is supposed to appeal to consumers between the ages of 5-17. The drink is double-carbonated and is called Belcher's soda. However, the drink is finding its way into adult bars where "burp" contests are now being scheduled. The Belcher Company has two soda pop drinks in distribution and is called Belcher's Gastro Grape and Loogie Lime.

ARTIFICIAL SWEETENERS MAY CAUSE BITTERNESS

If you purchase a soft drink that uses Nutrasweet as the artificial sweetener, the drink should be consumed within a 3-month period. After 3 months the sweetener may start to break down and impart a bitter taste to the soda.

COCA-COLA BOTTLE TO BE SMALLER

Coca-Cola may be marketing a new size resealable bottle in 2002. The bottle would be the height of a can and is being marketed to people with an active lifestyle that want to bring the small size with them in a pocket or pouch when they workout. The bottle will be recyclable.

WE ARE SETTING A WORLD RECORD

In 2001 Americans set an all time record for soft drink consumption. We averaged 542 sodas per person. That amounts to a 243% increase over 1958. This equates to about 51 gallons per year.

SOME USELESS FACTS

The National Beverage Corporation has stated that their annual usage of labels if placed on a roll would extend the combined length of the Nile, Mississippi and Amazon rivers…twice. They manufacture enough cans to circle the earth 5 times and if one years total number of bottle caps were placed on top of each other they would reach the height of Mt. Everest 740 times.

"DO THE DEW"

Mountain Dew originated in 1940 and was marketed as a lemon-lime soda to be used as a bar mixer. Since the name was related to hillbilly slang for moonshine, the soda was called the "zero proof hillbilly moonshine." In the late 1950's Mountain Dew was altered from the original lemon-lime formulation, re-formulated and in 1964 the rights were sold to Pepsi making it their second best selling soda.

The new slogan for Mountain Dew "Do The Dew" along with 30 vehicles have hit the road in 1998 in an advertising blitz centered around the skateboarders, snow-boarders, roller-bladers, and sky-surfers.

NEW SWEETENER

Diet RC Cola was the first carbonated-beverage to use a new FDA-approved, no-calorie sweetener, Sucralose.

PEPSI-COLA HITS THE SPOT, DIRT THAT IS

If you add one bottle of Pepsi to a load of really dirty clothes along with your detergent will really clean a load of greasy clothes.

GRANNY SMITH SODA

There is a new soda that will appear soon flavored like Granny Smith apples. It is an all-natural soda with no preservatives, no sodium, and natural flavor. The Elder Beverage Company of Bloomington, Minnesota is producing the soda.

WANT TO DRINK A SHRUB?

This is a sweet, drink that is made from fruit juice, sugar, apple cider vinegar and carbonated water. The early colonists drank the shrub to keep them cool when the weather became hot.

ESPRESSO SODA, WHAT'S NEXT?

A new carbonated beverage was recently released containing a very strong coffee flavor called Rageous Cool Bean Espresso Soda. The taste is similar to a double or triple espresso with a fairly pleasant honey flavor. It is a coffee lovers dream soda.

THE BEST ROOT BEER

At a recent food show Virgil's Root Beer beat out all contenders for the title of the best root beer. The root beer contains all natural ingredients and is slow brewed to bring out the flavor. The product is pasteurized to give it excellent shelf life and uses no preservatives. The sweetener is derived from pure unbleached cane sugar.

THE FOLLOWING IS A LIST OF THE INGREDIENTS AND COUNTRY OF ORIGIN OF THAT INGREDIENT:

Ingredient	Country
Anise	Spain
Licorice	France
Vanilla(Bourbon)	Madagascar
Cinnamon	Ceylon
Clove	Indonesia
Wintergreen	China
Sweetbirch	United States
Molasses	United States
Nutmeg	Indonesia
Pimento Berry Oil	Jamaica
Balsam Oil	Peru
Cassia Oil	China

The original root beer made in the United States by the colonists in the 1600's included sassafras root, water, sugar, and a small amount of ale or bread yeast placed in warm water. However, in recent years studies have shown that laboratory rats would develop cancer from consuming "safrole" which is the active ingredient in sassafras. The FDA has now banned sassafras from being sold other than as a raw food product by health food stores and use for tea.

ROOT BEER WITH CAFFEINE

Barq's Root Beer contains caffeine, about 13mg. per 6 ounces and must add a flavoring agent to counteract the bitterness of the caffeine.

THE TOP OF THE SODA POP HEAP

This is one of the highest quality soft drinks produced in the United States and is manufactured by the Yacht Club Bottling Works in Providence, Rhode Island. The company was founded in 1915 by Harry Sharp who was so fussy about the water that was to be used he drilled his own well into an artesian well 170 deep. The water used has been tested and tied with Perrier as one of the best sparkling waters in the world. The purity of the water has remained since the original well was drilled. The soda only uses pure cane sugar and will only sell the product in glass bottles. Their carbonation process utilizes dry ice, which they feel gives the soda its excellent flavor. Their Golden Ginger Ale is different from the ginger ales sold in supermarkets, which are produced and used as mixers. It has a darker color, more sweetness, and a more pronounce ginger flavor. Their White Birch Beer is similar in flavor to root beer but is clear.

WHAT'S IN A NAME?

New sodas are arriving daily and it is almost impossible to keep track of them. The following are a few of the new names reaching the market.

Keg Orange	Thai Lemongrass	Vermont Maple Ale
Peruvian Passion Flower	Honey Lemon Soda	Hazelnut Flavor
Twisted Bean Vanilla Bean	Raven	Lemon Beer
Siberian Sun Ginseng Brew	Venetian Creame	Brainwash Blue
Black Lemonade	Brainalizer	Wizard
The Drink	Dusk Til Dawn	Nestle Cosmo
Mega Melon	Hypnotonic	Mental Trick

TONIC WATER

A carbonated beverage that is usually flavored with fruit extracts, sugar, and quinine, which is a bitter alkaloid. Normally, sold and used as an alcoholic mixer.

THE GREAT BRAZILIAN SODA POP

One of the most popular sodas in South America is Guarana flavored and sold under a number of different names. The flavoring is difficult to explain but the flavor is very appealing. Guarana is also known as Brazilian Cocoa and the soda made from Guarana is produced and sold by the Crystal Beverage Corporation in the United States. Their product is called Guarana Brasilia and is excellent tasting soda.

Guarana is actually a seed of the plant Paullinia cupana that is high in caffeine (guaranine). The seed contains almost three times as much caffeine as a coffee bean. The soda contains about 55 milligrams of caffeine. The plant grows in the Amazon rain forest and has been a staple of the Indians living in that region for over 500 years. The vines of the plant may reach to 60 feet when climbing up a tree and the berries that the seeds are removed from may be found at the highest elevation.

- Guarana also has the reputation of being one of the world's most effective aphrodisiacs.

CARBONATION LASTS LONGER IN COLD SOFT DRINKS

The two most popular acids that are used to produce the carbonation in soft drinks are "citric acid" and "phosphoric acid." The carbon dioxide that is formed expands more in warmer beverages, the gas expands, and more of the gas escapes reducing the level of carbonation.

JUST THE FACTS

In a 24-hour period Coca-Cola is consumed 198 million times in 36 countries. Four caffeinated sodas will supply a child with the caffeine equivalent of 2 cups of regular coffee. When children are asked which beverage they prefer, they will say a soft drink over milk 75% of the time.

THE NEW ICE CRYSTAL BEVERAGE

A number of companies are now producing a beverage cup with a walled separation that contains a liquid that will easily freeze. The cups are to be stored in the freezer so that they will be ready to use and are perfectly safe. However, when you place the liquid in the cups, ice crystals tend to form and affects flavor and aroma of the beverage. A standard cup kept in the freezer will not produce the same effect on the beverage.

GREAT PUNCH TIPS:

- On a mild temperature day, a guest will drink about 2-3 cups of punch.
- One gallon of punch will make about 32 servings.
- Prepare a number of batches of punch and store in one-gallon containers.
- Use a block of ice not ice cubes. If possible freeze some of the punch in a $^3/_4$ gallon milk container to use in the punch bowl.
- Sweetness should be adjusted with sugar syrup, which is more easily absorbed.
- If possible chill the punch bowl.
- Never float too many pieces of fruit in the punch. This makes it hard to scoop out the punch and most people don't like it.
- Always add Champagne or any other carbonated beverage lasts since the carbonation will only last effectively for about 30 minutes at the most.
- Never place a hot punch in a glass bowl, always use metal.
- Prepare any mixed liquors or flavorings before hand and store.

I NEED SOME LIVENING UP

If your punch is too bland, try adding one of the following three seasonings: nut-meg, cardamom, or rosemary. Just dissolve 1 teaspoon of any one of these herbs to ½ cup of any hot fruit juice, then allow it to cool to room temperature before adding it to the punch.

NON-CARBONATED BEVERAGES

Since there is a segment of the population that would prefer a soft drink that is non-carbonated, a number of companies are capitalizing on this trend. The leader in this area is Snapple with Coca-Cola's Frutopia and Pepsi's Lipton Tea trying to play catch up. Snapple, however, is the market leader in this area by leaps and bounds. In November of 1994, the Quaker Oats Corporation purchased Snapple for a cool $1.7 billion. The original name of the company was the Unadulterated Food Products Company and was started by Arnold Greenberg, Leonard Marsh, and Hyman Golden on the Lower East Side, New York City in 1972.

FRUTOPIA

This soft drink was introduced to the public in March 1994 and was manufactured by the Coca-Cola Company to compete with Snapple's $6 billion market in non-carbonated beverages. The beverage is composed mainly of corn syrup and 5% fruit juice and not that exciting a drink. Coca-Cola improved the drink and introduced two "lighter-tasting" fruit flavors in November of 1994.

The bottles contain 20 fluid ounces and 225 calories. It is mainly a fruit-flavored sugar water drink with preservatives and artificial coloring. The only redeeming quality is that it contains 100% of your vitamin C minimum daily requirement in each serving. The taste leaves a lot to be desired and some flavors left an aftertaste. Could not be classified as a very nutritious or satisfying drink. Frutopia contains 8 times the sodium content of Snapple.

SNAPPLE

Snapple combines 5% natural juices with water and sugar, making it mostly a sugar-water drink. It is a satisfying drink that uses no preservatives and all-natural flavor extracts. It is a low sodium drink but does not contain any vitamin content of any significance.

PEPSI LIPTON TEA

Lipton tea is a water and sugar drink that contains a small amount of instant tea. It also contains both citric acid and phosphoric acid and 5 times the sodium as Snapple. It does not contain any fruit juice or vitamins of any consequence. It does, however, contain FD and C Red 40, which the National Cancer Institute reported that p-cre-dine, a chemical used in the preparation of Red 40 was carcinogenic in animals.

KOOL-AID

Edwin Perkins of Hendley, Nebraska invented Kool-Aid in 1920. The original product was a soft drink syrup called "Fruit Smack" and was sold in 4 ounce glass bottles. The original flavors were grape, orange, cherry, root beer, and raspberry. The syrup was in heavy glass bottles and Perkins started to sell the flavorings dehydrated in small packets. This made shipping less costly and resulted in a lower price for the product. In 1927 the name Kool-Aid originated and 1928 changed the name to Kool-Aid. The product was a big hit and Perkins gave up all other products and concentrated on selling the concentrated powdered flavoring.

Kool-Aid sold for 5 cents in 1933, a price which remained stable for 30 years. In 1953 Perkins sold the company to General Foods, which merged with Kraft Foods in 1988. Additional Kool-Aid products that are presently available are Kool-Aid Slushies, Kool-Aid Pops, Kool-Aid Bursts, and Kool-Aid Splash. The annual consumption of Kool-Aid is about 565 million gallons.

Today's Kool-Aid is a powdered flavoring to be added to water and sweetened with either sugar or an artificial sweetener. It contains preservatives and dyes such as Red 40. The vitamin C content is only 10% of the minimum daily requirement. The sodium content is low.

BUBBLY KOOL-AID

If you want to have a different type of Kool-Aid, just use club soda instead of water. Different and doesn't add calories.

O'SIPPIE

Excellent tasting, all-natural drink that has been pasteurized for a longer shelf life. It does not use Yellow food dye numbers 5 or 6, Red number 40 or Blue number 1. It is caffeine-free and uses the purest water available making the product sodium-free and is sold in four flavors; root beer, orange, black cherry and vanilla cream. For information call (888) 99-SIPME.

LEMONADE & LIMEADE

Lemonade and limeade prepared from a concentrate is a high calorie drink that contains a high degree of sweeteners to counteract the sour nature of the lemons. It is only a good source of vitamin C since the average glass only provides about 15% of the RDA unless the product has been fortified. Drinking too much could cause a tooth problem leading to sensitive teeth and even enamel corrosion. Lemonade and limeade prepared from a powdered mix also has a high sugar content and will end up to have less than 5% actual juice.

THE OLD FASHIONED WAY

To prepare the "real" lemonade or limeade, just squeeze the juice from enough lemons or limes to make 1/3 cup (no pits, please). Add 1 cup of water and 5 teaspoons of sugar or a sugar substitute. Mix together and pour over ice.

FLAVORED DRINKS

These drinks are usually sold in cans and may be called any one of a hundred different names, the most popular of which is "Orange Drink." These drinks are usually a diluted and sweetened form of the original juice and contain only a small amount of the healthy real fruit. A number of orange drinks may also contain a percentage of the orange peel, which has been known to cause allergic reactions in susceptible individuals.

DRINKS DESIGNED FOR CHILDREN

KIDZ WATER™

This new water is flavored and contains 1mg. of fluoride per liter of water. The drink is designed to appeal to children so that they will drink more water and get the fluoride to reduce the incidence of tooth decay.

TROPICANA BURSTERS

Tropicana has produced juice drinks that are bottled to appeal to children and contain all-natural ingredients. They are 100% juice and are a great soft drink alternative. They are packaged in convenient six-packs of 8 ounce bottles and reasonably priced. Most of the other juice drinks for children may only have 5% real juice. Chilled multi-pack children's drinks have grown in sales by over 139% since they were introduced in the mid-1990s.

COLORED SUGAR WATER

General Mills has a new drink for kids called "Sqeezeit®." It is advertised as a "fruit drink" and contains only 1% fruit juice.

RIP IT, SIP IT, AND SLURP IT

The Children's Beverage Group, Inc. is patenting a new type of opening beverage package for children. It is a self-contained fluid dispensing system called the "rip it sip it™" system. Wal-Mart will be one of the first companies selling the new packaging beverages.

NUTRITIONAL CONCERNS REGARDING SOFT DRINKS

There are two main carbonating agents used in soft drinks, phosphoric acid and carbonic acid. There have not been too many studies showing that there is any significant risk factors in the use of carbonic acid other than an article in the Pennsylvania Medical Journal a few years ago relating an increase in near-sightedness to overuse of the carbonating agent. Other studies may show that it is also related to reducing the effectiveness of certain vitamins depending on the number of sodas consumed per day.

However, the medical community is becoming more concerned about the carbonating agent, phosphoric acid. It would be best if you read the label of your favorite soft drink and at least be aware that consuming too many drinks that have phosphoric acid may upset the phosphorus/calcium ratio in your system. The concern is that if the ratio is upset it will result in a calcium deficiency, which is especially significant in middle-age women who may be at risk of osteoporosis. Kidney stone problems may also be related to excess intake of phosphorus.

The average American has a dietary phosphorus intake of about 1500-1600mg. per day. The recommended daily allowance of this mineral is 800mg per day. Soft drinks are a large contributor of this excess.

SOFT DRINK	MG. OF PHOSPHORUS PER OUNCE
Coca Cola	.69.9
Pepsi Cola	.57.2
Diet Cherry Coke	.55.7
Diet Pepsi	.49.3
Dr Pepper	.44.7
Tab	.44.4
Kool Aid (lemon flavored)	.31.6
Hires Root Beer	.22.4
Hawaiian Punch (lemonade flavor)	.16.7
7 UP	.3.0
Canada Dry Ginger Ale	.3.0
A & W Root Beer	.3.0

COLA DRINK FACTS

- In some states the police carry two gallons of cola in their cars to remove blood from the highways
- Cola will dissolve a T-bone steak in 2 days
- Cola is great for cleaning toilets and battery terminals and even for removing rust from car bumpers
- Cola will loosen a rusted bolt if allowed to remain for 10 minutes
- The active ingredient in most colas is phosphoric acid, which will dissolve a nail in about 4 days
- When transporting cola syrup (the concentrate), commercial trucks must use the Hazardous materials placard reserved for "highly corrosive materials."
- Cola is used to clean truck engines

EXTRACTS

Extracts are a relatively inexpensive method of making your own soft drinks at home. They have an excellent flavor and the cost is about 60% less than the super-market brands. The homemade sodas will also contain less sugar and the use of yeast will add a number of B vitamins. The formula is simple and all you have to do is add the extract, water, sugar, and yeast following the recipe to the letter.

The mixture is then placed into bottles and two days later; you have a carbonated soft drink. Hires Root beer extract is one of the oldest selling extracts in the United States and was one of the most popular for many years. Check the Yellow Pages for a home-brew supply house or just purchase the extract at the supermarket or health food store.

HOW ABOUT A SCUPPERNONG MUSCADINE COCKTAIL?

When the Pilgrims landed, one of their favorite foods was the muscadine berry, which were growing wild. It has a great-tasting tangy berry flavor and is made into juice, jams, syrup, and jellies in the Southern United States. The berries come in two varieties, the white or "scuppernong" and the red muscadines. Muscadine juice is the first new juice introduced to supermarkets since the 1930's. No sugar, coloring agents, or water is added to the juice and it is not bottled as a concentrate. It has a little punch to it and frequently replaces apple cider. To order the juice if it not available in your area just call: (800) 233-1736.

DURING WORLD WAR II COKE ALMOST WENT BATTY

In 1942 caffeine was becoming scarce due to the war and reduction of imports from foreign countries. The Coca Cola Company was considering the idea of extracting caffeine from bat guano (bat feces), however, they decided against it since they were afraid that if the public ever found out that Coke had bat excre-ments in it, Pepsi would have won the cola wars, hands down!

IS YOUR CALCIUM GOING DOWN THE TOILET?

Physicians are getting more and more concerned about the number of soft drinks women consume. Their concern stems from the fact that most of the more popular soft drinks contain "phosphoric acid" as the carbonating agent. Excessive amounts of phos-phorus can upset the calcium/phosphorus ratio in the body and may allow excess cal-cium to be excreted in the urine. Women who are near or who are going through menopause are especially at risk since osteoporosis is a major concern to this group.

Normally, we consume about 1500 mg. of phosphorus daily from the foods we eat. The normal daily, recommended allowance is 800 mg. The following soft drinks may contribute large amounts of phosphorus per ounce of the beverage; Coke 70 mg., Pepsi 57 mg., Dr. Pepper 45 mg., Hires Root Beer 32 mg. One 12-ounce Coke can provide 840 mg. of phosphorus.

A FEW HARD, SOFT DRINK FACTS

In a 24-hour period Coke is consumed 193 million times in 35 countries. Soft drinks, account for 25% of all sugar consumed in the United States. If a child drinks 4 colas per day they are taking in the equivalent caffeine in 2 cups of regular coffee. Soft drinks according to statistics are now the beverage of choice over milk with 3 times the dollars spent on soft drinks. This amounted to 56 gallons of soft drinks per person consumed in 2001.

DOES BLOWING ON HOT SOUP REALLY COOL IT?

Laboratory testing has shown that if a spoonful of very hot soup is held at room temperature for 45 seconds before it is consumed it will cool down to an acceptable temperature, one that will not burn the mouth. If the same spoonful is blown on to speed-up the cooling it will cool to the same acceptable temperature in 20 seconds. The fast moving air when blowing on the hot soup will carry heat away from the soup more efficiently by forcing evaporation from the surface.

WHO PUT THE POP IN SODA POP?

In 1822 a man by the name of Townsend Speakman living in Philadelphia developed the method of adding carbonation artificially to a beverage. He was asked to invent the process by none other than the father of surgery Dr. Philip Syng Physick who wanted to give such a beverage to his patients. The doctor charged his patients $1.50 per month for one drink a day. In 1878, the plain beverage was flavored and sold as soda water with a Hutchinson Bottle Stopper made from wire and rubber that would seal the carbonation into the bottle. When the stopper was moved to one side in order to drink the beverage, the gas escaped and caused the "pop" sound, thus the nickname "soda pop" was born.

FORMULA FOR LIMEADE

Squeeze out 1/3 cup of fresh lime, juice into 1 cup of water and add 5 teaspoons of sugar or equivalent of artificial sweetener.

HOW LONG WILL ORANGE JUICE CONCENTRATE LAST?

Orange juice has a higher acid content and therefore will last about a week after it is reconstituted. The nutritional value, especially of the vitamin C, however, will decrease rapidly and it would be wise to consume the juice in the first 3-4 days. Water contains oxygen, which is the enemy of vitamin C; that along with the airation of the mixing process adds a large amount of oxygen to the juice.

RAINBOW-COLORED BEVERAGES?

In case you haven't noticed children's foods are changing colors. Beverages are now all different colors with the most popular being blue. Kids will purchase blue drinks over any color and manufacturers are now going to make blue candy, cookies, ice cream, and even some foods. Studies performed at the University of Massachusetts showed that children "are open to the novelty of unnaturally tinted products." It was also discovered that color has an impact on how a food tastes to people. Kool-Aid now markets a green powder called Great Bluedini Punch that changes to blue when you add water.

HOW DID GATORADE ORIGINATE?

Gatorade originated in 1967 when researchers at the University of Florida decided that their football team, the Gators, needed to replace the minerals and fluids lost through strenuous exercise. In 1983 Quaker Oats purchased the brand name and sold the drink in different flavors. The drink was developed to provide water, sugar (energy), salt (fluid balance), and potassium (nerve transmission). At present: Gatorade has about 85% of the sports drink market of over $800 million dollars a year.

AVOID THE NEW BEVERAGE MUGS WITH A FREEZABLE LINING

A number of companies are producing a beverage mug with a walled separation that contains a liquid that will freeze. The mugs are to be kept in the freezer and used for any type of beverage. They are safe to use, however, when a beverage is placed in them, ice crystals are formed in the beverage reducing the palatability of the beverage. Even alcoholic beverages such as beer will develop ice crystals and reduce the flavor and aroma significantly. Soda will become crunchy and not very pleasant to drink. The mugs are fine if you are going to allow a beverage to sit for some time before you drink it. Standard mugs kept in the freezer do not produce the same problem.

THE FORMULA FOR COCOA

Just mix $2^1/_2$ tablespoons of unsweetened cocoa with 3 tablespoons of sugar and a dash of salt with $^1/_2$ cup of water, heat the mixture slowly until it is thick and starts to bubble then add 2 cups of low-fat milk and stir for a few minutes.

NUMBERS TO REMEMBER

Safe Water, Drinking Hot Line . . . .800) 426-4791. Ask for a free booklet.
Environmental Working Group . . .(202)667-6982
Natural Defense Council . . . .(212)727-2700
Greenpeace International . . . . . .202) 462-1177.

CHAPTER 8

A SPOT OF TEA

HISTORY OF TEA

Tea was probably first consumed in China around 2737 BC when the Chinese Emperor Shen Nung was boiling his drinking water and some leaves from the Camellia Sinensis plant accidentally dropped into his pot. The tealeaf was then commonly used to flavor water, which had a somewhat off taste after being boiled to purify it. The Emperor felt that the new beverage gave him added energy and called the new beverage the "vigor of the body."

Tea was introduced to Japan by the Chinese and was immediately hailed as a beverage of choice. Presently, the Island of Ceylon is the world's leading grower of quality tea. The tea is still picked by hand and an experienced picker is capable of picking 35-40 pounds of tealeaves per day.

The most popular tea in the United States is black tea with imports reaching about 168 million pounds in 2001. The annual consumption in the United States is now over 47.4 billion servings annually with the majority of the tea being imported from India. Tea is second only to water as the most popular beverage worldwide.

In 1904 iced tea was first sold at the Louisiana Purchase Exposition held in St. Louis, Missouri.

The average pound of tea will brew 200-250 cups. Brewed tea contains approximately half the quantity of caffeine as instant coffee. Tea has diuretic effects and should not be relied upon for providing your daily intake of water.

MAJOR VARIETIES OF TEAS

GREEN TEA

Green tea is mainly produced in China, Japan, India and Taiwan. Green is the natural color of green tea since oxidation does not affect the chlorophyll content of the tealeaf and the tea is not fermented. The manufacturing process has only three stages; first, the tealeaf is steamed to inactivate the enzymes and prevent fermentation and oxidation. Second, the leaves are rolled and dried over and over until they are crisp. This releases the juices, which are then held by the leaf. Third, repeated controlled firings then produces a stable, well-hardened tea that has retained its flavor and essential elements. The final product contains only 3% residual moisture, therefore is not capable of any further changes.

Chinese green teas are graded by age and style, with the finest being Gunpowder. Gunpowder is produced from tiny balls that are made from very young or at least medium-aged leaves. The next best is called, Young Hyson and finally, Imperial. The quality of Japanese green tea is graded as follows: Extra Choicest, Choicest, Choice, Finest, Fine, Good Medium, Good Common, Nibs, Fanning and Dust. Indian green tea is graded: Fine Young Hyson, Young Hyson, Hyson No. 1, Twankay, Sowmee, Fanning and Dust. The Encyclopedia of Chinese Teas lists 138 different varieties of green teas and 12,500 sub groups. However, only about 500 varieties are really recognized.

The following are some of the more common varieties of Chinese green teas:

Pouchong Used frequently to prepare jasmine tea. The leaves are oxidized to a greater extent than most green tea, leaves, which allow the leaf to retain the flavor of jasmine better. The jasmine flower has been imported from Persia for 1,000 years to flavor the tea.

Ching Cha This variety is grown in Mainland China and include some of the more famous and best tasting green teas such as Pi Lo Chun and Tai Ping Hou Gui.

Chunmee Grown in Yunnan province and has a somewhat plum flavor. Care needs to be taken so as not to over-brew, which is easily done.

Dragonwell This one of the favorite teas of Mainland China. It has a sweet, fresh taste and there are eight grades of Dragonwell with the highest grade called Qing Ming.

Emerald Tips A Dragonwell type of tea that is grown in an area, which borders the Dragonwell growing area. The quality is not as good; however, it is still a good quality tea.

Gunpowder First tea ever exported from China to Europe and is the most popular Chinese tea in Europe. If the tea, "pellets" are fresh, they will resist pressure and not easily crush.

The following are some of the more common varieties of Indian green teas:

Assam	The most plentiful tea in India accounting for $^1/_3$ of all tea produced. The tea is grown to produce a strong aroma and flavor and only a small quantity is grown for green tea.
Darjeeling	This tea is grown on the southern slopes of the Himalayan Mountains near Nepal. This variety has been called the champagne of teas and the finest grown in India. However, very little of the tea is produced as green tea. If you are lucky enough to find "single-estate" Darjeeling green tea you will enjoy an unusual cup of tea.

The following are some of the more common varieties of Japanese green teas:

Bancha	The most common tea sold in Japan. The green Bancha is actually somewhat bitter and not one of the better green teas.
Fukuiju	A higher quality green tea with a pleasant aftertaste.
Gyokuro	The highest quality green tea produced in Japan and is very fragrant and flavorful. It is sometimes mixed with lower grade teas to enhance their flavor and aroma.
Spiderleg	Another of the high quality green teas that has an excellent aroma and flavor. Occasionally found with a cherry aroma.

BLACK TEA

During the processing of tealeaves, the insides are exposed to oxygen, which causes oxidation and the darkening of the resulting tea. The actual steps involved are; withering, rolling, roll breaking, fermentation and finally firing. The withering process involves spreading the leaves on long tables and allowed them to remain for 18-24 hours. In India the climate is so dry that the leaves will actually wither on the vine. Natural withering is preferred because the leaf is never overheated. The leaf is now rolled which breaks up the plant's cells to release the juices and enzymes, which produce the flavor of the tea. When this is done the leaves will become somewhat twisted.

However, when the leaves are rolled they may become twisted and balled up too much and need to go through a roll-breaking process of vibrating the leaves. Fermentation is then introduced to the crushed leaves and the flavor process is completed. The final stage is the firing, which stops the fermentation process and further oxidation by totally destroying the enzymes and bacteria, which are responsible for fermentation.

The most common tea sold in the United States is black tea. Black teas are sometimes called red teas since their color is more reddish than black. The Chinese rarely drink black teas. Green teas are their choice with oolong coming in second. There are over 40 varieties of black teas with the best coming from Sri Lanka, China and India.

OOLONG TEA

This type of tea is only partially fermented and is a blend of black and green teas. It has a greenish-brown color and is usually grown in Taiwan and sold as Formosa oolong tea. One variety of oolong teas is Pouchong and is mixed with gardenia blossoms or jasmine flowers. Grades of oolong teas are really a mouthful and are: Choice, Finest to Choice, Finest, Fine to Finest, Superior, On Superior, Good to Superior, Good Up, Fully Good, Good, On Good and Standard.

MAJOR TEA PRODUCING COUNTRIES

INDIA

Produces about 1 billion pounds of tea annually on 900,000 acres. Since each Indian consumes about 1 pound of tea annually, India only exports about 50% of its tea. The United Kingdom purchases about 150 million pounds and the United States only buys about 17million pounds. Almost all the tea grown in India is manufactured as black tea.

CHINA

China produces about 350 million pounds of tea annually. China produces green, black, oolong and brick teas. The first plucking, which is the finest is called "show-chun." Most Chinese tea is a high quality tea.

JAPAN

The third largest tea producer: producing about 200 million pounds annually. Almost all of the tea is green tea and very little is exported since the Japanese are big tea drinkers. The finest Japanese teas are grown in the district of Yamashiro.

INDONESIA

The fourth largest tea producer: manufacturing about 170 million pounds of tea annually. Over 75% of the tea is grown in Java and the balance in Sumatra. Most of the Indonesian teas are used for blends and are black teas.

SRI LANKA (Ceylon)

Black tea is the most common tea produced in Sri Lanka. They produce over 500 million pounds annually utilizing 500,000 acres. They export over 400 million pounds with about 400,000 pounds going to the United States. If the tea was imported from Ceylon it will usually have a stamp stating that it was grown there. The color of most Celanese teas is a reddish-brown and most are excellent quality teas.

TAIWAN (Formosa)

Taiwan produces about 65 million pounds of tea annually with 85% of their crop being exported. They produce green, black and oolong teas. Formosa Oolong tea is a popular excellent quality tea sold in the United States. The tea is only grown on the northern tip of the island and is processed with great care to produce the high quality product.

BOTTLED AND CANNED TEAS

In supermarkets and health food stores tea is sold in bottles and cans with the addition of a number of herbs. These drinks are being sold as energy and sports drinks or supplement drinks using the various types of teas as their base. Many are high in sugar and contain preservatives and artificial coloring agents similar to soda water and it would be best to choose the all-natural beverages. Since there are hundreds of different teas presently on the market we will only discuss a few.

MAD RIVER TEAS

One of their popular teas blends two herbs: ginseng and ginkgo biloba, which are two energy providing herbs; that have been related to providing people with a sharper mental alertness. Other teas sold by this company include Green Tea with Lemon, Oolong Tea with Honey and Red Tea with guarana. All utilize pure cane sugar to enhance the taste. All their teas are infused with significant amounts of Echinacea purpurea to improve natural resistance to disease. No preservatives or artificial ingredients are used in the teas and they are one of the premium teas on the market.

BREWING METHODS

HOT, HOT, HOT

The following are temperatures that tea should be brewed at according to tea experts on two continents.

- Green tea: should be brewed between: 180°F to 200°F (82.2° C. to 93.3° C.)
- Oolong tea: should be brewed between: 185°F to 205°F (85° C. to 96° C.)
- Black tea: should be brewed between: 190°F to 210°F (87.8° C.– 98.9° C.)

The better quality teas should be brewed at a lower temperature since they will release their flavor more readily. The higher temperatures used in the lower quality teas tends to stimulate the release of the flavors.

BREW: LIKE YOU KNOW WHAT YOU'RE DOING

The following steps will lead you through the process of making the perfect cup of tea:

1. Use the best grade of tea that you enjoy.
2. Use pure quality cold water and bring it to a boil. Only use the water when it is bubbling rapidly. Never use water from a hot water under sink unit.
3. Rinse the teapot with the hottest water possible or use boiling water. The teapot should be warm before you add the tea.
4. When pouring the boiling water into the teapot, take the kettle to the teapot to assure that the water will be as hot as possible.
5. Brew the tea for 3-5 minutes depending on your taste and the type of tea. Most teas should never be brewed for more than 5 minutes.
6. Make sure that the brewing tea is kept as hot as possible as it is brewing.
7. Always have a removable tea leaf strainer that is easily removable to eliminate the tea leaf residues. Always stir the tea after removing the infusion.
8. If the tea cools after you pour it, it would be best to brew another batch and not try to re-heat it.

HOW TO MAKE A STRONG TEA

The problem most people have when trying to make a strong tea is that it usually turns out bitter. Never increase the steeping period; always add more tea, leaves. The longer the leaves remain in the hot water, the more polyphenols are released, thus producing a bitter tea.

TEA POTS & SUCH

One of the original teapots was more of a solo pot called a Yixing (E-ching). These small pots can be found in all different shapes. They may be in the shape of a vegetable or flower and were made from red clay that was only found in the Yunnan province of Mainland China. The Chinese only used one pot for one tea variety, which protected the pot from absorbing different flavors.

The red clay tended to hold the heat, keeping the flavor in and the tea hot for a long period of time. Since the clay did not conduct the heat well to the exterior of the pot, the outside was cooler and could be handled easily.

There are also small individual cups that are available in many different sizes and shapes. One of the more popular is the Chinese style "guywan" cup, which has a lid to keep the tea hot while the infusion process is taking place, releasing flavor into the water.

A quality teapot is crucial to enjoying the full flavor of the tea. Someone who really enjoys tea will never place a teabag in a cup and place it in the microwave.

THE STEAMING LEAVES

The reason why you would keep a cover on a cup or pot of steeping tea may seem simply that it keeps the heat in. However, another very important reason is that it traps the steam and dampens any tealeaves that are floating on the top, thus extracting their flavor.

STORAGE

MINE ENEMIES ARE LIGHT AND HUMIDITY

Loose tea should always be stored in a cool, dry location. Humidity and heat will reduce the quality of the tea significantly. A sealed container works well allowing as little oxygen to come into contact with the loose tea. Containers should only be large enough to hold the tea and be opaque since the light can have a negative effect as well. A large container will retain too much oxygen and may cause undue oxidation to take place. Teabags should be stored in the container they are purchased in and also stored in a cool, dry location.

CAFFEINE CONTENT

One pound of tea contains 205 grains of caffeine. The primary effects from the caffeine in tea lasts from 15-45 minutes depending on the individual sensitivity level to caffeine.

The following information is based on an 8-ounce cup of tea:

> Green Tea (5 minute brew) . . .35mg
> Black Tea (1 minute brew) . . .24mg
> Black Tea (3 minute brew) . . .41mg
> Black Tea (5 minute brew) . . .50mg
> Iced Tea 34mg
> Instant Tea 28mg
> Decaffeinated Tea . . . .~10mg

GROWING METHODS

The tea plant prefers a jungle climate with a continual level of heat and humidity and an elevation of 5,000 feet above sea level. The cool nights causes the plants to grow more slowly making them richer in flavor. The evergreen tree variety can grow as high as 30 feet, however, the quality of the tea decreases with the size of the tree. Ideally the rainfall where the trees are grown should amount to about 100 inches per year.

Tea is presently grown on small green bushes that stand about 3-4 feet high, which take about 2½ years to mature. Tea grows rapidly and can produce about 3500 bushels per acre. They are normally clipped flat on top, which give them the appearance of a hedge. The new growth leaves and buds are cut from the top of the hedge and are then brought to the manufacturing plant to be withered, cured, dried and packaged. Processing is performed at the site for the better quality teas; the freshness is significantly higher than that of the blends sold in supermarkets.

NUTRITIONAL INFORMATION

WHERE OH WHERE HAS MY FLUIDS GONE

Tea has a diuretic effect on the body and should never be relied upon as a source of liquid.

TEA AND CHOCOLATE ARE NOT GOOD FOR FIDO

Tea contains two alkaloids, theophylline and theobromine that relax the smooth muscles, while caffeine stimulates the heart and respiratory systems. Theobromine is also found in chocolate in amounts that are high enough to kill a dog if they ingest enough of it. If your dog got into a candy dish and show symptoms of excessive thirst, nervousness, urinary incontinence, spasms, seizures or diarrhea it would be best to take them to the vet immediately. Small amounts are not dangerous, but it would be wise to never give a dog any chocolate product. In humans high dosages of theobromine tend to have a diuretic effect and stimulate the heart to beat faster.

HEALTH BENEFITS OF GREEN AND BLACK TEA

There are numerous studies and articles that have been written regarding the health benefits of drinking green tea. Green tea has been used as a medicinal in China for over 4,000 years and was written about by the father of medicinal herbs, Shen-Nung. Recent literature has related green tea to lowering cholesterol and especially LDL, the bad cholesterol while increasing HDL, the good cholesterol. It has also been related to lowering blood pressure, acting as a blood thinner, lowering the risk of stroke, reducing the risk of cancer, improving the function of the immune system and even preventing cavities.

The active ingredients in the green tea are the "Catechins" a powerful antioxidant family. This family includes; epigallocatechin gallate (EGCG), epigallocatechin (EGO), epicatechin gallate (ECG), epicatechin (EC) and catechin. All are considered powerful antioxidants and free radical scavengers. The connection between these antioxidants and cancer is being investigated by a number of major universities. The effective amounts may be about 10 cups per day which is more than most of us will ever drink.

Tea brewed from black tea had the highest catechin content when brewed from tea bags. Decaffeinated tea had the lowest level of catechins. Black tea rivals green tea and has equal levels as long as you use the tea bags.

The M.D. Anderson Cancer Center in Houston and the Memorial Sloan-Kettering Cancer Center in New York are presently studying green tea extract for possible use in treatments.

HEALTH BENEFITS OF BLACK TEA

While a number of studies did not show any significant relationship between drinking black tea and disease prevention or cure, one study did show a positive correlation in the reduction of cholesterol levels and reduced risk of urinary and digestive disorders. Drinking 2.7 cups of black tea per day may also reduce the risk of stroke, when compared to men who only drank 2.6 cups per day. Black tea does contain antioxidants.

WHOOPS, THERE GOES SOME MORE IRON

There has never been a study that shows any risk factors in drinking tea, however, tea and red wine both contain tannins. Tannins have been known to interfere with the absorption of iron and certain B vitamins.

SPRUNG A LEAK?

A popular tea in Asia that is used as a diuretic is corn silk tea. It is one of the best diuretics that can be prepared from any herb. Corn silk tea has been proven to lower blood pressure. You might ask your doctor if he ever recommends that you take a diuretic if he would approve your trying corn silk tea first. He may get a surprise.

DANGER, TOXIC TEAS

There are a number of teas that do fall into the toxic category and should be avoided unless used in a prescribed manner by your physician or your herbalist.

Buckthorn	May cause diarrhea
Burdock	Blocks nerve impulses to organs
Comfrey	Can cause liver problems
Foxglove	May cause heart arrythmias
Groundsel	May cause liver problems
Hops	Can destroy red blood cells
Jimsonweed	Blurred vision and hallucination
Kava-Kava	May cause deafness and loss of balance
Lobelia	May cause liver problems
Mandrake	May block nerve impulses to organs
Meliot	Can cause tendency to hemorrhage
Nutmeg	Can cause hallucinations

Oleander.	Can cause heart stoppage
Pokeweed	May cause breathing difficulties
Sassafras	May cause liver cancer
Senna	May cause diarrhea
Thorn Apple	Blocks nerve impulses
Tonka Bean	Causes tendency to hemorrhage
Woodruff	Causes tendency to hemorrhage

One tea that you should stay away from is made from the germander plant (Teucrrium chamaedrys) and may still be used in some weight control products. Researchers in France have found that the tea will cause liver damage. A number of cases of hepatitis (liver disease) were reported in people consuming the tea for 3-18 weeks. Dosages ranged from 600 to 1,620mg per day when taken in capsule form. Teas will contribute enough germander to be considered dangerous as well. Herb shops are still able to sell the tea.

CAUTION: REGARDING TEA SOLD AS MEDICINAL TEA

Teas that are sold relating to cures or specific disease processes are not regulated by the FDA. These manufacturers do not have to prove their claims and the public is on their own when it comes to safety and effectiveness.

ALL NATURAL IS BEST

There is a substance in tea that has been isolated and is being studied in relation to cancer prevention. The substance is "polyphenol" and it is only found in sufficient quantities of tea that have not been processed. The high sugar content of canned or bottled teas reduce the effectiveness significantly.

DECAFFEINATION PROCESS

Tea is decaffeinated using the same chemical that is used to produce decaffeinated coffee. Ethyl acetate is used to bind the caffeine and it then removed by forced water filtration methods.

TAKING AN IRON SUPPLEMENT? DON'T TAKE IT WITH TEA

Studies show that taking an iron supplement with tea may block your body's ability to absorb the maximum amount available.

BOTTLED COMMERCIAL TEA VS. "REAL" HOME-BREWED TEA

The major antioxidants found in green or black tea are for the most part absent from commercial tea drinks. It would be best to brew your own tea and it doesn't matter whether it is hot or cold, you will still obtain the highest level of antioxidants. Commercial tea has higher sugar content.

VITAMINS, NUTRIENTS AND CHEMICAL COMPOUNDS IN TEA

SUBSTANCE	CONCENTRATION IN ABOUT 1 OUNCE OF TEA LEAVES
Antioxidants (polyphenols)	10-25%
Caffeine	25-30mg.
Carotene	14-30mg.
Flavenoids	0.6-0.7%
Fluoride	90-350ppm.
Glycosides	0.6%
Magnesium	400-2,000ppm.
Polysaccharides	0.6%
Saponins	0.1%
Selenium	1.0-1.8ppm.
Theanine (amino acid)	trace
Vitamin B2	trace
Vitamin C	150-200mg. Only in green tea not black tea
Vitamin E	25-70mg.
Zinc	30-75ppm.

Absorption of these nutrients when consumed in green tea is excellent compared to other forms of supplements. The only other tea, which is comparable to "real" green tea, is Mate tea.

TEA LEAF FACTS

THE #1 ORGANIC TEA

This tea comes from the oldest gardens in Darjeeling, the Makaibari Tea Estates. They grow the finest certified pure organic teas in the world. One of their most popular teas is the Makaibari Green, which has a taste of Darjeeling, however, it is still a green tea.

POUND FOR POUND DOES TEA OR COFFEE HAVE MORE CAFFEINE?

A pound of tea has almost twice the caffeine content than a pound of coffee. Tea goes farther making about 180-200 cups, compared to coffee only making about 40 cups. The taste of tea that is made with the equivalent measure of a coffee scoop would be too powerful to drink.

QUALITY MAKES A DIFFERENCE

The better the quality of the tea, the less you have to use per cup. Poor quality tea may take up to one teaspoon per cup to give the desired taste, while the higher quality green teas may only take half that much. Your typical supermarket teas may be a blend of 60 different teas and most people will never know what a good cup of tea really tastes like.

TEA OVERBOARD

Never drink hot tea from a Styrofoam cup with lemon added. The two acids, citric and tannic will react with the heat and eat a hole through the cup leaving a puddle on your desk and adding a number of carcinogens into the tea from the Styrofoam. If you don't believe it, try it for yourself. It only works with hot tea and lemon.

TEA IS SECOND ONLY TO WATER

Tea is the second most consumed beverage in the world.

BOY, I'M FRESH

If you want to test the freshness of tea, just close your fist very tightly around a small amount of tea or a tea bag and breathe in as you release your fingers. The aroma should be sweet and somewhat grassy. If you do not smell a strong aroma, the tea is probably old and should be thrown out.

TEA, GROWN IN AMERICA

There is only one tea grown in the United States, which is black tea grown near Charleston South Carolina on the island of Wadmalaw. Tea plantations were established in 1799 by a French botanist. The American Classic Tea has been the official tea of the White House since 1987. The tea is a traditional black tea and one of the finest black teas available. The first flush is harvested every May, with harvesting continuing every 15-18 days until October. The plantation prides itself on using no pesticides or fungicides, thus producing a high quality product. . For more information regarding the only American tea call (800) 443-5987.

HAVE A BRICK OF TEA

The leftovers from tea manufacturing are made into bricks of tea. The bricks are usually produced in China and shipped to Russia and Tibet, where small pieces are shaved off the bricks and used for tea. The bricks may contain twigs, leaves and even the stems of the bush.

THIS WILL FILL A FOOT-BALL STADIUM

The total tea production is about 2,130,000,000 pounds annually mostly from India and Sri Lanka. This will easily fill a football stadium.

DON'T BE A DUNKER

There is nothing wrong with purchasing a quality tea in a tea bag. They come in an odorless, tasteless filter paper that is very convenient and not as messy as loose tea. The mistake most people make is not using very hot, almost boiling water and then allowing the bag to remain in the water until the desired flavor is achieved. To dunk the teabag a number of times defeats the purpose of the teabag and does not result in a quality cup of tea. The water needs time to absorb the flavor and the cup should have a cover on it while it is steeping.

GREAT FOR HALLOWEEN

If you would like to firm up the skin on your face with a mask that really works, just mix 1 cup of mayonnaise with 1 heaping teaspoon of Matcha tea. Mix well, and apply evenly on your face, avoiding your eyes. Relax for about 20 minutes then rinse the mixture off with warm water. Pat your face dry using a soft towel and apply a soft moisturizer.

COLOR ME TEA GREEN

The color of tea can tell you a lot about the tea even before you drink it. Black tea should not have any greenish tint to it or it is indicative of an under-withered, over-fermented tea. Green teas should have a greenish-golden color. If the color of green tea is a somewhat brownish-yellow color this indicates that the tea is old or was produced from low-grade leaves. A good rule of thumb is the lighter the color, the higher the probability that it is a quality green tea.

GET OUT THE SPYGLASS

Since most tea is imported into the United States it must pass the stringent regulations, established by the Food and Drug Administration and is inspected by special "FDA Tea Examiners."

WHO INVENTED THE TEABAG?

The teabag was accidentally, invented in 1904 by Thomas Sullivan in New York when he was shipping tea samples to a customer. Samples were normally sent in small tins but he felt it would be less expensive to send them in small bags. He ordered hundreds of silk, hand-sewn bags, placed tea in them and shipped them out waiting for orders. The response was overwhelming when his customers found that by just pouring hot water over the bags they made their tea with no mess or fuss. Presently, teabags are used to prepare about 55% of all tea in the United States.

NO MORE MOSQUITOES

Place a fireproof bowl outside on the patio next time you have a barbecue and place some crushed dried green tea leaves in with one charcoal briquette and light it. The smoke will chase any mosquitoes or flies away.

CAN'T LIVE WITHOUT TEA

The British drink more tea than any group of people in any country in the world. The average Britisher drinks at least 4 cups of tea per day. Most of the tea is still made by infusion, however; teabags are coming on strong. The British consume about 8 pounds of tea per person annually.

WHAT IS BUBBLE TEA?

Bubble tea is a new beverage craze! The tea consists of a mixture of tea, milk, sugar and giant tapioca balls. The "bubble" refers to the foam that develops as a result of shaking the drink tea with ice. Other names for the tea are tapioca pearl drink, pearl shake, big pearl, milk tea, bubble drink or momi. The drink originated in Southwest Asia, probably Taiwan and has been popular for the last 15 years there.

WHY THE ENGLISH STARTED ADDING MILK TO TEA

The tea that was originally imported by England tended to be a bit astringent and this was not an acceptable quality, so the English tried adding a small amount of milk, which reduced the astringency caused by the higher tannic acid content. The milk protein would bind with the tannic acid. Another benefit is that by reducing the tannins, the tea became less constipating. Problems did arise, however, when the tea with the added milk had less aroma and flavor than they were used to. The habit stuck and a large number of the English still prefer their tea with milk.

LOOK INTO MY TEA

In many societies, reading tealeaves is serious business. The Chinese would read the patterns of the leaf residues left in the bottom of the cup to foretell future events in a person's life. In Scotland the tealeaf reader is called "spae-wife" who reads her tea leaves every morning to find out how the day would progress. To have sufficient tea leaves to read the tea must be prepared without an infuser.

The reading is always done from the left of the handle and progresses around the cup. If the symbols look like any of the following, it means that you will have good luck: anchors, stars, a leaf, tree, flower, a crown, cow, egg, heart-shape, dogs or a bridge. If the symbol looks any of the following, it means you will have bad luck: snakes, crosses, a coffin, rats, a church steeple, a weapon of any kind, ravens, monkeys, cats or a monkey.

USING YOUR GOOD CHINA, SPOON IT

When pouring hot tea into a good china cup, it would be a wise move to place the spoon in first. The spoon tends to absorb the heat first and you will not risk cracking the cup. Many of the cracks are micro-cracks and cannot be seen for many years. If they do appear, just boil a small amount of milk and pour it into the cup. Allow it to stand for about 20 minutes and the milk protein will seal the micro-cracks. Another method is to rinse the cup under very hot tap water before adding the tea or coffee.

MARBLING EGGS WITH TEA BAGS

A unique way to serve hard-boiled eggs is to marble them. The easiest method is to boil the eggs for 2 minutes, remove the eggs one at a time and just tap the shell to crack them. Continue cooking the eggs for 2 minutes more in the same water that has had 6 teabags added. Remove the egg and allow them to cool before removing the shells. The eggs will be marbled.

THE ALL AROUND TEA INFUSER

Almost any herb can be placed in a tea infuser and placed in your soup or stew to add the flavor of the spice without allowing the spice to fall apart and then be more difficult to retrieve. The infuser can even be used to stir your dish with while the flavor of the spice is being released.

TANNINS, BEGONE FROM MY TEAPOT

To remove the stains left by tannins, place $\frac{1}{2}$ cup of borax into a teapot full of boiling water, remove from the heat and allow it to stand overnight. Clean thoroughly before using.

CHINA TEAPOTS NEED CAREFUL CLEANING

To clean the inside of a china teapot, just place a small amount of baking soda on a damp cloth and rub firmly.

GETTING FOGGY IN HERE

If your tea is cloudy, just add a pinch of baking soda to the teapot.

TEAISTICS

The tea sales in the United States are increasing at an unbelievable rate. In 1991 tea sales were $1.9 billion and in 2001 grew to $4.7 billion.

ODORS A PROBLEM: GREEN TEA TO THE RESCUE

Litter Boxes	Green tea leaves should be crushed and sprinkled in a litter box to keep the odors away as well as any fleas.
Kitchen odors	If you want to get the smell of garlic or onions off your hands, try rubbing your hands with wet green tea leaves. The leaves can also deodorize your pan or bowl.
Pet Beds	Sprinkle some green tea leaves in your pet's bed.
Refrigerator	Keep a bowl with used green tea leaf bags in the refrigerator to eliminate odors. Works as good as baking soda.

THE PERFECT CUBE

Ice cubes used for iced tea or coffee should be made from the tea or coffee. Ice tea is diluted to a great degree and loses up to 40% of its flavor from the ice cubes.

CLEARING UP A PROBLEM

Cloudiness is common in iced tea but can be eliminated if you just allow the tea to cool to room temperature before placing it into the refrigerator. If the tea is still cloudy, try adding a small amount of boiling water to it until it clears up. A number of minerals are released when the tea is brewed which results in the cloudiness.

GETTING YOUR JOLT FROM TEA

If you want high caffeine tea, just have a cup of English Breakfast or Bigelow English Tea time. This tea has about 60 mg of caffeine per cup.

UP TO DATE

While the latest studies still show that there are no risk factors related to tea drinking the tannins found in tea and red wine can interfere with the assimilation of iron, thiamin, and vitamin B2 in the body.

CAN CORN SILK BE USED TO MAKE TEA?

On almost every continent corn silk has been used to prepare tea that has a diuretic effect. In fact, it is one of the best diuretics you can prepare from any herb. In some studies it was also shown that corn silk tea even lowered blood pressure, probably by controlling fluid retention.

SPECIAL NOTE:

- In recent literature tea has been discussed as a possible protective beverage for cancer. Research is presently being performed but there have not been any definitive, double, blind studies released that can provide information as to whether tea will act as a cancer preventive or cure.
- The substance in iced or hot tea is polyphenol that is suspect to have possible benefits. Canned iced teas would be the worst source of polyphenols due to the high sugar content, which reduces the potency of the chemical.

HERBAL TEA: THE FIRST TEAS

Herbs have been with us since the beginning of vegetation on earth. Early man probably placed the different plants or leaves in liquids or just ate them. Herbs have been used for medicinal purposes for thousands of years. There are only three ways to acquire herbs. You can grow them, forage for them or go to your local health food store or herbalist and buy them. The last, being the easiest method of obtaining your herbs. Herbs may be powdered and placed in capsules, made into tablets, liquefied or made into a tea. Tea will be discussed since it is one of the more common methods of obtaining herbs and their benefits. Every single herb has a story and historically has been used to cure some disease.

TYPES

The following herbs are some of the more common herbs used for teas. The medicinal uses for these herbs will be given for informational and historical purposes only and not for use as a medicine to cure any specific illness. The author does not recommend any of these herbs as a cure for any disease process.

Agrimony
This herb may go by a number of different names such as; cocklebur or sticklwort. It may be found in fields or along the road in North America and Europe, but is easily cultivated almost anywhere and can grow to a height of 3 feet. Both the leaves and flowers are used to make a tea that has a flavor similar to apricots. The tea was used to strengthen the liver, improve the skin, and cure colds and sore throats.

Alfalfa
May also be called Lucerne. Can be grown almost anywhere and can be found in the wilderness around streams and damp meadowlands. The plant grows to a height of 1-2 feet and was thought to be a vegetable by the Chinese. The tea is somewhat bland and grassy and is made from the leaves and flower heads. It is high in vitamins, minerals and digestive enzymes. It contains more protein than wheat and corn and the tea was used to cleanse the kidneys, cure ulcers, arthritis and to improve muscle tone.

Angelica
May also be called wild parsnip or archangel. The plant has bright green leaves that are 2-3 feet long and bears yellow flowers. It was originally only found in Europe but is now being grown in North America. The herb has had a history of being linked to angels in many languages and was said to help cure the plague. It was used as a remedy to fight witchcraft, rid the body of poisons, cure gout and lung diseases. Angelica was also known as the "Root of the Holy Ghost." The flavor of the tea is similar to juniper berries.

Anise
This herb may also be called: cumin or anise seed. Anise is somewhat sweet and tastes like licorice. The bible mentions anise as a protector against evil and especially the "evil eye." The tea has been used to cure gas, coughs and a number of digestive problems.

Balm
This is a very fragrant plant that is found in Southern Europe and grows to a height of 1-2 feet. It is easily grown in the United States and sometimes found wild in the woods of the northeast. Balm may also be called lemon balm or bee balm and has been known as the "elixir of life." Legend has it that it is the fountain of youth herb and has been used to assist in the healing of open wounds. It is very attractive to bees and therefore rubbed on beehives to keep the bees close to home. The tea is made from the flowering tops and the leaves. Other medicinal uses are for reducing fevers, improving nervous disorders and longevity.

Basil
Basil was originally found in India and was known as the "herb of hatred." It is now grown in a number of warm regions of the globe and was a sacred herb of the Hindu religion. History tells us that basil was buried with Hindus and used as their passport to paradise. The tea has a similar taste to anise and it has been used to treat nausea.

Bay
Known as the "herb of prophecy." It can grow to a height of 50-60 feet, but is usually controlled and grown as a bush. It is more common in the Mediterranean areas. The herb was a sacred herb to the Greek god Apollo and was made into wreaths and placed around the neck of victorious warriors and athletes. The tea has a pleasant aroma but is slightly bitter and was used to cure stomach upsets, ease the pain of childbirth, cure coughs and get rid of the cobwebs in the brain.

Bergamot
May also be called Horse Mint or Oswego tea and can grow to a height of 3-4 feet. They are members of the mint family and can easily be grown in your garden. The tea was commonly used by the Winnebago Indians to cure skin conditions and especially acne. The tea was also used to cure a variety of stomach disorders, bronchial problems and headaches.

Birch
Harvested from a tree that may be found in Europe, Iceland, Northern Asia and North America. Its nickname is "Lady of the Woods." The inner bark was powdered and was consumed with caviar by the Russians. The powder was also baked in bread and pastries by the Swedes and even made into a paste, rolled, dried and then smoked by Alaskan Eskimos. The tea has a somewhat wintergreen flavor.

Borage
The herb has also been called miner's candle, talewort and cool tankard. It has been known as the symbol of courage and brought increased energy levels to the Crusaders. The plant has beautiful blue star-shaped flowers and can be grown in most climates of the world. In many locations it grows wild and is regarded as a weed. The tea was used to relieve depression and tastes like fresh cucumber. The tea has also been used for bronchial problems, to increase the flow of mother's milk and as a diuretic.

Burnet
The tales of this herb dates back to medieval times when a Hungarian king was said to have cured the wounds of thousands of his soldiers that were injured in battle with the juice of the herb, burnet. The tea has been used to stop bleeding from open wounds and relieve diarrhea.

Chamomile
The herb has also been called: Manzanilla or sweet chamomile and has a reputation for its curative powers for thousands of years. It has a somewhat apple-like aroma but is somewhat bitter. The tea was used as a relaxant and to relieve stress. The herb has been used to soothe the effects of withdrawal from alcohol and drug addictions. Chamomile tea has also been used to soothe a baby's teething and restlessness.

Caraway
May be called kummel and is one of the oldest condiments having been found in archeological digs that were dated over 5,000 years old. The secret to your lover always remaining faithful is that they eat caraway seeds (it's that easy). The tea has a somewhat bitter flavor and tastes like parsley. It has been used to relieve a toothache and as a breathe freshener.

Catnip
This herb is a member of the mint family and is commonly found growing wild along the sides of the road. The tea has been used to flavor meats and is commonly used in salads. In England it was one of the favorite teas long before tea was imported from China as well as a favorite of the American colonists. The tea is normally prepared from the young leaves and flowering tops of the plant and has a slight bitter, mint-like taste. It has been used to relieve abdominal discomfort and to regulate menstruation.

Cinnamon
This herb is harvested from the evergreen tree that is a member of the laurel family. The inner bark of the tree is dried and becomes the cinnamon spice or herb we are familiar with. The most famous incident involving cinnamon was when the Emperor Nero burned a year's supply of cinnamon after his wife died to accentuate the level of his grief. The tea was used to relieve stomach problems and also as a stimulant.

Clover
May also be called red clover and has the motto "think of me." It was originally grown as a fodder plant and is one of the earliest cultivated herbs. A four-leaf clover is guaranteed to bring you good luck, especially in Las Vegas. The tea became popularized by the American Indians who ate the leaves and flowers raw. The tea is a soothing tea that has been used to treat ulcers, skin conditions and even cancer.

Cloves
Cloves are from clove trees that are for the most part grown in Southeast Asia. They are the dried seeds of the clove tree flowers that are harvested before they develop and their seeds removed. The trees will provide cloves for about 100 years. The Chinese called cloves the "chicken tongue spice" because of their shape. In Java they were smoked and in India they are chewed. They produce a strong, pungent tea that was also used as an antiseptic.

Coltsfoot
This herb grows wild in many areas of the United States and has been called coughwort and ass's foot. It has an asparagus-like stem and can grow to heights of 1-2 feet. The blossoms resemble a dandelion blossom, which is outlined by green leaves making it appear to look like a horse's hoofprint. The herb is commonly used in British tobacco products and was once thought of as the most powerful herbal medicine. The tea has been used for bronchial problems and coughs.

Comfrey
This herb is actually a weed that grows wild. It was used for thousands of years to cure battle wounds and even broken bones. The herb contains the chemical, Allantoin, which speeds up cell duplication and assists injured cells to heal faster. The tea has a mild flavor and is normally made from the leaves and ground root and used to heal ulcers and stop diarrhea.

Dandelion
The name originated because the yellow, jagged leaves resemble lion's teeth. Dandelions can be found almost everywhere and especially where you don't want them. The tea has been used in India for liver ailments and the flowers made into dandelion wine. The leaves are one of the more nourishing greens that can be found in the entire herb kingdom. It is high in vitamin A, calcium and potassium. The tea is somewhat bitter and has also been used to improve kidney and liver function.

Elder
Sometimes referred to as elderberry and grows wild in Europe. Legends surrounding the herb elder include the fact that the wood used in Pan's Pipes were made from the tree as well as the Cross of Calvary. Another legend is that Judas was hung from an elder tree. The berries are used to make elderberry wine and the tea has been used to cure the flu.

Fennel
Fennel is a member of the parsley family and originated in Southern Europe and Asia for the most part growing wild. Fennel is used on cow's utters to prevent the milk from becoming bewitched. The tea has a flavor similar to anise or licorice and has been used to improve memory, as an appetite suppressant and to stop a cough.

Fenugreek

This may also be called bird's foot and grows wild in the eastern Mediterranean area. The Egyptians used fenugreek as a food source and placed it in their "holy smoke." The sprouts were a popular favorite in salads and the powdered seeds were used to increase hair growth on bald men. The tea was used to lower fevers, soothe stomach disorders and help regulate blood sugar levels.

Flax

This is one of the most well known herbs in the world and is easily found in the wild. Some of the most significant uses of flax in history: The Egyptians who used the flax to wrap the mummies in, it was used in the Tabernacle in Exodus and the white sails in Homer's Odyssey. The tea has been used to relieve coughs and a remedy for colds and flu.

Ginger

The herb can be found in the wild throughout North America in cool, wooded areas and has been used in recipes for hundreds of years. Ginger and the tea have been used to relieve motion sickness and also effective for a number of stomach and digestive problems.

Ginseng

This herb has been known as the fabulous cure-all herb and has been written about in all literature that mentions healing and herbs for thousands of years. The root tends to resemble the human form and the more it resembles the more powerful it is said to be. Longevity and sexual prowess has always been associated with ginseng. Daniel Boone hunted and sold ginseng root to China when their supplies ran low. They made more money selling the root than they did from their fur trade. The Russian astronauts took ginseng with them into space to prevent infections. The tea is prepared from the root, which is ground up. The taste is similar to licorice and the tea is supposed to strengthen the cardiovascular system, cure diarrhea and even act as a pain suppressant.

Goldenrod

Also known as Blue Mountain tea, it grows wild in the northeastern United States. Because of the excellent quality of the tea, the tea was exported to China where it was a delicacy of the upper classes. The tea has been used to reduce fever, a digestive aide, to control nausea and even to dissolve kidney stones.

Hawthorn

Commonly called whitethorn or Mayblossom it is related to the apple tree and can grow to heights of 30 feet. The tree was considered a sacred tree since Christ's Crown of Thorns was made from hawthorn. If a hawthorn branch was brought into a home in medieval times it was thought to have foretold death. Tea is made from the berries and has been used to treat cardiac disease, kidney problems and cure sore throats.

Hollyhock

Originally grown in China but was found to grow wild in North America. The leaves were commonly used in Egyptian cooking. The tea was used for bronchial problems and to assist with digestion.

Hops
A vine: that has a tough, flexible stem. The herb has male flowers which are in loose bunches and female flowers that appear as small greenish cones. The female cones are used to brew beer and the pulp is sometimes used to produce paper products and even linen. The tea has a somewhat bitter flavor and is used to induce sleep and improve a person's appetite.

Horehound
Also called bull's blood and eye of the star by ancient Egyptian high priests and is a member of the mint family. Used in ancient times as an antidote for poisonings, it is one of the bitter herbs eaten at the Passover holiday by the Jews. Both the leaves and flowers are used to make a tea, which has been used to relieve coughs, help bronchial conditions and congestion.

Hyssop
Easy to grow garden herb, that was used by the ancient Hebrews to cleanse the lepers. Hyssop was also supposedly offered to Jesus at the time of the crucifixion to act as a relaxant. The tea has been used to regulate blood pressure and treat upper respiratory infections.

Lavender
Grows wild in many regions of the world and may have originated as a tea in India. Used by the ancient Romans as a perfume for their baths and potpourri bowls. The tea has a strong aroma and has been used as a mild sedative and to eliminate bad breath.

Lemon Verbena
This herb is mainly found in Central and South America and was a favorite tea in England in the 18th century. It is now grown in India and has a lemon flavor and aroma. The tea has been used for indigestion and as a relaxant.

Linden
May also be called lime or basswood and grows in Europe and North America. The inner bark of the tree has been used as an antiseptic. The linden tree blossoms produce one of the finest honeys in the world. The tea has been used as a relaxant and to relieve the cramps of menstruation.

Licorice
Sometimes known as Spanish juice or sweet root and a very desired herb by the Egyptian Pharoahs. In fact when Tutankhamen's tomb was opened a large quantity of licorice was found. Licorice is very sweet and tends to quench a person's thirst has been chewed as a treat for 2,000 years. The tea has been used for bronchial conditions and as an aid to assist people to stop smoking.

Mallow
May also be called marshmallow and is commonly found in swampy coastal areas. It has the reputation as being one of the oldest herbs that were used as a food and was mentioned in the Old Testament as a substitute for meat. It is also the ingredient used in marshmallows. The tea has been used to reduce mucous in the body and to alleviate the symptoms of colds and sore throats.

Marigold

This is one of the easiest flowers to grow in your garden. The plant is actually considered sacred in India and used to decorate temples and shrines. Gypsies claim that if you drink marigold tea you will have the ability to see fairies. However, if you are in Mexico or Germany it is the "insignia of death." The tea has been used to improve the complexion and treating ulcers.

Marjoram

May also be known as oregano and considered a sacred plant to some religions of India. The herb was planted on the graves of Romans to insure them a peaceful rest. It is one of the popular herbs used by European chefs and was called "the herb of grace" by William Shakespeare. The tea has been used as a relaxant, to relieve headaches and as a digestive aid.

Mate

– Mate is brewed from the dried leaves and stemlets of the perennial tree Ilex paraguarensis, also known as "Yerba Mate." The name Mate was derived from the gourd that the Indians drank the tea from. The plant only grows between the paralells 100 and 300 (South) and only grows in the Parana and Paraguay River basins. The plant requires 25 years to mature. The tea has a somewhat bittersweet flavor similar to alfalfa. The tea is said to be a natural stimulant with no side effects. The Guarani Indians use the drink to boost immune system response, as a blood detoxifyer, restore hair color, slow the aging process, fight fatigue, keep the mind sharp, as an appetite suppressant, reduce stress and eliminate insomnia. The tea also contains a number of vitamins.

Meadowsweet

The flower was always scattered on the floor of the apartment of Queen Elizabeth I and was her favorite flower. The herb can be grown worldwide in most temperate zones. The tea has been used to combat rheumatism and to relive an upset stomach.

Mint

One of the popular herbs for tea can be found in hundreds of varieties worldwide. In ancient times mint leaves were rubbed on a table before guests arrived as a gesture of friendliness. Mint leaves were considered a source of power and virility to the Greeks. The tea has been used to relieve the symptoms of arthritis, to increase ones appetite, cure nausea, and cure stomach problems.

Mugwart

The herb, mugwart is the symbol of "forgetfulness" and thought to ward off the devil and lightning. It was also a belief that if you place a small amount of mugwart in your shoes in the morning you will be able walk 40 miles before noon without tiring (wish I'd known that when I was in the army). The tea has been used to eliminate gallstones, cure serious skin rashes, and regulate the menstrual cycle.

Mullein

May also be called beggar's blanket or witch's candle and may grow to heights of 8 feet. Has been called the "herb of love" and in India the herb was thought to be protection against black magic and sorcery. The tea is somewhat sweet and must be strained since it may contain small fine hairs that cover the plant. It has been used to control asthma, relieve coughs, suppresses the effects of hay fever and as a relaxant.

Nettle

This is an unusual herb in that it contains small stinging hairs that contain formic acid. It is an irritant in the wild, however, it is high in iron, protein and vitamins A and C. In Scotland nettles were made into the finest linen and in England it was used as an important medicinal. The tea has been used to relieve bronchitis and as an appetite suppressant.

New Jersey Tea

This is one of the more popular American herbs and is also known as snowball or red root. It grows over most of the East Coast and was a popular beverage of the colonists, especially when it was difficult to get English tea during the great tea boycott. The taste is similar to black teas.

Nutmeg

A relative of the evergreen family, the nutmeg tree can grow to 60 feet and produces a yellowish fruit that resembles an apricot. Inside the seed, which is an oily dark brown color – the nutmeg. The nutmeg is considered to be a potent aphrodisiac by the Arabs. The tea has a somewhat sweet, spicy flavor and has been used to cure bad breath, headaches, fevers, and kidney problems.

Pennyroyal

In America it is called squaw mint and has a potent aroma and is a beautiful garden herb. It acts as a flea repellant and is popular with hunters. Early American colonists found the tea to be the most flavorful of the wild herb teas. The tea has been used to treat whooping cough, asthma, indigestion and headaches.

Purslane

May also be known as pigweed; and each plant may have as many as 50,000 seeds. The herb was grown in India and Iran over 2,000 years ago and used to line bedding with to ward off the devil. Commonly, used in salads and made into a popular tea by the American Indians. The tea has been used to lower fevers, stop coughs and cure insomnia.

Raspberry

There are hundreds of varieties of raspberries grown worldwide and one of the most popular berries. Many varieties grow wild and raspberry tea is one of the most popular. The tea has been used for hundreds of years to cure female problems, such as the discomfort of menstrual cycles, frigidity and labor pains.

Rose

Roses are one of the oldest know cultivated herbs with over 10,000 varieties worldwide. Their history can be traced back to Persia where it was called the mother of all nutritious fruits. Roses have been consumed as food for centuries in a variety of dishes and jellies. The end of the flower just under the end of the stem is the rose hip, which is exceptionally high in nutrient content, especially vitamin C. The tea has been used to strengthen the heart, cure colds and coughs and help memory.

Rosemary

This is an evergreen shrub that grows in most areas of the world, but is native to the Mediterranean region. It was highly regarded as a cure-all by the Romans. The color of the rosemary flower 2,000 years ago was said to have been white and changed to blue when Mary who was escaping from King Herod with the Christ Child washed her blue robe and hung it to dry on a rosemary bush. The next morning the flowers had turned from white to blue and have stayed that way ever since and were called "the rose of Mary." The tea has been used for digestive problems, a liver tonic to strengthen the heart action and as a relaxant.

Sage

Sage is a member of the mint family with over 700 varieties. The Romans placed sage in their baths to ease the pain of sore feet. The shoots are commonly added to salads in the Middle East. The tea, which is somewhat bitter, has been used to cure colds, relieve headaches, to strengthen muscles and nerves and to cure delirium tremors.

Sarsaparilla

Originally grown in Central and South America and exported to Europe from Mexico in the 1500's. This was the favorite drink of the pirates who thought that it would cure syphilis. The American Indians used the herb to cure arthritis and skin disorders. The tea tastes somewhat like bitter licorice and was used as a pain reliever, especially in the cervical vertebrae.

This herb has been used as a natural aphrodisiac for centuries. The plant contains chemical compounds that are similar in their action to testosterone and progesterone. Historically, the root was boiled in a pint of water for 30-45 minutes and 4 ounces were consumed daily.

Sassafras

May also be called cinnamon wood or smelling stick and is a member of the laurel family. This herb was one of the original exports from the Americas to Europe in the 1500's. The Spanish used sassafras for medicinal purposes. The tea has been used as a blood cleanser, relieve the pain of rheumatism, and to cure gout and diarrhea.

Savory

A peppery flavored herb that originated in Southern Europe and the Mediterranean and used by the Romans in meat and fish dishes. The use of savory declined as pepper became more readily available. During the Middle Ages drops of savory oil were considered a cure for earaches. The tea is not a very appealing tea with the flavor of pepper but was used to reduce fever, cure colds and soothe intestinal disorders.

Thyme

There are over 50 varieties of thyme with the most famous grown in Greece and used to produce some of the wold's finest honey. The Romans thought that by consuming thyme it would increase their bravery in battle. Thyme was also mentioned in the Bible to be in the straw in the manger of the Virgin Mary and the Christ Child. The tea was used to cure headaches and was used as an antiseptic for wounds.

Wintergreen

May also be called mountain tea or woodsman's tea and grows wild in North America. The oil contains the same chemical that is found in aspirin and the tea was used to relieve pain, cure colds, fight the flu and ease coughs.

Yarrow

This herb has also been called a bunch of daisies or soldier's woundwort, since it was used on soldier's wounds during the Trojan Wars. If brides carry a bouquet of yarrow when they get married, they are guaranteed seven years of wedded happiness. The American Indians used the herb for stomach upsets and toothaches. The tea has been used as an intestinal cleanser and to speed the healing of wounds.

PREPARATION OF HERBAL TEAS

If the herb is in the form of a flower or a leaf, an infusion ball may be used to make the tea. Place $1/4$ to $1/2$ teaspoon of the crushed herb, into the infusion ball and pour boiling water into the cup or pot, allowing it to steep for 10-15 minutes depending on the desired level of potency. If you are using one of the milder herbs, use $1/2$ to 1 teaspoon of the herb for the best results. If you make tea from the bark, seeds or the root of the herb, it would be best to use the decoction method. To prepare one pint of tea, just place 1 ounce of the herb in $1 1/2$-pints of pure water and boil for 30 minutes. Whenever possible use a teabag!

STORAGE

If you are purchasing dried herbs, they should be stored in a cool, dry location and in as airtight a container as possible. A well, sealed plastic container is usually the container of choice. If you plan on storing the herbs for a long period and not removing small amounts on a regular basis, then you should plan on purchasing an automatic heat sealer and plastic bags.

POISONOUS PLANTS

The following is a partial listing of some of the more popular plants whose parts are considered to be dangerous and could cause serious harm if consumed in any form.

PLANT/HERB	POISONOUS PARTS
Azaleas	Bulb
Buttercup	All Parts
Daffodil	Bulb
Elderberry	Shoots, Leaves and Bark
Fox Glove	Leaves
Hyacinth	Bulb
Iris	Roots
Jimson Weed	All Parts
Larkspur	Young Plants and Seeds
Lily-of-the-Valley	Leaves and the Flowers
Mistletoe	Berries
Narcissus	Bulb
Oak Trees	Leaves and the Acorns
Oleander	Leaves, Bark and Branches
Poinsettia	Leaves
Poison Hemlock	All Parts
Poison Ivy	All Parts
Potato	Leaves
Rhubarb	Leaves and Blade
Water Hemlock	All Parts
Cherry Trees	Branches and Leaves
Wisteria	Seeds and Pods

NUTRITIONAL FACTS

THE MYSTERY OF HERBS

Herbs were found to cure many diseases in ancient days and were hailed as magical potions. However, a study of the history of certain periods now tell us that diseases such as scurvy, poor eyesight, skin problems, etc. were for the most part due to vitamin deficiencies and were cured by consuming different herbs. The men who studied these illnesses and cured them had a very poor understanding of nutrients in herbs, but were smart enough to try different herbal remedies until they found one that worked; then used it for that illness all the time.

ON THE RUN AGAIN..........

When decaffeinated tea and coffee was introduced, a rumor started that since the caffeine was removed these beverages would not have the diuretic effect to the degree that they had. Sorry, wrong again! The caffeine did have a lot to do with the frequency of urination, however, there is another chemical that is still in tea and coffee called; theophylline which is a bladder stimulant.

VITAMIN AND MINERAL HERBAL SOURCES

Vitamin A . . . . Alfalfa, cayenne, garlic, kelp, marshmallow, parsley, raspberry, red clover, watercress and yellow dock.

Vitamin B1 . . . . Cayenne, dandelion, kelp, parsley and raspberry.

Vitamin B2 . . . . Alfalfa, dandelion, fenugreek, kelp, parsley, safflower and watercress.

Vitamin B6 . . . . Alfalfa.

Vitamin B12 . . . . . . Alfalfa and kelp.

Niacin . . . . Alfalfa, burdock, dandelion, kelp, parsley and sage.

Vitamin C . . . . . . Alfalfa, burdock, catnip, cayenne, dandelion, garlic, hawthorn, kelp, parsley, pokeweed, raspberry, rose hips, watercress and yellow dock.

Vitamin D . . . . Alfalfa and watercress.

Vitamin E . . . . Alfalfa, dandelion, kelp, rose hips and watercress.

Vitamin K . . . . Alfalfa, and plantain.

Calcium . . . . . . Alfalfa, chamomile, cayenne, dandelion, kelp, nettle, parsley, pokeweed, raspberry, rose hips and yellow dock.

Iodine . . . . Garlic, Irish moss, kelp and sarsaparilla.

Iron . . . . Alfalfa, burdock, cayenne, dandelion, kelp, mullein, nettle, parsley, pokeweed, rhubarb, rose hips and yellow dock.

Magnesium . . . . . . Alfalfa, cayenne, dandelion, kelp, mistletoe, mullein, peppermint, raspberry and wintergreen.

Phosphorus . . . . . . Alfalfa, caraway, cayenne, chickweed, dandelion, garlic, Irish moss, kelp, licorice, parsley, pokeweed, purslane, pokeweed, raspberry, rose hips and watercress.

Potassium . . . . Alfalfa, birch, borage, chamomile, coltsfoot, comfrey, dandelion, fennel, Irish moss, kelp, mullein, nettle, parsley, peppermint, raspberry, wintergreen and yarrow.

Selenium . . . . Kelp.

Sodium . . . . Alfalfa, dandelion, dulse, fennel, kelp, parsley and willow.

Sulfur . . . . Alfalfa, burdock root, cayenne, coltsfoot, fennel, garlic, kelp, nettle, parsley, raspberry, sage and thyme.

Zinc . . . . Kelp and marshmallow.

NOTE: The best herb source for trace minerals is kelp.

CHAPTER 9

IT'S COFFEETIME

THE STORY OF COFFEE

The coffee tree is believed to have originated in Central Africa where the natives would grind the coffee cherries into a powder and mix it with animal fat, then roll it into small balls, which they would take with them on long journeys or hunting trips. Raw coffee is high in protein (until it is diluted with water) and when combined with the fat provided adequate calories and a stimulant.

The first factual information relating to the actual drinking of the beverage is by the Arabs in the Middle East. The Arabs protected the coffee bean seed to such a degree that they would not allow it to be exported under the threat of death. However, in 1660 some of the coffee seedlings were smuggled into Holland and then transported to Brazil in 1727 where the climate was more favorable. The climate and soil conditions were ideal and the coffee trees thrived.

Coffee trees need an annual rainfall of over 70 inches of rain with every tree only producing about 2,000 "coffee cherries" to make one pound of coffee. The United States consumes 50% of the world's coffee, which amounts to 400 million cups every day. The average coffee drinker drinks 3 cups per day. Eight out of 10 adults drink at least one cup of coffee daily.

Coffee prices have risen dramatically since 1994 due to major frosts in Brazil, which destroyed 1 billion pounds of coffee, about 10% of the world's coffee supply.

COFFEE PRODUCING COUNTRIES

BRAZIL

For the last 100 years Brazil has led the world in coffee production. Almost 650 million acres can be planted in coffee trees, however, only the areas least likely to be hit by frost are being planted at present. All coffee grown in Brazil is Aribicas and if you wish to try a Brazilian coffee it would be best to try a Brazilian Bourbon Santos. While most Brazilian coffee is only considered a fair quality coffee, the Santos is produced using a high quality bean grown in the Sao Paulo region deriving its flavor from the rich soil, called "terra roxa."

COLOMBIA

Presently, Columbia is the second largest exporter of coffee in the world. The quality is excellent since the majority of the coffee is grown at high elevations. Columbia has over 2 billion coffee trees. The United States purchases about 50% of all coffee grown in Columbia. The top grade of coffee is the "Supremo" and if you can purchase a 100% Supremo Colombian coffee you will really be able to tell the difference from any other coffee you have been drinking. The best Colombian coffee to try is the Colombian Medellin Excelso.

COSTA RICA

Costa Rican, coffee is grown at high altitudes and is all Aribicas, and one of the more popular coffees of Europe. The coffee is graded depending on the hardness of the bean. The higher the altitude the harder the bean and the better the quality of the coffee. The best quality is called the "Good Hard Bean (GHB)" and is grown at altitudes of over 4,000 feet.

DOMINICAN REPUBLIC

Most of the Dominican Republic crop is sold to the United States with the best grade called "Barahonas." The coffee is only rated fair.

UNITED STATES

Coffee is only grown on the slopes of the Mauna Loa volcano at elevations of 1,500 to 2,000 feet. The volcanic soil produces a coffee tree that is never bothered by disease, which is unique in the world. The average crop per acre on Hawaii is about 2,000 pounds compared to only 650 pounds in Latin American countries. The total production, however, is only about 30,000 bags.

JAMAICA

Jamaican coffee is grown on the slopes of a mountain ridge at an elevation that reaches 7,000 feet. Jamaican coffee is rated as one of the finest in the world. If you can find Jamaican Blue Mountain or High Mountain Supreme coffee you might want to try it.

AFRICA

Africa is now one of the largest growers of coffee in the world and increasing their market share every year. One of their best coffees is 100% Robusta, which is difficult to find as a 100% Robusta and not part of a blend. Angola is actually the fourth largest coffee exporter in the world.

There are a number of other countries that grow coffee, these include: Mexico, Puerto Rico, Indonesia, Ecuador, El Salvador, Guatemala, Haiti, Peru, Venezuela, India, and Yemen.

ROASTING THE BEANS

Raw coffee beans must be roasted to change an unappetizing seed into a beverage that is desired by 80% of all adult American. Roasting shrinks the bean about 15% and increases its size by 50% in a process similar to popcorn popping without the full explosion. The longer a bean is roasted, the darker it becomes. Darker roasts do not necessarily produce a stronger coffee. The following are the steps the bean is subjected to during the roasting process.

1. The roasting process applies heat to the bean in such a manner as to assure that every surface area of the bean receives the same amount of heat. Even heating is important.

2. The heat is applied at the lowest temperature to perform the roasting and for the shortest period possible.

TYPES OF ROASTS

Light City Roast The bean is not fully matured with a cinnamon color instead of brown. The flavor is somewhat weak.

Standard City Roast Most popular roasted bean sold in the United States. It may be sold as the American roast or just the brown roast. The beverage that is brewed is somewhat dull and a little on the flat side.

Full City Roast A popular roast on the East Coast. It is roasted for a slightly longer period than the standard roast, which produces a darker cup of coffee. The coffee bean is a dark brown with no hint of oil on the surface. Most specialty coffee shops on the East Coast will carry this roast.

Brazilian Roast No relation to Brazilian coffee. The bean has been roasted a bit longer than the full city roast and the coffee has a darker color and a flavor that starts to taste like a very dark roast.

French Roast The bean has an oily appearance on the surface and the color is a somewhat dark, golden brown. The coffee has a smooth rich flavor and is easily distinguished from the lighter roasts.

French/Italian Roast Called: Spanish or Cuban roast. The bean is roasted darker than the French roast and this coffee makes excellent espresso.

Italian/Espresso Roast Darkest roast possible without carbonization of the bean or roasting it to death. The bean has a shiny, oily surface and looks black.

ESPRESSO BEVERAGES

The smaller Pavoni espresso machines were first used but were only capable of producing about 150 cups per hour. Since this was not sufficient to serve larger crowds, a bigger version called the "La Victoria Arduino" machine was invented which was capable of producing about 1,000 cups per hour. This is the reason for the size of some of the older machines. These early machines, however, had the tendency to over-extract and pull too much coffee out of the grounds, scalding the coffee and producing a somewhat bitter espresso.

The machines that are now in use utilize a horizontal water boiler, which allows the steam and water to mix more efficiently. The steam and hot water is forced through the coffee under high pressure, producing an excellent tasting cup of espresso with good strength and taste.

ESPRESSO

The beverage is prepared by "rapid infusion" which forces the coffee through almost boiling water. A high-quality dark, fine, gritty ground (never powdered) coffee should be used. The darker the coffee, how dense it is packed and the amount of water being forced through will determine the strength of the final product. Always use the recommended amount suggested by the manufacturer of your machine, never less. Espresso should never be served with cream.

WE'LL I'LL BE

A new espresso beverage has recently been introduced, called Sunrise Espresso. Espresso in a bottle is a pre-brewed beverage that is 100% natural, full strength espresso. A problem with espresso is that it takes too long to brew, however, Sunrise states that their product will compete with the fresh brewed product and can be ready in 10 seconds. Their product is prepared from the finest Aribica beans and prepared by master coffee roasters.

CAPPUCCINO

Prepared by combining one shot of a strong espresso with very hot steamed milk and topped with a layer of frothy milk.

CAFFE MOCHA

Prepared using one shot of espresso and topped off with the froth from hot chocolate. A somewhat sweet coffee drink, that tends to taste similar to hot chocolate.

CAFFE LATTE

Prepared using one shot of espresso with about 4 ounces of steamed milk. Usually, has extra milk added instead of more cappuccino and topped off with a large head of foam.

MACCHIATO

Prepared using one shot of espresso with a very small amount of foam on top.

LATTE

Prepared with a small amount of espresso on top of a glass of steamed milk.

CAFÉ AU LAIT

Espresso is not used, however, it is prepared with a very strong coffee blend and steamed milk. It will occasionally be served in a bowl.

DECAFFEINATION PROCESS

The chemical process to decaffeinate coffee was actually invented in 1900 but was not used since there did not seem to be the need to produce decaffeinated coffee and the chemicals and the cost were somewhat prohibitive. The actual process of decaffeination starts with a raw green bean, which is softened with steam and water, allowing the bean to double in size.

The beans are then doused with a chemical solvent, originally chlorine, which had the ability to soak completely through the bean. The beans are vibrated for about an hour in the solvent, which loosens the caffeine and combines it with the chlorine. The solvent is drained off, the beans are heated and dried with steam until all traces (we hope) are removed.

However, this process must be repeated dozens of times on the same beans to produce a bean that is almost completely decaffeinated. Needless to say all this processing takes its toll on the flavor of decaffeinated coffee, which is why some people will never drink it.

1973
The first chemical used to decaffeinate coffee was trichloroethylene. However, 2 years later it was found that it caused cancer of the liver in mice and use was discontinued.

1975
Processors switched to methylene chloride in 1975, however, this was also found to cause cancer in mice. The FDA said that the residues that did reach your coffee cup, was found to be minimal and concern was low that it posed a human health risk.

1981
In 1981; coffee companies decided to use ethyl acetate, a chemical that is also found in pineapples and bananas. However, studies showed that when used in concentrated form the vapors alone were causing liver and heart damage in laboratory animals. This chemical is also used as a cleaning solvent for leathers and production of plastics. This chemical is still in use today.

1984
Two companies have developed methods of decaffeinating coffee using water. Swiss and Belgium companies use water to harmlessly remove the caffeines, however, there is a small amount of flavor loss. A number of U. S. companies are working with the method but production is still low and more expensive than using a solvent. When purchasing coffee, try choosing a coffee that states that it has been decaffeinated using a "water process."

WATER IN, FLAVOR OUT

The safest method to remove the caffeine from coffee was invented by the Swiss, using water. This process soaks the green coffee cherries in water for several hours which will removes about 97% of the caffeine as well as some of the flavor components. The liquid is then passed through a carbon filter that removes the caffeine and the flavor components. The water is then added back to the beans before they are dried.

A GOOD GAS

Another method that is becoming popular is the carbon dioxide method. The green beans are dampened with water; then placed into a pot that is then filled with carbon dioxide. The carbon dioxide has the ability to draw 99% of the caffeine out of the bean. The beans are then dried to remove the excess moisture. Both methods are safe and should be the only two methods used.

COFFEE CAFFEINE SENT TO POP MAKERS

The caffeine that is extracted from coffee and tea is sent to soft drink and drug manufacturers to be used in their products.

BREWING METHODS

DOUBLE-BOILED WATER, A NO, NO

Never use water that has been previously boiled and cooled to make coffee or tea. The water will lose a good percentage of its oxygen content and produce a somewhat flat, tasting beverage.

SAVING THE TASTE

One of the major problems with poor tasting coffee is that the pot is dirty. The preferred method of cleaning is to use baking soda and hot water. Never use soap, since the slightest hint of soap scum will alter the taste of the coffee. If you are using an aluminum pot, which has black stains, just boil a small amount of rhubarb juice in the pot and the stain will disappear.

CLEANING THE COFFEEMAKER

Most coffeemakers build up hard water residues and should be cleaned often. The easiest method is to run straight apple cider vinegar through a cycle, then run water through the cycle twice to clean out the vinegar.

TEMPERATURE IS IMPORTANT

When you brew coffee, it is necessary to have the proper temperature, which will allow the maximum extraction of the caffeol compounds, which are the taste and aroma enhancers. The proper temperature also protects the coffee from producing an overabundance of polyphenols (tannins), which will give the coffee a somewhat bitter taste.

Professional coffee brewers will keep the brewing temperature between 185°F–205°F (85°C–96.1°C). If the temperature is too low, the coffee grounds will not release sufficient caffeols and if too high the tannins take over.

THE PERFECT TEMPERATURE FOR DRIP COFFEE

Studies have proven that the ideal temperature for drip coffee making is 95° to 98°F (35°C. to 36.7°C). If the water is any cooler it will not extract enough caffeine and essential oils from the coffee bean. Coffee that is brewed above the ideal temperature range will contain too high a level of acidity.

GREAT CUP OF COFFEE: VS. HEALTH RISK

The cafetiere or French coffee press (plunger pot) is the hottest craze to hit the coffee-making industry in years. A number of retailers are advertising the cafetiere as the "perfect method of brewing coffee ever invented." The unit does not use a filter; it just presses the coffee and water into a cup. However, studies are showing that if you drink 5-6 cups of pressed coffee per day it could increase your cholesterol levels by as much as 10% and raise the bad cholesterol (LDL) by 14% in some cases. Using the standard filter method allows the cafestol and kahweol, two of the harmful ingredients in coffee to be removed. Espresso is also guilty of high levels of these two compounds.

PAPER TOWEL TO THE RESCUE

If you ever run out of coffee filters try using a piece of plain white (no design) paper towel. Cloth filters work very well, however, a new cloth filter should be washed before using it.

IF YOU GRIND IT, USE IT, OR LOSE IT

When coffee beans are ground, a large percentage of their surface is exposed to the air, thus allowing the breakdown of the flavor components and their rapid destruction. The process is called oxidation and takes its toll on all surfaces of every food when you expose their delicate innards to the air. The other problem that occurs is that the longer the ground up bean is stored the more carbon dioxide is going to be lost, which also contributes to the aroma and flavor of the bean. If you do grind up more than you can use, store the remainder in a well-sealed container in the refrigerator and use as soon as possible.

DIFFERENT GRINDS FOR DIFFERENT BREWING METHODS

Coffee should be ground to match the method of brewing that is desired. A very coarse grind is best for a French press, a medium grind for vacuum pots and finer grinds for manual drip methods of brewing.

MAKING THE PERFECT CUP

There are a few factors that you need to be aware of in order to prepare the perfect cup of coffee:

- The freshness of the ground beans, always grind the beans just before you are ready to use it.
- How long ago the bean was roasted. Is the coffee bean fresh?
- Cleanliness of the brewing equipment.
- The quality of the bean.
- The quality of the water.

The most critical of these factors is the freshness of the ground, cleanliness of equipment and the water quality.

THE RIGHT POT MAKES ALL THE DIFFERENCE

Metal coffee pots, may impart a bitter or metallic taste in your coffee. A glass or porcelain pot is recommended. If you are going to use a metal pot, the only one that is acceptable is a stainless steel one. Copper and aluminum are not recommended at all. If you are using a percolator the brewing time should be no more than 6-8 minutes, while a drip pot should take about 6 minutes and vacuum pots about 1-4 minutes.

TREAT YOUR COFFEE POT WITH TLC

At least once each week you should clean out your coffee pot and filter holder. Bitter oils that are released will make their home on the walls of glass containers and plastic filter holders. They should both be washed with soap and hot water. Rinsing will not remove the bitter oils. The taste of the coffee will be noticeably improved.

TAP, TAP, NEVER USE HOT TAP WATER

If your tap water is not filtered, it is not a good choice for coffee making. Hot water from the tap tends to pick up a number of metals and chemicals that will more easily be absorbed by hot water and won't by cold water. The best water for coffee is pure water, if you would like a clean, fresh taste.

COFFEE CHANGES COMING IN NEIGHBORHOOD STORES

Watch out Starbucks, you're hurting the small neighborhood convenience markets and service station coffee business and they will be fighting back. Both types of mini-market operations by 2002 will be offering gourmet coffees in a number of flavors with personnel to assist the coffee drinker.

HOPE YOUR NOT USING A PERCOLATOR ANYMORE

If you like a bitter cup of coffee, then use a percolator. This type of coffee maker can boil coffee for 7-15 minutes, which is long enough to cause even the best coffees to turn bitter. The aroma of the coffee is also adversely affected, since the coffee is exposed to the air for too long a period.

FLAVOR YOUR OWN COFFEE

When grinding your coffee beans, try adding a small amount of any spice or herb that you like so that the coffee and the herb blend well before brewing the coffee. The coffee grinder can also blend a number of different spices before you add them to a stew or soup to release the flavors more efficiently. However, make sure you clean the grinder thoroughly before grinding coffee.

DON'T BUY SPECIAL FILTERS

Special water filters are being sold to remove the chlorine from the water when preparing coffee. These are really not needed, since chlorine will be released into the air as soon as the water is heated high enough to prepare the coffee. There will not be enough chlorine left to affect the taste.

BUYING & STORAGE

BUY IT RIGHT

When you purchase coffee, it would be best to purchase it in a vacuum sealed container. If you do purchase coffee that is made from freshly roasted beans, be sure that it is packed in non-airtight bags to allow the carbon monoxide that is formed during the roasting process to escape. If the carbon monoxide does not escape, it will adversely affect the flavor of the coffee.

KEEP IT COOOOOL

When storing coffee the ideal method is to place the unused coffee in a well sealed glass jar in the refrigerator. The glass will not impart any flavor like metal will. This is recommended for fresh coffee beans. The grounds can be stored this way but must be used ASAP. Coffee beans can also be frozen for no more than 6 months, but must be sealed really tight.

COFFEE FACTS

FRESH GROUND COFFEE BEANS, BREW IT FAST

When coffee beans are ground, a large percentage of their surface is exposed to air allowing oxidation to take place at a rapid rate as well as causing some of the natural aromatics to be lost. Another problem is that the longer the fresh ground beans sit, the more carbon dioxide is lost which contributes to the coffee's body and aroma. Coffee beans should be stored in the refrigerator and only the quantity that is needed removed and ground. The vacuum packed cans should be stored upside down to preserve the taste and flavor longer. By placing the can upside down you reduce the amount of oxygen that had contact with the surface of the coffee slowing down oxidation.

SURVIVAL & REVIVAL

When you keep coffee warm in a coffee pot on a warming unit, it will only stay fresh for about 30 minutes after it is brewed. If your coffee needs to be freshened up, try adding a dash of salt to your cup then reheat it.

SO WHAT'S A FEW WRINKLES

New studies report the caffeine and nicotine may cause your skin to age prematurely. These chemicals tend to cause the skin to dehydrate at a faster than normal rate.

THE CASE OF THE FLOATING CREAM

Almost every coffee drinker at one time or another has been irritated by the presence of floating cream. A thorough investigation was conducted and the results are in. The stronger the coffee, the more acid that may be formed and if the cream is not very fresh it will contain just enough lactic acid to cause a reaction with the coffee and rise to the top. However, if the coffee is too acidic it may cause even the freshest cream to go bad almost instantly and thus rise to the top.

AMERICA'S BEST

Hawaii is the only state that is capable of growing coffee. The Island of Hawaii is the home of the fabulous Kona coffee. The soil is rich in minerals from the volcanic soil and the rainfall is sufficient to provide the trees with just enough moisture. In fact, in taste tests, Kona coffee was judged to be almost equal to the finest coffees in the world. The coffee is now being exported to the continental United States but try and purchase the pure coffee, not a blend. If you do purchase the 100% pure Kona, you will use less than you normally would.

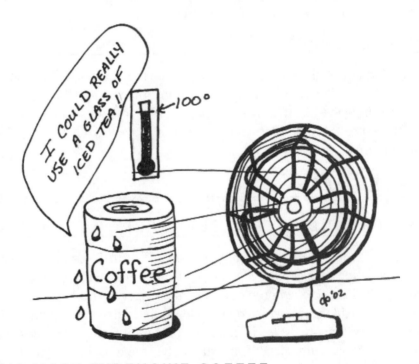

WORLD'S MOST EXPENSIVE COFFEE

The most expensive coffee in the world is from Indonesia. It sells for $300 per pound and is called: Kopi Luwak.

IN COFFEE BEANS, SIZE DOES MAKE A DIFFERENCE

The size of the grind does make a difference, both in taste and the caffeine content. Espresso should be made with a fine ground, while Turkish coffees need an even finer ground. The majority of American coffee is ground into a "drip grind" providing the maximum, surface area, which makes the richest coffee and never bitter. However, if the grinds are micro-fine, the water will take longer to filter through and this will result in an increase of tannins (polyphenols), which produce a bitter taste.

ONE CUP OF COFFEE, HOLD THE ACID

If you have a problem with over acidity or are overly sensitive to acidic beverages, just add a pinch of baking soda to the drink. Baking soda is a mild base and will neutralize a small percentage of the acid.

WHERE DID "CUP OF JOE" ORIGINATE FROM

Alcoholic beverages used to be allowed on board U.S. Naval vessels, However, this practice was discontinued when Admiral Josephus "Joe" Daniels became Naval Chief of Operations. He discontinued all alcoholic beverages with the exception of special occasions. The seamen then took to drinking their second choice beverage, coffee and nicknamed coffee, "a cup of Joe" as a bit of sarcasm directed at the Admiral.

SUPERMARKET COFFEE

Most supermarket coffee brands usually contain too much debris. The cost of producing a fresh quality coffee is too high for markets to produce and the price will be more than most people will pay. Most supermarket coffee is a combination of Aribica and robusta beans. Coffee houses usually only sell Aribica. Robusta beans are higher in caffeine and less expensive to produce. Look for 100% Aribica for a great tasting coffee. Vacuum packed coffee in a supermarket must have an expiration date, which should be checked before you purchase it.

TYPES OF ACIDITY

If the coffee you are drinking leaves dryness on the top of your mouth or on your tongue it is usually due to acidity levels in the coffee. This not necessarily a negative, since some people like a coffee that is somewhat dry, similar to a dry wine.

COFFEE TOO HOT, SIP IT

Your ability to drink burning hot coffee that is capable of burning you and not your mouth is easily explained. When you sip a very hot cup of coffee, you tend to suck in more cool air than you ordinarily would. This instantly lowers the temperature of the hot coffee through convection (air currents) as well as evaporation. Another factor is also at work, and that is the saliva, which is being released tends to partially coat the inside of the mouth, insulating it against a burn.

WHERE DID THE NICKNAME "JAVA" COME FROM

The island of Java, which is part of Indonesia produced some of the finest coffee in the world and was well known during World War II when the coffee plantations were devastated by the war. Some companies use the name "Java" to denote a good coffee but they are restricted from using the name Java Robusta, which can only be used on the "real" Java coffee.

FRAPPE COFFEE

Frappe coffee is more popular in Europe and Latin America than the United States. It is prepared by shaking 1-2 teaspoons of instant coffee with $\frac{1}{2}$ teaspoon of sugar water and ice cubes. It is usually served in a tall glass with ice and sometimes a small amount of milk is added. If shaken properly it will have thick foam on top.

QUICK, SERVE THE COFFEE

The longer the coffee remains on a warmer, the more the oils tend to impart a bitter taste and a percentage of the aroma is lost.

LOOK! THE ACID IS EATING MY STYROFOAM

We know that hot tea with lemon has the ability to corrode away Styrofoam and place carcinogens in your tea, but now there are studies that show that if the coffee has a high enough acid content it will chew away at the Styrofoam as well. We really don't need additional carcinogens in our lifestyle than we already get from all the contaminants we already come into contact with. Use a glass cup, it's safer and the coffee will taste better.

THE ALL AROUND COFFEE GRINDER

A coffee grinder can be used to grind herbs and spices. To clean the grinder and rid it of the coffee aroma, just grind up a few pieces of bread before you grind your herbs or spices.

SUGAR CUBES = FRESH SMELLING COFFEEPOT

To stop the musty smell in a coffeepot between uses, just place a few sugar cubes into the pot and store it without the lid. Sugar cubes have the ability to absorb moisture, which causes the musty odor.

HERE YE, HERE YE, LAMB LOVES COFFEE

Coffee tends to bring out the flavor in lamb. Next time you prepare lamb stew, add a cup of black coffee to the stew as it is cooking. It will enhance the flavor and give the sauce a richer color.

COFFEE CAN REPLACE ALCOHOL

If you don't want to use alcohol when preparing chocolate dessert, try substituting the same quantity of black coffee. You will be amazed at the flavor of the dessert compared to the same dessert using alcohol.

CAFÉ COCOA BEAN

If you would like to try a different cup of coffee, try adding a small piece of plain chocolate in the coffee filter. A piece of vanilla bean works great too.

TASTE BUDS GOING CRAZY

Coffee can elicit a number of different taste sensations depending on the brand you choose. Most people will choose the pure coffee or blend they enjoy the most. The taste can be sweet; caused by sucrose, sour: caused by tartaric acid, salt: caused by sodium chloride, or bitter; cause by quinine.

REALLY HOT BEANS

When coffee beans are roasted to a temperature of 465°F (240°C) chemical changes occur and the beans are capable of emitting their own heat, which then causes the temperature of the roasting oven to increase. This process is called: pyrolysis.

THE LATEST CRAZE

Bottled coffee drinks; is the latest craze in coffee. One of the innovators was Starbucks with Nestle following close behind. One of Starbucks best sellers is Frappuccino, which is sold in 9.5 ounce bottles. Starbucks has more calories, 190 compared to Nestle's 140 and less fat. The taste of Nestle's is weaker than Starbucks but makes it more palatable. The difference in the calories is due to higher sugar content in Starbucks. Neither could be classified a nutritious drink by any stretch of the imagination.

CURDLING UP WITH CREAM

If you want to stop cream from curdling up in your coffee, just add a pinch of baking soda to the cream before pouring it in. The baking soda will neutralize the acid in coffee just enough so as not to alter the flavor, but will eliminate the curdling.

NUTRITIONAL INFORMATION

HAVE A FEW WRINKLES WITH YOUR COFFEE

The latest studies now show that both caffeine and nicotine may cause your skin to dehydrate and cause premature wrinkling. If you drink more than 2 cups of coffee per day or smoke more than 4 cigarettes per day, it would be wise to be sure and drink sufficient water. Remember coffee may have a diuretic effect on your system.

MEDICAL WARNING

One cup of coffee has enough caffeine to keep your brain alert for about four hours in the average person who does not consume large quantities. If you are going to consume coffee, which has not been decaffeinated, try not to drink any after about 4PM. However, the more coffee you drink the higher your tolerance will be to caffeine. Also, if you suffer from stomach ulcers, coffee has been shown to reduce healing time.

COFFEE MAY LOWER RISK OF GALLSTONES

The Journal of the American Medical Society reported in an article; that three cups of regular coffee may lower the risk of gallstones. The reason may be either the caffeine or the caffeic acid that has antioxidant properties.

MEN, TOO MUCH CAFFEINE MAY = USING THE LITTLE GREEN PILL

Studies show that excessive caffeine consumption may cause reduction in zinc absorption and a lower man's sex drive. It may also adversely affect the prostate gland and cause increased stress levels.

ARE HOT DRINKS BODY WARMERS?

Other than a psychological response, hot drinks do not actually increase the body temperature at all. The U.S. Army Research Institute of Environmental Medicine conducted testing and discovered that in order to raise body temperature with liquids a person would have to drink 1 quart of a liquid at 130°F. They also stated that it would be difficult to retain that much liquid at one time. The hot beverages do cause a dilation of the surface blood vessels, which makes you feel warmer as the blood flow increases; however, this will soon make you lose warmth.

WHOOPS, THERE GOES MORE CALCIUM

Studies from the University of Washington stated that regular coffee drinking may lead to an excessive loss of calcium through the urine. This loss amounts to 7mg of calcium for every cup of coffee or 2 cans of caffeinated soda pop. However, if you consume 2 tablespoons of milk for each cup of coffee you drink or 1 tablespoon for every soft drink that will offset the loss.

CAFFEINE CONTENT

BEVERAGE	PER 8 OUNCE SERVING
Espresso	.350-400mg
Drip Coffee	.178-200mg
Percolated	.80-156mg
Instant Coffee	.90-112mg

DRUG WITHDRAWAL AND CAFFEINE

If you decide to give up caffeine be prepared to go through a withdrawal period of about 12-16 hours. The symptoms may be headaches, irritability, depression, runny nose, dizziness and fatigue. Best if you cut back gradually, unless you leave home for a couple of days and spare the family the aggravation.

CAFFEINE CAN KILL

The lethal dosage of caffeine for 50% of the population is about 10 grams if administered orally. This varies widely depending on a person's weight with the dosage of 15 grams capable of killing most people. The lethal dose for coffee varies from 50 cups to 200 cups to be lethal. Since no one drinks 50-200 cups of regular coffee per day, I don't think we need to worry. Children can show signs of toxicity after only 3.5 grams per day and should not be given high caffeinated drinks.

PREGNANCY AND CAFFEINE

Evidence shows that excessive caffeine ingestion will cause malformations in rats when they ingest the equivalent of 70 cups of coffee per day for a human. Since this is more than anyone ever drinks there is probably no harm in consuming a reasonable level of coffee per day until better scientific evidence is released. Studies have shown that caffeine will reduce sperm motility, which may lead to a lower rate of fertility.

OSTEOPOROSIS AND CAFFEINE

Studies have shown that the more caffeine is ingested, the lower the bone density is at the hip and spine. However, if a person's calcium consumption is kept up, there is no difference. One glass of milk a day can make a difference.

COFFEE DRINKING AND SUICIDES

Studies have shown that there are fewer suicides among coffee drinkers; than those who do not drink the beverage. This study was performed on 130,000 Northern Californians with records of 4,500 who died.

CAFFEINE MAY INCREASE METABOLISM

Caffeine tends to cause an increase in the level of circulating fatty acids in the bloodstream. This leads to an increase in the oxidation of these fats for fuel. Caffeine; is used by some runners to enhance fatty acid metabolism and increase endurance levels. This is one reason why caffeine is included in a number of diet pills.

CAFFEINE AND MIGRAINES

Migraine sufferers have been aware for years that by consuming a cup or two of regular coffee lessens the severity of the headaches. The reason for this is that caffeine tends to increase the effectiveness of the drugs used to treat migraines, mainly ergot alkaloids.

STORING COFFEE

Opened coffee cans, should be stored upside down in the refrigerator. The coffee will retain its freshness and flavor for a longer period of time.

Ground coffee oxidizes and loses flavor, it needs to be used within 2-3 days for the best results. Best to buy coffee vacuum, packed. Fresh-roasted beans are usually packed in non-airtight bags to allow the carbon monoxide formed during the roasting process to escape. If the carbon monoxide doesn't escape, the coffee will have a poor taste.

If you run out of coffee filters, try using a piece of white paper towel with no colored design. Clean your coffee pot regularly, the slightest hint of soap or scum will alter the taste. Baking soda and hot water work well.

WHAT IS THERE, IN COFFEE AND TEA THAT ACTS AS A DIURETIC?

Many people switched to decaffeinated beverages so that they would stop running to the bathroom as often and were surprised that the problem was still with them. Unfortunately, many people over a period of years get used to going to the bathroom after drinking coffee and tea that their body just tells them they need to continue doing that even though it isn't necessary. Caffeine does have a diuretic effect on many people, but unfortunately even when it is removed from tea there is still another diuretic agent that remains called theophylline that may stimulate the bladder.

ARE THERE ANY SAFE METHODS OF DECAFFEINATING COFFEE?

The only safe methods are the Swiss water method and the carbon dioxide method. The Swiss Water Process method the green coffee beans are soaked in water for several hours which will remove about 97% of the caffeine as well as a few of the flavor components. The water is then passed through a carbon filter, which removes the caffeine and leaves the flavors. The same water is then added back to the beans before they are dried.

In the carbon dioxide method, the green beans are dampened with water, then placed into a pot that is then filled with pressurized carbon dioxide. The carbon dioxide has the ability to draw the caffeine out of the bean and can remove almost 100% of the caffeine. The coffee beans are then dried to remove the excess moisture. Both methods employ only natural elements to decaffeinate the coffee beans.

DOES THE GRIND-SIZE OF COFFEE BEANS MAKE A DIFFERENCE?

The size of the grind does make a difference in the taste and level of caffeine in a cup of coffee. Espresso should be made with a fine ground, and Turkish coffee needs to have an even finer ground. Most American coffee is ground into a "drip grind." This provides the maximum surface area and will brew a rich cup of coffee that is not bitter. However, if the grinds are ultra-fine the water will take longer to filter through and this will result in an increase in polyphenols (tannins) and bitter tasting coffee.

ARE THEY REALLY MAKING CAFFEINATED WATER

Yes, it's true and it's being sold under the names of "Water Joe" and "Java Johnny." It is being advertised as the latest cure for sleepiness when you are driving. When you go to a restaurant they will soon be asking you whether you want your water "caffeinated" or "plain."

REDUCING ACIDITY IN BEVERAGES

Acid levels can easily be reduced in a number of common beverages since certain people are overly sensitive to these high acid content beverages. To reduce acidity in most beverages just add a pinch of baking soda to the drink, especially coffee. Other high acid foods as well can have their acidity levels reduced with baking soda.

DOES COFFEE KEEP YOU UP AT NIGHT?

Coffee will only keep you up if you are not used drinking a large amount in most instances. The more coffee you drink, the higher your tolerance will be to caffeine and the more it will take to keep you awake. Some individuals are actually born with a high tolerance and are never kept awake. Studies have also found that the thought of the fact that coffee is supposed to keep you awake at night is enough to make people think it is true.

SHOULD YOUR COFFEE MAKER; HAVE A THERMOMETER?

When brewing coffee it is necessary to have the proper temperature to allow the extraction of the maximum amount of caffeol compounds (taste and aroma enhancer) and the lowest level of polyphenol compounds (tannins) that tend to give coffee an off-taste. A professional coffee brewer will keep the temperature of coffee that is brewing between 185^0-205^0 F. If the temperature is too low the coffee grounds will not release adequate caffeol compounds and if gets too high the tannins are released. Caffeine in coffee has very little to do with the taste.

THE LATEST COFFEE CRAZE, THE CAFETIERE

The cafetiere or French coffee press or plunger pot is the latest craze in the United States. A number of coffee product retailers are touting the cafetiere as the "preferred method of brewing." The unit does not use a filter it just presses the coffee and water, which is then poured into a cup. Studies, however, indicate that this is not a preferred method and if people drink 5-6 cups of pressed coffee a day since it may increase cholesterol levels by about 10% and the "bad" cholesterol (LDL) by 14% in some cases. The standard American method of brewing coffee by pouring water through a filter removes two of the risk ingredients that are implicated in raising cholesterol; cafestol and kahweol. These compounds are also found in other non-filtered coffee products such as espresso, which is produced by forcing steam or water through finely, ground coffee.

COFFEE BITTER?

The best flavor will be from freshly ground coffee and always use filtered water. Coffee should never be boiled, the longer it is boiled the more tannins are released.

CAFFEINE CONTENT IN COMMON FOODS AND DRUGS

BEVERAGE	PER 8 OZ. SERVING
Drip Coffee	178-200 mg.
Instant Coffee	90-112 mg.
Black Tea 5 Minute Brew	32-78 mg.
Iced Tea	34-65 mg.
Instant Tea	20-34 mg.
Cocoa	6-8 mg.
Jolt Cola	58 mg.
Diet Dr. Pepper	55 mg.
Mountain Dew	42 mg.
Coca Cola	38 mg.
Diet Coke	38 mg.
Dr. Pepper	37 mg.
Pepsi Cola	29 mg.
Diet Pepsi	28 mg.
DRUGS	**PER TABLET**
Weight Control Aids	250 mg.
Vivarin	200 mg.
NoDoz	100 mg.
Excedrin	65 mg.
Vanquish	38 mg.
Anacin	35 mg.
Midol	32 mg.
Soma	31 mg.
CHOCOLATE	
Milk Chocolate (1 oz.)	5-6 mg.
Semi-Sweet Chocolate (1 oz.)	20-35 mg.

Caffeine is the most popular drug in the United States and can be derived from 60 different plants. It is found naturally in cocoa beans, cola nuts, tea, leaves and coffee beans.

Caffeine is a stimulant to the central nervous system and is capable of warding off drowsiness and increasing alertness. It does, however, reduce reaction time to both visual and auditory stimuli.

Studies have shown that caffeine does not cause frequent urination, but does cause an acid increase in the stomach after just two cups. Chronic heartburn sufferers should avoid coffee completely. Caffeine intake should be restricted to 300 mg. per day.

The latest information on pregnancy and caffeine consumption is relating to studies performed at U.C. Berkeley recommending that pregnant women should try and limit their caffeine consumption to a maximum of 300 mg. per day.

CHAPTER 10

SUBSTITUTIONS AND MEASUREMENTS

SUBSTITUTIONS

If your using a cookbook and it was published in England, the following information will be very useful since many of the common cooking ingredients are called by different names.

BRITISH FOOD	AMERICAN FOOD
Plain Flour	All-Purpose Flour
Wholemeal Flour	Whole Wheat Flour
Strong Flour	Bread Flour
Single Cream	Light Cream
Double Cream	Whipping Cream
Castor Sugar	Granulated Sugar (10X)
Demerara Sugar	Brown Sugar
Treacle Sugar	Molasses
Dark Chocolate	Semi-Sweet Chocolate
Sultanas	White Raisins
Courgettes	Zucchini
Swedes	Turnips
Gammon	Ham

ACTIVE DRY YEAST (one package)
1 cake compressed yeast

AGAR-AGAR
Use gelatin

ALLSPICE
$1/4$ teaspoon cinnamon & $1/2$ teaspoon ground cloves or
$1/4$ teaspoon nutmeg for baking only
or Black pepper other than baking

ANISE (use equivalent amount)
Fennel or dill or cumin

APPLES
One cup of firm chopped pears and one tablespoon of lemon juice.
1 pound of apples = 4 small, 3 medium, or 2 large or $2^3/4$ cups sliced or 2 cups chopped

ARROWROOT
Flour, just enough to thicken, should take a few tablespoons.

BAKING POWDER (one teaspoon, double-acting)
$1/2$ teaspoon cream of tartar plus $1/4$ teaspoon of baking soda or
$1/4$ teaspoon baking soda; plus $1/2$ cup of sour milk, cream, or buttermilk.
Must take the place of other liquid or
4 teaspoons of quick-cooking tapioca

BAKING POWDER (one teaspoon, single-acting)
$3/4$ teaspoon double-acting baking powder

BASIL (dried)
Tarragon or
Summer savory of equal amounts or
Thyme or
Oregano

BAY LEAF
Thyme of equal amounts

BLACK PEPPER
Allspice in cooking providing salt is also used in the dish

BORAGE
Cucumber

BRANDY
Cognac or rum

BREAD CRUMBS ($1/4$ cup, dry)
$1/4$ cup cracker crumbs or
$1/2$ slice of bread, may be toasted or crumbled or
$1/4$ cup rolled oats or
$1/4$ cup of matzo meal or
$1/4$ cup of sifted flour or
$1/4$ cup of corn flakes

BULGUR
Use equal amounts of:
Cracked wheat, kasha, brown rice, couscous, millet, quinoa

BUTTER (in baking)
Hard margarine or shortening
DO NOT USE OIL IN BAKED PRODUCTS
1 pound = 2 cups
1 cup = 2 sticks
2 tbl = $\frac{1}{4}$ stick or 1 ounce
4 tbl = $\frac{1}{2}$ stick or 2 ounces
8 tbl = 1 stick or 4 ounces

BUTTERMILK
One cup of milk plus $1\frac{3}{4}$ tablespoons of cream of tartar or equivalent of sour cream

CAKE FLOUR
Use 1 cup of all-purpose flour minus 2 tablespoons

CAPERS
Chopped green olives

CARAWAY SEED
Fennel seed or cumin seed

CARDAMOM
Cinnamon or mace

CAYENNE PEPPER
Ground hot red pepper or chili powder

CHERVIL
Parsley or tarragon (use less) or anise (use less)

CHIVES
Onion powder (small amount) or leeks or shallots (small amount)

CHOCOLATE, BAKING, UNSWEETENED (one ounce or square)
3 tablespoons of unsweetened cocoa plus 1 tablespoon of butter or
3 tablespoons of carob powder plus 2 tablespoons of water

CHOCOLATE, BAKING, UNSWEETENED (one ounce pre-melted)
3 tablespoons of unsweetened cocoa plus 1 tablespoon of corn oil or melted Crisco

CHOCOLATE, SEMI-SWEET (6 ounces of chips or squares)
Nine tablespoons of cocoa plus 7 tablespoons of sugar plus 3 tablespoons of butter

CILANTRO
Parsley and lemon juice or orange peel and a small amount of sage or lemon grass with a small amount of mint

CINNAMON
Allspice (use a small amount) or cardamom

CLOVES (ground)
Allspice or nutmeg or mace

CLUB SODA
Mineral water or seltzer

CORNMEAL
Grits (corn) or polenta

CORNSTARCH
Flour, a few tablespoons for thickening, usually no more than two

CORN SYRUP (one cup, light)
1¼ cups granulated sugar or
1 cup granulated sugar plus ¼ cup of liquid

CREAM CHEESE
Cottage cheese mixed with cream or cream with a small amount of butter or milk

CREME FRAICHE
Sour cream in a recipe or ½ sour cream and ½ heavy cream in sauces

CUMIN
⅓ anise plus ⅔ caraway or fennel

DILL SEED
Caraway or celery seed

EDIBLE FLOWERS (garnish)
Bachelor buttons, blue borage, calendula petals, chive blossoms, mini carnations, nasturtiums, pansies, rose petals, snap dragon, or violets.

EGGS, WHOLE (one)
2 tablespoons water plus 2 tablespoons of flour plus ½ tablespoons of Crisco plus ½ teaspoon of baking powder or
2 yolks plus 1 tablespoon of water or
2 tablespoons of corn oil plus 1 tablespoon of water or
1 teaspoon of cornstarch plus 3 tablespoons of water if part of a recipe
1 banana (best for cakes and pancakes)
2 tablespoons of cornstarch or arrowroot starch
¼ cup of tofu (blend with liquid ingredients before adding to any dry ingredients)

EVAPORATED MILK
Light cream or half and half or heavy cream.

FLOUR (thickeners, use up to 2-3 tablespoons only)
Bisquick, tapioca (quick cooking), cornstarch, arrowroot (use small amount), potato starch, mashed potato flakes, or pancake mix

GARLIC (equivalent of 1 clove)
¼ teaspoon of minced, dried garlic or
⅛ teaspoon of garlic powder or
¼ teaspoon of garlic juice or
½ teaspoon of garlic salt (omit ½ tsp salt from recipe)

GHEE
Clarified butter

HONEY (one cup in baked goods)
$1^1/_4$ cups granulated sugar plus $^1/_4$ cup water

JUNIPER BERRIES
A small amount of gin

LEMONGRASS
Lemon or lemon rind or verbena or lime rind

LEMON JUICE
Use $^1/_2$ teaspoon of white vinegar for each teaspoon of lemon juice, unless the flavor is required.

LOVAGE
Celery leaves

MARJORAM
Oregano (use small amount) or thyme or savory

MASA HARINA
Corn flour

MASCARPONE
Cream cheese, whipped with a small amount of butter

MEAT
Tempeh (cultured soybeans provides a chewy texture)
Tofu (after it has been frozen)
Wheat gluten

MILK, EVAPORATED
Light cream or half and half or heavy cream

MILK (in baked goods)
Fruit juice plus $^1/_2$ teaspoon of baking soda mixed in with the flour

MILK (one cup)
$^1/_2$ cup evaporated milk plus $^1/_2$ cup of water or
3 tablespoons of powdered milk: plus 1 cup of water. If whole milk is called for add 2 tablespoons of butter

MOLASSES (one cup)
1 cup of honey

NUTMEG
Allspice or cloves or mace

NUTS (in baked goods only)
Bran

OREGANO
Marjoram or rosemary or thyme (fresh only)

PANCETTA
Lean bacon (cooked) or very thin sliced ham

PARSLEY
Chervil or cilantro

POLENTA
Cornmeal or grits (corn)

POULTRY SEASONING
Sage plus a blend of any of these: thyme, marjoram, savory, black pepper, and rosemary

ROSEMARY
Thyme or tarragon or savory

SAFFRON (¹/₈ teaspoon)
1 teaspoon dried yellow marigold petals or
1 teaspoon azafran or
1 teaspoon safflower or
¹/₂ to 1-teaspoon turmeric (adds color)

SAGE
Poultry seasoning or savory or marjoram or rosemary

SELF-RISING FLOUR (one cup)
1 cup all-purpose flour plus 1 teaspoon of baking powder, ¹/₂ teaspoon of salt, and ¹/₄ teaspoon of baking soda

SHALLOTS
Small green onions or leeks or standard onions (use small amount) or scallions (use more than is called for)

SHORTENING (one cup in baked goods only)
1 cup butter or
1 cup hard margarine

SOUR CREAM (one cup)
1 tablespoon of white vinegar: plus sufficient milk to make 1 cup. Allow the mixture to stand for 5 minutes before using or
1 tablespoon of lemon juice plus enough evaporated milk to make 1 cup or
1 cup of plain yogurt if it is being used in a dip or cold soup or
6 ounces of cream cheese plus 3 tablespoons of milk or
¹/₃ cup of melted butter plus ³/₄ cup of sour milk for baked goods

TAHINI
Finely ground sesame seeds

TARRAGON
Anise (use small amount) or chervil (use larger amount) or parsley (use larger amount) or a dash of fennel seed

TOMATO PASTE (one tablespoon)
1 tablespoon of ketchup or
$^1/_2$ cup of tomato sauce providing you reduce some of the other liquid

TURMERIC
Mustard powder

VANILLA EXTRACT (in baked goods only)
Almond extract or other extracts that will alter the flavor

VINEGAR
Lemon juice in cooking and salads only or grapefruit juice, in salads or wine, in marinades

YOGURT
Sour cream or creme fraiche or buttermilk or heavy cream or mayonnaise (use in small amounts)

COMMON LIQUID SUBSTITUTIONS

The following substitution may be used for liquids that are not available at the time the recipe is being prepared. However, it is always better to use the ingredients called for in the recipe for the best results.

LIQUID INGREDIENT	ADEQUATE SUBSTITUTION
1 cup barbecue sauce	1 cup ketchup + 2 tsp. Worcestershire sauce
1 cup broth	1 bouillon cube dissolved in 1 cup of water
1 cup butter	1 cup vegetable shortening + 2 Tbsp. water
1 cup buttermilk	1 Tbsp. lemon juice + balance of cup in milk, then allow it to stand for 5 minutes before using or add 1 Tbsp. of vinegar to 1 cup of evaporated milk and allow to stand for 5 minutes before using.
1 cup chili sauce	1 cup tomato sauce + $^1/_2$ cup sugar + 2 Tbsp. vinegar
1 cup corn syrup	$^3/_4$ cup sugar + $^1/_4$ cup water
1 cup creme fraiche	$^1/_2$ cup sour cream + $^1/_2$ cup heavy cream
1 egg	1 banana or 2 Tbsp. cornstarch or arrowroot starch or $^1/_4$ cup tofu blended into liquid ingredients well
1 cup evaporated milk	Equal amount of light or cream or half and half
1 cup heavy cream	$^3/_4$ cup whole milk + $^1/_3$ cup of butter

1 cup light cream	1 cup milk + 3 Tbsp. butter
1 cup ketchup	1 cup tomato sauce + 4 Tbsp. sugar + 2 Tbsp. vinegar + $1/4$ tsp. ground cloves
1 cup honey	$1 1/4$ cups granulated sugar + $1/4$ cup water
1 tsp. lemon juice	1 tsp. of vinegar
1 cup molasses	1 cup honey
1 cup whole milk	4 Tbsp. dry whole milk + 1 cup water or 1 cup buttermilk + $1/2$ tsp. baking soda
1 cup non-fat milk (skim)	4 Tbsp. nonfat dry milk + 1 cup water
1 cup sour milk	1 Tbsp. lemon juice or vinegar + additional milk to fill 1 cup, allow to stand for 5 minutes
2 drops of hot pepper sauce	A dash of cayenne or red pepper
2 tsp. tapioca	1 Tbsp. all-purpose flour (more if desired)
1 cup tomato juice	$1/2$ cup tomato sauce + $1/2$ cup water
1 Tbsp. tomato paste	1 Tbsp. tomato ketchup
1 cup tomato puree	6 ounce can of tomato paste + 6 ounces of water
1 Tbsp. Worcestershire sauce	1 Tbsp. soy sauce + dash hot sauce
1 cup wine	1 cup apple juice or apple cider or 1 part of vinegar, diluted in 3 parts of water
1 cup yogurt	1 cup buttermilk or sour cream

EXTRACTS AND ESSENCES

LIQUID INGREDIENT	**ADEQUATE SUBSTITUTION**
Angostura Bitters	Orange Bitters or Worcestershire sauce
Anise Extract	Anise Oil (only use 50%)
Cinnamon Extract	Cinnamon Oil (only $1/4$ as much)
Ginger Juice	Place minced ginger in cheesecloth and squeeze out the juice.
Oil of Bitter Almonds	Almond Extract (use 50% more)
Peppermint Extract	Peppermint Oil (use $1/4$ as much)
Rose Water	Rose Syrup (2-3 drops)

OILS AND COOKING SPRAYS

Almond Oil ....Walnut Oil or Extra Virgin Olive Oil
Canola Oil ....Corn Oil or Safflower Oil
Clarified Butter ....Butter (foods may overbrown)
Coconut Oil ....Canola Oil or Corn Oil
Corn Oil ....Canola Oil or Soybean Oil
Ghee ....Clarified Butter or Canola Oil
Grapeseed Oil ....Avocado Oil (very high smoke point)
Peanut Oil ....Corn Oil Or Canola Oil
Schmaltz ....No known substitute when prepared right
Soybean Oil ....Corn Oil

VINEGAR SUBSTITUTES

Apple Cider Vinegar ...Wine Vinegar
Balsamic Vinegar .....Sherry Vinegar
Champagne Vinegar ...Apple Cider Vinegar
Raspberry Vinegar ....Red Wine Vinegar
Red Wine Vinegar .....Balsamic Vinegar
Rice Vinegar ....Apple Cider Vinegar
White Vinegar ....Apple Cider Vinegar (canning only with at least
..................5% acidity)

ALCOHOL SUBSTITUTIONS FOR RECIPES

AMARETTO	Use non-alcoholic almond extract, orgeat Italian soda syrup or marzipan.
APPLE BRANDY	Use unsweetened apple juice or cider.
APRICOT BRANDY	Use the heavy syrup from canned apricots or apricot preserves.
BOURBON	Use non-alcoholic vanilla extract.
CHAMPAGNE	Use sparkling apple cider or grape juice.
CHERRY LIQUEUR	Use heavy syrup from canned cherries or cherry preserves.
COFFEE LIQUEUR	Use non-alcoholic coffee extract.
CRÈME DE CACAO	Use non-alcoholic vanilla extract
CRÈME DE MENTHE	Use non-alcoholic mint extract
MUSCAT	Use white grape juice.
ORANGE LIQUEUR	Use unsweetened orange juice concentrate.
PEACH BRANDY	Use heavy syrup fron canned peaches.
PORT	Use Concord grape juice.
RED WINE	Grape juice
RUM	Use non-alcoholic vanilla or rum extract.
SHERRY	Use non-alcoholic vanilla extract or coffee syrup.
VERMOUTH	Use apple cider.
VODKA	Use white grape juice.
WHITE WINE	Use white grape juice.

I CAN SEE A RAINBOW, SEE A RAINBOW......

Liquid food colorings are sold in small bottles since a little goes a long way. Food coloring is composed of water, propylene glycol and artificial colors, many of which are suspect in relation to laboratory studies pertaining to cancer in mice. However, the small amount that is used should pose no health risk. A new addition to the colorings is decorative gels, which are composed of corn syrup, water, modified corn starch, salt, carrageenan gum, citric acid, preservatives and of course those artificial dyes. Liquid food colorings have a safe shelf life of about 4 years if stored in a cool, dry location.

MEASUREMENTS

THESE LIQUIDS DO MEASURE UP

60 drops	=	5 ml. or 1 Tsp.
3 Tsp.	=	1 Tbsp.
2 Tbsp.	=	30 ml. or 1 fl. oz.
8 Tbsp.	=	$^1/_2$ cup
5 Lg. Eggs	=	1 cup
2 Tbsp. butter	=	1 oz.
1 oz.	=	30 grams
Juice of 1 orange	=	5-6 Tsp.
8 Fluid Ounces	=	1 Cup
16 Fluid Ounce	=	2 Cups (1 pint)
32 Fluid Ounces	=	4 Cups (1 quart)
4 Quarts	=	6 Cups (1 gallon)

CHAPTER 11

RESTAURANTS & FAST FOOD

FAST FOODS, THE GOOD AND THE BAD

Fast food restaurants over the past 5 years have had to make a number of changes and are now offering a number of low-fat alternatives to their usual fare of high-calorie, high-fat foods. The level of education and media information that has been released has had an impact and raised the public's level of health consciousness.

IT'S THE REAL THING, OR IS IT?

If you're going to Arby's to get a "real" roast beef sandwich you are in for a surprise. According to Arby's, the roast beef is just processed ground beef, water, salt, and sodium phosphate. It is lower in cholesterol and fat than "real" roast beef or the average hamburger; making it still a good choice for fast food fare. Arby's also has an excellent roasted chicken sandwich.

BIOSENSORS TO CAPTURE BACTERIA

Biosensors have been invented that will detect bacteria on food in restaurants and slaughterhouses. Microelectronics have made it possible to produce a sensor that can capture bacteria in a repeating pattern similar to a bar code, which will read the information with a laser beam. Specific antibodies are actually stamped on the sensor and form a pattern that is read with the laser beam. The device will detect even minute bacteria. A hand-held device may be available by 2001 to easily monitor bacterial contamination of foods before you eat the food. Automated systems may also be in use by 2002.

ORGANIC WASTE CONVERTED INTO ETHANOL

Converting biomass, which consists of waste organic material, scrap foodstuff, sugar cane residues, rice hulls and wood wastes can now be converted into a usable product called ethanol. Ethanol is a relative of alcohol and can be used as a clean-burning fuel or industrial chemical. A genetically modified, bacteria has been developed by the University of Florida that converts the biomass into ethanol. This is the fist economical conversion process ever developed.

NEW VEGETARIAN MENU ITEMS

Restaurants will be offering more vegetarian foods and meatless entrees than ever before by 2001. Expect to see separate menus that will cater to the growing segment on non-meat eaters.

AUTOMATED ORDERING

By the year 2005 most restaurants will have a menu that will allow you to choose your food by touching the item with a special pen attached to the menu. You will also be able to write a special request and the information will be delivered to an employee in the kitchen that will pass the order on by electronic pencil to the chef.

BURGER BUN FACTOID

There are approximately 180 sesame seeds on a McDonald's Big Mac bun.

RESTAURANTS TO GET BUSIER

The food service business is expected to reach $800 billion by 2005 with a good part of the growth expected to be from free-standing kiosks, food chains that feature broad menus and supermarkets that sell prepared foods. The traditional grocery store will eventually be a thing of the past.

RESTAURANTS TO OFFER PHARMAFOODICALS

You're going to start seeing the term "pharmafoodicals" more and more as we approach 2003. Restaurants will be carrying foods that have been altered into "pharmafoodicals." These foods will give your specific levels of additional nutrients and are basically "functional foods." Staying healthier and living longer will be on everyone's minds.

DRIVE-THRU QUALITY FOOD – THE FUTURE TREND

More and more of your favorite restaurants will be installing drive-thru windows to cater to the breadwinner that is heading home and picks up dinner on the way. Even high-end restaurants will be making this service available.

THE DINKS WILL BE ORDERING HOME DELIVERY THE MOST

The "double-income with kids" (DINKS) will be at the forefront of purchasing from restaurants that deliver. You might even see some of the fast food chains like McDonald doing home delivery by 2003. The term DINKS originated with ABC news. The home delivery business is expected to expand to 20% of the market share.

KOREAN ALCOHOLIC ICE CREAM

Korean restaurants are now serving alcoholic ice cream, which is basically different wines and ice cream powder prepared into 10 different ice creams. The new treat is becoming increasingly popular throughout Korea and will probably making its way to the United States by late 2002. The ice cream has been described as fresh and very thirst quenching. The special secret formula is also prepared from standard ice cream, slush and sherbet. The Brewery Company that will be producing the treat is Bae Young-ho Brewery of Seoul, Korea.

BURGER CHAINS WILL SELL SOYBURGERS

A number of fast food restaurants that tried to sell the public on the use of meat substitutes in their burgers a few years ago failed horribly. However, with all the new studies appearing in the newspaper and TV shows relating soy to reducing the incidence of heart disease, the public is changing their minds and restaurants are selling more veggie burgers than ever before. One of the leaders in the new soy burger revolution will be Boca Burger,

SALT SHAKE?

Most thick shakes contain so many additives that are derived from sodium that they contain more sodium than an order of French fries.

SLOP ON THE CHOCOLATE FAT

When they dip a soft-serve ice cream product into a vat of chocolate coating, they are actually dipping it into; a high-fat product made from oils that have a very low melting point.

YUM, YUM, FRIED CHICKEN FAT

When the skin and special coatings are consumed on your fried chicken, the product ends up providing you with more fat and calories than a regular hamburger.

GEE, WE GOT FOOLED AGAIN, SO WHAT'S NEW

The fast food restaurants are now advertising that they do not use any animal product to fry in. However, what they neglect to mention is that some are using tropical oils such as coconut and palm oils, which are both high in saturated fat. Also, some chains are pre-frying their fries to reduce cooking time. The pre-frying may be done in high saturated fat oils.

NUMERO UNO FRENCH FRIES

The number one fast food, restaurant French fry: is made by the In-N-Out Burger restaurant chain. They are never fried twice and always cut up fresh and fried immediately.

THE GOOD IS OUT, THE BAD IS BACK

McDonald's removed the McLean hamburger, which had only 350 calories and 12 grams of fat and replaced it with the Arch Deluxe hamburger, which contains 570 calories and 31 grams of fat. Taco Bell removed the Border Light Taco from its menu, which had only 140 calories and 5 grams of fat and replaced it with the Big Border Taco, which has 290 calories and 17 grams of fat.

WELL SHIVER MY TIMBERS

If you are ordering a fried fish sandwich, be aware that the coating and frying oil make the sandwich a 50% fat meal. Might as well eat a burger.

HAR, HAR, HAR

Baked fish is available at Long John Silvers, a reduction of over 200 calories over fried fish. Even the sodium content is in an acceptable range of 361mg. instead of the usual 1200mg.

THIS WILL MAKE YOU POP-UP

Make sure you use a "lite" dressing and the shrimp salad at Jack-In-The-Box will only have 115 calories and 8% fat.

ONE FATTY CHICKEN

If you think you are getting a low-fat meal by ordering the Burger King chicken sandwich, think again. It contains 42 grams of fat and can be compared to eating a pint of regular ice cream in one sitting.

THE ROASTED CHICKEN INVASION

KENNY ROGERS ROASTERS — $1/2$ chicken with skin contains 750 calories and 8.7 teaspoons of fat.

KENTUCKY FRIED CHICKEN — $1/2$ chicken with skin contains 670 calories and 9.0 teaspoons of fat.

There isn't enough difference to really make an intelligent choice. Kenny Rogers Roasters in my opinion has the best, flavored product and the best, side dishes as long as they are kept fresh.

GREAT BUNS

Fast food restaurants are finally getting more health conscious and offering multi-grain buns, which are an excellent source of fiber.

ALL OF ME, WHY NOT TAKE ALL OF ME

When you see an advertisement that reads "100% pure beef" and your biting down on unusually chewy material it might be almost any part of the beef. Legally, bone, gristle, fat, and almost any other part of the animal can be ground up and used in a number of processed meat products. It is sometimes referred to as "edible offal."

GOOD GOING JR.

If you go to a Carl's Jr. you may see a number of small red hearts next to an item. They have a few sandwiches that are actually approved by the American Heart Association.

A small order of McDonald's Chicken McNuggets (6): have 21.3 grams of fat, 36.5% of which is saturated.

COMMON FAST FOOD MEAL

FOOD	CAL.	CHOL.	SODIUM	FAT
Hamburger on a bun	550	80mg.	800mg.	57%
Regular Fries	250	10mg.	115mg.	52%
Thick Shake	350	31mg.	210mg.	8%
Apple Pie	260	13mg.	427mg.	21%
	1,410cal.	134mg.	1,552mg.	

HOLD THE BAD STUFF

When ordering in a fast food restaurant always order your food "special order" so that you can tell them that you do not want the special sauce (fat), ketchup (sugar), mayonnaise (fat), and pickles (salt).

EASILY BEATS THE BURGERS

Pizza is the most popular fast food in America (44,000 units) and pepperoni is the number one topping. In Japan the favorite pizza topping is tuna and scallops.

STUFF IT

The new "stuffed pizza crusts" add 13-23 grams of fat to the pizza and an additional 400-500 calories.

FAST FOOD FRYERS

Fast food frying vats use about 50 pounds of shortening per fryer. A few new pounds are added every day to replenish the losses and the old fat filtered. The fat is usually changed every 4-7 days and is kept at 335°F for about 16-20 hours that the restaurant is open. Best to get your fries on the day they change the oil, not he 4-7th day.

FAT CITY

If you really want a high-fat meal, try Carl's Jr. Double Western Cheeseburger. This one is on top of all charts with over 1,000 calories and 63 grams of fat, half of which is saturated. If you want to double the fat just add a thick shake and a large order of fries. Jack in the Box, however, has the "Ultimate Cheeseburger" at 69 grams of fat.

SALAD FAT?

If you think that a salad is a better meal: try adding one packet of ranch dressing to a McDonald's Chef's Salad, it will have more fat than a Big Mac.

HEALTHY CRUST OR UNHEALTHY CRUST?

Nutritionally, pizza may or may not be reasonably healthy. Some restaurants use flour that is NOT "enriched" since it is the cheaper product.

IT'S A HOLY CATASTROPHE

In 2001 we ate over 11.9 billion doughnuts. 90% of Americans eat doughnuts on a regular weekly basis.

KEEPING YOUR CARDIOLOGIST BUSY

Between McDonald's, Burger King, and Wendy's, they sell almost 4 million pounds of French fries daily that contain a total of 1 million pounds of saturated fat.

HIGH FAT SALAD

One of the worst salads found at a fast food restaurant was the Taco Bell Taco Salad containing 838 calories and 55 grams of fat, 16 grams of which is saturated.

THE UNINFORMED LEADING THE ADULT

In over 83% of American families, kids make the decision as to which fast food restaurant to go to. The deciding factor is the toy promotion.

COOKING WITH BASIC INGREDIENTS FOR CHEF'S ONLY

Predictions are that few Americans will have ever cooked using basic ingredients by the year 2005. Ready-prepared meals will be such a big business that most families will not bother cooking anymore. The quality of these meals will be high and the prices very affordable.

CRISPY VEGGIES TO BE MORE POPULAR

Expect to see more and more vegetables to be made into crisps. Genetically modified vegetables will be able to retain their flavor when fried or dried. This will increase their appeal, even to the youngsters. Vegetables that will appear first will be watermelon, radishes, celery and tomatoes.

CHIPS TO BE MADE FROM PASTE

The method of producing chips will be changing by 2001 and almost all chips will be made from a vegetable paste that is fortified with nutrients and will be naturally low fat, even though they are fried. The chips will be pressed from the paste with added natural binders and flavor enhancers.

MOVE OVER POTATO CHIPS

A reduced-fat apple chip will be on the market in early 2002 called "Seneca's Apple Chips." The apple chips are fried in fat-reduced oil called "Salatrim" that is metabolized by the body into a fat and carbohydrate. Salatrim is produced from "real" fat and has no relationship to Olestra, which must have a warning label on the packages of chips. Therefore, the new apple chip will not carry a warning label stating that it will cause digestive problems if you eat a large serving.

PITA BREAD SNACK FOOD

The "Pita Puffs" are coming to town and will be a big snack success. The Puffs will only have 110 calories and 2 grams of fat in 35 puffs compared to one ounce of potato chips, which contain 150 calories and at least 10 grams of fat. They can also be used to replace croutons on salads and in soups and even as a stuffing mix.

A SNACK EXPLOSION

A new refrigerated snack will be released in early 2002 or before. The new food will be called "FruitJelite®" and is based on a new food technology. This new technology allows the food to be packaged in a form that will separate when consumed into individual citrus "cel sacs" of the fresh fruits. The "cel sacs" break apart in the consumer's mouth and releases the flavors. The product has been 3 years in research and development.

WHO'S RUNNING THE SHOW?

Over 2 million children every day eat in a fast food restaurant. In most cases they are given the right to choose what food they will order and usually order whatever has a prize in it, which are all high fat meals. The sad part is that the adults will allow a six-year old to determine what is healthy and not healthy for them. In 85% of families the children even choose the restaurant.

THE ADULT'S FAVORITE

The most popular fast food chain with the adults is Burger King. Burger King's Weight Watcher's Fettucini Broiled Chicken, however, is 33% fat by calories.

ADDING THEIR OWN TOUCH

If you are curious about additives in fast foods you might send away for the list of ingredients in the fast foods. You may be surprised at the number of additives such as MSG in chicken and roast beef seasonings, yellow dyes in shakes, soft ice cream, chicken nuggets, hot cakes, and sundae toppings, etc., etc.

RATING THE FAST FOODS

FOOD	BEST RESTAURANT
1. Pizza	Fasolini's Pizza (Las Vegas, NV)
2. Rotisserie Chicken	Kenny Rogers Roasters
3. Roast Beef Sandwich	Roy Rogers
4. Hamburger (single)	In-N-Out Burgers
5. French Fries	In-N-Out Burgers
6. Baked Fish Sandwich	Long John Silver's
7. Chicken Sandwich (grilled)	McDonald's

GREATEST PIZZA AND ITALIAN FOOD IN NORTH AMERICA

This is without a doubt the finest hand-made pizza and homemade Italian food in America, prepared with all fresh ingredients. Many pizzas are unique to The Fasolini's Pizza Café and my favorite is the garlic tuna. The blend of seasonings is a family secret formula that has been handed down since the beginning of pizza, making. Next time you visit Las Vegas, this is a must stop for the taste sensation of the finest Italian food you will ever taste. For information on a true gourmet pizza, call Josie or Jim Fasolini at (702) 877-0071.

REASONABLE FAST FOOD CHOICES

FOOD	CALORIES	TEASPOONS OF FAT
BURGER KING		
Plain Bagel	270	1.0
Chef's Salad	178	1.9
Garden Salad	95	1.3
Side Salad	25	0.0
Tater Tenders	213	2.6
CARL'S JR.		
Chicken Salad	200	1.8
Hamburger, Plain	320	3.2
DOMINO'S PIZZA		
Cheese Pizza (2 lg. slices)	375	2.3
Ham Pizza (2 lg. slices)	417	2.5
HARDEE'S		
Chicken Fiesta Salad	280	3.4
Chicken Stix	210	2.0
Fried Chicken Leg(no skin)	120	1.1

Garden Salad	210	3.2
Grilled Chicken Sandwich	310	2.0
Roast Beef Sandwich (reg.)	310	2.7

JACK IN THE BOX

Chicken Fajita Pita	292	1.8
Hamburger, Plain	265	2.5
Hash Browns	115	1.6
Taco	190	2.5

KENTUCKY FRIED CHICKEN

Baked Beans	133	0.4
Chicken Little Sandwich	169	2.3
Cole Slaw	119	1.5
Corn on the Cob	75	0.7

LONG JOHN SILVER'S

Catfish Fillet (1pc)	180	2.5
Chicken Plank	110	1.4
Chicken, Baked	140	0.9
Clam Chowder Soup (w/cod)	140	1.4
Cod, Baked	130	0.0
Hushpuppies	70	0.5
Rice Pilaf	250	0.7
Seafood Salad	270	1.6
Vegetables	120	1.4

McDONALD'S

Apple Bran Muffin	190	0.0
Chunky Chicken Salad	140	0.8
Garden Salad	110	1.5
Hamburger, Plain	260	2.2
Hashbrown Potatoes	130	1.7

SUBWAY

Ham Sandwich	360	2.5
Roast Beef Sandwich	375	2.5
Turkey Sandwich	357	2.3

TACO BELL

Pintos and Cheese	190	2.0
Chicken Taco, Soft	210	2.3
Steak Taco, Soft	218	2.5
Taco	183	2.5
Tostada	243	2.5

WENDY'S

Chili	220	1.6
Garden Salad	102	1.1
Grilled Chicken Sandwich	340	3.0
Jr. Cheeseburger	310	3.0
Jr. Hamburger	260	2.1

Almost everyday fast food restaurants are changing their menus: many of these changes are low-calorie and low fat. Send for their up-to-date nutritional information brochure or ask for one at any restaurant.

If you would like a copy of the list of ingredients in your favorite fast food, just write to the restaurant chain listed below:

Arby's
Ten Piedmont Ctr.
3495 Piedmont Rd. NE
Atlanta, GA 30305

Burger King
P.O. Box 520783
General Mail Facility
Miami, FL 33152

Burger Chef
College Park Pyramids
P.O. Box 927
Indianapolis, IN 46206

Church's Fried Chicken
P.O. Box BH001
San Antonio, TX 78284

Hardee's
1233 N. Church St.
Rocky Mount, NC 27801

Jack In The Box
Foodmaker Inc.
9330 Balboa Ave.
San Diego, CA 92123

Kentucky Fried Chicken
P.O. Box 32070
Louisville, KY 40232

Long John Silver's
P.O. Box 11988
Lexington, KY 40579

McDonald's
McDonald Plaza
Oak Brook, IL 60521

Pizza Hut
P.O. Box 428
Wichita, KS 67201

Roy Rogers
Marriot Corp.
Marriot Dr.
Washington, D.C. 20058

Wendy's
4288 W. Dublin Granville
Dublin, OH 43017

Kenny Rogers Roasters
899 West Cypress Creek Road, Ste #500
Fort Lauderdale, FL 33309
(305) 938-0330

CHAPTER 12

SHELF LIFE OF COMMON FOOD ITEMS

BAKING RELATED

All-purpose flour .....unopened 12 months, opened 6-8 months
Whole Wheat flour   unopened 1-2 months, opened 6 months if refrigerated
Granulated sugar .....unopened 2 years, opened 6 months
Brown sugar   unopened 4 months, opened 4 months if stored in freezer
Confectioners sugar ...unopened 18 months
Solid shortening ......unopened 8 months, opened 3 months
Cocoa ....unopened 2 years, opened 1 year
Baking soda ....unopened 18 months, opened 6 months
Baking powder ....unopened 6 months, opened 3 months
Cornstarch ....18 monhs opened or unopened

SPICES

Whole spices ....2-4 years, opened or unopened, away from heat
Ground spices ....2-3 years, opened or unopened, away from heat
Paprika ....2-3 yers if refrigerated
Cayenne pepper, ...2-3 years if refrigerated
chili powder

CANNED GOODS (HIGH ACID)

Tomato products ......1-2 years unopened
Fruit juices ....1-2 years unopened

CANNED GOODS (LOW ACID)

Soups ....3-5 years unopened
Meats ....2-4 years unopened
Gravy ....3-5 years unopened
Vegetables ....3-4 Years unopened

MISCELLANEOUS

Pasta (no eggs) . . . . . . .unopened 2 years, opened 1 year
Dry egg noodles . . . . . .unopened 2 years, opened 1-2 months
Salad dressing . . . . .unopened 1 year, opened 3 months if refrigerated
Honey . . . . .1 year opened or unopened
Ground coffee   2 years unopened, 2 weeks in refrigerated if opened
Coffee (instant) . . . . . . .1 year unopened, 3 months opened
Bottled water . . . . .2 years unopened, 3 monhs opened
Jams, jellies, preserves . .1 year unopened, 6 months opened if refrigerated
Peanut butter . . . . .6-9 months unopened, 2-3 months opened

CHAPTER 13

REPAIRING FOODS – QUICK REFERENCE

ANCHOVIES

TOO SALTY
Soak them in cold tap water for 10-12 minutes. If you are not going to use them immediately, store them for 1 day in fresh extra virgin olive oil in the refrigerator.

APPLES

Poor Flavor
Quarter the apples and dip them in powdered anise or sprinkle them with cinnamon.

ARTICHOKES

Falling Apart
Cannot be fixed. Best to wrap the artichoke in cheesecloth before you cook it and then remove the cheesecloth just before serving.

Too Bland
Sprinkle a small amolunt of fennel in the cooking water, about $1/8$th teaspoon should do the trick.

ASPARAGUS SPEARS

Not Sweet Enough
Asparagus tends to lose sweetness the older it gets. Add a small amount of sugar to the cooking water and if they are too old, add $1/4$ teaspoon of salt to the water to help them retain their color.

Overcooked
Cannot be revived, best to cut up and use in soup.

AVOCADOS

Not Ripe Enough
Place the avocado in a wool sock and place in a dark location for 24-30 hours.

BEETS

Discoloring
If you see the color fading, just add 1 tablespoon of lemon juice or white vinegar to the cooking water.

Too Bland
Usually only occurs when beets get too old. Just add a pinch of allspice to the cooking water. You can also add a small amount of sugar to the cooking water to sweeten them up.

BERRIES

Bland
Berries may get a little bland if they are too many days old. Just sprinkle them with brown sugar to perk them up.

Overripe
Not much you can do except to make an ice cream topping.

BREAD

Dried Out
Try wrapping the bread in a very damp kitchen towel and refrigerate overnight, remove the towel and bake in a 350°F oven for no more than 5 minutes.

BREADING

Won't Stay Put
Make sure the food is dry before placing it in the breading mixture. Place the food in the refrigerator for 45 minutes before cooking.

BROCCOLI

Cooked Too Much
Broccoli will only store in the refrigerator for 3-4 days.

Too Bland
To perk up broccoli, just add a small amount of mustard seed to the cooking water.

Too Salty
Rinse the broccoli gently under hot water; then continue cooking for a short period of time.

BUTTER

Burned
Discard it; there is no way to save it. Next time add a little canola oil to raise the smoke point.

CABBAGE

Overcooked
Cannot be revived, use in soup.

Purple Color
If this occurs when cooking red cabbage, just add 1 tablespoon of white vinegar to the cooking water and in a minute or so it will turn red again. If it turns blue this will work as well.

CANDY

Sugaring
If chocolate candy starts to sugar during cooking, just add a small amount of whole milk and continue cooking until the candy returns to the proper temperature.

CARROTS

Limp
Soak the carrots in ice water overnight in the refrigerator with 1 tablespoon of concentrated lemon juice.

CAULIFLOWER

Discolors
If you notice the cauliflower getting darker when you are cooking it, just add a very small amount of white vinegar to the boiling water.

Too Salty
Place the cauliflower into fresh boiling water for 1-2 minutes.

CHEESE

Dried Out/Hard
Grate it and use it for a topping.

Moldy
Remove at least $1/2$ inch or more from the mold area before using.

Rubbery
Place the cheese into a food processor and chop into small bits, then place it in the top of a double boiler and cook slowly. This usually occurs when too high a heat is used or cheese is cooked too fast.

COCONUT

Got Stale
Place the shredded coconut in a bowl and add $\frac{1}{8}$th teaspoon of sugar and enough whole milk to cover. Allow to stand for 3-4 minutes, then drain well.

COOKIES

Burned
Stop using brown cookie sheets, use shiny ones. Make sure that the cookie sheet is full and does not have just a few cookies on it.

Dough Crumbly
Allow the dough to remain at room temperature for 30 minutes and cover the dough with a lightly dampened kitchen towel.

Dough Stcks to Hands
Place your hands in a bowl of ice water (with ice cubes) for 20 seconds.

Dough Sticks to Rolling Pin
Store the rolling pin in the freezer.

CORN

Overcooked
Cream the corn.

CRACKERS

Soggy
Place the crackers on a shiny cookie sheet in a 350ºF oven for 3 minutes.

CREAM

Getting Sour
Place a pinch of baking soda in the cream and it will sweeten for a day or two.

CUCUMBERS

Too Soft
Place the cucumbers in a large bowl if ice water in the refrigerator for 1-2 hours.

DATES

Stuck Together
Place the dates on a lined cookie sheet and place in a warm oven for 2-3 minutes.

EGGS

Undercooked
If you crack open an undercooked egg, just place it in aluminum foil and twirl the ends, then place it back in the water to finish cooking.

EGGPLANT

Discoloring
If eggplant starts to discolor while it is cooking, just add a small amount of salt to the water.

Hard to Skin
Slice the eggplant into quarters and then peel the skin off.

FISH

Too Salty
Soak raw fish in cold water for 10-12 minutes, then change the water and store it in water if you are going to cook it soon.

GELATIN

Won't Set-Up
Place the gelatin in an ice cold bath. A bowl with ice cubes set under the gelatin until it sets up.

GRAVY

Lumpy
Place the gravy in a blender for a few seconds.

Not Brown Enough
Add 1 teaspoon of instant decaf coffee to the gravy and cook for a few minutes more.

Not Thick Enough
Use instant potato powder, arrowroot or cornstarch.

GREENS

Badly Wilted
Submerge the greens in hot water, then immediately in ice water that contains $1/8$th teaspoon of white vinegar. Shake off the excess liquid and place into the refrigerator for about an hour before serving.

HAM

Too Salty
Place the ham in the oven and cook for $\frac{1}{2}$ the time, remove and pour a can of gingerale over the ham and then rub salt on the outside and finish cooking. The gingerale and salt will draw salt water out of the ham.

ICE CREAM

Melted
Best not to re-freeze ice cream.

MAYONNAISE

Separated
Place 1 teaspoon of prepared mustard in a warm bowl, then add 1 teaspoon of mayonnaise and beat until creamy. Continue adding 1 teaspoon at a time of the mayonnaise and beating until it is all back in suspension.

Curdled
Place 1 large egg yolk in a cold bowl and VERY slowly add the mayonnaise while continually stirring. Add a small amount of boiling water to the mixture and continue to mix. Mayonnaise should not be made on humid days.

Too Thick
To retain the creaminess, thin it out with cream or evaporated milk.

MERINGUE

Condensation Droplets
This tends to occur when the meringue is cooled too fast. Try turning the oven off just before it is done and allow it to cool somewhat in the oven.

MILK

Soured
Place 2 teaspoons of baking soda in each quart of milk and that will extend the life for 1-2 days.

MUFFINS

Moist Bottoms
Muffins were allowed to remain in the pan too long and moisture from condensation occurred. Muffins should be removed from the pan and cooled on a wire rack.

Stuck to Pan
Place the pan on a wet towel for 2-3 minutes to cool the pan and release the muffins.

Too Tough
This is caused by beating the dough instead of folding it. They can't be fixed, just slice them up and toast them.

MUSHROOMS

Shriveled
All you have to do is peel the outer covering off.

Too Light
Cook them in an iron pan and use real unsalted butter.

Too Dark
Add 4-5 drops of concentrated lemon juice to the butter and cook for a few minutes longer.

ONIONS

Difficult To Peel
Place the onion in boiling water for 8-10 minutes.

PUNCH

Too Bland
Give it a boost with $\frac{1}{2}$ cup of powdered cardamom dissolved in $\frac{1}{2}$ cup of very warm fruit juice or use use 1 teaspoon of rosemary dissolved in the same fruit juice before adding to the punch.

PANCAKES

Sticking to Griddle
Add more shortening to the next batch.

PASTA

Sticks Together
Place the pasta back into boiling water for a few seconds. A small amount of olive oil in the water helps so does a warm colander.

POPCORN

Will Not Pop
Soak the kernels in warm water for 4-5 minutes before trying again.

POTATO CHIPS

Too Soggy
Place on cookie sheet in a 350°F oven for 5 minutes.

PRUNES

Too Hard
Place them into a pot and cover with boiling water; then place them in the refrigerator overnight.

PUDDINGS

Curdling
As soon as curdling begins, stop the cooking and place the pan into a cold water bath. Beat the pudding with a whisk or eggbeater until smooth.

Skin Has Formed
Remove skin and place a piece of plastic wrap on top if it not too hot to eliminate another skin forming.

QUICHE

Crust is Soggy
Usually caused by using vegetables that have not been properly drained and dried off before being added. Many vegetables are naturally high in moisture and ruin the crust.

RAISINS

Sinking to the Bottom
Because of their weight, they need to be coated with flour so that they will adhere to the dough or batter better.

Sticking Together
Place the mess of raisins on a cookie sheet in a 300°F oven for 2 minutes.

SOUFFLES

Browning Too Soon
Make a tent with aluminum foil and cover, but do not remove from oven (going to be tricky).

SOUPS

Cloudy Bouillon
Place a number of eggshells in and continue cooking. Strain through fine sieve or cheesecloth: before you serve it.

Too Salty
There are a number of solutions: you can add tomatoes, some brown sugar, or a piece of raw potato to sop up the excess salt.

SQUASH

Very Stringy
Place the squash in a food processor or electric mixer for a few seconds.

STEW

Burned
Carefully remove the portion that was not burned and put it into another pot using a wooden spoon. Adding onions will overcome any burnt flavor or odor that remains.

TOMATOES

Can't Get The Skin Off
The easiest method is to pour boiling water over the tomatoes and allow them to stand for 3-4 minutes.

VEAL

Too Dark a Color
If you want the veal to be nice and white, just soak it overnight in whole milk in the refrigerator.

WHIPPED CREAM

Beat It Too Long
Enjoy the homemade butter.

Difficult To Whip
Make sure all utensils and bowls are ice cold.

CHEF'S SECRETS OF COOKING AND PREPARATION

VEGETABLE COOKING

www.gallawa.com

www.landaui.phys.virginia.edu

www.national.sidewalk.msn.com

www.topsecretrecipes.com

www.shorelunch.com

www.goodnuke.com

www.dickerinc.com

www.sciencedaily.com/releases/1998/06/980623045258.html

www.canolainfo.org/htm/frg.html

www.canolainfo.org

http://pages.ivillage.com/fd/angel_luv/SpicyFries.html

www.yumyyum.com

http://antoine.fsu.umd.edu/chem/senese/101/liquids/faq/oil-and-defoaming.shtml

www.comfort.site.yahoo.net

www.faberonline.com

www.sniffies.com

www.excite.com/lifestyle/food

www.geocities.com

www.foodsafety.org

www.wa.beeftips.com

www.geocities.com

www.goerie.com/newsonly/life/food

www.spud.co.uk

www.thomasland.org

www.makenets.com

www.home.naxs.com/puckett/casseroles

www.bakels.com/bakelsab/custard.html

www.foodland.net

www.food6.epicurious.com

www.fmi.org/foodkeeper.com

www.webfoodpros.com

www.3.epicurious.com

www.dairytechnology.com

www.goodnuke.com

PREPARATION OF FOODS

www.fanafana.com/consumers

www.geocities.com

COOKWARE, CURRENT Y2K FACTS

www.ultranet.com/~jkimball/Biologypages1A/Aluminum.html

http://mayohealth.org/mayo/askdiet/html/news/gd980304.html

www.lodgemfg.com/why.html

www.globaloutlet.com/store/304.html

www.silverstone.com

www.eternity-enamle.com

www.tauinton.com/fc/features/kitchen/10pans.html

www.globalgourmet.com

www.happycooker.net

www.worldkitchen.com

www.discountcookware.ehome-women.com

www.switcheroo.com

BARBECUING FOOD FACTS

www.barbecuen.com/alphaf1.com/barbecue

http://members.aol.com/stephndon/tips.html

http://smokehousenews.com/home_pages/grill_tips.html

www.southerngrill.com

SAUTÉING

www.sunsite.unc.edu/expo/restaurant/chef/sauteing

www.wegmans.com

www.taunton.com/fc/admin/foodscience

www.goodcooking.com

NUTRIENT LOSSES

http://seflin.org/drjason/drjafood.14.html

www.cakeemporium.com

www.nncc.org/Nutrition/fd.safe.crosscontam.html

www.worldkitchen.com www.thrive.net/eats

www.dupps.com/boil/poin.html

www.womanmotorist.com

www.ichef.com

www.crisco.com

www.eatright.org

www.naturalhealthinfo.com

www.healthychoice.com

www.nal.usda.gov/ttic/tektran/data/ooooo7/94

www.techultant.com www.canola.com

www.goodcooking.com

www.homebooks.home.mindspring.com/craft/candykit.htm

www.cooking.com/advice

TESTING YOUR METAL

Copper

www.forum.epicuean.com/pots_N_pans

Aluminum

www.alumaworksinc.com

www.corningware.com

www.donskitchen.com

www.hosewarehouse.com

www.gourmet.org

www.foodwine.com

www.globalgourmet.com

SALTING YOUR COOKING WATER

www.leskincaid.com/food

BOILING POINT VS. ALTITUDE

www.30daygourmet.com

www.chemistry.co.nz/cooking-altitudes.htm

HOW A CONVECTION OVEN WORKS

www.csw.com/apogee/cookhtm/ccotc.htm

MAKING THE BREADING STAY PUT

www.ichef.com

HOW DOES HEAT COOK FOOD?

www.housecenter.com

NEVER USE PLASTIC WRAP IN A MICROWAVE

www.hermes.ecn.purdue.edu:800/linjs/fnspec_mg/0492.html

SOLVING PROBLEMS THAT MAY OCCUR IN SAUCE BEARNAISE

www.wolfi.chemie.unibas.ch

www.premiersystems.com/recipes/sauces

www.momscooking.com

WHY CHEF'S LEAVE THE BROILER DOOR AJAR

www.simplyseafood.com

IS GAS OR ELECTRIC COOKING BEST?

www.gasco.com

www.homearts.com/cooking/front/08fb0d16.htm

MICROWAVE

www.chefskitchen.com

www.geocities.com

http://more.abcnews.go.com/sections/tech/Geek/geek10.html

www.gallawa.com/microtech.mwfaq.html

WOKS

www.theironworks.com

www.happycookers.com

SELF-CLEANING OVENS, IT'S HOTTER THAN HADES

www.electricnet.com

QUICHE

www.kashrut.com

www.geocities.com

TOASTER

www.toaster.org/faq.html

http://inventors.about.com/msub12_2a.html

CROCK POT AKA SLOW-COOKER

www.fatcatcafe.com

www.earthlink.net

www.culinary.net

THE CUTTING EDGE

www.knifeshop.com

www.delightfulthings.com

www.knifeoutlet.com

www.chippingaway.com

www.up-north.com/edgemaker

www.tastetheworld.com/p4online/wu9piecsetw.html

www.bullmancutlery.com

BOILED FOODS TAKE LONGER TO COOK ON BAD WEATHER DAYS

www.ichef.com

HOW TO CHECK YOUR OVEN TEMPERATURE WITHOUT A THERMOMETER

www.happycooker.com

www.jensco.com

www.onlinechef.com

THE COLD FACTS AND FOOD STORAGE

www.fanafana.com/Consumers/Food-and-Nutrition/Food
www.spingree.cals.wisc.edu/farmmarket/freeze.html
www.spectre.ag.uiuc.edu/~robsond/solutions/nutrition/f
www.members.aol.com/OAMCLoop/freeze.html
www.scana.com/sce%26g/home/rekitp.htm
www.cec.uga.edu/Family/soeasy/he445.html
www.ces.ncsu.edu/depts/foodsci/agentinfo/org/
www.foodsafety.com
www.cadersky.cz/himedia/food3.htm
www.nal.usda.gov/fnic/etext/oooo28.html
www.publications.unsw.edu.au/handbooks/science/sub

FREEZING BAKED GOODS

Biscuits
www.foodsafety.org/he/he486.htm

Doughnuts
www.oznet.ksu.edu/dp_fnut/HRAP/STORAGE/freezesto.htm

Bread (homemade)
http://cafecreosote.com/Reference/FreezingTips.html

Sandwiches (closed)
http://agschool.fvsc.peachnet.edu/html/publications/telet
www.birdseye.com

NEGATIVE EFFECTS OF FREEZING FOODS

www.ctipubs.com/feofq.htm
www.ag.uiuc.edu/~robsond/solutions/nutrition/docs/janan316.html

www.fmi.org/foodkeeper/freezing.htm

www.taunton.com/fc/features/foodscience/3freeze.htm

www.eec.lt/en/p_saldytuvai.html

www.taunton.com/fc/features/foodscience/3freeze.htm

www.epicurious.com/e_eating/e02_secrets/l/539.html

http://207.153.213.131/

www.sciencedaily.com

www.sescoappl.com/ses7.htm

www.yourview.com/0/12/5/Comments.flame

www.ag.uiuc.edu/~robsond/solutions/nutrition/food_

SMOKE CURING FOODS

www.usersuniserve.com/~bleathem/books.html

NEW STORAGE BAGS, A MUST FOR EVERY KITCHEN

www.thepeacenetwork.com/Storagebags3.htm

www.greenbags.com

STORING MARGARINE

www.geocities.com

www.ig.csic.es/Revisi/Fas48i/Abs48i/Ab48if21.htm

FREEZER STORAGE TIMES AT ZERO DEGREES FAHRENHEIT

www.ameriplas.org/benefits_your_life/Refrigerator/

REFRIGERATED STORAGE TIMES FOR VEGETABLES

www.netnow.micron.net/~eduun/y2kveggies.html

www.stretcher.com

www.mayohealth.org/mayo/961/htm/stor_sb.htm

www.msue.msu.edu/msue/imp/modc4/62994009.html

STORAGE TIMES FOR FRESH FRUIT

www.mycpc.com/shelflife.html

STORAGE TIMES FOR NUTS IN THE SHELL

http://forums.cosmoaccess.net/forum/survival/prep/pfs/016

STORAGE TIMES FOR REFRIGERATED DAIRY PRODUCTS

http://agschool.fvsc.peachnet.edu/html/publications/telet

STORAGE TIMES FOR CHEESES

www.countrylife.net

www.tasteofamerica.com

www.idealcheese.com

www.newenglandcheese.com

STORAGE TIMES FOR MEATS

www.ontimecooks.com/Tips/FrozenFoods.htm

www.hotbags.com

www.switcheroo.com

WHICH IS BETTER, A THERMAL BOTTLE, OR A VACUUM BOTTLE?

www.vita-tec.com

www.chefskitchen.com

THE DANGERS IN RAW FOODS

www.safefoods.com

www.rawfoods.com

COLD FACTS

www.fanafana.com

KEEPING FROZEN FOODS MORE PALATABLE

Meats & Fish

www.ag.ohio-state.edu/~ohioline/hyg-fact/5000/5334

http://ag.arizona.edu/NSC/class/meat.htm

Vegetables

http://spectre.ag.uiuc.edu/~vista/abstracts/aPREPVEG.html

Freezing Salsa

www.globalgarden.com

Fruit

www.homearts.com/gh/food/79peac76.htm

Eggs

www.food.epicurious.com/e_eating/e02_secrets/l/522

Dairy Products

www.fanafana.com/Consumers/Food-and-Nutrition/Food

Emulsified Sauces

www.foodsafety.org

Starchy Sauces

www.pan.co.yakima.wa.us/wsuext/coop/food/frztomat

Baked Goods

www.foodsafety.org/he/he384.htm

Soups & Casseroles

www.nsac.ns.ca/nsdam/pt/hort/garden95/gg95-75.htm

COLD AND FREEZING FACTS

http://csf.colorodo.edu/perma/frugal/august97/msg00910.html

www.omsi.edu/sln/air/science/density/more.html

www.occc.com/abc/dry-ice.htm

www.madsci.com

www.uiuc.edu

http://207.153.213.131/

www.sciencedaily.com

http://207.153.213.131/ www.sciencedaily.com

http://seamonkey.ed.asu.edu/~storslee/aloe.html

www.nsac.ns.ca/nsdam/pt/hort/garden95/gg95-75.htm

www.foodsafety.org/he/he384.htm

www.foodsci.purdue.edu/publications/foodsafetyday/slide042.html

www.foodsafety.org

www.foodsafety.org/he/he387.htm

http://agschool.fvsc.peachnet.edu/html/publications/spani

http://foodsci.orst.edu/sugar/corn.html

ELIMINATING BROWN OUT #1

www.foodsafety.org

ELIMINATING BROWN OUT #2

http://207.153.213.131/

www.acs.org

www.sciencedaily.com

BLANCHING IN A MICROWAVE

http://207.153.213.131/

www.uiuc.edu www.sciencedaily.com

http://207.153.213.131/

www.sciencedaily.com

FREEZING YOUR CORN

www.neosoft.com/recipes/preserving/freezing-corn.html

COOKING FROZEN VEGGIES

http://spectre.ag.uiuc.edu/~vista/abstracts/aPREPVEG.html

COOKING MEATS THAT HAVE BEEN FROZEN

www.foodsafety.org/il/il018.htm

TO RE-FREEZE OR NOT TO RE-FREEZE, THAT IS A HEALTH QUESTION

www.foodsafety.org/he/he485.htm

CONDIMENTS, SAUCES AND SUCH

HOW FOODS BECOME EMULSIFIED

www.surfacants.net/emulsion.htm

www.greatlakesgelatin.com

www.dynagel.com

www.stock-talk.com/talk/HNZ/84.shtml

www.heinz.com

THE JELLY THICKENER

www.countrylife.net

www.scs.bg/pectin/offer2.htm

www.nsac.ns.ca/~piinfo/hort/garden95/gg95-63.htm

NEW SALT SUBSTITUTE

http://web.net-link.net/preparedfoods/1999/9902/9902newprod.htm

HERBS TO BATTLE HARMFUL BACTERIA

www.ift.org

www.sciencedaily.com/releases/1998/07/980721081028.htm

www.japanscan.com

HOT PEPPER SAUCES

www.northcoast.com/~alden/Hotsauce.html

www.tabasco.com

http://ashleyfood.com/liquid.htm

www.firegirl.com/preserving/freezing2.html

www.wiw.org/~cory/chile/scoville.html

www.cajunproducts.com/FAQ_Scoville.htm

www.chiletoday.com

KETCHUP

www.ketchup.wonderland.org/facts.html

VINEGAR

www.vinegar.at/

www.interlution.com/quicktips/R1013.htm

www.4vinegar.com

www.cyber-north.com/tipnet/vinegar.html

www.rawfoods.com/articles/vinegartruth.html

www.vinegarman.com

SOME DIFFERENT TYPES OF COMMERCIAL VINEGAR

Apple Cider Vinegar

www.ezlinks.com/herbal/cider.htm

Balsamic Vinegar

http://balsamic.com

www.table.mpr.org/articles/97_065.htm

www.balsamicvinegar.nature-greatergood.com

www.colombini.it/barrell.htm

Cane Vinegar

http://betterbaking.com/baker2/ingrsteen.html

Champagne Vinegar

www.farawayfoods.com/fruitvinegars.html

Distilled Vinegar

www.belton.com/vinegar.htm

Fruit Vinegar

www.vinegar.at/

Malt Vinegar

www.vegweb.com/glossary/docs/janan389.shtml

Raspberry Vinegar

www.naefusa.com/vinegar.html

Rice Vinegar

http://brewery.org

Wine Vinegar

www.winevinegar.locate-ishophere.com

www.midihaven.com/facts1.html

www.isbe.accessus.net/~090/awh/trivia.html

http://azcentral.webpoint.com/food/ckfixit.htm

http://allthingsfrugall.com/vinegar.htm

http://secure.valley-internet.com/~palnet/private/vinegar.htm

http://frugalliving.about.com/library/b/vinegar.htm

www.powerup.com.au/~swimskins/index2.html

www.stretcher.com/stories/970811c.cfm

www.go-symmetry.com/apple-vinegar.htm

http://members.aol.com/frugally4u/frugaltips.html

BALSAMIC GRAPE BREW

www.geocities.com/NapaValley/4079/balsamic.htm

www.nfm-online.com/nfm-backs/Mar_95/Food_Focus.htm

HOUSEHOLD CLEANING USES FOR VINEGAR

Polish Leather Furniture

www.msue.msu.edu.msue/imp/mod02/01500631.htm

Remove Carpet Stains

www.cyber-north.com/tipnet/vinegar.html

Chewing Gum Remover

http://frugalliving.about.com/library/b/vinegar.htm

Decal Remover

www.msue.msu.edu/msue/imp/mod02/01500631.html

Mildew Remover

www.members.tripod.com/Howtuzz/vinegar.html

Plastic Upholstery Cleaner

www.stretcher.com/stories/970811c.cfm

Metal Cleaner

www.powerup.com.au/~swimskinsf/household_hints_tips.html#vinegar

Clean Aluminum Pot Stains

http://secure.valley-internet.com/~palnet/private/vinegar.htm

Wash Windows

www.powerup.com.au/~swimskins/household_hints_tips.html#vinegar

Grease Cutter

www.geocities.com/Heartland/Hills/9684/vinegar.html

Crystal Clear Glassware

www.stretcher.com/stories/970811c.cfm

Remove Lime Residue

www.msue.msu.edu/msue/imp/mod02/01500631.html

Drain Cleaner

www.wackyuses.com/heinz.html

Clean Shower Head

www.members.tripod.com/Howtuzz/vinegar.html

Weed Killer

www.geocities.com/Heartland/Hills/9684/vinegar.html

Pet Flea Killer

www.makestuff.com/vinegar.html

Cement Remover

www.interlution.com/quicktips/R1013.htm

Ant Remover

www.geocities.com/Heartland/Hills/9684/vinegar.html

Remove Scorch Marks

www.wackyuses.com/heinz.html

Brighten Clothes

www.msue.msu.edu/msue/imp/mod02/01500631.html

Remove Crayon Stains

www.cyber-north.com/tipnet/vinegar.html

Eliminate Deodorant Stains

www.wackyuses.com/heinz.html

Ink Stain Remover

www.stretcher.com/stories/970811c.cfm

Rust Remover

www.interlution.com/Quicktips/R1013.htm

MEDICINAL USES FOR VINEGAR

Dandruff

www.geocities.com/Heartland/Hills/9684/vinegar.html

Nail Polish Saver

www.apex.net.au/~jokers/handyhints.htm

Sunburn Reliever
www.go-symmetry.com/apple-vinegar.htm

Athletes Foot
www.members.tripod.com/Howtuz/vinegar.html

Morning Sickness
http://secure.valley-internet.com/~palnet/private/VINEGAR.htm

Indigestion
www.freeyellow.com/members/lomike

A BUNION SANDWICH
www.wackyuses.com/heinz.html

AROUND THE KITCHEN WITH VINEGAR

Storing Pimientos
www.members.tripod.com/Howtuz/vinegar.html

Flavor Enhancer
www.makestuff.com/vinegar.html

Over-Salted Foods
www.cyber-north.com/tipnet/vinegar.html

Mold Eliminator
www.spots.ab.ca/~ics/green.htmlodors

Vegetable and Fruit Wash
www.stretcher.com/stories/970811c.cfm

Stops Food Discoloring
http://allthingsfrugal.com/vinegar.htm

Great Mashed Potato Trick
www.cyber-north.com/tipnet/vinegar.html

Firm Gelatin
www.makestuff.com/vinegar.html

www.geocities.com/Heartland/Hills/9684/vinegar.html
www.members.tripod.com/Howtuzz/vinegar.html
http://members.tripod.com/Spunky_Ang/mycookbook/SweetfpickledEggs.html

STEAK SAUCE

www.foodexplorer.com/product/NEWPROD/PF07874g.HTM

www.cuisinenet.com/glossary/worcstr.html

SOY SAUCE

www.foodexplorer.com/product/NEWPROD/FF09777a.HTM

MUSTARD

www.mustard-place.com/content2.htm

MARINADES

www.culinarycafe.com/Barbecue/About_Marinades.html

www.baychef.com/stockpot/questions.html

www.rmc.com/wrap/good_food/recipe_box/rec/gril_mrb.html

MAYONNAISE

www.embassyofheaven.com/kcp/mayonnai.htm

http://soar.berkeley.edu/recipes/condiments/homemademayonnaise1.html

www.food.epeicurios.com/e_eating/e02_secrets/e/262.html

http://ndsuext.nodak.edu/extnews/askext/freezing/4451.htm

www.idahonews.com/111198/FOOD-AND/28768.htm

www.cdkitchen.com/rfr/data/937048720.htm

http://ndsuext.nodak.edu/extnews/askext/freezing/4451.htm

www.embassyofheaven.com/kcp/mayonnai.htm

www.ichef.com/ichef-recipes/Dips-dressings/dressings/19495.html

www.neosoft.com/recipes/sauces/tartar-sauce02.html

www.topsecretrecipes.com/recipes/1000isle.htm

www.betterbaking.com/caesarerem.html

SAUCES

www.aloha-city.com/chef_kitchen/sauces.html

Arrowroot

http://soupsong.com/bthicken.html

Tapioca

http://soupsong.com/bthicken.html

Vegetable puree

www.taunton.com/fc/features/techniques/28puree.htm

A FEW OF THE COMMON GRAIN THICKENERS

Cornstarch

www.northcoast.com/~alden/Thicken.html

All-Purpose Flour

www.flourr.com/bakers/glossary.htm

Rice Starch

www.riceland.com/rice/milling.html

Mung Bean Starch

www.itah.net/malayasia-industry/mygrmung.htm

PECTIN

www.phys.com/b_nutrition/03encyclopedia/02terms/p/pectin.html

COMMERCIAL THICKENERS

www.thickandeasy.com/aip-T%26E.html

www.foodstarch.com/25c6.htm

www.foodexplorer.com/product/industry/Fi02845.htm

INSTANT STARCH

www.amescompany.com/productspecs/clearjel1.htm

www.amescompany/productspecs/Fact%20sheets/fact_she1.htm

www.cfs.purdue.edu/fdsnutr/fn453/addstarch.htm

www.kbnet.net/r/eggat/photo/history/gelatin.htm

www.epicurious.com/HyperNews/get/archive_swap13901_14000/13909/2/1.htm

www.eatethnic.com/ga-archives.htm

http://dailies.about.com/recipes

REGULAR FLOUR VS. INSTANT FLOUR

www.naturalland.com/cv/soy/sfb.htm

www.germandeli.com

http://soar.berkeley.edu/recipes/sauces/mock-hollandaise1.html

http://library.ncsu.edu/marion/AJ1-1565

www.charlottesgardens.com/recipe.html

www.taunton.com/fc/features/techniques/custards/1.htm

www.food-guide.com/Cooking_Tips_And_Advice/cooking_tips/more2.html

www.food.epicurious.com/e_eating/e02_secrets/g/313

http://asia.yahoo.com/Society_and_Culture/Food_and_drink/cooking/recipes/cheese

www.foodwine.com/destinations/poland/easterch2.html

http://homearts.com/depts/food/03basib1.htm

www.cannongas.com/dinner/sauce_stuffing_10.html

FREEZING WHITE SAUCE

http://ndsuext.nodak.edu/extnews/askext/Freezing/4451.htm

WINE SAUCE

www.oregonlive.com/foodday/features/99/05/25/fd_ti

SPEEDY, ALMOST INSTANT SAUCES

Beef Sauce

www.recipe-world.com/recipes/beef.html

Chicken Sauce

www.parentsplace.com/readroom/recipes/carischx.html

Fish Sauce

www.topsecretrecipes.com/recipes/r/tartar.htm

Lamb Sauce

www.lambchef.com/flavprof.html

Low-fat Sauce

www.healthychoice.com/

Pork Sauce

http://bbq.miningco.com/library/recipes/b1072697.htm

Vegetable Sauces

www.titanic.kn-bremen.de/sauce48.html

LOWER-FAT SAUCES

Barbecue Sauce
www.lombardia.com/kitchen/barbeque/recipe153.html

Bordelaise
www.geocities.com/NapaValley/3774/recipes36.html%recipe008748

Bourguignonne
www.bienpublic.com/rubrig/cuisine/somcui.html

Coulis
http://foodwine.com/food/recipes/coulis.html

Demi-Glace
www.globalgourmet.com/food/egg/egg1196/espagnol.html

Marinara
http://cdkitchen.com/recipes/ot/sauce/ot-sau003.shtml

Sweet and Sour
http://minto.sd74.bc.ca/html/recipes/sweet.html

Veloute
www.ja.mlive.com/dining/recipes/19980405veloute.html

HIGHER-FAT SAUCES

Alfredo
www.cdkitchen.com/rfr/data/939660542.html

Bechamel
http://gr.mlive.com/dining/recipes/19980405bechamel.html

Bernaise
www.geocities.com/NapaValley/3774/recipe36.html#recipe008739

Bolognese
www.jonsilver.com/jon/recipes/bolognese.htm

Hollandaise
http://homepages.lycos.com/JeffCombs/lyrecipe/index-6.html

Mole
www.ramekins.com/mole/recipesmole.html

Pesto
www.cyberdiet.com/cgi-bin.uncgi/ddf

Ragu
www.4pasta.com/fun.shtml

Vinaigrette
http://globalgourmet.com/food/egg/eggslds/eggs017/vinaigre.html

TOMATO SAUCES

www.cs.csmu.edu/~mjw/recipes/pasta/frsh-tom-sauce-s

www.ichef.com/icheff-recipes/Saucesmarinades/sauce

www.httpbusycooks.miningco.com/b/recsauces.htm

BARBECUE SAUCE

www.grampysbbq.com/

www.lombardia.com/kitchen/barbecue/recipe190.html

COMMERCIAL TERIYAKI SAUCE

www.foodexplorer.com/product/NEWPROD//FF09783a.HTM

www.ramekins.com/mole/recipesmole.html

SWEET SAUCES

CUSTARD

www.bawarchi.com/cookbook/sauce6.html

http://iurwww.unl.edu/pubs/foods/g944.htm

CHOCOLATE SAUCE/SYRUP

www.bhglive.com/food/cookhelpers/melting.htm

www.culinarycafe.com/Desserts/chocolate_Ganache_G

www.neosoft.com/recipes/sauces/hot-fudge04.html

www.chocolatier-electro.com

www.cannylink.com/agriculturetrade.htm

www.womenswire.com/livinglarge/grub/souffle.html

www.bhglive.com/food/cookhelpers/quick.htm

COOKING EXTRACTS

VANILLA EXTRACT

http://web.net-link.net/preparedfoods/1998/9808/9808chocnvanil.htm

www.saffron.com/vanhistory.html

www.taunton.com/fc/features/techniques/9infuse.htm

GOOD FATS, BAD FATS & OILS

FATS (LIPIDS)

http://esg-www.mite.edu:8001/esgbio/lm/lipids/lipids.html

http://foodsci.orst.edu/l/lowfat/izzo.html

www.mayohealth.org

www.eatright.org

www.sciencenet.org.uk

www.uwinnipeg.ca/~byard/macro/tsld013.htm

www.diabetes.org.uk

THE THREE MAJOR TYPES OF FATS

POLYUNSATURATED FATS (PUFA) GOOD FATS

www.dietsite.com

www.cyberparent.com/nutrition/goodfats.htm

MONOUNSATURATED FATS (MUFA) GOOD FATS

www.nutritionnewsfocus.com/archives/MonoFat.html

SATURATED FATS (SFA) BAD FATS

www.caregroup.org

www.hsu.edu/faculty/engmanj/bio2114/power/maroweb

MEDIUM CHAIN TRIGLYCERIDES (MCT)

www.vegsource.com/articles/koop_index.htm

ESSENTIAL FATTY ACIDS (EFA)

www.ellmer.netmegs.com/cggb.html

HYDROGENATION

www.hhp.ufl.edu/hse/faculty/sdorman/nutrit/tsld026

THE BAD PARTS OF A GOOD FAT

www.phys.com/d_magazines/01self/fats/fats.html

www.nutrionnewsfocus.com/archive/MonoFat.html

Cis-Form Fatty Acids

www.nutrition.psu.edu/undergrad/courses/nutr251/nutr25

Trans-Form Fatty Acid

www.flora.net.au/html/body_trans.htm

COMMON COOKING OILS

Almond Oil
www.nutristrategy.com/fatsoils.htm

Avocado Oil
www.wsus.com/fishfat.html

Canola Oil
www.canolainfo.org/html/culinary.html

SHOOT THAT RAPESEED PLANT

Smoke Point – 525[0] F. (273.9[0] C.)
www.worldyellowpages.com/chiapsh

Coconut Oil
www.hippocrates.com.au/coconut.html

Corn Oil
Smoke Point – 475[0] F. (246.1[0] C.)
www.biotechknowledge.com/showlib.php3?1458

Cottonseed Oil
www.nutristrategy.com/fatsoils.htm

Flaxseed Oil

www.veg.on.ca/newsletr/janfeb97/best_oil.html

Grape-seed Oil

www.healthstar.com/Pages/GS02.html

Hazelnut or Filbert Oil

www.nickleranch.com/eatright/bdiet2.htm

Hemp Oil

www.ellmer.netmegs.com/dtcf.html

Olive Oil

www.human.cornell.edu/dns/nutriquest/043099/oils.html

Smoke Point – 375^0 F. (190.6^0 C.)

Palm Oil

www.mayohealth.org/mayo/askdiet/htm/new/qd70521.htm

Peanut Oil

Smoke Point – 440^0 F. (226.7^0 C.)

http://ohio.com/bj/features/food/docs/008446.htm

Safflower Oil

Smoke Point – 510^0 F. (265.6^0 C.)

www.deliciousdecisions.com/cb/hhc_easy_fats.html

Sesame Oil

Smoke Point – 420^0 F. (215.6^{0}C.)

http://thehealthnetwork.com/nutrition/fnarticle2.htm

Soybean Oil

Smoke Point – 495^0 F. (257.2^0 C.)

www.bberson.com/sic20/sic202075.html

Sunflower Oil

www.worldyellowpages.com/chiapsh

Walnut Oil

www.naturalhealthvillage.com/newsletter/990415/nut

METHODS OF REFINING AND EXTRACTING OILS

www.unece.org/stats/econ/iwg.agri/handbook.vegetable.htm

REFINED OILS

www.dsuper.net/~styan/oils.htm

UNREFINED OILS

www.florainc.com/united_states/html/perfected_blen

EXPELLER-PRESSED EXTRACTION

www.soyatech.com/glossary.html

COLD-PRESSED EXTRACTION

www.soyatech.com/Glossary.html

CHEMICAL SOLVENT EXTRACTION

www.frontierherb.com/aromatherapy/aro.glossary.html

www.food4.epicurious.com/HyperNews/get/archive_swap22701

www.geocities.com/HeartlandHills/7799/tkfiagm.html

STORING OILS

www.foodscience.afisc.csiro.au/oilvine.htm

DIGESTION OF FATS

http://tqjr.advanced.org/4245/intestine.htm

ESSENTIAL FATTY ACIDS

www.ellmer.netmegs.com/cggb.html

OMEGA 3 FATTY ACIDS

www.americannutrition.com/max_epa.htm

OMEGA-6 FATTY ACIDS

www.eatright.org/pr/press103097e.html

FLAXSEED OIL

www.michaeldale.org/spinner

SALAD DRESSING MAY BE GOOD FOR YOUR HEART

www.dietians.ca/eatwell/english/kitchen/recipes

TRANS-FATTY ACIDS

www.healthcastle.com/trans.shtml

www.umich.edu/~newsinfo/MT/96/Fall96/mta2f96.html

www.ifrn.bbsrc.ac.uk

www.admin.uiuc.edu/NB/98.10/foodtip.html

www.sciencedaily.com/releases/1998/10/981002081406.htm

http://outreach.missouri.edu/hesnutrnews/98-2/98-2.htm

www.margarine.org

www.foodforhealth.com

www.pmac.net/canola.htm

http://phys.com/b_nutrition/03encyclopedia/02terms/m/mod

www.oliveoilsource.com/store.htm

www.obs-us.com/obs/english/books/pg/pg193.htm

www.pointest.com

www.csiro.au

www.sciencedaily.com/releases/1999/03/990311055719.htm

www.inel.gov

http://navigator.tufts.edu/general/margarin.htm

http://news.foodingredientsonline.com/industry-news/19990504-337.html

www.msnbc.com/news/218236.asp

www.healthestores.com/racer/sectogoodhea.html

http://ukdb.web.aol.com/hutchinson/encyclopedia/41/m00208

www.Life-enhancement.com/N40website/n40FATS.html

http://borntoexplore.org/omega2.html

www.allergyhomecare.com/feeding.htm

www.margarine.org

www.colostate.edu/Depts/CoopExt/PUBS/COLUMNNN/NN97

CHEF'S FRYING SECRETS

www.compsoc.net/~Kake/Cooking/Techniques/fatfree-s

www.cp-tel.net/smokin/sgumbo.html

FAT FACTS

www.popcorn.org/mpindex.htm

www.foodfunfacts.com/foodhistory.htm

www.ntwrks.com/~mikev/chart4a.htm

http://forums.co5moaccess.net/forums/survival/prep/pfs/01600839.htm

www.flipnfry.com

http://www.aeb.org

www.6.phys.com/b_nutrition/03encyclopedia/02terms/t

www.smartpages.com/sil/ca/v/cityguides/ar/little_r

www.elenigourmet.com/

www.geron.uga.edu/~rob/cb/deep_fat.html

http://answersleuth.com/food/mayonnaise.5.shtml

www.thorncrestoutfitters.com/products/f-shortening

www.usoil.com/uslab/wote/wodyimain.html

www.butterdish.com

www.scan-mall.com

www.butterdish.unique-hammacher.com

www.goodcooking.com www.winecountrycooking.com

www.food6.epicurious.com/e02_secrets/j/434.html

www.butterinstitute.org

REDUCED FAT VS. STANDARD FOOD

www.purelyorganic.com

www.theolivestore.com

www.olivegroves.com

www.ukdb.web.aol.com/hutchinson/encyclopedia/15/m00391

www.tassos.com/health.htm

www.benbest.com/health/transfat.html

www.geron.uga.edu/~rob/cb/deep_fat.html

www.aocs.org/prdeepfr.htm

www.miroil.com

http://healthyideas.com/cooking/recipes/meat/porkloin.html

www.users.york.ac.uk/~socsl6/prod/lard.htm

www.soar.berkeley.edu/recipes/appetizers/salmon-pate1.rec

www.mayohealth.org

www.foodsupply.com

www.penpages.psu.edu/penpages_reference/1210/1210

www.2.hawaii.edu/lynn/chapter6.html

www.lattaplantation.org/sugarpop/htm/pigs_ina_bla

www.healthyway.hypermart.net/fatcont8.htm

www.vegweb.com/glossary/buttermilk.shtml

www.eatright.org/womanshealth/osteoporosis.html

www.healthyideas.com

www.aeb.org/eggcyclopedia

www.asa.europe.org/soja/soyoil.htm

www.olive-oil.com

www.madsci.org/posts/archives/may98

www.ptc.dcs.edu/HASP/FoodChem/int11.html

www.nirpublications.com/abs/j3_219_225.html

www.humorscope.com/herbs/carob.html

www.margarine.com

www.butterbuds.com

www.opus.simplenet.com/recipes/recipes31.htm

www.embassyofheaven.com/kcp/mayonnai.htm

www.hhp.ufl.edu/fit/article/butter.htm

www.madsci.org/posts/archives/oct98/907166532.ag.r

http://k2.kirtland.ccmi.us/~balbachl/lowfat.htm

www.ifwmusic.com/fastfood/tacobell.html

www.medicaltalk.com/7256.html

www.mpopc.org.my/abtenbopo4.htm

www.nutrition.psu.edu/nutrmag/fatty.html

www.iseo.org/iseo/statisti.htm

www.margarine.org

www.sln.fr.edu/biosci/healthy/hints.html

www.heartinfo.com/nutrition/fat/0924.htm

www.canola.com www.canolainfo.org

www.jeffline.tju.edu/CWIS/OAC/demos/cd_demo/HTML/ADIP/

www.phys.com/b_nutrition/02solutions/03rx/insomni/

www.usatoday.com/snapshot/life/snap019.htm

www.stairway.org/tickle/recipes/caesar.txt

http://spectre.org.uiuc.edu/~robson/solutions/nutrition/d

www.eatright.org www.nalusda.gov/fnic/dga/dguide95.html

www.biophase.com/new_web_site/mcts.html

www.onweb.es/nutrispot/english/catalogo/mct.htm

www.madsci.org

FAT-REPLACERS

www.aip.org/inside_science/html/80.html

PROTEIN-BASED FAT-REPLACERS

Simplesse®
www.autrasweetkelco.com/ingred/sim.htm

www.nutritionnewsfocus.com/archive/FatRepSimp.html

Dairy-Lo®
www.dalya.com/tur/bes/696_fat.html

K-Blazer®, Lita®
www.caloriecontrol.org/frgloss.html

CARBOHYDRATE-BASED FAT-REPLACERS

Avicel®, Methocel™
http://vm.cfsan.fda.gov/~dms/ga-adf7.html

Slendid™ (1991)
http://nutrition.hhdev.psu.edu/undergrad/courses/nutr251/chapt4-8.htm

Fruitafit®
www.caloriecontrol.org/frgloss.html

Oatrim, Beta-Trim™
www.ars.usda.gov/is/pr/1998/981204.htm

Z-trim™
www.wral-tv.com/features/healthteam/1996/0826-New

Nu-Trim™
http://www.acs.org

http://207.153.213.131/

www.sciencedaily.com

FAT-BASED REPLACERS

Olestra (Olean®) (1996)
www.foodfuture.org.uk/ffoods2.htm

www.olean.com www.cspinet.org/olestra/

Salatrim, Benefat™
www.foodexplorer.com/product/NEWPROD/ff08660A.htm

Caprenin™ (1992)
http://nutrition.hhdev.psu.edu//undergrad/courses/nutr251/chapt4-8.htm

FAT BY THE TEASPOON

www.healthychoice.com
www.tgir/advanced.org/3646/nutrition/nutrients/calorie
www.genovese.com/health/nutrition4.htm
www.qualityoflife.org
www.technultant.com/mhc/food/health/fatallow.htm
www.criscokitchen.com/products05.shtml
www.your-kitchen.com/htm/meredith/bookbake.htm
www.geron.uga.edu/~rob/lcb/dcep_fat.html
www.ukdb.web.aol.com/hutchinson/encyclopedia/41/Moo208
www.canolainfo.org
www.statcom-online.com/canolahome/canolanews4.html

THE DIFFERENCE BETWEEN FATS AND OILS

www.chebucto.ns.ca/Health/CPRC?nutritn.html
http://ukdb.web.aol.com/hutchinson/encyclopedia/15/m00391
www.mayohealth.org/mayo/askdiet/htm/new/qd70709.htm
www.northcoast.com/~alden/oils.html
http://www.aust-agbiz.com.au/economic_statistics.htm
www.ag.uiuc.edu/~robsond/solutions/nutrition/docs/janan123.html

NUTTY OILS

http://sunzine.net/bundaberg/goldmac/pgeight.html
www.oldhawaii.com/igd/htm/macoil.htm
http://azcentral.webpoint.com/food/ckoils.htm
http://starnews.webpoint.com/food/ckoils.htm

GRAVY

www.real-home-cooking.com/gravy-recipes/gravy-rec
www.womensinfo.com/Recreation/Cooking
www.highplacesdesign.com/kitmisc/misctips.html
www.highplacesdesign.com/kitmisc/misctips.html
www.messygourmet.com/creations/issue9.html
www.taunton.com/fc/features/techniques/17gr

FAT FACTS

www.urbanext.uiuc.edu/champaign/4Hse/fat.html

www.ams.usda.gov/howtobuy/butter.htm

www.pbs.org/newshour/forum/december97/fat5.html

www.foodsafety.org/or/or001.htm

www.crisco.com/usingoil/hints.htm

www.compsoc.net/~Kake/Cooking/Techniques/FatFree-s

www.xe.net/lowfat/tips/tip_0001.htm

www.psychichotline.net/bookd.html

www.foodexplorer.com/product/NEWPROD/pf09895b.htm

www.foodexplorer.com/product/NEWPROD/FF09789a.HTM

www.foodexplorer.com/product/NEWPROD/FF09667c.HTM

www.switcheroo.com/ct/fatsoils.htm

www.golden.net/~escl/bird/request.htm

www.foodwine.com/food/egg/egg1296/schmaltz.html

www.highplacesdesign.com/kitmisc/misctips.html

www.oldhouseweb.net/stories/Detailed/726.shtml

http://homecooking.about.com/library/weekly/aa090597.html

www.detroitnews.com/menu/stories/43108.htm

www.funnygirls.com/rosemary/recipe.html

www.survival-center.com/foodfaq/ff10-fat.htm

www.canolainfo.org

www.thriveonline.com/eats/experts/Joan/Joan.04-14

www.washingtonpost.com/wp-srv/Wplate/1999-03/24/0271-032499-idx.html

www.geocities.com/NapaValley/4722/ghee.html

www.hugs.org/DRAWN_BUTTER.shtml

www.betterbaking.com/library/weekly/aa060899.htm

www.expage.com/page/brownbutterfrosting

www.eatdangerously.com/thorough-cook/sauces/black-butter.html

SAUTÉING SECRETS

www.wegmans.com/kitchen/howto/tech/sauteing.htm

www.mardiweb.comlowfat/cooktip.htm

SPICES, SEASONINGS & HERBS

www.thefoodstores.com/thp/html/herbfaq.htm
www.msue.msu.edu/msue/imp/mod03/03900064.html
www.consumersinternational.org/campaigns/irradiati
http://hometown.aol.com/jdelcambre/cajun.html
www.spiceman.com
www.spiceadvise.com
www.pallensmith.com/features/highlights98/hd2301d.html

THE WORLD OF SPICES

http://ukdb.web.sol.com/hutchinson/encyclopedia/13/M00193
www.azuswebworks.com/herbs/anise.htm
www.twilight.org/store/anise.htm

BASIL

www.eat.com/cooking-glossary/basil.html
http://food.homearts.com/food/cooking/front/08fbdn16.htm

BAY LEAF

www.indianspices.com/htm/s062jbay.htm

CAPERS

www.fawcett-bros.com.au/aristocrat/capers.htm

CARAWAY SEEDS

www.jwkc.com/encyclopedia/low/articles/c/c00400071
www.azuswebworks.com/herbs/caraway.htm

CARDAMOM SEED

www.thriveonline.com/health/Library/vitamins/vitam
www.avalon.net/~slainte/cardamon.html

CAYENNE PEPPER

www.answersleuth.com/food/cayenne-pepper.shtml

www.potentherns.com

http://ukdb.web.aol.com/hutchinson/encyclopedia/69/M00193

CELERY SEED

www.spiceadvise.com

CHERVIL

www.hydrogarden.com/gardens/food/chervil.htm

CHILI PEPPERS

www.smartbasic.com/glos.herbs/capsicum.html

CHILI POWDER

www.hotchili.com

www.netchef.com/chilie/recipes/chilipow.asp

CHIVES

www.naturalland.com/gv/hg/chv.htm

www.dansgardenshop.com/gardenshop/chives.html

CILANTRO

www.vegweb.com/glossary/cilantro.shtml

CINNAMON

www.americanspice.com

CLOVE

www.spiceguide.com

www.spicetec.com

CORIANDER SEED

www.pinn.net/~swampy/coriander.html

www.natashascafe.com/itemdetails/cumin.htm

CUMIN SEED

www.asiangrocery.com/itemdetails/cumin.htm

CURRY POWDER

www.oein.ucdavis.edu/~britt/recipes/OLD_BOMBAY_CURR

DILL

http://dillsauce.search-greatergood.com

FENNEL

http://dansgardenshop.com/gardenshop/fennel.html

www.encarta.com/index/conciseindex/50/05064000.htm

FENUGREEK

www.vegweb.com/glossary/fenugreek.shtml

www.theuae.com/~forever/Dishes/DP/halba.html

GARLIC

www.garlicpage.com

www.gilroygarlicfestival.com

www.thegarlicstore.com

www.garlicpage.com/recipes/kitchen.html

www.mostlygarlic.com

www.mistral.co.uk/garlic/research.htm

www.sciencedaily.com/releases/1998/11/981117075803.htm

www.pacificpud.org/~opchamber/garlic

GINGER

www.spiceadvice.com

MACE

www.spiceguide.com

www.astaspice.org/spice/sp_nutmeg.htm

MARJORAM

www.tones.com/spiceadvice/durkee/spices_atoz/marjo

MINT FLAKES

www.vegweb.com

MUSTARD

www.mustardfestival.com

http://rayesmustard.com

www.mustardstore.com

www.americanspice.com

http://agrolink.moa.my/comoditi/doa/sa_tek.html

http://soar.berkeley.edu/recipes/condiments/chinese-musta

Dijon Mustard

www.rolandfood.com/spotdijo.htm

German Mustard

www.chefshook.com/fwgermanmustard.htm

www.st7.yahoo.net/t-e-x-a-s/tergermus.html

NETTLE

www.revivarantg.com/nutrition/nettles.htm

NUTMEG

www.astaspice.org/spice/sp_nutmeg.htm

OREGANO

www.produceoasis.com/items_folder/HerbMisc/Oregano.html

PAPRIKA

www.americanspice.com

PARSLEY

www.hernoutlet.com/parsley

PEPPER

www.m-mueller.com/new24207.html

PEPPERCORNS

www.northstarnet.org/evkhome/spices/muntokwhilepep

PEPPERMINT

http://home.vicnet.au/~woodlink/pepper.htm

POPPY SEED

www.thespicehouse.com

http://www.aaohn.org

www.board/direct_care/messages/136.html

POULTRY SEASONING

www.spiceadvice.com

ROSEMARY

www.hydrogarden.com/gardens/food/rosemary.htm

www.weslynfarm.com/year.html

SAFFRON

www.saffron.com

www.saffroninfo.com

www.menlo.com/folks/adamm/recipes/tips/saffron.html

SAGE

www.geocities.com/HotSprings/8300

SALT (Sodium Chloride)

www.mortonsalt.com

www.mayohealth.org

www.solvay.com/salt/usefood.htm

www.swmed.edu/library/consumer/lowsalt.htm

www.mortec.com/diet1.htm

www.mothernature.com/ency/Dietary-Sodium.asp

www.adam.com/ency/article/002415fod.htm

http://ej.bergen.org/Magnifique/Health/salt.html

www.medco.com/oh/hf/cfif.htm

www.medicinegarden.com/archive/00001394.htm

GENERAL SALT INFORMATION

TYPES OF SALT:

Canning Salt

www.vegweb.com/glossary/docs/janan233.shtml

Kosher Salt

www.food.epicurious.com/e_eating/e02_secrets/9/745.html

Pickling Salt

www.2.nishikigoi.or.jp/bbs-a/messages/470.html

Rock Salt

www.makeicecream.com/sendicecream/howdoesrocsa.html

Sea Salt

www.hawaiisalt.com

www.mos.org/sln/slm/ksalt.html

www.cetic-seasalt.com

Iodized and Non-Iodized Salt

http://bluecrab.richmaond.edu/morton_salt.htm

REPAIRING OVER-SALTED FOODS

http://hometown.aol.com/gjda.page99.html

SAVOY

www.spiceadvice.com

SESAME

www.americanspice.org

TARRAGON

http://ukdb.web.aol.com/hutchinson/encyclopedia/55/P00025

THYME

www.herbsherbals.com

www.kypros.org/Projects/Laona/thyme.html

TURMERIC

www.culinarycafe.com/Spices_Herbs/Turmeric.html

VANILLA

www.spice-islands/our_spices...tones.com/spiceadvice

www.voicenet.com/~tjohn/herb/van.html

www.chem.uwimona.edu.jm:1104/lectures/vanilla.html

PURE EXTRACT

www.icdc.com/~vanilla/vanilla.htm

MEXICAN EXTRACT

www.mayo.ivi.com/mayo/9702/htm/2nd_op2.htm

SUBSTITUTING HERBS

www.ailenes-heavenlywebs.com/personal/cooking/Herbs

www.dehnsgardenherbs.com/

www.internetgarden.co.uk/herb/fragrence.htm

www.eat.com/cooking-glossary/pesto.html

http://soar.berkeley.edu/recipes/pesto

www.licorice.org

www.foodsafety.org/or/or001.htm

www.vegweb.com/glossary/janan123.shtml

http://dansgardenshop.com/gardenshop/herbgardening.html

CHINESE FIVE-SPICE POWDER

http://soar.berkeley.edu/recipes/ethnic/chinese/five-spic

www.nsn.org/evkhome/spices/chinesefivespicepowder.htm

www.azuswebworks.com/herbs/cloves.htm

www.spiceadvice.com

UNSAFE HERBS

www.cell2000.net/~users/joef/newpage72.htm

www.sbherbals.com/AvoidInPregnancy.html

www.parentsplace.com/fun/gardening/gen/0%2C3476%2C

www.ipm.ucdavis.edu/PMG/WEEDS/black_nightshade.html

BLOODROOT, RED PUCCOON

http://botanical.com/botanical/mgmh/b/bloodr59.html

BUCKEYES, HORSE CHESTNUT

www.potentherbs.com

BURNING BUSH, WAHOO

http://tncweeds.ucdavis.edu/esadocs/euonalat.html

DEADLY NIGHTSHADE

www.erowid.org/plants/belladonna/belladonna.shtml

EUROPEAN MANDRAKE

www.acsu.buffalo.edu/~insrisg/nature/nw98/mandrake.html

HELIOTROPE

http://encarta.msn.com/index/conciseindex/44/0447e000.htm

HEMLOCK, SPOTTED HEMLOCK, CALIFORNIA OR NEBRASKA FERN

http://w3.uwyo.edu/~caps/poison/poison.html

HENBANE, HOG'S BEAN, DEVIL'S EYE

http://ukdb.web.aol.com/hutchinson/encyclopedia/58/P00048

INDIAN TOBACCO, ASTHMA WEED, EMETIC WEED

www.holoweb.com/vit/herbs98.shtml

JALAP ROOT, HIGH JOHN ROOT, ST. JOHN THE CONQUEROR ROOT

http://search1.healthgate.com/vit/herbs98.shtml

JIMSON WEED, THORNAPPLE, TOLGUACHA
http://medhlp.netusa.net/glossary/new/gls_2565.htm

LILY OF THE VALLEY, MAY LILY
www.ansi.cornell.edu/plants/lilyofthevalley.html

AMERICAN MANDRAKE, MAY APPLE, WILD LEMON
www.healthherbs.com/sing250.htm

MISTLETOE
www.personalhealthzone.com/mistletoe.html

MORNING GLORY
www.ansi.cornell.edu/plants/morningglory.html

PERIWINKLE
www.healthy.net/library/books/hoffman/materiamedic

POKEWEED, SKOKE, PIGEONBERRY
http://sac.uky.edu/~mthom0/pokeweed.htm

SCOTCH BROOM, BROOM
www.ces-ncsu.edu/depts/hort/consumer/poison/images

SWEET FLAG, SWEET ROOT, SWEET CANE, SWEET CINNAMON
www.altnature.com/Library/sweetfla.htm

TONKA BEAN
http://rain-tree/cumaru.htm

WATER HEMLOCK, COWBANE, POISON PARSNIP, WILD CARROT
http://w3.uwyo.edu//~caps/poison/poison.htm

WHITE SNAKEROOT, SNAKEROOT, RICHWEED
www.fwkc.com/encyclopedia/low/articles/w/w02800069

WOLF'S BANE, LEOPARD'S BANE, MOUNTAIN TOBACCO
www.ansci.cornell.edu/plants/Kevgoat/alkal.htm

WORMWOOD, MADDERWORT, MUGWORT
http://search1.healthgate.com/mdx-books/vit/herb194.shtml

YOHIMBE, YOHIMBI
www.mothernature.com/ency/Herb/Yohimbe.asp

HIDDEN DANGERS IN ADDITIVES

http://vm.cfsan.fda.gov/list.html
www.cspinet.org/additives
www.lumenfds.com/fdachem.htm
www.oznet.ksu.edu/library/fntr2/samplers/ncr438.htm
http://ifse.tamu.edu/CKNOWLEDGE/FoodAdditives.html
http://gopbi.adam.com/ency/article/002435.htm
www.fanafana.com/Consumers/Food-and-Nutrition/Food

Antioxidants
www.foodsafety.org/cresi1.htm

Coloring Agents
http://crucial.ied.edu.hk/Foodchem/certifi.html

Flavor Enhancers
www.allergy.pair.com/additives.flavor620-637.htm

Texturizers
www.biz-lib.com/ZBUFoo7.html www.tandfdc.com/JNLS/fac.htm

HIDE AND SEEK
http://cpl.lib.uic.edu/008subject/009scitech/cooking.html

COMMON FOOD ADDITIVES

ACETIC ACID
www.lj.eb.com:82/index.htcl/thisRow/361/aDB/articl

ACID-MODIFIED STARCHES
www.penford.com/apps/starch02/Sto2_crown.asp

ALUM

www.fwkc.com/encyclopedia/low/articles/a/a00100131

AMMONIUM BICARBONATE

www.ahperformance.com/preoducts/ambi.html

AMMONIUM CHLORIDE

http://ukdb.web.aol.com/hutchinson/encyclopedia/44/M00226

AMYLASE

http://apnet.com/inscight/01061997/amylase.htm

BETA-CAROTENE

www.hcrc.org/faqs/beta-car.html

BHA AND BHT, FRIEND OR FOE

www.feelhealthy.com/bha.htm

www.pueblo.gsa.gov/cic_text/food/foodpres/foodpres.txt

BROMELAIN

www.mothernature.com/ency/Supp/Bromelain.asp

CAFFEINE

www.termisoc.org/infoserv/drugs/graphical/grphcaff

CALCIUM CARBONATE

http://ukdb.web.aol.com/hutchinson/encyclopedia/61/M00304

http://phys.com/b_nutrition/03encyclopedia/02terms/c/cak

CALCIUM HYPOCHLORITE

http://vvvvv.8m.com/Calcium_hypochlorite.html

CALCIUM LACTATE

http://www6.phys.com/b_nutrition/o/self_analysis/02calcium

CALCIUM PROPIONATE

http://www.eatingsmart.com/bread/18001.shtml

CALCIUM SULFATE

http://mineral.galleries.com/minerals/Sulfates/Anhydrit/A

CARRAGEENAN

http://foodsci.orst.edu/gums/carr.html

CHLORINE GAS

http://nobel.scas.bcit.bc.ca/resource/ptable/cl.htm

CHLOROPHYLL

http://scifun.chem.uisc.edu/chemweek/chlrphyl/chlrphyl.html

http://pgjr.alpine.k12.ut.us/science/whitaker/Chlorop

COLORINGS

http://phys.com/b_nutrition/03encyclopedia/02terms/c/colo

DISODIUM PHOSPHATE

http://www6.phys.com/b_nutrition/03encyclopedia/02terms/d

ETHYL ACETATE

www.yourfuture.pg.com/schldays/fnb/41001.htm

www.osha-slc.gov/SLTC/healthyguidelines/ethylacetate

ETHYL VANILLIN

www.food.us.rhodia.com/brochures/romexpvn/page3.htm

EUCALYPTUS OIL

www.azuswebworks.com/herbs/eucalpts.htm

www.healthherbs.com/sing224.htm

GLUTEN

www.fwkc.com/encyclopedia/low/articles/g/g01000025

www.freybe.com/nutri/gluten/avoid.html

GUM ARABIC

www.foodexplorer.com/product/apps/NEWPROD/F106618B

www.redbay.com/plthomas/arabic/

HYDROGENATED OIL

www.womens-health.com/health_center/nutrition/nfaq

INVERT SUGAR

http://ukdb.web.aol.com/hutchinson/encyclopedia/68/M00517

LECITHIN

http://stratsoy.ag.uiuc.edu/archives/experts/health/1997/

www.upnatem.com/lecithin.htm

MALIC ACID

www.mothernature.com/ency/Supp/Malic_Acid.asp

www.trans-japan.com/test/fuso_chem/products/acid/a

MANNITOL

www.phys.com/b_nutrition/03encyclopedia/02terms/ml

METHYLENE CHLORIDE

http://gala.cchs.ca/oshanswers/chemicals/chem_profiles/m

MODIFIED STARCH

www.foodstarch.com/23ab.htm

www.foodexplorer.com/products/apps/NEWPROD/F106618B

MONOSODIUM GLUTAMATE (MSG)

http://crucial.ied.edu.hk/Foodchem/msg.html

www.202.org/members/holland

www.msgfree.com

NITRATE

http://ukdb.web.aol.com/hutchinson/encyclopedia/21/M00262

NITRITE

http://ukdb.web.aol.com/hutchinson/encyclopedia/86/M00100

http://darwin.apnet.com/insciht/06131997/nitrite1.htm

PAPAIN

www.cof.orst.edu/cof/teach/for442/hawaii/papaya.htm

PECTIN

http://www6.phys.com/b_nutrition/03encyclopedia/02terms/p

www.nsac.ns.ca/nsdam/pt/hort/garden95/gg95-63.htm

www.cfs.purdue.edu/fdsnutr/fn453/addpectn.htm

PEROXIDE

www.fwkc.com/encyclopedia/low/articles/h/h01100174

SODIUM BENZOATE

http://hive.lycaeum.org/messages/2449.html

SODIUM BISULFATE

www.koiusa.com/question/530r.htm

SODIUM CARBONATE

www.adam.com/ency/article/002486.htm

SODIUM CASEINATE

www.casein.com

SODIUM CITRATE

www.alka-seltzer.com/alka_symt/symptom_heartburn.htm

TANNIC ACID

http://family-e-docs.com/qtannic.html

www.geocities.com/Yosemite/5609/tannicacid.html

SORBITOL

www.1st-nutrition.com/ingredients/ing_160.html

SULFITES

www.mayo.ivi.com/mayo/9708/htm/sulfites.htm

www.pueblo.gsa.gov/cic_text/food/foodpres/foodpres.txt

SULFUR DIOXIDE

http://gala.ccohs.ca/ashanswers/chemicals/chem_profiles/s

LIQUID FACTS

WATER

www.ces.ncsu.edu/depts/fcs/docs/he393.html

www.cleanwater.gov/progress/keyact.html

www.epa.gov/OGWDW/dwinfo.htm

www.water.com/need.html

BOTTLED WATER

www.bottledwater.org

or by calling 1 (800) WATER-11.

FLOURIDE

www.bottledwater.org

CRYPTOSPORIDIUM

www.ces.ncsu.edu/depts/fcs/docs/he393.html

www.bottledwater.org/public/Crypto.htm

ADDITIVES

www.bottledwater.org

STORAGE

www.bottledwater.org

TYPES OF BOTTLED WATER

SPRING WATER:

www.bevnetmarketplace.com/news/4_14_97/akva.asp

MINERAL WATER:

www.bottledwater.org

SPARKLING WATER:

www.bottledwater.org

TAP WATER

www.water.com/need.html

www.mayohealth.org/mayo/askdiet/htm/new/qd970611.htm

HARD WATER

http://phylogeny.arizona.edu/AZWATER/Glossary/hardwater.html

HEALTH CAUTION:

http://dailynews.yahoo.com/headlines/hl/story.html?s=v/nm/19981223/hl/mag2_1.html

OXYGENATED WATER

www.hiosilver.com/cgi-bin/webc.exe/hiosilver/public_htm/InfohiO.html

LIFE O2 SUPER OXYGENATED WATER

http://bevnet.com/reviews/life-o2/

GINSENG SPRING WATER

http://bevnet.com/reviews/ginspring/index.asp

CAFFEINATED WATER

http://bevnet.com/reviews/aqau

ACIDULATED WATER

www.epicurious.com/e_eating/e02_secrets/r/852

WATER PURIFICATION METHODS

www.fc.net/~tdeagan/water/

Activated Charcoal Filtration Units

www.lungusa.org/pub/cleaners/air_clean_chap3.htm

Chlorination

www.eng.rpi.edu/dept/env-energy-eng/WWW/DISINFECT/

Multi-Stage Filtration

http://water.com/systems.html

Microstrainers

www.tetranet.net/users/maddox/envtek.html

Reverse Osmosis

www.naturalpurewater.com/reverse_osmosis_method.htm

Distillation

www.californiacentralcoast.com/busi/epa/epa.html

Aeration

www.wateronline.com/storefronts/wet.html

Ultraviolet Radiation Purifiers

www.rexuv.com/ www.ultraviolet.co.za/ultra_violet_av.html

Ozonators

www.enviro.org/Ozone.html

www.poolcenter.com/ozone_poolstor.htm

Carbon Filters

http://healthnet.simplenet.com/mp/carbon.htm

Magnetic Water Conditioners

www.csisun.com/gmx/main.htm

CHECKING YOUR OWN TAP WATER

www.siouxlan.com/water/faq.html#stain

www.usatoday.com/news/special/water002.htm

COMMON CONTAMINANTS IN TAP WATER

Copper

www.siouxlan.com/water/faq.html#t6

Fluoride

www.bottledwater.org/public/fluoride_fact_sheet.htm

Chlorine

www.c3.org/

Lead

www.drkoop.com/news/focus/feb/lead.html

Drugs

http://biz.yahoo.com

www.siouxlan.com/water/faq.html

HEALTH FACTS

DEHYDRATION

http://water.com/news.html

www.cspinet.org/sodapop/liquid_candy.htm

WATER AND AGING, A SERIOUS PROBLEM

http://water.com

http://encarta.msn.com/index/conciseindex/15/0150Food.htm

WATER AND ATHLETES

www.water.com/athlete.html

WHERE IS YOUR WATER FROM?

www.ces.ncsu.edu/depts/fcs/docs/he393.html

RISK OF DYING FROM PESTICIDES IN WATER SUPPLIES

www.ga.usgs.gov/publications/acfpest/acfpest.html

YOUR TAP WATER MAY BE DRUGGED

www.monitor.net/rachael/r614.html

www.ces.ncsu.edu/depts/fcs/docs/he393.html

WET FACTS

THE NATIONAL CANCER INSTITUTE REPORTS

www.wessexwater.co.uk/factsstats/

www.bottledwater.org/public/Crypto.htm
www.mindbodyhealth.com/health-talk/index.html
www.pastrychef.com/htmlpages/archives.html
www.water.com/choice.html
http://family.drkoop.com/conditions/encyclopedia/articles
http://water.com
http://ucrwcu.rwc.uc.edu/koehler/biophys/8d.html
www.perrier.com/perrier/OUTPUT/hist1.html
www.cbn.org/newsstand/stories/990208d.asp
www.nsda.org/softdrinks
www.bodyisland.com/balance/97/1_3/sports/water.htm
http://encarta.msn.com/index/conciseindex/12/0123Doou.htm
http://multipueco.com/p12.htm
http://encarta.msn.com/index/conciseindex/12/0123D000.htm
http://comptonsv3.webaol.com/encyclopedia/ARTICLES/012
www.washingtonpost.com/wp-srv/Wplate/1999-04/07/1931-040799-idx.html
www.marinemedical.com/water.htm
www.perrier.com/perrier/OUTPUT/hist1.html
www.totalwater.com/facts.htm
www.purewateriac.com/html/about_distillation_.htm
www.medicaltalk.com/6880.html
www.cdc.gov/travel/foodwater.htm
www.garlic.com/~pburnett/formtrav.htm
www.cgi.chi.il.us/WorksMart/Water/html/Trivia.html
www.obs-us.com/obs/english/books/pg/pg175.htm
www.butterisbest.com/
www.science.uva.nl/beta/istitutes/cma/english/products/ipc4229.html
www.newscientist.com/lastword/answers//wa230bubble
www.howstuffworks.com/question205.htm
www.personal.psu.edu/users/j/p/jph10
www.helico.com/newsite//inks.html
www.bottledwaterweb.com/news/nw_110198.html
www.beveragesdirect.com/products/life02/index.ask
www.purestwaters.com/fct.htm
www.nsda.org/softdrinks/

FLUID BALANCE

www.bodyisland.com/balance/97/1_3/sports/water.htm

www.mayohealth.org/mayo/9909/htm/water.htm

http://multipurco.com/p12.htm

http://homearts.com/gh/health/11wateb3.htm

www.H2OforSale.com

www.mrwa.com/waterfac.html

www.pueblo.gsa.gov/cic_

http://homeart.com/gh/health/11wateb3.htm

www.marinemedical.com/water.htm

www.medicaltalk.com/6880.html

www.mayohealth.org/mayo/askdiet/htm/new/qd980121.htm

www.totalwater.com/facts.htm

www.purewaterinc.com/html/about_distillation_.htm

www.waterinfo.org/cnsrb.html

www.geocities.com

http://family.drkoop.com/conditions/encyclopedia/articles

http://water.com

www.soundwaters.org/make/water.htm

www.browardarts.net/wsi01800.htm

www.healthinc.com/healthynyou/library/nutrition/wat1

www.eatright.org/feature/080198.htm

http://erwin.phys.virginia.edu/Education/Teaching/HowThin

http://homearts.com/gh/health/11wateb3.htm

www.geocities.com/researchtriangle/9514/lead.htm

http://homearts.com/gh/health/11wateb3.htm

http://rville.k12.mo.us/Cave/caveForm1.html

www.colorodo.edu/Geo/Sci/courses/GEOL1010-1/G1010/

http://watercure2.com

www.bottledwater.org/public/water_use.htm

COOKING WITH WATER

www.taunton.com/fc/features/techniques/26poach.htm
www.mtsu.edu/~kgregg/dmir/08/0822.html
www.voicenet.com/~tjohn/gloss.html
www.washingtonpost.com/wpsrv/Wplate/1999-04/1931-040799-idx.html
www.samcooks.com/Newsletter/1999February.htm
http://west.uwyo.edu/food/Publications/Adjust7.htm
http://food.homearts.com/food/cookings/techn/29vt5a12.htm
www.taunton.com/fc/features/techniques/26poach.htm
www.taunton.com/fc/features/techniques/custards/1.htm

STORING WATER FOR EMERGENCIES

www.baproducts.com/water.htm

SHORT HISTORY OF CARBONATED BEVERAGES

www.sodafountain.com/softdrnk/vernors.htm
www.xensei.com/users/iraseski
http://webster.unh.edu/~sfl/moxie.html
www.drpeppermuseum.com/history.html
www.sodafountain.com/softdrnk/7_up.htm
http://brewery.org/cm3/recs/12_11.html
www.sodafountain.com/softdrnk/eggcreamhistory.htm
http://web.net-link.net/preparedfoods/1998/9807/9807marketwa.htm

THE HISTORY OF THE SODA FOUNTAIN

www.sodafountain.com/history/hisfirst.htm
www.sodafountain.com/history/hismineral.htm
www.sodafountain.com/history/hisliquid.htm
www.sodafountain.com/history/hismass.htm
www.sodafountain.com/history/his1stfn.htm
www.sodafountain.com/history/hisdrank.htm
www.sodafountain.com/history/hisflavor.htm
www.sodafountain.com/history/hislunch.htm
www.sodafountain.com/history/histufts.htm
www.sodafountain.com/history/hisrefrig.htm

www.sodafountain.com/history/hisfront.htm
www.sodafountain.com/history/hiscalls.htm
www.sodafountain.com/history/hisdeath.htm

CARBONATED BEVERAGES IN 2000

www.fas.usda.gov/info/agexporter/1997/asiadrin.html
www.edweek.org/ew/vol-17/30cola.h17

CAFFEINE CONTENT OF SOFT DRINKS (12 OUNCE SERVINGS)

www.wco.com/~booyah/dew/dewcaffeine.html
www.gocarolinas.com/living/health/nutrition/1998/0
www.consrv.ca.gov/dor/
www.madsci.org/posts/archives/aug97/872289138.Me.q.html
http://web.net-link.net/preparedfoods/1999/9903/9903newprod.htm
http://dem0nmac.mgh.harvard.edu/forum/Addictionf/
    dietcoke-ArtificialSweeteners.html
www.5aday.com/schools2.html
www.albion.edu/students/jstanisz/softdrink.html
www.nbcfiz.com/index2.html
www.sodafountain.com/softdrnk/mountain_dew.htm
www.bevnetmarketplace.com/news/october97/10/dew.asp
www.bevnetmarketplace.com/news/98/4/23-rc.asp
http://jacksonville.com/tu-online/stories/041798/bus_1c8DietS.html
www.hints-n-tips.com/household.htm
www.bevnet.com/revoews/batch_no6/index.asp
www.cyberholics.com/coffeetime.html
http://bevnet.com/reviews/rageous/index.asp
www.sodafountain.com/softdrnk/AboutVirgils.htm
http://aomt.netmegs.com/coffee/coffag.html
www.sodafountain.com/softdrink/rootbeer.htm
www.perrier.com www.sodafountain.com/softdrnk/yachtclub.htm
http://micro.magnet.fsu.edu/micro/gallery/softdrink/soft4
www.sodafountain.com/softdrnk/guaranalegend.htm
www.sodafountain.com/softdrnk/guarana_brazilia.htm
http://sundae.roanoke.edu/~jsteele/chem103/data13.htm
www.neuronic.com/caffeine.htm
www.swmed.edu/library/consumer/caffkid.htm
www.epicurious.com/d_drinking/d03_punch/punchtips.html

NON-CARBONATED BEVERAGES

www.snapple.com/index.cgi?loadpage=TRUE&/home/snapple/
snapple_ht.../history.html

www.altculture.com/aentries/f/frutopia.html

www.altculture.com/aentries/s/snapple.html

www.altculture.com/aentries/f/frutopia.html

www.snapple.com

www.pepsico.com/Web_pages/pcnews2.html

www.kraftfoods.com/kool-aid/html/history/ka_pitcher.html

http://web.net-link.net/preparedfoods/1999/9902/9902newprod.htm

www.osippie.com/NATURAL

www.starchefs.com/Summer/99/Slukins/recipes.html

www.momsonline.com/homespace/dishitup/article.asp

DRINKS DESIGNED FOR CHILDREN

www.bottledwater.org/public/fluoride_fact_sheet.htm

www.kidzwater.com/product.html

www.bursters.com.

www.gmifs.com/

http://biz.yahoo.com

NUTRITIONAL CONCERNS REGARDING SOFT DRINKS

www.phys.com/b_nutrition/03encyclopedia/02terms/p/

www.msds.org/oshanswers/chemicals/chem_profiles/phosphoric/
phosphor.htm

EXTRACTS

www.hbsmarketing.com/carbonator.html

www.ars.usda.gov/is/np/fnrb/fnrb198.htm

www.sodafountain.com/softdrnk/cokecp.htm

http://parentsplace.com/expert/nutritionist/adults/ga/0%2

www.nsda.org/softdrinks

http://inventors.about.com/library/inventors/b/cocacola.htm

www.scienceuva.nl/beta/institutes/cma/english/products/ipc4229.html

http://inventors.about.com/library/weekly/aa091699.htm

http://inventors.about.com/gi/dynamic/offsite.htm?site=http

www.webtender.com/db/drink/4851

www.epicurious.com/d_drinking/do2_non_alc/quench/l

www.detnews.com/1998/health/981103/food/food.htm

http://answersleuth.com/food/juice.9.shtml

www.colormatters.com/bubdarc9a-physio.html

http://klingon.iupucs.iupui.edu/~creagan/list.html

http://sciencekennesaw.edu/~mhermes/gatorade.htm

www.hersheyscocoarecipea.buycouponsresource.com

www.hugs.org/Cocoa.shtml

http://cocoarecipe.betterthantherest.net/

A SPOT OF TEA

HISTORY OF TEA

www.enteract.com/~robchr/tea/faq.html

www.farsinet.com/hottea/

MAJOR VARIETIES OF TEAS

www.elitehealthshop.com/Articles/Grn_Tea.html

www.gourmetcoffeeroaster.com/cafemaison/poucgreent

www.stashtea.com/w-111002.htm

www.stashtea.com/w-111218.htm

www.teaboard.com/assam.html

www.teaboard.com/darjling.html

www.gray-seddon-tea.com/japanese_green_tea.htm

http://efr.org/~sundance/Tea.html

www.sally-place.com

www.enteract.com/~robchr/tea/faq.html

MAJOR TEA PRODUCING COUNTRIES

http://ukdb.web.aol.com/hutchinson/encyclopedia/48/M00144

http://tea.hypermart.net/countries/indonesiafacts.html

www.teatalk.com/general/regions.htm

www.worldbank.org/html/extdr/extme/1441.htm

www.taiwantrade.com/agricultural

BOTTLED AND CANNED TEAS

www.bevnetmarketplace.com/news/98/1/29-mad_river.asp

BREWING METHODS

www.taooftea.com/cgi-bin/teashop.cgi?page=brewing.html

www.greentea.com/teachat/messages/708.html

http://stashtea.com/teafaq.htm#4

http://web.net-link.net/preparedfoods/1999/9904/9904japan.htm

TEA POTS & SUCH

www.asiancities.com/Teapots/about_yixing_teapots.htm

http://stashtea.com/teafaq#4

STORAGE

www.teleport.com/~tea/teatimes.htm

CAFFEINE CONTENT

www.coffeescience.org/other.html

GROWING METHODS

http://world.std.com/~pemtea/pemlinks.htm

NUTRITIONAL INFORMATION

www.cis.ohio-state.edu/hypertext/faq/usenet-faqs/html/caffeine-faq/faq.html

www.ars.usda.gov/is/np/fnrb/fnrb199.htm

www.ag/uiuc.edu/~ffh/abstracts/Abstracts47.html

www.ecologystore.com/bhteasmain.htm

www.epicurious.com/db/dictionary/terms/t/tannin.html

www.herbsherbal.com/cornsilk.html

http://internalmedicine.medscape.com/MedscapeWire/1998/10.98

http://web.net-link.net/preparedfoods/1999/9904/9904japan.htm

www.celestialseasonings.com/research/abouttea/decaffeination.jhtml

www.rdi.gpo.or.th/NetZine/V2N43/tea.htm

TEA LEAF FACTS

www.strandtea.com/organic.htm

www.teatime.com/tea/caffeine.html

www.fda.gov/fdac/features/296_tea.html

www.sallys-place.com/beverages/tea/american_classic.htm

http://stashtea.com/teafaq.htm#4

www.teatime.com/tea/consumption.html

http://channelone.com/pop/connection/beautyrecipes/1.html

http://flushitsolutions.com/teadescription.htm

www.fda.gov/opacom/backgrounders/miles.html

www.fda.gov/fdac/features/296_tea.html

www.easc.indiana.edu/Pages/EASC/curriculum/china/1

www.iht.com/IHT/TB/98/tb063098.html

www.willa.com/tealeaves

http://newage.about.com/culture/newage/library/wee

www.craftsforkids.about.com/library/weekly/mcurrent.htm

http://flushitsolutions.com/infuser.htm

http://agschools.fvsc.peachnet.edu/html/publications/telet

www.teacouncil.co.uk/

www.food.epicurious.com/e_eating/e02_secrets/i_ind

www.cw-usa.com/brewhints.html

www.nsplus.com/lastword/answers/1wa1087mysteries.htm

www.teatime.com/tea/caffeine.html

www.bigelowtea.com

www.celestialseasonings.com/

www.erowid.org/chemicals/caffeine/caffeine.shtml

www.herbsherbal.com/cornsilk.html

www.teahealth.co.uk

http://web.net-link.net/preparedfoods/1999/9904/9904japan.htm

http://mecenter.medscape.com/MedscapeWire/1998/10.98/ACG

www.loop.com/~bkrentzman/sup.vitamin.alt/herbs/her

KITCHEN BASICS & SOLUTIONS

HERBAL TEA: THE FIRST TEAS

TYPES

www.aabhealth.com/herbsdefined.htm#AGRIMONY

Alfalfa

www.viable-herbal.com/herbdesc/1alfalfa.htm

Angelica

www.aabhealth.com/herbsdefined.htm#ANGELICA

Anise

www.egregore.com/herb/Anise.htm

Balm

www.egregore.com/herb/Balm.htm

Basil

www.angelfire.com/sys/popup_source.shtml?category=basil

Bay

www.spiritonline.com/wicca/herbs.html

Bergamot

www.wic.net/waltzark/herbencb.htm

Birch

www.viable-herbal.com/herbdesc/1birchba.htm

Borage

www.viable-herbal.com/herbdesc/1borage.htm

Burnet

http://www.io.com/~wilsone/shadysweeties.htm

Chamomile

http://192.225.33.129/magazine/foods/body/factoids/0,1088,25,00.html

Caraway

www.aabhealth.com/herbsdefined.htm#CARAWAY

Catnip

www.gardenguides.com/herbs/catnip.htm

Cinnamon

www.viable-herbal.com/herbdesc1/1cinnamo.htm

Clover

www.aabhealth.com/herbsdefined.htm#REDCLOVER

Cloves

www.egregore.com/herb/Cloves.htm

Coltsfoot
www.viable-herbal.com/herbdesc1/1coltsfo.htm

Comfrey
www.aabhealth.com/herbsdefined.htm#CONFREY

Dandelion
www.aabhealth.com/herbsdefined.htm#DANDELION

Elder
www.egregore.com/herb/Belderberry.htm

Fennel
www.egregore.com/herb/Fennel.htm

Fenugreek
www.viable-herbal.com/herbdesc1/1fenugre.htm

Flax
http://pages.ivillage.com/fb/cindy711/links.html

Ginger
http://www.io.com/~wilsone/shadysweeties.htm

Ginseng
www.aabhealth.com/herbsdefined.htm#GINSENG

Goldenrod
www.aabhealth.com/herbsdefined.htm#GOLDENROD

Hawthorn
www.wic.net/waltzark/herbench.htm

Hollyhock
www.dehnsgardenherbs.com/products/edible.html

Hops
www.viable-herbal.com/herbdesc2/1hops.htm

Horehound
www.aabhealth.com/herbsdefined.htm#HOREHOUND

Hyssop
www.thefamilysolution.com
www.aabhealth.com/herbsdefined.htm#HYSSOP

Lavender
www.viable-herbal.com/herbdesc2/1lavende.htm

Lemon Verbena
www.gardenguides.com/herbs/lemon.htm

Linden

http://herbal-solutions.com/herbdesc2/1linden.htm

Licorice

www.herbsherbals.com/licorice.html

Mallow

www.aabhealth.com/herbsdefined.htm#MARSHMALLOW

Marigold

www.egregore.com/herb/Marigold.htm

Marjoram

www.adelaide.park.org/Pavilions/FoodandMarket/herbs/gr_039.htm

Mate

www.healthfree.com/herbgarden

Meadowsweet

http://herbal-solutions.com/herbdesc2/1meadows.htm

Mint

www.swedeponic.com/us-products-id09.htm

Mugwart

http://maxpages.com/witch1garden/Herb-Use

Mullein

www.aabhealth.com/herbsdefined.htm#MULLEIN

Nettle

http://herbal-solutions.com/herbdesc3/1nettle.htm

New Jersey Tea

www.yale.edu/fes5056/njt.html

Nutmeg

www.culinarycloset.com/nutmeg.html

Pennyroyal

www.viable-herbal.com/herbdesc3/1pennyro.htm

Purslane

http://healthgate.com/vit/herb151.shtml

Raspberry

www.aabhealth.com/herbsdefined.htm#RASPBERRY

Rose

www.wic.net/waltzark/herbencr.htm

Sage

www.aabhealth.com/herbsdefined.htm#SAGE

Sarsaparilla

www.viable-herbal.com/herbdesc3/1sarsapa.htm

Sassafras

www.aabhealth.com/herbsdefined.htm#SASSAFRAS

Savory

www.culinarycloset.com/savory.html

Thyme

www.viable-herbal.com/herbdesc4/1thyme.htm

Wintergreen

www.aabhealth.com/hicpain.html

Yarrow

www.viable-herbal.com/herbdesc4/1yarrow.htm

PREPARATION OF HERBAL TEAS

www.seedman.com/index/herbtea.htm

STORAGE

www.teleport.com/~tea/teatimes.htm

POISONOUS PLANTS

http://cal.vet.upenn.edu/poison www.ansci.cornell.edu/plants.html

NUTRITIONAL FACTS

http://my.webmd.com/medeast_toc/pdr_herbs_and_vitamins
www.cis.ohio-state.edu/hypertext

VITAMIN AND MINERAL HERBAL SOURCES

www.selfgrowth.com/articles/lee25.html
www.3w.net/timeless/vitamin-xdpp.html
http://games.go.com/WebDir/Health/Drugs/Minerals
www.kmxg.com/hrbmoore/ManualsMM/BadForm.txt

IT'S COFFETIME

THE STORY OF COFFEE

www.cosic.org/caffeine/index.html

www.gmabrands.com/facts/foodbytes/9904.cfm

www.sallys-place.com/beverages/coffee/whats_goes_up.htm

COFFEE PRODUCING COUNTRIES

BRAZIL
www.wildbill.com/current/Brazil-174.html

COLOMBIA
http://coffee.com/bean/bean_8.htm

COSTA RICA
http://coffee.com/bean/bean_6.htm

DOMINICAN REPUBLIC
http://lazarus.elte.hu/~zetor/cia95/rg.html

UNITED STATES
www.hawaiicoffeeassoc.org/ www.coffeetimes.com

JAMAICA
http://coffee.com/bean/bean_1.htm

AFRICA
www.nwlink.com/~donclark/java/javafaq.html

ROASTING THE BEANS

www.cis.ohio-state.edu/hypertext/faq/usenet-faqs/html/caffeine-faq/faq.html

TYPES OF ROASTS

www.nwlink.com/~donclark/java/world.html

http://cnn.com/FOOD/resources/food.for.thought/beverages/
coffee/roast.html

http://cnn.com/FOOD/resources/food.for.thought/beverages/
coffee/roast.html

www.nwlink.com/~donclark/java/world.html

www.nwlink.com/~donclark/java/world.html

http://cnn.com/FOOD/resources/food.for.thought/beverages/
coffee/roast.html

www.illuminatus.com/fun/agoago/bean.html

ESPRESSO BEVERAGES

www.salls-place

www.sallys-place.com

http://sunrise-espresso.com/LiquidFuture.htm

www.sallyhs-place

www.nwlink.com/~donclark/java/recipes.html

www.geocities.com/Paris/Salon/2549/glossary.html

www.geocities.com/NapaValley/8118/coffee3.html

www.btinternet.com/~roastandpost/Glossary.html

DECAFFEINATION PROCESS

www.sallys-place.com/beverages/coffee/decaffeinated.htm

http://ag.arizona.edu/AZWATER/glossary/trich.html

www.planetroasters.com/double.htm#howdo

www.1st-line.com/coffee/defmthds.htm

www.1st

www.sallys-place.com

www.cs.unb.ca/~alopez-o/Coffee/coffag.htm#decaf

http://olive-live.webnet.advance.net/foodday/features/99/

BREWING METHODS

www.planetroasters.com/doyou.htm#shouldi

www.jamaicancoffee.gov.jm/brewing.html#CareofUtensils

www.cs.unb.ca/~alopez-o/Coffee/coffaq.html#HowtoBrew

www.nwlink.com/~donclark/java/best.html

www.nwlink.com/~donclark/java/javafaq.html

http://192.225.33.129/magazine/foods/body/factoids/0,1088,25,00.html

www.nwlink.com

www.sallys-place.com/beverages/coffee/perfect.htm

www.supramatic.com/help.htm

www.manyhits.com/gate/1/coffee.shtml

http://web.net-link.net/preparedfoods/1998/9807/9807lastbite.htm

www.geocities/Paris/Salon/2549/faqs.html

http://copeland.udel.edu/~mmcoffee/

www.quakerbonnet.com/coffeetc.htm

BUYING & STORAGE

www.jamaicancoffee.gov.jm/brewing.html#storageofcoffee

www.coffeeuniverse.com/tips.html

COFFEE FACTS

www.cw-usa.com/faqs.html

http://beta.go.com/WebDir/Living/Food_and_Drink/Beverages

www.hoosiertimes.com/stories/1999/03/24/lifestyle.990324

http://software2.bu.edu/COHIS/smoking/upsmoke/nicsigns.html

www.american

www.funtrivia.com/Food/Coffee.html

www.jamaicancoffee.gov.jm/brewing.html#coffeetips

www.coffeeuniverse.com/tips.html

www.coffeeuniverse.com/university_taste.html

www.geocities.com/Paris/Salon/2549/faqs.html

www.sally-place.com/beverages.coffee/supermarket.htm

http://coffee.com/bean/bean_2.htm

www.cs.unb.ca/~alopez-o/Coffee/coffaq.html#Frappe

www.coffeeuniverse.com/tips.html

www.epicurious.com/e_eating/e02_secrets/u/959.html

www.cis.ohio-state.edu/hypertext/faq/usenet-faqs/html/caffeine-faq/faq.

http://homearts.com/rb/food/02chocb1.htm

www.skyisland.com/i/coffee/links-green.html

http://bevnet.com/reviews/frappuccino/index.asp

NUTRITIONAL INFORMATION

www.cosic.org/caffeine/index.html

www.coffeescience.org/studies.html#gall

http://ificinfo.health.org/brochure/caffeine.htm

http://onhealth.com/ch1/columnist/item%2c47177.asp

CAFFEINE CONTENT

http://aomt.netmegs.com/coffee/caffaq.html

http://mayohealth.org/mayo/askdiet/htm/new/qd970312.htm

http://demOnmac.mgh.harvard.edu/forum/HeadacheF/12.3.978

http://ificinfo.health.org/ganda/gach.html

http://aomt.netmegs.com/coffee/caffaq.html#HowDoesCaff

www.coffeescience.org/women.html

www.cis.ohio-state.edu/hypertext/faq/usenet-faqs/html/caffeine-faq/faq.html

http://cnn.com/HEALTH/9603/coffee_suicide

www.cis.ohio-state.edu/hypertext/faq/usenet-faqs/html/caffeine-faq/faq.html

http://pharminfo.com/pubs/pnn/pnn22_14.html

www.mrcoffeehouse.com/storage1.htm

www.thriveonline.com/eats/experts/joan/joan.12-09

www.oberlin.edu/~ssteiman/caffeine.htm#decaffeinate

www.ivillage.com/food/qas

www.nwlink.com/~donclark/java/java

www.albany.net/~dsissman/caffeine

www.metroactive.com/papers/cruz/07.03.97/caf-water

http://onhealth.com/ch1/columnists/item%2c47177.asp

www.oberlin.edu/~ssteinman/caffeine.htm

www.tdo.com/features/stories/1111coffeebox.htm

www.rpi.edu/~ellwad/coffee/home.htm

http://aomt.netmegs.com/coffee/coffaq.thm

www.manyhits.com/gate/1/coffee.shtml

CAFFEINE CONTENT IN COMMON FOODS AND DRUGS

www.wilstar.net/caffeine.htm

www.joltcola.com/cola.html

www.coffee

www.coffeereview.com

http://www2.lucidcafe.com/lucidcafe/glossary.html

SUBSTITUTIONS AND MEASUREMENTS

www.foodsubs.com/Thicken.html
www.switcheroo.com/ct/thicken.htm
www.foodsubs.com/Herbseur.html
www.mathes.carleton.edu/stats/ConsumerEconomics/bu
www.foodies.com/Tips/tips.html#outof
www.swticheroo.com/ct/thicken.htm
www.aginfo.psu.edu/news/march99/flowers.html
www.chefjob.com/foodtalk
www.mayohealth.org/mayo/9604/htm/serv_sb.htm
www.maxpages.com/vegancookery3/Milk_and_Cream
www.food.epicurious.com/e_eating/e02_secrets/n/631.html
http://southernfood.about.com/library/info/b/cooks.htm
www.foodsubs.com
www.cei.net/~terry/auntedna/utilities.html

COMMON LIQUID SUBSTITUTIONS

www.foodsubs.com
http://imgworks.adbureau.net/accypiter/adclick.exe/site=ma

EXTRACTS AND ESSENCES

www.northcoast.com/~alden/Extracts.html

OILS AND COOKING SPRAYS

www.mnsinc.com/cornucopia/ingsubs.htm

VINEGAR SUBSTITUTES

www.ichef.com/ichef-recipes/Sauces-marinades/sauce
www.faq.org/faq/cooking/faq/

RESTAURANTS & FAST FOOD

FAST FOODS, THE GOOD AND THE BAD

www.dietition.com/fastfood.html

www.rdserv/.rd.msu.edu/enved/curric/water/kidsshalima

www.phys.com/d_magazines/05allure/traps/foodtrap

www.cornell.edu www.sciencedaily.com

www.ifas.ufl.edu

www.sciencedaily.com/releases/1998/10/981020074004.htm

http://web.net-link.net/preparedfoods/1999/9904/9904procmeat.htm

http://web.net-link.net/preparedfoods/1998/9809/9809meatyveg.htm

www.mckinseyquarterly.com/food/saam96.htm

http://web.net-link.net/preparedfoods/1998/9807/9807funcfood2.htm

www.ifrn.bbsrc.ac.uk

www.pb.net/spc/mii/990377.htm

www.abcnews.com

http://cnn.com/FOOD/news/9903/09/alcoholic.ice.cream/index.html

www.healthy.net/library/books/haas/kitchen/poultry

www.seattletimes.com/extra/browse/html97/fatt_1120

www.in-n-out.com

www.tacobell.com www.mcdonalds.com/food/nutrition_facts/sandfries

www.ljsilvers.com/nutrit.htm

www.jackinthebox.com/menu/nutrition/menu_index.html

www.burgerking.com/nutrition.sandwich.htm

THE ROASTED CHICKEN INVASION

www.kfc.com
http://dfmusic.com/fastfood/kfc.html

www.mcdonalds.com/food/ingredient_list/sandwiches

www.dietriot.com/fff/rest.html
www.olen.com/food/book.html
www.worldcrawl.com/Recreation/Food
www.hpm.com/HOD2/general/weight-dinin
http://rcc.webpoint.com/fitness/badfoods.htm
www.fatchicks.com/fastfood/carls.html
www.dfwmusic.com/fastfood/burgers.htm
www.mcdonalds.com/food/nutrition_facts/salads/ind
www.pizzahut.com/NUTRITION98/DEFAULT.HTM
http://soar.berkeley.edu/recipes/nutrition
www.virginia.edu/~dining/nutrition/foodfact.html
www.worldcrawl.com/web/Recreation/Food/Fast_food
www.cyberdiet.com/ffq/show_results.cgi
www.mcspotlight.org/media/press/rollingstone1.html
www.fas.usda.gov
www.onhealth.com/ch1/in-depth/item/item.39963_1_1.asp
www.burgerking.com/home.htm
http://dfwmusic.com/fastfood www.dietriot.comfff/rest.html
www.burgerking.com/home.htm
www.hardees.com
www.jackinthebox.com
www.kfc.com
www.ljsilvers.com
www.mcdonalds.com
www.tacobell.com
www.wendys.com/index0.html